TRIANGLE REPUBLICS

TRIANGLE REPUBLICS

CROSS-BORDER LITERARY
TRANSITS BETWEEN THE COLD
WAR KOREAS AND JAPAN

I JONATHAN KIEF

Columbia University Press
New York

Columbia University Press
Publishers Since 1893
New York   Chichester, West Sussex

Copyright © 2025 Columbia University Press
All rights reserved

Library of Congress Cataloging-in-Publication Data
Names: Kief, I. Jonathan author
Title: Triangle republics : cross-border literary transits between the Cold War Koreas and Japan / I Jonathan Kief.
Description: New York : Columbia University Press, 2025. |
Includes bibliographical references and index.
Identifiers: LCCN 2025005048 (print) | LCCN 2025005049 (ebook) |
ISBN 9780231219846 cloth | ISBN 9780231219853 trade paperback |
ISBN 9780231562935 ebook
Subjects: LCSH: Korean literature—20th century—History and criticism | Japanese literature—20th century—History and criticism | Literature and society | Politics and literature | Korean literature—Korea (South)—20th century—History and criticism | Korean literature—Korea (North)—20th century—History and criticism | LCGFT: Literary criticism
Classification: LCC PL958.7 .K44 2025 (print) | LCC PL958.7 (ebook) |
DDC 895.7/4—dc23/eng/20250520

Cover design: Chang Jae Lee
Cover image: Han Youngsoo, *Mapo*, Seoul,
1956–1963 © Han Youngsoo Foundation

GPSR Authorized Representative: Easy Access System Europe,
Mustamäe tee 50, 10621 Tallinn, Estonia, gpsr.requests@easproject.com

FOR MY FAMILY:

"I FIND YOU EVERYWHERE
(IN UNDERSTANDSTANDING)"

CONTENTS

Acknowledgments   ix
Note on Names, Spelling, and Transliteration   xiii

INTRODUCTION   1

1. REVERBERATIONS: SOUTH KOREAN LITERATURE BETWEEN 1950s–1960s NORTH KOREA AND JAPAN   24

2. MOTHER(S) OF THE SOUTH: FIGURES OF REVOLUTION AND FRACTURE BETWEEN THE 1960s–1970s KOREAS AND JAPAN   94

3. CRITICAL CONNECTIONS AND CRITICAL LIMITS IN 1950s SOUTH KOREA: THE HUMAN AND NONHUMAN ACROSS THE COLD WAR AND EAST SEA DIVIDES   141

4. TRAGIC RETURNS: WRITING BORDER-CROSSING PASTS IN 1960s–1980s SOUTH KOREA   207

EPILOGUE: THE COLD WAR IN KOREA: SUSPENDED ANIMATION   256

Notes   263
Bibliography   309
Index   333

ACKNOWLEDGMENTS

This book is the product of many years of work, and I would not have been able to complete it without the help and inspiration of many individuals. First, I would like to thank Theodore Hughes, whose class I wandered into as a curious yet clueless sophomore. The spark of interest that he lit that semester continues to motivate me, and I am extraordinarily grateful for all of the patience, kindness, and generosity that he has shown me over the years. I would also like to express my heartfelt thanks to JaHyun Kim Haboush, who taught me that the past is always more complex—and radical—than we expect. It was Professor Haboush's support that allowed me to visit Korea for the first time, and for this I will always be grateful. In addition, my many years at Columbia University would not have been the same without the guidance of the faculty members who taught and challenged me: Paul Anderer, Katherine Biers, Kim Brandt, Souleymane Bachir Diagne, Shigeru Eguchi, Marwa Elshakry, Carol Gluck, Matthew Jones, Beom Lee, Lydia Liu, Samuel Moyn, Jisuk Park, Tomi Suzuki, EunYoung Won, and Hyunkyu Yi. It would also not have been the same without the many colleagues, teaching assistants, and role models who showed me how to learn, grow, and collaborate: Eunsung Cho, Hwisang Cho, KumHee Cho, Ksenia Chizhova, Dajeong Chung, Jae Won Edward Chung, Charles Kim, Cheehyung Harrison Kim, Jimin Kim, Jisoo Kim, Sun-Chul Kim, Sung Eun Kim, Yumi

Kim, Jenny Wang Medina, Peter Moody, Se-Mi Oh, Alyssa Park, Mi-Ryong Shim, Sixiang Wang, and Christina Yi.

I am also extremely grateful to the faculty members who welcomed me and guided me during my time as a student in Seoul: Baek Moonim, Chang Seijin, Hwang Jongyon, Jeong Jong-hyun, Kim Jae-yong, Kim Yerim, Kwon Boduerae, Lee Sang-kyung, Shin Hyung-ki, So Young-Hyun, and the instructors at the Sogang University Korean Language Education Center. Likewise, I send my sincere thanks to all of those who welcomed and supported me at the University of Michigan and the University of Southern California, where I completed postdoctoral fellowships at the Nam Center for Korean Studies and the Korean Studies Institute: Juhn Ahn, Jiun Bang, Youngmin Choe, SE Kile, Jae Kyun Kim, Linda Kim, Gloria Koo, Nojin Kwak, Minna Lee, Hiroaki Matsusaka, Do-Hee Morsman, Se-Mi Oh, Sunyoung Park, Youngju Ryu, and Irhe Sohn. These years in Seoul, Ann Arbor, and Los Angeles were funded by fellowships from the Fulbright Program (US Student Program), the Korea Foundation (Language Training Fellowship, Fellowship for Field Research, Postdoctoral Fellowship), and the Academy of Korean Studies (Postdoctoral Fellowship, 53-4816-0003), for which I express my gratitude. An Academy of Korean Studies Research Fellowship (2021–2022) and a grant from the Northeast Asia Council of the Association for Asian Studies (2016) also supported my research at the book and dissertation stages of this project, respectively.

Since arriving at the University of North Carolina at Chapel Hill, I have had the great fortune to work and teach alongside a wonderful group of colleagues in the Department of Asian and Middle Eastern Studies. I would like to thank all of my colleagues in the department, especially the fabulous faculty in the Korean Program: Dongsoo Bang, Ji-Yeon Jo, Eunji Lee, and Giseung Lee. It has been my honor to contribute to the program that you have built at UNC. I would also like to send my gratitude to the Carolina Asia Center and its staff for their support for my research and teaching, to the Institute for Arts and Humanities for its partial subvention of this book's publication, and to all of my graduate and undergraduate students, who have taught me a great deal over the years.

In the field of Korean studies, more broadly, my research has benefited immensely from the insight of many colleagues and mentors. Throughout my academic career, I received unwavering and deeply meaningful support from Jin-kyung Lee, to whom I am extremely grateful, and I received invaluable feedback on early versions of the proposal for this book from Jae Won Edward Chung, Susan Hwang, Pil Ho Kim, Aimee Kwon, and Sunyoung Park. I also express my gratitude to Cheehyung Harrison Kim and Immanuel Kim for supporting me as I stumbled into the study of North Korea, and I thank Chris Hanscom, Susan Hwang, Ji-Eun Lee, Hyun Seon Park, Si Nae Park, Jooyeon Rhee, Haerin Shin, Ivanna Yi, and Dafna Zur, who have been wonderful and inspiring colleagues to work with on the LLC Korean Forum at the Modern Language Association. I am also extremely grateful to all of those who have provided feedback on my work at conferences or invited me to take part in academic events, translation anthologies, or edited volumes: Ruth Barraclough, Gregg Brazinsky, Heekyoung Cho, Kyeong-Hee Choi, Steven Chung, Dongyoun Hwang, Kelly Jeong, Jina Kim, Jisoo Kim, Young-Key Kim-Renaud, Youngju Ryu, Toba Koji, Ethan Waddell, Yoon Sun Yang, and Theodore Jun Yoo.

This book is also indebted to the generosity and patience of Christine Dunbar, Alex Gupta, and Leslie Kriesel at Columbia University Press, who supported the project despite many delays. Lis Pearson and Mamta Jha offered much appreciated indexing and copyediting. I am likewise indebted to the kindness of KumHee Cho, John DiMoia, Matthieu Felt, Iris Kim, Song Hyewon, Susan Su, and Sonagi Village (the Hwang Sunwŏn Literary Village), who shared essential research materials with me. I would also like to thank Cambridge University Press, Duke University Press, and Routledge for their permission to reprint the portions of this book that appeared in earlier forms. Portions of chapter 2 appeared in "In the Southern Half of Our Republic: Cross-Border Writing and Performance in 1960s North Korea," *Journal of Asian Studies* 81, no. 1 (February 2022): 81–100. Portions of chapters 1 and 2 appeared in "Reading Seoul in Pyongyang: Cross-Border Mediascapes in Early Cold War North Korea," *Journal of Korean Studies* 26, no. 2 (October 2021): 325–48. Portions of the Introduction, chapter 1, and chapter 4 appeared in "Closed Borders and Open Letters in the Postcolonial Koreas," my contribution to the *Routledge Companion to Korean Literature*, ed. Heekyoung Cho (New York: Routledge, 2022), 427–40.

Finally, I would like to express my deepest gratitude to the members of my family, without whom none of this would have been possible. Although they are no longer with us, my grandparents—Doris, Isaac,

Hadassa, Nina, Jarma, and Fay—showed me how to live. From my mom, who always believes in me even when I've lost faith, I learned passion, devotion, and love. From Cindy and my dad, the contrarian, I learned to be contrary—and the opposite. From Byeon Jaeseon, I learned the essentials of Taegu dialect, how to listen and listen again, and to always wait for Kuro. From Bae Bong Sik and Son Jumok, who always welcomed, loved, and supported me, I learned happiness—pure happiness—and its poetry. From Nicole, Mo, and Rose, I learned how to navigate academia, how to make outstanding sandwiches, and how to enjoy ice cream in three dimensions. From Anna, Coco, Jesse, and Jake, I learned to imagine other paths and their crossings. From Minwook and Dajeong, I learned that the day has more than twenty-four hours—and they're all brimming with energy. From Kyoungjin, I learned history and just about everything else. So, Kyoungjin, my beginning and my end, I thank you forever, right here—at the end.

NOTE ON NAMES, SPELLING, AND TRANSLITERATION

This book must deal with a number of complex issues relating to spelling and romanization. For references to writers in the Koreas, I romanize names according to the conventions of the place where the individual was living at the time (or most recently lived). Therefore, in my discussions of the era after 1948, when new spelling and pronunciation rules were promulgated north of the thirty-eighth parallel, I use word-beginning Rs for the names of those active there (such as Rim Hwa and Ri T'aejun) but not for the names of those in the South (such as Yŏm Sangsŏp and Yi Ponggu).

To remain consistent and avoid confusion, I implement this rule not only for my own writing about the post-1948 era but also for my discussions of others' writing from that era. When discussing texts about authors in the South, I use the South Korean spellings for these authors' names regardless of where the text was produced, and when discussing texts about those in the North, I use North Korean conventions for their names regardless of where the text was produced. For quotations, I also add the spelling/pronunciation that the author of the text would have used in brackets. The only exceptions appear in the transliterated titles in the notes and bibliography, where I use the spelling that the author of the text would have used and place the "corrected" spelling in brackets.

For those in Japan, I follow North Korean conventions for the names of Chongryon authors writing in Korean. For ethnic Korean authors who write in Japanese, I follow their preferences to the extent possible. Therefore, when discussing those who prefer the Korean reading of their names (such as Kim Sŏkpŏm and Hŏ Namgi), I romanize accordingly. For those who prefer the Japanese reading (such as Ri Kaisei), I do the same.

Throughout the book, I romanize Korean according to the conventions of the McCune-Reischauer system, and Japanese according to the conventions of the modified Hepburn system. The names of commonly known places (Seoul, Pyongyang, Tokyo, and Osaka) appear without diacritics, except in the transliterated titles of texts.

INTRODUCTION

NATIONAL DIVISION AND BEYOND

In February 1972, the veteran critic Kim Kijin published an open letter to the novelist Ri Kiyŏng, his old friend and colleague in the North, in the new South Korean journal *Pukhan*.[1] Appearing alongside others in a feature titled "Letters Sent to the North" ("Puk ŭro ponaenŭn p'yŏnji"), Kim's message was, as we might expect, an ideological utterance. It was an utterance whose public articulation rather than private transmission dramatized the distance between Kim, its writer, and Ri, its intended recipient, and it was based upon the assumption that Ri, in the North, was living incommunicado in a "completely closed off environment," a "serial drama of lies, fabrication, deception, cruelty, revenge, and purges."[2] The letter, as such, was one that mourned division, looking forward to a day, not far in the future, "when the thickly frozen ice on the Taedong River [would] melt and spring [would] come to Pyongyang."[3]

At the same time, however, Kim's letter also undercut this image of a frozen, isolated, and closed off world in the North. Although Kim expressed confidence that his friend was still the man he remembered—a man who, having "lived uprightly since youth, accompanied only by poverty, consciences, and justice," must have found life in the North to be "internally nauseating, detestable, and exasperating"—he also knew this to be far from the truth.[4] "A number of years ago," Kim confessed in his opening paragraph, "I got the news that a 60th birthday congratulatory conference was held elaborately in your honor," and he was thus keenly aware of the position of influence and leadership that his friend had attained in the North.[5]

Kim's letter, in other words, was motivated by the presence rather than absence of information about his friend, and the source of this news that had crossed the border was likewise significant. As Kim made clear, he had become aware of Ri's 60th birthday congratulatory conference "upon seeing a text and photograph published in Japan," and his letter thus highlighted the dual particularities of inter-Korean communications during the early decades of the Cold War era: that is, not merely their emergence at points of border porosity, where connections were simultaneously both restricted and transmitted, but also their movement and dissemination through the third, mediating space of Japan.[6] In other words, what Kim's letter highlighted was the ongoing yet incomplete nature of division during these decades, when those in North and South Korea could not communicate directly but were nevertheless linked via a network of cross-border media streams whose bounds exceeded the space of the Korean peninsula.

This book is a history of the complex and multidimensional interactions between North and South Korean literature that were formed and transformed via the mediation of colleagues in Japan during the decades between the 1950s and the 1980s. Although the division of the Korean peninsula, implemented by the United States and Soviet Union in 1945 and consolidated with the formation of two separate Korean states in 1948, remains a firm reality eight decades later, the two Koreas and their cultural domains have never been completely isolated from each other. On the contrary, as this book demonstrates, writers in the two postcolonial Koreas engaged, throughout these years, in triangular relations of dialogue flowing through the third space of Japan. These triangular interactions were long-standing and powerful, yet they were far from uniform: they moved in multiple directions across these three locations; they flowed through different sets of colleagues—and different languages—in Japan; and they operated in collaboration with official policies as well as in ways that challenged them. They thus took diverse shapes—and they likewise shifted over time.

In fact, this dimension of historicity was evident in the Kim Kijin letter mentioned above. The text and photograph that Kim was referring to from Japan seems to have been a pair that had appeared in the Japanese journal *Shin Nihon bungaku* in August 1955 with a preface by the novelist Kim Talsu.[7] Kim, as Christina Yi has noted, was "an active member of the Japan Communist Party and Shin Nihon Bungaku Kai," the leftist Japanese literary organization that published *Shin Nihon bungaku*, who would later be acknowledged "as the first and foremost *zainichi* (resident) Korean author of the postwar period."[8] He also played an important role in the publication world of the pro-Pyongyang General Association of Korean Residents in Japan (Kr. Chae Ilbon Chosŏnin Ch'ongnyŏnhaphoe, Jp. Zai-Nihon Chōsenjin Sōrengōkai; hereafter, Chongryon, following the organization's usage). Therefore, he would have served as a key link between the journal and the literary domain in the North, and indeed, his preface noted that the text about Ri had been sent directly from the "homeland" (*hongoku*) alongside others. At the time of its original publication, then, this text and image would have been politically sensitive and beyond the bounds of acceptable discourse in South Korea.

By 1972, however, the situation would have changed. By this time, as discussed in chapter 4, Kim Talsu had parted ways with Chongryon and had begun making new connections with South Korean literature. On the Korean peninsula, the two Koreas had begun a historic series of talks and negotiations in September 1971, culminating in the historic joint communiqué of July 1972, which, alongside the establishment of diplomatic relations between the United States and the People's Republic of China around the same time, led to a temporary thawing of Cold War hostilities. Moreover, the South Korean state, bolstered by steady economic growth that had finally brought South Korea's gross domestic product close to the North's (it would surpass it in 1974), had begun an ideological offensive that included promoting co-optive engagements with those in the North in journals like *Pukhan* and beyond.[9]

By 1972, therefore, links to texts by Kim Talsu as well as to figures in the North had entered the sphere of politically acceptable—even politically useful—discourse, producing a pivotal moment of transformation in South Korean literature's relationship to the "other side" of the Cold War divide. At stake in this transformation was not merely access but also practice. In looking back to his colonial-era relationship with Ri, Kim Kijin not only invoked their past friendship but also their writerly connection, and he here made a provocative claim: that he had responded to Ri's own request for assistance by "writing more than thirty installments of and completing" Ri's *Hometown* (*Kohyang*, 1933–1934), a canonical work of colonial-era proletarian literature.[10] While the veracity of this claim is hard to evaluate, its public articulation in this open letter is nevertheless significant. In this moment, Kim not only laid claim to a portion of this central text of the colonial-era proletarian heritage but also positioned himself and Ri as collaborators in its production.

The textual links invoked in Kim's letter were thus not simply links of reception and communication but also links of creative interaction. And as we will see, such interactions—in addition to being elements of memory—were also ongoing practices on both sides of the thirty-eighth parallel. Yet these practices, as well as the broader cluster of interrelations and connections discussed above, have long been hidden from scholarly view. They only come into focus—individually and in their interrelation—when we consider national division and its impact on Korean literature from new perspectives that look beyond totalizing visions of the thirty-eighth parallel as blockage, beyond the boundaries of the Korean peninsula, beyond monolingualism, beyond the confines of discipline and genre, and beyond the reduction of creativity to originality.

BEYOND DIVISION AS ISOLATION

In February 1949, the North Korean journal *T'aep'ung* published an essay by Yun Namhŭi recalling her experience crossing the thirty-eighth parallel from the South. As she recounts it, the journey is a difficult one that requires travel by freight train, by foot, and by boat. It is also one that almost ends in failure, as the small boat carrying Yun and her companions on the last leg of their trip is intercepted by two South Korean police officers as they approach the border. This was not, as Yun's essay makes clear, their first encounter with state controls on movement. Throughout the trip, they have had to circumvent the "tediously watching eyes" of those keeping tabs on arrivals and departures at Yun's home station; the "unpleasant-feeling gazes" of those checking the identities of individuals on board the trains; and the "venomous looks surrounding passengers like a pack of wolves" as they disembark in Kaesŏng. Yet this is the first time that they have actually been stopped, and they thus quake in fear "as if their whole bodies were being run through by electricity."[11]

This encounter near the border, however, ends much differently than expected. Yun and her companions have not been traveling alone but rather with a guide experienced in such journeys, and when the police officers board the boat, the guide takes them aside and offers them a bribe. The police officers readily accept, and they send them on their way with wishes to "take care" that sound, to Yun, strangely "kind."[12] In place of crackdown, there is commerce—a moment of exchange that transforms the police officers from agents of blockage to well-wishers facilitating passage. In this moment, the essay's vision of border control takes on a dimension of fluidity and porousness, one that is only heightened by the fact that Yun and her companions, when they finally do cross the thirty-eighth parallel, do not know this until the boatman tells them. The border, as such, is not a proverbial line in the sand but rather a space of flow whose differentiations are only legible to someone with extensive border-crossing experience.

In Yun's essay, therefore, the domains of border crossing and control are domains of flow, exchange, and interconnection rather than simple rigidity, differentiation, and blockage, and this characterization intersects with central currents in recent research in the field of border studies. As such work has made clear, borders and boundaries are by no means self-contained, stagnant entities. On the contrary, they are domains of linkage shared in common by the two spaces, places, and entities that they supposedly separate.[13] They are also nodes of action; they are sites, as recent scholarship has noted, where practices of bordering take place, where both difference and identity are produced via processes of filtering—that is, both blockage and flow, both interruption and exchange.[14] The same holds true for the vision of the thirty-eighth parallel in Yun's essay, and it was far from alone in presenting such a characterization.

In Korea, ideological division did not begin in 1945. On the contrary, it could be traced back to contrasting visions of anti-colonial resistance developed in the 1920s.[15] While those on the burgeoning Left saw imperialism as an outgrowth of capitalism and thus linked anti-colonial resistance to internationalist class struggle, cultural nationalists who occupied a spectrum to their political right foregrounded national identity and cross-class national resistance to imperialism. These two positions formed the bedrock of the social, cultural, and political fields of the colonial era in Korea, and debates between them reemerged in 1945 after the fascist restrictions on speech and press of the late colonial era were lifted.

Simultaneously, however, they also became territorialized: that is, linked to two different parts of the Korean peninsula. This territorialization was an outcome of division. On the evening of August 14, 1945, the day before the Japanese surrender that ended the Second World War, Dean Rusk and Charles Bonesteel met in Washington, D.C., with a *National Geographic* map to set a dividing line between two postwar spheres of Allied occupation.[16] Unable to "find a natural geographic line," as Monica Kim has relayed from Dean Rusk's memoirs, they instead chose the thirty-eighth parallel, a line of demarcation subsequently accepted by the Soviet Union, which would occupy the northern half of the peninsula while the Americans occupied the southern half.[17]

As such, the surrender of the Japanese Empire did not return the Korean colony to a sovereign Korean government, which Korean political leaders were then in the process of organizing. On the contrary, the Korean peninsula was split into two zones in which one foreign occupation would be replaced with a pair of new ones. Moreover, since these postwar occupations were not only dual but dueling—that is, engaged in an emerging Cold War rivalry—the thirty-eighth parallel became a boundary tethered to ideological differences and their enforcement. In the southern zone, the Americans preserved the economic order of the colonial era and suppressed a variety of political challenges from the Korean Left: the people's committees that had emerged in tandem with Liberation; labor strikes; leftist political parties; and critiques of American power in the press. In tandem, they gave support to political allies who envisioned a capitalist, anti-communist future for Korea.[18] In the northern zone, the Soviets facilitated the rise of actors seeking a socialist future for Korea, and they supported a revolutionary program that included thoroughgoing land reform, labor reform, the nationalization of industry, and legal prohibitions against gender inequality.[19]

In this way, Left-Right ideological divisions among Koreans were territorialized, and this produced not only strife but also movement. In the years after 1945, millions moved across the Korean peninsula. Some of these migrants were returnees from abroad—those who had been mobilized to the far reaches of the former Japanese Empire—who crossed the thirty-eighth parallel in order to reach their hometowns. Many others, however, crossed from one side of the peninsula to the other because of these dueling systems and the frictions they produced. Indeed, those who were persecuted by or otherwise unhappy with the system in which they found themselves in the post-1945 era relocated en masse. The division of Korea, therefore, was not only a process of blockage but also one of circulation; the institution of the border was not only something that prevented people from moving but also something that compelled them to do so.

After arriving in Korea, the new occupying powers quickly interrupted existing transportation networks and established roadblocks to prevent movement across the thirty-eighth parallel. However, this prohibition was not yet legally institutionalized, and it was also piecemeal in its coverage and enforcement.[20] As such, crossing the thirty-eighth parallel itself remained possible. Newspapers like the Seoul-based *Tonga ilbo* thus carried, for example, a December 1945 article explaining how to cross the thirty-eighth parallel from the south. Based, it said, upon information gleaned from visits to the border by employees of a travel agency based at Seoul Station, the article explained that to get to Pyongyang, for example, one should do the following: from Kaesŏng Station, which was then in the southern zone, hitch a ride on a freight-carrying truck to Ch'ŏngdan; at Ch'ŏngdan, hire a guide for help crossing the border to Hakhyŏn; at Hakhyŏn, board a train to Sariwŏn; at Sariwŏn, transfer to a train to Pyongyang.[21] With transportation networks interrupted, traveling from one zone to another was difficult and at times dangerous. Yet it was done, even necessitated—and this continued even after increasing controls on movement were instituted.

As Chŏng Pyŏngjun, Taeyoung Oh, and others have noted, the outbreak of cholera in Korea in early 1946 served as the impetus for the legal codification of restrictions on crossing the thirty-eighth parallel, and in May of that year, crossings were legally banned.[22] This institutionalization of border controls, however, still did not stop people from crossing. On the contrary, it gave rise to more complex and robust networks of navigation facilitated by the types of guides mentioned in Yun's narrative. According to journalist dispatches from the front lines of the divide, these guides were mostly local farmers who, initially offering their advice for free, had decided to profit off of their knowledge of the geography of the area around the border, and over time, they created a profitable cottage industry.[23] The hardening of the border, in this respect, gave rise to new structures of migrant circulation.

It also produced new structures of material circulation. "Borders," as Elisabeth Leake has noted, "can create new opportunities and new economies,"[24] and indeed, the thirty-eighth parallel not only interrupted transportation networks for people but also for goods and resources. The result was comparative shortages, gluts, and differences in price between the two halves of the peninsula, and in response, traders began crossing the border with goods to exchange.[25] At first, such trading activities were done illicitly, and they took the form of barter exchanges (*mulmul kyohwan*) with brokers sometimes acting as intermediaries.[26] However, this soon changed. With the institutionalization of border restrictions in May 1946, such illicit trade become more difficult, and shortages, gluts, and price instability became even more drastic.[27] The authorities on the two sides of the peninsula thus agreed to set up a legal structure of trade across the thirty-eighth parallel divide, something that began with an agreement for shipborne trade in late 1946 and expanded to overland trade via licensed merchants in mid-1947.[28]

This system, at least in part, came to an end in 1949.[29] However, in one fashion or another, North-South trade appears to have continued until at least 1953. In October 1953, the US Central Intelligence Agency reported that the goods shipped to the South included "ginseng, silver, gold, medicine herbs, Korean silk, and furs" while those sent North included "rubber shoes, lighter flints, cosmetics, textiles, dyes, bicycle tires, medicines, and marine products."[30] The hardening of the border unleashed new structures of exchange across it, and this included the development of an alternative currency and trade in it. As the *Tonga ilbo* journalist Kim Hojin reported in late 1947, since traders from north of the thirty-eighth parallel could not return home with the newly issued currency from the southern zone, traders from both sides would exchange their currency for black-market notes, paying a commission to the money traders who specialized in these exchanges.[31]

The variety of people put in motion by division was thus accompanied by things—by goods in the case of traders—and also by texts. Although postal service between the two sides of the peninsula was originally interrupted alongside transportation and trade networks, weekly postal exchanges were established in March 1946 and they lasted, with some interruptions, until the outbreak of the Korean War.[32] This postal flow, alongside the continued flow of people and goods, meant that publications, too, crossed borders during these years. In early 1947, the literary critic Yi Wŏnjo, then in the northern occupation zone, wrote to his colleagues in Seoul in an open letter published in the April 1947 issue of the Seoul-based journal *Munhak*, the official organ of the Korean Writers' Alliance (Chosŏn Munhakka Tongmaeng).[33] Echoing a similar letter by the novelist Yi T'aejun published the previous year, this communication was, in part, a belated farewell. "When I left," Yi Wŏnjo wrote, "I was not able to meet you, and even when I arrived, I was unable to convey news to you."[34] In this way, the letter began by invoking the pain of separation and distance, going on to express, in its conclusion, a hope for a day in which Yi, the letter writer, would return to engage in "one fight" together with his colleagues.[35]

Nevertheless, the relationship with the literary field in Seoul that Yi's letter outlined was significantly more complex than this framing let on. This was not simply because the letter, dated January 30, had succeeded in crossing the border that its author decried as boundary. It was also because Yi's letter, a call to further develop the movement to "popularize" (*taejunghwa*) literature, was voiced in response to his reading of *Munhak*'s most recent issue. "I read the second [November 1946] issue of *Munhak*," Yi wrote, "and although I know that it is the crystallization of many comrades' hard work and should not be subjected to selfish complaints from outside, for the official organ of the Alliance, the creative work was somewhat weak."[36] While framed in terms of division, Yi's communiqué thus staked out enduring connections as well, and it did not do so alone, as side by side with Yi's text appeared a second letter by Yi T'aejun that likewise conveyed the feeling of joy that its author had experienced upon reading the journal's previous issue, which, he told his colleagues, had been like "seeing your faces."[37]

This cross-border movement of publications, moreover, continued beyond the formation of two separate states in 1948. We can glean this, for example, from statements like the following from the critic Cho Yŏnhyŏn, who, in early 1949, wrote in the South Korean journal *Taejo*:

From what we hear from the countless cultural producers who come South practically every day and from what we read in the various North Korean newspapers and magazines that are smuggled into the country, we are aware of how the North Korean cultural movement is progressing. Of course, we are not foolish enough to blindly believe every word and story that we hear. But we have sufficient material to be able to understand the fundamental methods and goals according to which the North Korean cultural movement is progressing.[38]

We can also get a sense of this continued cross-border circulation of texts from Pyongyang-based publications like *T'aep'ung*, a magazine focused on issues of division published between 1948 and 1950. From its earliest issues, *T'aep'ung* included data, anecdotes, and other information from a wide variety of broadcast as well as textual news sources from south of the border, citing these publications explicitly in recurring features like "Broadcast Room on Paper" ("Chisang pangsongsil"), "Collection of Palm-of-the-Hand True Stories" ("Sirhwa changp'yŏnjip," 實話 掌篇集), "Collection of True Stories" ("Sirhwa"), "Reflective Lens" ("Pansagyŏng"), and "Poster Board" ("Pyŏkpop'an"). The cross-border circulation of texts, like that of people and goods, thus operated hand in hand with division even as it interrupted traditional communication networks.

It would be easy to dismiss the above as a phenomenon confined to a bounded period before the Korean War (1950–1953), and indeed, the existing scholarship generally views the years after 1945 as a "liberation space" (*haebang konggan*)—a momentary space for exchange, flexibility, communication, and compromise—that gradually closed with the establishment of separate states in 1948 and the outbreak of full-scale warfare in 1950. In reality, however, what the years between 1948 and 1950 witnessed was not simply a rigidification of the border but also the opposite: the increasing contestation of it by the two Korean states themselves; and the mass migration of people with the moving warfront of the first year of the Korean War. Moreover, even after the flow of people reduced to a trickle with the military stalemate in 1951 and the establishment of the heavily guarded armistice line in 1953, certain flows continued. As this book makes clear, flows of media—texts, images, and more—continued to link the two Koreas throughout the subsequent decades.

The division of the Korean peninsula between 1945 and 1948 has produced deep and painful cleavages in Korean culture, politics, and society. Yet to cleave does not only mean to split but also to adhere, and indeed, the thirty-eighth parallel has never simply divided the two halves of the Korean peninsula but also, at the same time, sutured them together in relations of co-optive, competitive, and transformative interaction and exchange. Recent scholarship in Korean studies has demonstrated how writers in the two Koreas have represented each other, how they have engaged with global literary trends shared in common, such as science fiction, and how particular filmmakers like Sin Sangok have crossed the thirty-eighth parallel divide.[39] Additionally, recent research has also begun to explore how texts crossed the thirty-eighth parallel divide in the 1980s–1990s.[40] Drawing upon such work, this book goes one step further to highlight direct interactions between texts from North Korea, South Korea, and Japan across the Cold War decades. As we will see, these interactions have taken diverse forms across a range of historical periods, and they varied from highly visible to hardly perceptible. In all cases, however, they have been integral to the constitution and transformation of postcolonial Korean literature—something that cannot be understood as a purely peninsula-bound affair.

BEYOND THE KOREAN PENINSULA

In April 1965, North Korea's *Munhak sinmun* newspaper, the official organ of the Central Committee of the Korean Writers' Alliance, published a South Korean poem titled "Come Smash the Altar" ("Wasŏ chedan ŭl pusura") in order to commemorate the upcoming fifth anniversary of the April Revolution of 1960, when student-led protests pushed South Korea's first president, Syngman Rhee (Yi Sŭngman), and his Liberal Party from power.[41] Written by the poet and critic Ku Chungsŏ, the poem had originally appeared in the Seoul-based *Han'guk ilbo* newspaper on April 18, 1963, as part of a larger feature looking back at the events of April 1960, and it had subsequently appeared in the North's *Chogukt'ongil* newspaper in June 1963 before being reprinted again, as mentioned above, in the *Munhak sinmun* in April 1965.⁴² Yet even before crossing into the Democratic People's Republic of Korea (DPRK), Ku's poem had already traversed borders in a different direction. After being published in the *Han'guk ilbo* on April 18, 1963, it had been picked up and reprinted less than a week later by the *Chosŏn sinbo* newspaper, the official organ of Chongryon.⁴³ The poem's path to the North had thus been triangular; it had traveled across the East Sea from South Korea to the DPRK-affiliated press in Japan before making the transit a second time to Pyongyang.

The triangular path that Ku's poem took from South Korea to North Korea via Japan was by no means unique. On the contrary, as the thirty-eighth parallel divide hardened on the Korean peninsula, the space of Japan emerged as a primary circuit of transfer and exchange between the two Koreas. While it may seem, therefore, that the hardening of the thirty-eighth parallel produced isolation between the two Koreas, the reality is that it produced something quite different: triangulation. This book, therefore, looks beyond the Korean peninsula to Japan, showing how ethnic Korean residents in Japan as well as Japanese writers, scholars, and publishers played vital roles in both mediating inter-Korean relations and transforming them.

While there is a robust literature on colonial-era Korean-Japanese connections, less attention has been given to postcolonial interactions. Yet the surrender of the Japanese Empire on August 15, 1945, did not suddenly isolate these two territories or populations. At the end of the Second World War, there were more than a million Japanese civilians and soldiers in Korea and more than two million Koreans in Japan.⁴⁴ It took years for all of the Japanese citizens in the former colony to leave; in the northern half of the peninsula, some technicians stayed or were kept in place even after the founding of the DPRK.⁴⁵ Likewise, repatriation of Koreans from Japan took many years, and a sizable population never left, forming the significant ethnic Korean population in postcolonial Japan.⁴⁶

There were also new connections and exchanges that emerged after Liberation. Indeed, if there continued to be a Japanese presence in Korea even after 1945, this was not only because portions of the colonial-era population stayed but also because new individuals entered for the first time. In the northern half of the peninsula, Japanese individuals not only took up residence in Korea on their way home from China and other parts of the former empire but also—and quite remarkably—were recruited from

Japan to work as technicians as well as medical professionals like doctors and nurses.[47] This occurred via ongoing trade links to Japan, which were illicit yet continuous and robust. Indeed, as the US Central Intelligence Agency reported in April 1950, the Korean Commercial Company (Chosŏn Sangsa), one of the primary actors in this trade, had brought Japanese technicians from the North to Osaka to help recruit new technicians in 1949.[48]

Japanese residents and workers do not appear to have stayed in the southern zone as long as they did in the northern one. However, the joint occupation of the southern zone and Japan by the US military—alongside a range of illicit trade and repatriation activities—meant that the two territories continued to be closely linked via people, mail, and things. Moreover, although the majority of the transit of Koreans was from the Japanese archipelago, there were also Koreans moving illicitly in the opposite direction: those who found the economic and political situation trying in Korea; those seeking out family and business improvement; those looking for educational opportunities; those fleeing violence on Cheju Island.[49]

All of these flows, moreover, took on new contours with the outbreak of the Korean War. As will be discussed in chapter 3, Japan was the primary site for military procurement and personnel staging on the US and UN side during the conflict. This expanded traffic across the East Sea, and it also brought Koreans to Japan to work in psychological warfare and other endeavors. This meant that it was not only technicians and official personnel who made the journey but also individuals from the cultural and intellectual arenas, and this produced lasting effects on the cultural and intellectual spheres of the South. In the North, too, the Korean War era gave new importance to Japan. The North's invasion of the South had been an attempt to reunify the country by force. Once the course of the war turned to stalemate, however, DPRK authorities turned to other means of expanding the revolution. In particular, they looked to the ethnic Korean population in Japan. As will be discussed in chapter 1, new links were established in 1952 and institutionalized in 1955 with the founding of Chongryon, an organization that played a central role in North Korean engagements with the South.

In staking out this set of connections, this book draws upon recent scholarship in the postcolonial history of Korean and Japanese relations,[50] expanding the scope of this research to relations with the North and inter-Korean relations. It also builds upon the robust scholarship that has developed in recent decades on the ethnic Korean population in Japan.[51] In particular, this book seeks to expand the focus of such research from analysis of the community's place within Japan to its broader place in the region: that is, in the triangular relations between the two Koreas and Japan. In this way, this book adapts Sunhee Koo's recent discussion of "diasporic agency" in relation to the ethnic Korean minority in China, and it likewise draws upon David S. Roh's vision of "triangulating" literary production across diaspora-mediated borders.[52] By reimagining the Korean diasporic community in Japan as a crucial hinge of regional interactions linking North Korea, South Korea, and Japan, this book aims to underline the community's historical and cultural centrality rather than its marginality.

In doing so, moreover, this book also contributes to a new vision of Cold War studies in the region. In recent years, scholarly interest in inter-Asian connections has grown markedly. Linked to a broader turn toward emphasizing South-South interactions, exchanges, and solidarities, this growing interest has transformed a variety of fields, including that of Cold War studies. In the past, scholarship in Cold War studies operated firmly within a superpowers framework focused on the relationships between the United States, the Soviet Union, and the countries in their respective blocs. As a result, the center of gravity for scholarly analysis of the Cold War era remained fixed around the United States and the Soviet Union, and studies of other locations recurred to an explanatory mode focused on these locations' relationships to or interactions with one or both of these superpowers.

With the growth of interest in inter-Asian connections, however, scholarship has begun approaching the Cold War differently: in the words of Rosie Bsheer and Mohammed Alsudairi, "as less of a struggle emanating from Europe and engulfing the 'peripheries' through the instigation of the super powers and more as an instance of 'intercontinental synchronization of hostilities' catalyzed by local and regional actors, struggles, and dynamics."[53] The result is a new type of Cold War scholarship that recognizes the presence of multiple "regional, sub-systemic, Cold Wars" and responds to Lorenz Lüthi's call "to change the focus—or better adopt multiple foci—in order to decenter the Cold War in a systematic fashion, to move structural developments into the foreground, to restore middle powers and smaller actors to visibility, and to link events horizontally to each other (and not only vertically to the great powers)."[54]

Showing how diasporic Koreans in Japan played a key, mediating role in the Cold War–era triangular interactions between North Korea, South Korea, and Japan, this book contributes to this decentering of Cold War studies and the concomitant turn toward inter-Asian connections. That is, by reframing the Cold War conflict in Korea in terms of regional interactions, this book neither isolates the Koreas nor reduces them to mere proxies for the superpowers. In tandem, it also challenges the monolingualism inherent in much of the existing scholarship on this era.

BEYOND LINGUISTIC BOUNDARIES

On December 30, 1952, the Tokyo-based *Haebang sinmun* newspaper published an essay by the resident Korean writer Kim T'aegyŏng on "The *Haebang sinmun* and the Study of Our National Language."[55] In the essay, Kim—a daily reader, he said, of a range of Japanese newspapers—described a recent encounter with an issue of the *Haebang sinmun* that he had discovered on the floor of a Korean restaurant where he had been eating. For Kim, this was the first Korean-language newspaper that he had seen in several years, and his encounter with it was thus "extremely moving."[56] It also produced a change in his life. Having become a regular reader of the *Haebang sinmun* after this encounter, Kim—perusing the paper with a dictionary by his side—had acquired a new urge to improve himself. For him, it was not just a vehicle of news. It was an elixir of life in the foreign land of Japan: one that gave new hope and meaning and identity; and it was one that had to be treated differently, with reverence.

He was not alone in his reverence for the paper. He was also not alone in the importance that he placed on the Korean language and knowledge of it. At the time, most resident Koreans in Japan spoke Japanese, and those who had received an education either in Japan or in Korea during the colonial period also read and wrote Japanese. At the same time, a significant portion of this population also spoke Korean, and resident Korean activists—especially those on the political Left—increasingly saw use and knowledge of written and spoken Korean for children as well as adults as a priority for the community's growth, development, and strengthening of relations with the homeland. Korean-language outlets like the *Haebang sinmun* published regular exhortations on this issue, and it even became a regular part of the popular comic, *Ttolttoli*, that appeared daily in the newspaper.[57] Moreover, the community soon began publishing a range of Korean-language outlets, including ones that extended beyond the leftist community.

This is not unknown; on the contrary, recent research has highlighted the complexity and importance of debates over language use in the resident Korean community and its literary world, especially after the formation of Chongryon, which called upon writers to primarily use Korean rather than Japanese.[58] Nevertheless, most scholarship in English has continued to focus on Japanese-language works rather than Korean-language works in narrating the history and culture of the community. Or rather, it has generally separated the two, rather than looking across the linguistic divide. This book takes a multilingual approach in order to take these works seriously and show how writing from Japan, in both Japanese and Korean, transformed the literary domains in North and South Korea and the relationship between them. It also takes such an approach because this was not the only multilingual population. As noted above, the Japanese presence on the Korean peninsula did not disappear all of a sudden on August 15, 1945. Likewise, the decades of knowledge and use of the Japanese language that Koreans had developed between 1910 and 1945 did not vanish into thin air. On the contrary, more than an entire generation of Koreans had been schooled in Japanese rather than Korean, and this had a lasting effect on their thoughts, lives, and experiences, something that Serk-Bae Suh has shown in detail in his work on the poet Kim Suyŏng.[59]

It also made possible a whole range of cross-border interactions that have largely been ignored in the existing scholarship. Although the use of Japanese was stigmatized and people rarely discussed their continued abilities in the language, this does not mean that it was not in fact used. On the contrary, there is ample evidence that it was used—on both sides of the thirty-eighth parallel—for a range of activities from popular reading to scholarship to interpreting to the translation of foreign works. When the Japanese novelist Hino Ashihei, for example, wrote of his 1956 visit to North Korea, he noted the ease with which he was able to communicate with Han Sŏrya, the foremost writer in the North at the time, who, Hino said, spoke excellent Japanese.[60] Likewise, when North Korean works of literature entered the South for what was perhaps the first time in 1957, they did so via a Japanese-language anthology compiled by the Chongryon writer Hŏ Namgi in Japan.[61] As such, the scope of postcolonial Korean reading interests cannot be thought of in isolation from the colonial past. Japanese publications continued to inform Korean texts and discussions in robust and complex ways, providing alternative visions of the Cold War order, access to works from across the Cold War divide, and even new ways of thinking about Korean identity and the Korean past. None of this would be visible without a consideration of how texts, ideas, and imaginations crossed linguistic boundaries.

BEYOND THE CONFINES OF GENRE AND DISCIPLINE

In January 1973, the popular South Korean magazine *Sindonga* published a Korean translation of an essay by the Japanese historian Ueda Masaaki on Nara's Isonokami Shrine and a particular artifact housed there: the Seven-Branched Sword (Kr. Ch'iljido, Jp. Shichishitō), an ancient product of the Korean peninsula's kingdom of Paekche supposedly given to a Yamato king at some point between the third and sixth centuries.[62] The essay was published as part of a special feature on ancient Korean-Japanese relations, and it was a text whose concerns would seem distant from the topic of this book.

Ueda's essay, however, was translated from a Japanese-language publication called *Nihon no naka no Chōsen bunka*, a loosely Chongryon-affiliated journal edited by Kim Talsu, the novelist mentioned at the outset, who Ueda quoted directly in the essay.[63] Moreover, as will be discussed in chapter 4, this topic of ancient Japanese-Korean relations was one that had garnered enough public interest since the 1972 discovery of the Takamatsuzuka Tumulus in Japan to warrant a special feature in a popular magazine, and even more importantly, it would also go on to inspire a range of literary works including Ch'oe Inho's multiyear work, *The Lost Kingdom* (*Irhŏbŏrin wangguk*, 1985–1988), which brings together scholarship from South Korea, North Korea, and Japan.

As this case demonstrates, literary production from these years cannot be understood in isolation, and this book thus follows literary transits across boundaries of discipline and genre. During these years, novelists, poets, and playwrights did not restrict their reading or writing to literary publications, and they did not live lives isolated from concerns and discussions that exceeded the bounds of their literary profession. To understand their work, therefore, scholarship must cross borders alongside them. Otherwise, it would decontextualize them; it would rob them of their multidimensional relationship to the world, and, in the case of Ch'oe's *The Lost Kingdom*, completely obscure the innovative and challenging ways in which literature crossed borders of genre and discipline as a means of establishing triangular networks of interactions between those in North Korea, South Korea, and Japan.

There are also material reasons why literary texts should not be understood in isolation. Since *Sindonga* was a popular magazine, it published a range of types of work that attracted public interest, from works of scholarship to poetry to essays to fiction and more. The issue that carried Ueda's article, therefore, not only exposed readers to perspectives on ancient history but also exposed them to a range of other types of work: fiction, poetry, photography, a discussion of the war in Vietnam, a discussion of the new Yusin Constitution in South Korea, a discussion of North-South relations on the Korean peninsula, and more. As such, literary texts not only engaged with and drew upon other types of texts in their content and imagination but also moved through textual fields as parts of multigenre, multidisciplinary publications that brought various types of works together in their pages. When a publication like *Sindonga* traveled across borders, it brought literature, comics, photographs, news items, opinion pieces, and more all packaged together. To ignore this, once again, is to decontextualize—to literally rip works from the pages on which they were published.

BEYOND CREATIVITY AS ORIGINALITY

In October 1961, North Korea's *Munhak sinmun* newspaper published an open letter by the veteran poet Ri Chŏnggu to an unnamed "southern Korean writer." Addressed simply to "Brother R," the letter called upon its intended recipient to reject the American presence on the Korean peninsula and turn instead toward solidarity with the North. "Brother R," the letter said, was like "a boat without a captain—a boat just floating along as the wind blows,"[64] and it thus came to a pointed conclusion: "What you need, brother, is a captain. As you abandon that cursed shore and depart for a new one, what you need is a captain who can find that new, happy shore for you. I feel the urge, in particular, to tell you that it is precisely because of this that one side of our fatherland has been turned into a heaven on earth [*chisang rakwŏn*]."[65]

Ri's letter here took up a form of ideological exhortation that resembled the one seen in the Kim Kijin open letter discussed at the beginning of this introduction. It likewise invoked, as in Kim's letter, an experience of cross-border reading. "Brother R," Ri's letter began, "A while ago I happened to read your text, 'Silent Protest,' which was published in a certain southern Korean journal, and I could not sleep for nights because the scenes of your wretched life and the image of your resentment-ridden face kept appearing before my eyes like phantoms [*hwanyŏng*]."[66]

Despite these similarities, however, there was one aspect of Ri's letter that was quite different. The letter's description of recent events in "Brother R's" life makes it clear that the individual being addressed in the text was not, as in the case of Kim's letter, a friend. In fact, the individual being addressed was not even a real person but rather a character in a South Korean short story. More specifically, "R" was the narrator-protagonist of Im Suil's "Record of White Clothes" ("Paegŭi ŭi sugi"), a short story published in the May 1961 issue of the South Korean journal *Hyŏndae munhak* and later republished in the North's *Munhak sinmun* in 1962.[67] Ri's call to pair "Brother R's" boat with a northward-looking captain was thus not a demand for direct political action but rather a demand for literary action: that is, a call for transformation in a literary character produced by a colleague in the South.

Ri's letter, in other words, was an attempt at creative, literary engagement. And as we will see over the course of this book, other writers—from North Korea, South Korea, and the diasporic community in Japan—translated this call into direct action in their work. In various ways, that is, writers in these three locations took up practices of cross-border writing: the integration of pieces of texts from across borders into new literary works; and, at times, the creative reimagination and rewriting of such texts in a more comprehensive fashion. In drawing out the border-crossing history of such practices, this book takes an expansive vision of their literary significance. Instead of seeing such borrowing and adaptation as a sign of literary derivativeness—that is, a lack of creativity—I understand such textual borrowing and refashioning as means of creative engagement. As scholars in adaptation studies and beyond have noted, to borrow, adapt, and rewrite is to engage in intertextual dialogue, to begin a conversation with the original text and its author, bringing them into new contexts and taking them in new directions.[68]

This is precisely what the writers discussed in this book accomplished via their practices of cross-border writing—and it was not, to be sure, a result of lack of creativity. It was also not uniform in its meaning or purpose. Although all of the writers discussed in this book sought out cross-border connections, they did so toward different ends. Korea, as it was understood at the time, had long been—and continued to be—a single country. The thirty-eighth parallel divide thus could not be seen or accepted as an actual border dividing foreign countries, and this was a conviction that was shared across political and ideological lines. In fact, it was also a conviction shared by the two Korean states established in 1948, each of which refused to recognize the other and instead claimed legitimacy over the entire peninsula—hence the lack of "North" and "South" in the official names of each state.

Yet what this overwhelming agreement produced was a complex and conflicted political calculus. On the one hand, the two Korean states sought unification because they each rejected the legitimacy of the other side. This gave rise, at certain points in time, to ideological offensives in which writers were encouraged to look across the border and engage in co-optive practices of engagement. At the same time, however, the two Korean states found themselves tasked with policing the boundary at the thirty-eighth parallel. This made them the enforcers of division alongside their respective Cold War allies, and it meant that those who sought to resist the Cold War–state system and the violence and repression that it authorized also called for reunification.

Therefore, while this book deals continuously with attempts to make connections across the thirty-eighth parallel, it does not flatten the important political differences between these different attempts and the different contexts, motivations, and subject positions that produced them. We will see, therefore, how state-aligned practices of cross-border engagement in South Korea and Japan have coexisted and/or alternated with oppositional practices of cross-border engagement that sought to push back against state projects in critique and resistance. Additionally, we will see how practices of cross-border engagement in North Korea, while echoing state-sponsored projects in South Korea and Japan, have not emerged in a parallel oppositional vein. As such, we will see how practices of cross-border reading, writing, and engagement both link these contexts and demonstrate their cleavages.

CHAPTER SUMMARIES

Chapter 1 discusses the consumption and creative adaptation of South Korean literature in 1950s–1960s North Korea, emphasizing the pivotal role in developing these practices played by writers and publications from the Korean leftist community in Japan. As the chapter makes clear, the institutionalization of national division did not stop South Korean texts from entering the North. On the contrary, North Korean practices of citation and reference show that South Korean media continued to be available, that their presence grew over time, and that the type of interaction that North Korean literature engaged in with them gradually became more robust and creative. The chapter then turns to the activities of the Korean Left in Japan, eventually organized under the umbrella of Chongryon, in order to show how these developments in North Korean literature became possible because of the way in which writers and activists in Japan engaged with the South and because of the tightening relations between those in Japan and those in the North.

Chapter 2 picks up on the discussions of the previous chapter by focusing on a particular example of North Korean literature's creative engagement with South Korean literature: that of Kim Myŏngsu's 1965 play *Mother of the South* (*Namnyŏk ŭi ŏmŏni*), which drew directly upon the South Korean short story "Hope" ("Hŭimang," 1963) by An Tongnim, among other texts. The chapter then shows how the vision of the militant mother developed in Kim's play made its way not only into North Korean representations of the Korean revolution's colonial-era history but also into the Chongryon imagination in Japan. The chapter thus shows how influence moved not only from Japan to North Korea but also in the opposite direction, and it also shows how this influence both consolidated the relationship between the literary field in the DPRK and produced new cleavages. In particular, the chapter ends with a consideration of the Chongryon literature of "repatriation" (*kwiguk*) and the problematic figure of the deferrer who emerged with it, showing how this figure—officially sanctioned by Chongryon at first—also became linked to the literature of those who, leaving the organization in the late 1960s and 1970s, gradually developed new types of interaction with South Korean literature.

In chapters 3 and 4, this book turns to South Korean literature, showing the multistep process through which writers reengaged with the writing of those across the border in the North. Chapter 3 focuses on South Korean literature and criticism of the 1950s: in particular, the way in which it deployed literary and intellectual currents from Japan to find a way out of the Cold War binary and reengage with both Marxism and with the banned, colonial-era writing of those who had gone North after 1945. Unlike chapters 1 and 2, this chapter focuses on interactions with texts by Japanese writers rather than resident Korean writers in Japan, and it emphasizes the surprising yet robust way in which South Korean writers used these texts to challenge state policy and discourse rather than reinforce it, as done in the North. Additionally, the chapter notes the counterintuitive role of the United States and the United Nations, whose infrastructure Korean writers used to import a variety of works of Japanese Marxism and Marxist existentialism.

Finally, chapter 4 demonstrates how South Korean literature of the 1960s, 1970s, and 1980s gradually moved from challenging the Cold War binary and looking back to colonial-era works by modernists who had gone North after 1945 to more robust forms of cross-border engagement.

First, the chapter shows how colonial-era proletarian writers like Rim Hwa reemerged, again with help from Japanese writing, in South Korean works and discussions of the 1960s, allowing for new ways of engaging with the work of those who had gone North, including, to a limited extent, their post-1945 writings. It then turns to Cho Haeil's 1970s–1980s rewriting of the canonical colonial-era work *Im Kkŏkchŏng*, written by Hong Myŏnghŭi, later the North Korean vice premier, to show how even those nonmodernists who were never purged were able to be brought back into textual visibility. Finally, it discusses the multivolume 1980s novel *The Lost Kingdom* by Ch'oe Inho, which uses the lens of ancient Korean-Japanese relations to link together works from North Korea, South Korea, and the resident Korean community in Japan.

1

REVERBERATIONS

South Korean Literature Between 1950s–1960s
North Korea and Japan

In August 1961, the North Korean youth magazine *Sae sedae* published an open letter written by Min Sukcha, a student in the city of Hamhŭng, to her older brother in the South. Written in tandem with the sixteenth anniversary of Korea's liberation from the Japanese Empire on August 15, 1945, Min's letter began with the following words:

> Elder brother!
>
> Holidays are always joyous days.
>
> For us Koreans, everyone's heart flutters with new joy and emotion each time the 8.15 holiday approaches.
>
> [But] the more fully I partake in the joy and emotion of the 8.15 Liberation and the more freely I sing the song of learning, the more unable I am to control my feelings of sorrow and lamentation.
>
> For days now, I have been sick with this feeling of lamentation, so I once again write this letter that cannot be sent.¹

For Min, the August 15 anniversary was a time of mixed emotions: a time to both recall the joy of Liberation and remember, with sorrow, those in the South who had not yet tasted its rightful fruits. For Min, in other words, it was a time that highlighted the stark contrast and division between the current realities of the two sides of the Korean peninsula.

Min's letter, however, was not only a lamentation of distance. After recounting a recent encounter with Kim Il Sung (Kim Ilsŏng), who, during a visit to Min's school, had encouraged her to seek vengeance upon her family's American enemies, the letter turned to the text of a recent South Korean poem—reproduced almost in its entirety within the text—that likewise inspired Min to call upon her brother to rise up against the South Korean state and its American allies. This poem, Kang Myŏnghŭi's "Why My Brothers and Sisters Bled" ("Oppa wa ŏnni ka wae p'i hŭllyŏnŭnji"),[2] was a work written by a South Korean elementary school student in the immediate aftermath of the South's April Revolution of 1960, when a monthslong series of demonstrations against corrupt elections and authoritarian rule led primarily by students succeeded in forcing the first president of the Republic of Korea (ROK), Syngman Rhee, from power, and what its presence in the letter signaled was the robust way in which cultural producers in the North engaged with South Korean literature as a vehicle of both connection and collaboration. Indeed, echoing the poem's characterization of April 19, 1960, as "unforgettable," the letter used the same description for the poem, establishing a point of linkage and dialogue between the two writers and the two texts.

The emergence of such direct engagements between North Korean and South Korean texts is the subject of this chapter. Yet it also emphasizes the multivalent trajectories of connection and exchange that made them possible. Min was likely familiar with Kang's poem from its reprint in the August 1960 issue of the North Korean children's magazine *Adong munhak*,[3] where it appeared as the first—but, as we will see, by no means last—South Korean poem to be republished in the North. Yet the appearance of this poem in *Adong munhak* was itself mediated, as it had been picked up from two earlier republications in Japan. In May 1960, just weeks after the April Revolution, Kang's poem had already appeared in the pages of the *Chosŏn minbo*,[4] the Korean-language newspaper of the Chongryon organization, and it appeared again, in July 1960, in the Chongryon-affiliated, Japanese-language journal *Atarashii sedai*.[5] Finally, at the roughly the same time as it appeared in *Adong munhak* in

North Korea, it appeared again in a Chongryon-edited, Japanese-language monograph called *An April of Blood: The Southern Korean People's Uprising* (*Chi no shigatsu: Minami Chōsen jinmin hōki*),[6] published by the Chōsen Bunkasha in Tokyo, where Kang's poem appeared side by side with a range of others from the South that would soon be recirculated in the North.

The set of transits behind Min Sukcha's letter of August 1961, therefore, was not bilateral but trilateral. Indeed, the relationship of connection that it produced—despite the ongoing reality of national division—was one that both engaged directly with South Korean literature and emerged out of larger circuits of texts that were triangular in shape, passing across the East Sea from the South and then back again to the North. In order to follow these transits, this chapter begins by showing how South Korean texts continued to be read in North Korea despite the advent of national division. Looking at the literary sphere in particular as well as the broader publishing world, it shows how South Korean texts were not only read and cited in increasingly robust ways over the course of the 1950s and 1960s but also how they came to be reprinted in North Korean publications, where they were identified as targets for revolutionary engagement. It then turns to Japan, showing how the influence of the Chongryon publishing sphere played a vital role in this transformation in South Korean literature's reception in the North, highlighting the novel forms of cross-border writing and creative textual engagement developed by writers across the East Sea. Finally, it demonstrates how North Korean writers—learning from and then going beyond their colleagues in Japan—produced novel practices of cross-border writing that reimagined South Korean literature and its relationship to the North.

CROSS-BORDER READING I

The establishment of a separate state north of the thirty-eighth parallel was a piecemeal process. As Kim Chaeyong has noted, one of the first decisive steps in this direction was taken on February 7 and 8, 1946, with the formation of the Provisional People's Committee of Northern Korea (Pukchosŏn Imsi Inmin Wiwŏnhoe).[7] This body, as Kee Kwang-seo has put it, was the "first central authority organ in North[ern] Korea," and it immediately moved to remake the nation, beginning with the March 5, 1946, declaration of the Land Reform Act, which, as Cheehyung Harrison Kim has noted, redistributed approximately 2.45 million acres of land "in just a little more than three weeks."[8] The Land Reform Act, as Kim has further noted, provided the "724,522 households receiving land for free . . . [with their] first sweet taste of socialism," and it was soon followed, in June, July, and August, respectively, with new regulations on labor, gender equality, and the nationalization of industry.[9]

On the heels of these transformational policies enacted by the Provisional People's Committee of Northern Korea, the more durable structures of rule that would gird the formation of the DPRK emerged in rapid succession. Late August 1946 witnessed the establishment of the Workers' Party of Northern Korea, which would subsequently merge with the Workers' Party of Southern Korea to form the DPRK's ruling Workers' Party of Korea. February 1947 brought the establishment of the People's Assembly of Northern Korea (Pukchosŏn Inmin Hoeŭi), a representative body made up of delegates from the People's Committees elected in November 1946 that, in turn, founded the People's Committee of Northern Korea (Pukchosŏn Inmin Wiwŏnhoe), a new "supreme executive organ" led by Kim Il Sung.[10] And February 1948 witnessed the founding of the Korean People's Army and the composition of the first drafts of the DPRK's constitution.[11]

As such, when the Democratic People's Republic of Korea was finally proclaimed in September 1948, it stood on the foundation of years of sociopolitical developments that took the area north of the thirty-eighth parallel in a dramatically different direction than the area south of it. Once again, however, this institutionalization of division—the establishment of a separate state in the North, and to parallel it, a separate state in the South—did not simply produce isolation but also confrontation, as each state claimed to be the legitimate government of the entire peninsula. These two states were not only dual but also dueling, and this meant that they continuously looked over the border in a confrontation that suffused politics, media, and culture.

In the North, this was a confrontation that, from the very beginning, relied upon and propagated practices of cross-border reading. In August 1949, the National People's Publishing Company in the North released a monograph called *Collection of Materials about the Southern Half [of our Country]* (*Nambanbu e kwanhan charyojip*). Intended for those engaged in the work of ideological training and guidance, this nearly 200-page book was produced, its authors noted, by compiling "materials...from southern Korean newspapers and wire services as well as from 'declarations' and 'conversations' released by the traitors themselves."[12] And indeed, in offering evidence of the many crises engulfing the contemporary South, it not only marshaled a wide array of South Korean sources but also cited them with dates in each instance throughout the text.

For example, the text's third chapter, "The Pitiful State of Southern Korea's Society and Culture," began with a discussion of the excessive taxes imposed upon ordinary citizens in the South. "In the second half of 1948 alone," it explained, "the puppet 'government' has accrued a deficit of 10.7 billion [wŏn], so in order to make up for this, it has decided to increase its tax revenues by 3 billion [wŏn] through raises of various taxes, and it has even reached the point of collecting 100% of real earnings through income tax (*Chayu sinmun*, March 24, 1949)."[13] The text then went on to demonstrate the extent to which tax demands exceeded the ability for citizens to pay:

> From late March 1949 to [early April 1949], the amount of delinquent taxes was more than 3.6 billion [wŏn], and combined with the previous amount, the total comes to more than 5.6 billion [wŏn] (*Yŏnhap sinmun*, April 9, 1949). The number of delinquent tax cases in downtown Seoul alone is 1,000,000 (*Tonga ilbo*, March 8, 1949). As a result of the type of delinquent taxes mentioned above, the number of cases of [asset] seizure by the Taegu tax authorities alone in just two weeks between March 7 and March 20 was 5,000 (*Chayu sinmun*, March 26, 1949).[14]

Such formal taxes, moreover, were just the beginning, and the text thus continued: "Besides these [taxes], there are more than fifty types of contributions (*Chosŏn chungang ilbo*, March 29, 1949), and these contributions and fees exceed [the above tax amounts] by many times. Regarding these various, forcibly imposed fees...according to the report given in the 'National Assembly' by Yi Hun'gu [Ri Hun'gu] and 71 others, they include the following... (*Chosŏn chungang ilbo*, April 22, 1949)."[15] Of course, the text's goal here was to demonstrate the difficult situation in the contemporary South. Yet what it demonstrated, in tandem, was the extensive access to South Korean news sources that existed in the North.

Moreover, this access was evident not only in texts published for state and party operatives but also in texts published for a wider audience. Already in 1947 and 1948, similar practices of citation from South Korean journalistic publications were present in various North Korean serials. They were evident, for example, in installments of the "Southern Korean News" ("Namchosŏn sosik") corner published in the August 1947 issue of the journal *Podo*. They were also evident in a running feature called "Broadcast Room on Paper" ("Chisang pangsongsil") in the journal *T'aep'ung*. This feature, which had existed since the publication's inaugural issue and focused on news from the South, began including citations from South Korean news sources in October 1948, and this was something that continued under the title "Poster Board" ("Pyŏkpop'an") after February 1949. Additionally, by August 1949, the publication had also begun printing a similar feature called "Reflective Lens" ("Pansagyŏng") in the front matter of each issue.

By the late 1940s, therefore, North Korean practices of cross-border reading had become a regular presence in North Korean publications, and this extended to the main, state-sponsored daily, the *Rodong sinmun* newspaper, as well. On January 28, 1949, the *Rodong sinmun* published an article titled "A Dismal Social Landscape of Degeneration and Prostitution" ("T'oep'ye wa yullak ŭi amdamhan sahoesang") alongside a cluster of other pieces focused on the sorry state of contemporary South Korea.[16] After comparing the Syngman Rhee state to its Japanese colonial predecessor, the article cited a set of South Korean newspapers—the *Minju ilbo*, the *Segye ilbo*, the *Kukche sinmun*, and the *P'yŏnghwa sinmun*—to highlight the destitute condition of ordinary citizens in the South: the many frozen bodies found in Seoul; the empty ration stations unable to satiate the hunger of the starving; the rash of suicides among destitute laborers, farmers, postcolonial returnees, and opiate addicts; the succession of corpses run over by US military vehicles; and the profusion of brothels frequented by US personal and corrupt officials of the ROK state.

From this article and similar ones that appeared around this time,[17] it is clear that writers at the *Rodong sinmun*, like their colleagues at other publications, had wide-ranging access to South Korean sources, and this was a wide-ranging access that, in the post–Korean War years, would extend increasingly further. "The Pitiful State of Southern Korean Children," a 1956 article by the journalist Hong Tuwŏn, demonstrates this well.[18] According to Hong, South Korea was a "terrifying living hell and prison not only for adults but also for children," and in order to substantiate this he presented a range of evidence: regarding the situation of orphans, Hong reported, "According to the *Tonga ilbo*, greater than 97% of the children receiving 'protection' in the custody of so-called 'orphanages' have some sort of frightening disease"; regarding homeless children, he reported, "According to the southern Korean magazine *Hyŏndae kongnon*, southern Korea's juvenile vagrants now number approximately 50,000"; and regarding child and infant mortality, he reported, "Conveying the wretched state of the starving residents of Pusan, the *Pusan ilbo* [states] that the situation is one in which 50% of those born in the city 'die within the first year of their birth due to disease or their mother's malnutrition,'" and likewise, "According to the 1955 issue of *Han'guk yŏn'gam*, babies and children under the age of four accounted for 43% of total deaths and the mortality rate for children under the age of 14 amounted to 52.4% of total deaths."[19]

These statistics are just a sampling of those that Hong relayed to readers alongside a photo attributed to South Korea's *Han'guk hwabo*. Yet they give us a sense of how the range of South Korean publications being consumed and deployed in the North expanded over time to not only include Seoul-based dailies like the *Tonga ilbo* but also Pusan-based dailies like the *Pusan ilbo*, intellectual journals like *Hyŏndae kongnon*, and annuals like *Han'guk yŏn'gam*. Indeed, as shown in table 1.1, these years witnessed a remarkable broadening in the field of North Korean journalists' citations in the *Rodong sinmun*, incorporating increasing numbers of daily newspapers, regional newspapers, popular culture publications, and specialized publications including those oriented toward writers, intellectuals, businesspeople, teachers, legal professionals, and more. Quite clearly, then, the entrenchment of national division did not stop the flow of publications over the border. Journalists continued reading South Korean sources—in fact, a widening array of them—and the same held for those in the literary domain.

CROSS-BORDER READING II

On December 25, 1946, the *Rodong sinmun* carried a long-form work of criticism by the poet and critic Paek Injun under the title "Literary Arts Must Serve the People." Extending across two of the four pages of the newspaper, the article offered a strident critique of *Ŭnghyang*, a collection of poetry that had been published in the northern city of Wŏnsan the preceding August. "These days," Paek wrote:

> it is common knowledge—not merely for writers and artists but also for members of the general populace—that literary arts must go amongst the people. Yet the poetry collection *Ŭnghyang* . . . does not merely lack any sense of connection to the line of the Northern Korean Literature and Arts Alliance, but in fact opposes it, and the phenomena that come with this are present. More than half of the poems included in the poetry collection *Ŭnghyang* are in fact expressions of the "completely degenerate [*t'arakchŏk*] and decadent [*malsegijŏk*] customs [*yusŭp*] left behind by Japanese imperialism" and the "efforts and ideas of reactionary art."[20]

In its damning assessment of *Ŭnghyang* and its poems, Paek's article spoke in unison with a formal statement by the Standing Committee of the Northern Korean Literature and Arts Alliance (Pukchosŏn Munhak Yesul Ch'ongdongmaeng Chungang Sangim Wiwŏnhoe). Published in the *Rodong sinmun* the day before, this statement, which appeared alongside an article about *Ŭnghyang* and a related message circulated to provincial authorities, noted that the Standing Committee had not only determined that the majority of the poems in the collection displayed "skeptical, fantastical, degenerate [*t'oet'oejŏk*], escapist, and even despairing tendencies in relation to the [revolutionary] Korean present" but also called for a range of responses, including the prohibition of the sale of the collection and the dispatch of a team of "censors" (*kŏmnyŏlwŏn*) to Wŏnsan to assess the situation, facilitate self-critique, and right the local literary world's ideological course.[21]

The late-December publication of Paek's article and the Standing Committee's decision—which, as Kim Sŏngsu has recently noted, took place months before previously known—was transformational.[22] Indeed, the so-called "*Ŭnghyang* Incident," which O T'aeho has described as "a symbolic event amounting to a critical juncture in North and South Korean literature,"[23] demonstrated that writers and literary organizations whose work did not meet the contemporary call for a "literature that serves the people" would become targets of sustained public critique. And indeed, references to *Ŭnghyang* as counterexample reverberated throughout literary criticism north of the thirty-eighth parallel across subsequent years, serving as a point of connection linking successive waves of critique and crackdown. These were waves of critique and crackdown that, engulfing some of the most prominent writers then in the North, increasingly narrowed the space of acceptable literary discourse in the DPRK. Yet they were also waves of critique and crackdown that, perhaps counterintuitively, opened up new spaces for discussion of South Korean literature.

The early years of the northern literary world were defined by the successive waves of writers who traveled north across the thirty-eighth parallel between 1945 and 1950. During these years, transplants were quickly integrated into the growing literary and cultural sphere centered in Pyongyang, and they took up an array of positions of influence. However, these early years of integration and accommodation came to an end in 1952, when the group of writers who had first established the post-Liberation literary field in Pyongyang began turning against those who had come north in subsequent years. As Tatiana Gabroussenko and Brian Myers have discussed in detail, this campaign was conducted under the banner of the critique of "naturalism" (*chayŏnjuŭi*) and "formalism" (*hyŏngsikchuŭi*), and by 1953, it had resulted in the denunciation of some of the most influential writers of the colonial and postcolonial eras, including Kim Namch'ŏn, Rim Hwa, and Ri T'aejun.[24]

Not surprisingly, these events were bound up with the return of critical references to *Ŭnghyang*, albeit in a somewhat different guise. This was evident in a January 1952 article by the critic Ŏm Hosŏk titled "The Struggle Against the Remnants of Naturalism and Formalism in Our Literature" ("Uri munhak e issŏsŏ ŭi chayŏnjuŭi wa hyŏngsikchuŭi chanjae waŭi t'ujaeng").[25] Published in the *Rodong sinmun*, Ŏm's article played a key role in highlighting "naturalism and formalism" as pressing ideological and artistic concerns for the nation. It also framed them as issues of long-standing significance by linking them back to *Ŭnghyang*, whose offenses were now characterized in noticeably different terms: not decadence but rather "the remnants of naturalism and formalism," as Ŏm put it.[26] The critique of *Ŭnghyang* was here repackaged for a new political moment, and it was done so in a way as to link it to a new set of offending texts, including, in this particular article, Kim Namch'ŏn's "Honey" ("Kkul," 1951).[27]

Ŏm's article was not alone in making such connections. In 1953, the critic Han Hyo serialized a four-part article titled "Korean Literature in the Struggle Against Naturalism" ("Chayŏnjuŭi rŭl pandae hanŭn t'ujaeng e issŏsŏ ŭi Chosŏn munhak") in *Munhak yesul*, the official organ of the Korean Writers' Alliance. Extending across more than one hundred pages, Han's article gave canonical form to the denunciations of Rim Hwa, Kim Namch'ŏn, and Ri T'aejun that had emerged in the previous year. It also returned to the critique of *Ŭnghyang*, whose offenses it linked to the work of Ri T'aejun. Indeed, in its third installment, after discussing *Ŭnghyang*, it turned directly to Ri, who it characterized as "one who has openly spread the poison of naturalism in the prose domain with the intention of paralyzing the consciousness of the people of northern Korea, who are on the path to creating a new way of life, and implanting the ideology of distrust and despair."[28]

Once again, the specter of *Ŭnghyang* was revived in order to mark contemporary works as unacceptable. This resulted in the further narrowing of the bounds of acceptable discourse in the North. Yet counterintuitively, it also made possible new forms of connection across the thirty-eighth parallel. In fact, when Han's article critiques Kim Namch'ŏn, Rim Hwa, and Ri T'aejun, it not only links their work to *Ŭnghyang* but also to contemporary texts from Seoul. Indeed, it connects Rim Hwa's post-Liberation calls for a "national literature in the modern sense" to the call for a "global, universal national culture" articulated by Cho Kyudong in an early 1950 issue of the Seoul-based journal *Sinch'ŏnji*,[29] and it then goes on to link Cho's vision of "national spirit" to the use of "naturalism" in contemporary South Korean literature: in particular, the works of Yu Ch'ijin, Hŏ Yunsŏk, Yŏm Sangsŏp, Kim Chinsu, Kim Yŏngnang, Kim Kwangsŏp, Yi Ponggu, Kwak Hasin, Yu Chuhyŏn, Hwang Sunwŏn, and Mo Yunsuk.[30]

Han's article, therefore, demonstrates not only the enduring significance of *Ŭnghyang* but also the enduring importance of—and familiarity with—South Korean literature in the North. Indeed, Han's discussion of South Korean literature—in particular, his mention of Yŏm Sangsŏp's short story "The Coveted Shack" ("T'amnaenŭn hakkobang," 1951) and Kim Chinsu's play *The Flower that Bloomed on the Roadside* (*Kilka e p'in kkot*, 1952)—demonstrates that publications from the South continued to cross the thirty-eighth parallel after the stabilization of the battlefront in 1951. Once again, even after people stopped moving across the thirty-eighth parallel, texts clearly continued to do so, and this continued throughout the postwar period. In fact, discussions of such texts increased over time, becoming regular presences in North Korean publications.

In mid-1956, the critic Kye Puk published in article in *Chosŏn munhak* focusing on "southern Korea's reactionary, bourgeois aesthetics." "A class undergoing demise," Kye wrote, "does not exit the stage of history voluntarily but attempts to sustain its dying fate and, writhing and railing, mobilizes all of its ideological tools."[31] He then presented a damning indictment of the uses toward which South Korean literature was being mobilized, writing, "While trying to eliminate and eradicate everything in art that is advanced, new, and accords with the interests of the people, the American imperialists and the Syngman Rhee cabal use southern Korean's reactionary, bourgeois aesthetics and art as an ideological weapon in their attempt to provoke a 'drive north' war [i.e., a new Korean War] as well as a new world war."[32]

For Kye—as for his readers—there would have been no question of South Korean literature's reactionary stance and significance. And yet, his article nevertheless mobilized a plethora of evidence to support this claim. In addition to discussing the works of American and British literature and criticism published in Korean translation in South Korean publications, Kye here offered critiques of works of literature, literary history, and criticism by a wide range of contemporary South Korean authors: Yi Muyŏng, Pak Chonghwa, Yu Ch'ihwan, Kim Yunsŏng, Paek Ch'ŏl, Son Usŏng, Kim Yangsu, O Chongsik, Kim Kijin, Cho Yunje, Hong Hyomin, and Cho Yŏnhyŏn. Drawing from a range of literary and nonliterary publications—the journals *Munhak yesul*, *Munye*, *Hyŏndae munhak*, *Sasanggye*, *Munhwa segye*, and *Sint'aeyang* as well as the *Chosŏn ilbo* newspaper—Kye critiqued these writers for their "Neo-Platonic" detachment from reality, their facile, nihilistic naturalism, their denigration of Korean literary tradition, and their "cosmopolitan" servility to the foreign. In doing so, he demonstrated the robust extent of his access to South Korean publications and helped pave the way for many similar articles that would follow.

Such articles, however, did not appear exclusively in *Chosŏn munhak*. Instead, after its founding in late 1956, they appeared most frequently in the *Munhak sinmun* newspaper, the official organ of the Central Committee of the Korean Writers' Alliance. And in particular, the multiple-issue-per-week publication schedule of the *Munhak sinmun* allowed such articles to become not only increasingly thorough in their coverage of the wide breadth of South Korean literature but also increasingly engaged in an in-depth fashion with very recent publications from across the border. This was evident, for example, in an April 12, 1959, critique of recent South Korean poetry published in the newspaper by Wŏn Sŏkp'a. "Recent southern Korean poetry," Wŏn wrote, was "characterized by its walking of an even more heinous, antipeople path [than before]."[33] Using the "tone of sorrow, futility, lamentation, and eroticism" to "render the southern Korean people's spirit of struggle numb and addicted," South Korean poetry, Wŏn argued, faithfully fulfilled the function given to it by "American colonial policy," and he then proceeded to analyze a set of particular works, including poems by Kim Kyŏngsu and Yi Chonghak, which had only recently been published in the February 1959 issue of the South Korean journal *Hyŏndae munhak*.[34]

This demonstrates the speed with which such publications were crossing the border to the North, and such rapid transits, it is clear, were happening on a regular basis. For example, a month later, in May 1959, the *Munhak sinmun* published an article by Ri Hyŏn focused on the short story "At a Certain Point" ("Ŏttŏn chijŏm esŏ") by Yi Ukchong. In this article, Ri reprised the basic characterizations and assertions mentioned above, describing the text in question as "spreading poison" and "betraying human reason and ethics" in its vision of "immorality and eroticism." It also mirrored Wŏn's article in the rapidity of its response, as Yi's "At a Certain Point" had only been published two months prior in the March 1959 issue of the South's *Hyŏndae munhak*.[35]

Such articles were not confined to literary publications. As early as 1954, the *Rodong sinmun* had carried these types of critiques of South Korean literature,[36] and in the late 1950s and early 1960s, they spread to a range of other nonliterature-focused publications as well. Such publications included popular magazines like *Ch'ŏllima*, which published recurring articles on South Korean literature in the 1960s, such as a November 1961 text by Ro Kŭmsŏk that highlighted the reactionary "nihilism" and "existentialism" espoused in recent fiction by Yŏm Sangsŏp, Song Sugyŏng, and Kim Kwangju.[37] They also included journals like *Kŭlloja*, the official organ of the Central Committee of the Korean Workers' Party, which likewise published a succession of such pieces, including a 1964 critique of the influence of "Freudianism" on contemporary South Korean literature. Written by Kim Haegyun, this article discussed fiction by O Yugwŏn, Sŏ Kŭnbae, Yi Pŏmsŏn, and Hyŏn Chaehun, linking these works, their stream-of-consciousness style, and their eroticism to the "decaying, licentious lifestyle of the bourgeoisie" and the "contradictions of imperialism."[38]

As this makes clear, North Korean publications throughout these years presented ample evidence of the robust presence and consumption of South Korean publications. This presence and consumption were widespread among writers affiliated with an array of different publications, and these writers' access to South Korean publications diversified in its scope and accelerated in its rapidity over time. By the mid-1960s, writers in North Korea seem to have had access to virtually all publications being produced in the South and they were able to respond to them with minimal lag time.

At the same time, not all of the responses to South Korean publications that North Korean writers penned during these years were of the same character. Although all of the articles mentioned above made use of South Korean texts more or less exclusively as evidence of depravity across the border, this was not the only approach that writers took. Indeed, beginning in the late 1950s, there emerged a parallel stream of discourse in the North that identified "progressive" elements in South Korean texts and pointed to them as evidence of the growing spirit of critique in the South. This alternative stream of discourse emerged hand in hand with shifts in DPRK policy, and it also gave birth to new practices of reprinting such "progressive" South Korean texts in North Korean publications.

SPROUTS OF CRITIQUE

In September 1958, the critic Ch'ŏng Am published an article called "The Literature of the Slave and the Literature of Resistance: The Essence of Bourgeois Humanism" ("Noye ŭi munhak kwa panhang ŭi munhak:

Purŭjyoajŏk hyumanijŭm ŭi ponjil") in *Chosŏn munhak*.³⁹ Opening on a familiar note, the article decried "The various [forms of] ... decayed bourgeois, reactionary thought ... flowing through southern Korea like a dirty, turbid river."⁴⁰ It then proceeded to a critique of recent works by Im Okin, Ch'oe Inuk, Pak Yŏngjun, Yŏm Sangsŏp, and Pak Yonggu, linking their fiction to "bourgeois humanism" and its moral corruption, its individualism, and its function as an alibi for expropriative violence and abuse.

At this point, however, the article took a striking turn. After these writers in terms of their "naturalist" aesthetics, Ch'ŏng contrasted their "literature of the slave" (*noye ŭi munhak*)—which simply describes reality without changing it—with an alternative vision: the "literature of resistance" (*panhang ŭi munhak*). Unlike the "literature of the slave," this "literature of resistance," Ch'ŏng said, refuses naturalism's "accommodation to reality" (*hyŏnsil t'ahyŏp*) and instead takes up the cause of "exposing and revealing" (*chŏkpal kwa p'ongno*) the injustice of the present. And it was precisely this type of literature, Ch'ŏng argued, that "ha[d] recently begun to emerge in southern Korea."⁴¹ Ch'ŏng here offered a quite different vision of South Korean literature, drawing it out with a discussion of recent fiction by Kim Sŏnghan, among others, and urging it on toward more radical development.

As striking as this new vision of South Korean literature was, Ch'ŏng was not presenting it alone. In May 1958, as Balázs Szalontai has noted, Han Sŏrya "declared that the DPRK's cultural policy had ... been wrong to assume that South Korean literature was merely a tool of imperialism ... for there were also several progressive writers in the South, persons who deserved Pyongyang's support."⁴² And in fact, moves in this direction had already been taking shape for multiple years. Beginning in 1955, as Szalontai has likewise noted, the DPRK initiated a series of calls for inter-Korean economic and cultural exchanges, all of which were rejected by the ROK.⁴³ The following year, in July 1956, the North Korean state mobilized a group of influential current and former leaders of "southern Korean origin" to establish the Northern Council for the Promotion of Peaceful Unification (Chaebuk P'yŏnghwa T'ongil Ch'okchin Hyŏbŭihoe), which signaled the opening of a new wave of attempts at co-option of individuals in the South. And at the Second Congress of Korean Writers, held in October 1956, the poet Cho Pyŏgam, in a speech calling for "cultural exchange" (*munhwa kyoryu*) with writers in the

South, noted, "We are well aware that, although a handful of reactionary writers in the southern half [of our country] are completely estranged from the people and aid the American imperialists' colonial policy and the Syngman Rhee cabal's traitorous policy, the writers with a conscience in the southern half [of our country] are, on the other hand, standing and fighting on the side of the people."[44]

This was the context in which Ch'ŏng Am wrote the article mentioned above with its vision of a new "literature of resistance" in the South, and it was followed by many others. A mid-1959 article in the *Munhak sinmun* by O Chŏngsam thus appended its critique of "reactionary" fiction by pointing toward the "progressive literature that, in opposition to southern Korean reactionary literature, had recently emerged in a notable way."[45] And in particular, he singled out three recent stories by Chŏn Kwangyong—"Stratum" ("Chich'ŭng"), "Thunder" ("Pyŏngnyŏk"), and "G.M.C."—as representative of this new "undeniable" trend that "struggles to seek out the new and carries robust critical depth in relation to the pitiful state of its society."[46] Likewise, a 1962 article in *Ch'ŏllima* by Ro Kŭmsŏk differentiated the "song of conscience" found in poems by South Korean writers like Yi Insŏk, Kim Suyŏng, Chŏn Yŏnggyŏng, and more from the facile, reactionary "formalism" of others in the South.[47] Writing in the *Munhak sinmun* in 1963, Kim Kyŏngho likewise praised the line of recent South Korean literature that "stood firmly in real life and spoke on behalf of the people's hearts," pointing in particular to poetry by Yi Insŏk and Kim Chaewŏn as well as fiction by O Yŏngsu and Chŏn Kwangyong.[48] And in *Chosŏn munhak*, Kim Haegyun drew upon fiction and poetry by Nam Chŏnghyŏn, An Tongnim, Paek Inbin, O Sangwŏn, Song Sangok, Chŏng Hansuk, Chŏng Kuch'ang, Im Suil, Hwang Kŭmch'an, Cho Pyŏnghwa, and Chŏng Kongch'ae to demonstrate that "Today, the progressive literary elements of southern Korea occupy a clear position in southern Korean literature, and the line between these progressive literary elements and reactionary literature is sharply drawn."[49]

For all of these writers, South Korean literature was no longer a wholly bourgeois or reactionary entity. On the contrary, it included a thriving community of "progressive" writers who stood with the people and against the forces of the United States and the ROK state, writing critically engaged literature that was not only worthy of praise but also of engagement and amplification. And indeed, as North Korean writers and critics took up the cause of such "progressive" South Korean writers, the publications for which they wrote also began reprinting this literature. An experimental foray in this direction appeared in June 1957, when *Chosŏn munhak* reprinted the South Korean novelist and playwright Kim Song's 1956 short story "Green Frog" ("Ch'ŏnggaeguri").[50] Yet it was not until the early 1960s that such reprints became common features in North Korean publications, and the turning point in this spread of reprint practices was the April Revolution of 1960.

In April 1960, as noted above, a monthslong series of protests against corrupt elections and authoritarian rule in the South came to a head, pushing South Korea's first president, Syngman Rhee, from power in a movement that was led primarily by students and subsequently became known as the April Revolution. This was a momentous time in South Korea: one likened by some at the time, as Charles R. Kim has noted, to a "second liberation" and looked back on as an origin point for subsequent waves of democratization.[51] It was also a time when those across the thirty-eighth parallel divide saw new hope and possibility for the overthrow of the South Korean state as a whole and the reunification of the country under the North's leadership.[52] Within this context, those in the North took up the task of fanning the flames of revolution. They did this, as previous scholarship has shown, via an outpouring of literature heroizing the revolution's participants.[53] They also did this, however, by amplifying critical voices from the South in their own publications.

The fact that such republications occurred is not entirely unknown. As Theodore Hughes has discussed in detail, the South Korean writer Nam Chŏnghyŏn was prosecuted by the ROK state because his 1965 story, "Land of Excrement" ("Punji"), was republished in the North.[54] Yet what has not been discussed is the surprising scale and breadth of this phenomenon. Although Nam appears to be the only writer prosecuted as a result of such republication, his work's presence in the pages of North Korean publications put him in relatively good company. As table 1.2 shows, the reprinting of South Korean texts in the North provided readers in the DPRK with access to the works of an eclectic range of South Korean cultural producers ranging from poets to fiction writers to playwrights to memoirists and from young writers to veterans.[55]

Reaching the height of their visibility between 1962 and 1965, these works of South Korean literature were disseminated to North Korean readers in a range of different types of publications, where they appeared either alone or in groups. They were not, moreover, the only types of South Korean texts to be reprinted there. In fact, the same mid-1950s change in perspective noted above in relation to the literary domain also occurred in the broader publishing sphere. In March 1958, for example, the *Rodong sinmun* published an extended synopsis of a recent article by the South Korean opposition party lawmaker Kim Sangdon that had appeared in the December 1957 issue of the journal *Sasanggye*.[56] Characterized by its unnamed interpreter in the North as an "indictment of the fact that the Rhee Syngman clique's political corruption and fascist oppression of the people is becoming harsher by the day,"[57] the article was described as a blistering call for change that highlighted the political, economic, and social depravity of the contemporary scene in the South. It was taken up, as such, not simply for the evidence of depravity across the border that it offered but also for the perspective on this depravity that it articulated. Indeed, its final word was that the current state of the ROK had "come to a situation in which one could not live with a sense of conscience," a position that, the text suggested, was compatible with southward visions from the DPRK.[58]

Moreover, after the April Revolution of 1960, such practices of paraphrase, summary, and synopsis by North Korean journalists transformed into practices of republication in a steady and sustained manner that mirrored the literary domain.[59] Once again, the goal of such republication was to emphasize the presence of critical perspectives in the South and the emerging overlap between North and South Korean sensibilities. This was evident, for example, in the March 1963 *Han'guk ilbo* editorial "Only an Autonomous [*chaju*] Spirit, Autonomous Judgment, and Autonomous Treatment—Principles that Cannot be Conceded—Are Capable of Leading an Autonomous Nation-State Autonomously," which was reproduced in the *Rodong sinmun* in April 1963.[60] Echoing many North Korean commentaries on the current state of affairs in the South, the editorial began with an invocation of emotive resonance, "We cannot help but admit that when we encounter [news] reports, we become mired in conflicted feelings that are quite difficult to describe."[61] It then went on to critique the United States' outsized role in Korean affairs and the dependency that it had created via its foreign aid practices, and it concluded by calling on "the political leaders in the ruling party [to] pay close attention to ensure that the type of toadyist disposition [*sadae kŭnsŏng*] that welcomes foreign interference is not able to take root."[62]

Highlighting such critiques from the South became a recurring part of republication practices in the *Rodong sinmun*. In November 1963, the newspaper serialized a two-part article from the magazine *Han'guk kyŏngje* on the creation of economic dependency in the ROK,[63] and the following month, it republished an article from the magazine *Sedae* on a similar topic.[64] The next month, in January 1964, it again republished a South Korean article on this topic, this time from the magazine *Sinsegye*. Originally titled "Does the United States Know South Korea's Troubles?" the article had been published the month before in the South, and it began with the recognition that the United States offered foreign aid to advance its own interests—not, as the article's author, Kim Chongt'ae, put it, "out of good will or the sole benefit of the country being aided."[65] As Kim noted, the amount of aid the United States had offered had been tremendous, yet its focus on providing consumer goods and its failure to fund the building of productive industries had produced dependence rather than stability. This meant, first and foremost, that "what we need to understand anew is that even if we must undergo all kinds of difficulty, we cannot delay in focusing our work—for the good of economic capacity, the basis of all development—on the formation of a self-sufficient economy."[66]

Such republication practices, moreover, were not confined to the *Rodong sinmun*. On the contrary, South Korean texts appeared in a wide range of North Korean publications during these years, many of which placed South Korean texts of different types side by side. The women's magazine *Chosŏn nyŏsŏng* offers an instructive example. Although the magazine had begun making sporadic references to South Korean publications in the mid-1950s, such citations became regular fixtures in its pages by 1963. The next year, it also began republishing South Korean texts. In April 1964, on the fourth anniversary of the April Revolution, the magazine published a 1960 poem by Chang Habo as well as a similar one written by Ko Yangsun, the sister of Ko Wan'gi, a high school student who was killed during the protests on April 19, 1960.[67] In September 1964, the magazine reprinted a pair of letters first published in the *Taegu maeil sinmun* accompanied by a selection of South Korean current events comics, and in December, it reprinted an extended article by the activist and philosopher Ham Sŏkhŏn that had first appeared in *Sasanggye* in April of the same year.⁶⁸

Republications continued to expand the next year. In February 1965, the magazine republished Kim Sangwŏn's poem "Unification of the Ancestral Land" ("Choguk t'ongil") as well as a cluster of short excerpts of reunification-related articles drawn from a wide range of South Korean daily, regional, and student newspapers.⁶⁹ In April 1965, it republished Pak Yŏngil's short story "Gold Ring" ("Kŭm panji") from the South Korean literary journal *Hyŏndae munhak*.⁷⁰ The next month, it began a three-month serialization of the South Korean novelist O Yŏngsu's "Anna's Will" ("Anna ŭi yusŏ"),⁷¹ often publishing other South Korean texts in the same issue. While this is just a sampling of the emerging presence of South Korean texts in *Chosŏn nyŏsŏng*, it gives a sense of the range and frequency with which they began to appear, and it signals the extent to which the general reading public was proactively brought into the intersecting textual networks of North and South Korean publications.

Something similar happened at the youth magazine *Sae sedae*. Although some republications from the South appeared as early as mid-1963, it was in the following year that they became regular presences. In March 1964, for example, in addition to the Yi Insŏk poem "Bridge" ("Tari") from the South Korean journal *Chayu munhak*, the magazine reprinted a student essay from the *Kyŏnghyang sinmun* and a "gibberish" (*hoengsŏl susŏl*) column from the *Tonga ilbo*.⁷² The next issue, too, included a student essay from the South Korean student magazine *Hagwŏn*, and so did the following issue, which carried an essay from the *Chosŏn ilbo* newspaper alongside a South Korean children's poem.⁷³ Such practices continued at a steady pace in the second half of the year: the June issue included a South Korean poem; the July issue republished a version of a *Chosŏn ilbo* article alongside another South Korean poem; the October issue included two articles from the *Pusan ilbo*, one article from the *Han'guk ilbo*, and one article from the *Kyŏnghyang sinmun*, alongside a South Korean poem; November included a *Han'guk ilbo* article as well as a feature mixing North and South Korean comics; and December included a pair of *Kukche sinbo* articles.⁷⁴ This continued in 1965, providing young readers in the North with unprecedented access to writing from across the border.

What this demonstrates, once again, is the robust presence that South Korean texts accrued in North Korean publications during these years.

Although North Korean publications continued to cite and quote South Korean texts as evidence of depravity across the border, they also reimagined them as progressive forces to reference and reprint. In tandem, the revolutionary possibilities of the South and the bounds of the proper readership of South Korean texts were rethought—and so too were the shifting relations between the two Koreas and the Korean diasporic population in Japan. Indeed, the Korean resident population in Japan affiliated with the Chongryon organization played a central role in the development of the cross-border printing practices mentioned above, and they likewise played a central role in the emergence of cross-border writing practices, which I will discuss later in the chapter.

CROSS-SEA ENGAGEMENTS

As Avram Agov has written, the "establishment and affirmation of the North Korean state ... are inseparable from the country's system of alliances with the Soviet Union, China, and other Socialist countries."[75] Indeed, from the early days of regime's formation under the Soviet Civil Administration to the years of the Korean War, when the DPRK received crucial assistance from both the Soviet Union and China, to the period of postwar economic reconstruction, when China, the Soviet Union, and an array of Eastern European socialist allies contributed vitally to the rebuilding of the nation,[76] North Korea charted a course of growth and development that went through—rather than beyond—networks of international alliances. And likewise, in subsequent years, when the DPRK turned, as Benjamin Young and Moe Taylor have suggested, toward emphasizing alliances with Third World nations rather than Beijing and Moscow, it did so within the context of an emerging vision of new forms of anti-colonial solidarity across boundaries of nation and continent.[77] Nevertheless, North Korea never completely severed its interactions with countries outside the networks mentioned above; this was the case, as we have seen, with South Korea, and it was also the case with Japan.

Although the majority of South Korean texts and images appeared in North Korean publications as onetime phenomena, some were republished more than once, shuffled between different DPRK outlets. One of the earliest South Korean poems by a professional writer to be republished in the North, Yi Insŏk's "Bridge" ("Tari"),[78] first appeared in the *Munhak sinmun* in July 1962, then again in the *Choguk t'ongil* in January 1964, and one more time a few months later in the youth magazine *Sae sedae*.[79] Sin Tongmun's "Ah, My Ancestral Land" ("Aa nae choguk"), originally published in *Sasanggye*,[80] was first republished in May 1963 in the *Minju ch'ŏngnyŏn* newspaper and then handed off to a long list of publications: *Choguk t'ongil, Rodongja sinmun,* and *Munhak sinmun*.[81] For its part, Nam Chŏnghyŏn's June 1964 story, "Letter to Father" ("Pujujŏn sangsŏ"),[82] was republished virtually simultaneously in three newspapers, appearing in the *Munhak sinmun* on September 18, 1964, in the *Choguk t'ongil* in two installments published on September 16 and 19, 1964, and in the *Rodong sinmun* on September 21, 1964.[83]

South Korean texts also moved across the peninsula's boundaries in their republication. Yi Kŭnbae's poem "On 4.19" ("4.19 e puch'yŏ"), originally published in the South's *Kyŏnghyang sinmun* on April 18, 1964,[84] was republished in the North the following month in the *Choguk t'ongil* newspaper before appearing again the following year in *Ch'ŏllima*.[85] Around the same time, however, the poem also crossed the East Sea to Japan, where it was republished in the Chongryon organization's *Chosŏn sinbo* on the fifth anniversary of the April Revolution.[86] Similarly, Yi Insŏk's "A Human Has the Right to Live" ("In'gan ŭn sara issŭl kwŏlli ka itta"),[87] which was republished in the North in the pages of the *Choguk t'ongil* and *Munhak sinmun* newspapers, also appeared in Chongryon's *Chosŏn sinbo* in Japan in between these two republications.[88]

However, the relationship between Chongryon's reprinting practice and the North's was not simply derivative. In fact, South Korean poems not only traveled from North Korean publications to publications in Japan but also in the opposite direction, something that happened in the case of Ku Chungsŏ's "Come Smash the Altar" ("Wasŏ chedan ŭl pusura").[89] This poem, too, appeared multiple times in North Korea: once in the *Choguk t'ongil* newspaper in June 1963 and then again in the *Munhak sinmun* newspaper in April 1965.[90] Yet it first appeared in the *Chosŏn sinbo*, where it was republished on April 24, 1963—just six days after its original publication in the South Korean newspaper *Han'guk ilbo*.[91] Writers and editors at the *Chosŏn sinbo* thus intervened in the process of inter-Korean exchange, and they played a key role in the emergence of this practice.

As we saw in Min Sukcha's open letter referenced in the beginning of this chapter, the first South Korean poem to be reprinted in the North was actually taken up via prior, multilingual republication in Japan, and this was not the only way that Chongryon-affiliated writers intervened; they also set the stage for the process of creative response and coproduction that would soon emerge in the North.

The sizable ethnic Korean population in Japan was, in part, a legacy of the colonial era. At the time of Japan's surrender on August 15, 1945, there were more than two million Koreans in the Japanese home islands.[92] By the spring of 1946, as Sayaka Chatani has noted, approximately three quarters of the Korean population in Japan had packed up their belongings and left for the Korean peninsula, with others continuing to leave in smaller numbers in subsequent years.[93] Yet, due to a variety of familial, economic, and political concerns—including the division of the Korean peninsula—hundreds of thousands decided to stay, at least for the time being, and they were joined by a significant yet not precisely known number of Koreans who, finding conditions in their newly divided homeland difficult, either returned to Japan after having been repatriated or decided to move to Japan for the first time during these years. And so, although the ethnic Korean population in Japan shrunk rapidly during this time, it retained a significant presence and continued to support a robust organizational life and media ecosystem.

In the period immediately following Liberation, the League of Koreans (Kr. Chae Ilbon Chosŏnin Yŏnmaeng, Jp. Zai Nippon Chōsenjin Renmei) stood at the center of this organizational life in Japan. Inaugurated in October 1945, the league emerged, as Deokhyo Choi has noted, out of the mutual assistance groups that had been established by Koreans immediately following the Japanese surrender, and by January 1946, it had "established a total of forty-seven local chapters across Japan."[94] Using this network of local chapters, the league pursued a range of activities, including assisting Koreans in seeking compensation for their experiences as forced laborers and organizing a Peace-Preservation Corps to keep public order in Korean neighborhoods.[95] It also played a central role in the process of postcolonial repatriation. In addition to facilitating unofficial, ad hoc repatriation transits via small, private boats,[96] the league also took on a role in the official repatriation program overseen by the US occupation and the Japanese government; between November 1945 and May 1946, it served as the authority responsible for issuing repatriation certificates to Koreans who desired to return to the peninsula.[97]

However, the relationship between the League of Koreans and US occupation authorities soon soured. The league's post-Liberation activities had included organizing a network of Korean schools for children, and "By October 1947," as Hiromitsu Inokuchi has written, "the league had built 541 elementary schools, seven junior high schools, twenty-two adolescent schools, and eight high schools."[98] In April 1948, however, US occupation authorities in Japan outlawed the league's Korean schools, declaring that all resident Korean children would be required to attend Japanese schools. This led to a series of protests by tens of thousands of resident Koreans across the prefectures of Yamaguchi, Hiroshima, Okayama, Hyōgo, and Osaka. The largest of these protests were in the cities of Kobe and Osaka, and in one of these protests in Osaka, the Japanese police—responding to an order from the US military—opened fire on the group, killing one teenager.[99]

These events produced deep hostilities between the league and the US occupation authorities, which only intensified with the establishment of two separate states on the Korean peninsula. With its strong relationship with Japanese Communist Party, the league recognized the DPRK as the legitimate government of Korea immediately after it was founded in September 1948.[100] Use of the DPRK flag, however, was banned by US occupation authorities, and violent repression ensued when it was flown by a local branch of the league in Osaka and a public gathering organized by the league in Sendai.[101] Tension between the league and the US occupation authorities thus not only intensified but also became explicitly linked to the Cold War ideological conflict and the division of the Korean peninsula, and the league was finally dissolved by occupation authorities and their Japanese allies in September 1949.

This set the stage for future links between the Korean resident community in Japan and their colleagues in North Korea. The dissolution of the league and the subsequent entry of a large segment of its membership into the Japanese Communist Party temporarily interrupted the formation of direct institutional ties between the North Korean state and the Korean resident population in Japan; instead, leftist outlets like the *Haebang sinmun* called upon its readership to "go broadly within the Japanese people."[102] However, with the January 9, 1951 founding of the United

Democratic Front of Koreans in Japan (Kr. Chaeil Chosŏn T'ongil Minju Chŏnsŏn, Jp. Zainichi Chōsen Tōitsu Minshu Sensen; hereafter, Minjŏn), an attempt to establish such ties reemerged. As Chin Hŭigwan, building on the pioneering work of Chŏn Chun, has discussed, the seventy-three representatives who founded the organization in Edogawa included in its founding principles[103] the dedication to "Defending at any cost [sasu] the Democratic People's Republic of Korea."[104]

This statement, as Chin and Chŏn have further noted, produced controversy among those most closely allied with Japanese Communist Party,[105] and indeed, the Korean Left during these years attempted to balance solidarity with Japanese colleagues and expanding ties with North Korea. Yet those in favor of deepening ties with the DPRK ultimately succeeded in setting the future direction for Minjŏn, and this had profound consequences that extended far beyond the language of official declarations. In late June 1950, after the outbreak of the Korean War, the *Haebang sinmun*, the most influential resident Korean newspaper in Japan,[106] which had been associated with the league before its dissolution, ceased publication. In May 1952, however, it reappeared in Japanese under the influence of Minjŏn, whose leader offered a congratulatory statement for the front page, where it was printed underneath a picture of Kim Il Sung. What was significant about this congratulatory statement was not simply its presence front and center but also the way in which its language situated the paper and its readers in relation to the DPRK.

Kim Hun, the leader of Minjŏn who wrote the message, here described the *Haebang sinmun* as a "newspaper with the glory [eiyo] of citizens [kōmin] of the Democratic People's Republic of Korea."[107] By asserting this citizenship link to the DPRK, Kim's formulation varied significantly from existing framings of resident Koreans in Japan as "overseas compatriots" (kaigai dōhō) of a shared "ancestral land" (sokoku), and it was further reinforced by other statements in this inaugural issue of the reissued newspaper. The editors' "reissue message," which quoted from Kim Il Sung's May Day message of that year, likewise referred to "compatriots in Japan" (zainichi dōhō) as "citizens [kōmin] of the glorious [kōei] DPRK,"[108] and the appeal to all Koreans in Japan from the Minjŏn Central Committee, published on the second page of this issue, called on the resident Korean community to develop "patriotism and revolutionary heroism as citizens [kokumin] of the DPRK."[109] This trio of statements clearly positioned resident Koreans in Japan as overseas citizens of the DPRK, asserting a formal link between the community and the North Korean state.

At stake here, however, was not simply the political meaning of the relationship between the resident Korean community in Japan and the DPRK but also its textual dimensions. More or less in tandem with its return to publication, the *Haebang sinmun* began including a significant amount of North Korean literature in its pages alongside the resident Korean work that it had already featured. This began even before the paper's return to Korean-language publication in September 1952, with the serialization of a Japanese translation of Ri Pungmyŏng's Korean War short story "Devils" ("Angma"), which began on June 28, 1952, and it was accompanied, in its second installment on July 5, with a selection from Cho Kich'ŏn's *Paekdusan*. On its own, this serialization was not entirely novel; in 1950, for example, the newspaper had already published one of Cho's other poems. However, the constant flow of North Korean literature that this serialization inaugurated signaled a new orientation. In subsequent months and years, the newspaper would print a steady stream of North Korean works by authors including Rim Sundŭk (1952), Kim Saryang (1952 and 1952–1953),[110] Ŏm Hŭngsŏp (1953), Pak Ch'anmo (1953), Ri T'aejun (1953), Ch'oe Myŏngik (1953), Sin Pulch'ul (1953), Min Pyŏnggyun (1953–1954), Han Sŏrya (1954), and Hwang Kŏn (1954), and this increased availability produced a new set of links between North Korean literature and readers and writers in Japan.

Moreover, beginning around the same time, resident Koreans in Japan also gained additional means of accessing North Korean texts. In August 1952, a group including Ri Chin'gyu, who would later take on a powerful role in Chongryon, opened a bookstore and publishing house called Hagu Sŏbang (Jp. Gakuyū Shobō) in the Chiyoda region of Tokyo.[111] Although details regarding the operation of the company are not available, advertisements and book reviews in the *Haebang sinmun* newspaper demonstrate that the store—in addition to acting as a source for educational texts for schools—played a vital role for the community as a source for North Korean texts of a range of genres: literature by Han Sŏrya, Ri T'aejun, Cho Kich'ŏn, Ch'oe Myŏngik, Yu Hangnim, and others;[112] collections of songs and children's literature produced in the North;[113] works of history by prominent North Korean scholars like Kim Sŏkhyŏng and Pak

Sihyŏng;[114] and works of state-produced ideology, including an abbreviated biography of Kim Il Sung.[115]

The store, moreover, also sold a range of texts produced in Japan by resident Koreans and others, including a journal called *Chosŏn munje yŏn'gu*,[116] a publication of the Research Institute on the Korean Problem, founded in November 1952 by Han Tŏksu, an activist who would become the longtime leader of Chongryon.[117] This publication, which released its first issue in the same month that the institute was established, focused on the republication of necessary materials from the North, which included statements of policy and vision culled from a range of official publications. Through this journal, Korean residents in Japan could access in-depth explications of policy from the North that went far beyond the scope of access offered by a newspaper like the *Haebang sinmun*.

Finally, Hagu Sŏbang also offered services through which books that were not available at the store—either Korean-language materials or Japanese-language materials related to Korea—could be ordered on the customer's behalf.[118] Based on advertisements, it is unclear whether the Korean-language materials referred to included materials from the DPRK. However, this was precisely the service that became available in 1954 with the advent of another bookstore and publishing house that played an instrumental role in the Korean resident community: Kuwŏl Sŏbang (Jp. Kugatsu Shobō).[119] These two bookstores worked together to provide access to DPRK publications for resident Koreans in Japan. A December 1954 advertisement, for example, noted that magazines and books imported (via Hong Kong) from the DPRK by Kuwŏl could be bought from Hagu.[120] Eventually, however, Kuwŏl—which began in a small, rented room on the second floor of a building in Chiyoda[121]—became the central location for resident Koreans' access to general texts from the DPRK, and Hagu, in turn, came to focus primarily upon educational materials for schools.

With the establishment of Kuwŏl Sŏbang, the importation of texts from the DPRK expanded dramatically, and it came to include a wide range of serial publications imported on a regular basis. From newspapers like *Rodong sinmun*, *Minju Chosŏn*, *Minju ch'ŏngnyŏn*, *Kyowŏn sinmun*, *Sonyŏn sinmun*, and *Choguk chŏnsŏn* to monthly journals and magazines like *Chosŏn nyŏsŏng*, *Chosŏn munhak*, *Adong munhak*, *Cho-Sso ch'insŏn*, *Sonyŏndan*, *Inmin*, *Kŭlloja*, *Ch'ŏngnyŏn saenghwal*, *Uri choguk*, *Kyŏngje saenghwal, Kyŏngje kŏnsŏl,* and *Kwahagwŏn hakpo,* Kuwŏl Sŏbang connected resident Korean readers to contemporary discussions across a wide swath of the North Korean mediascape.[122] By exposing readers to a variety of materials issued in the North, it facilitated new modes of ongoing engagement spanning the East Sea divide.

The early to mid-1950s thus witnessed a dramatic deepening of links between the Korean Left in Japan, organized around Minjŏn, and the DPRK, and this trend was further consolidated in 1955 with the establishment of Chongryon as a replacement for Minjŏn. As previous scholarship by Sonia Ryang has discussed, the founding of the Chongryon organization marked an important point of inflection in the history of the Korean Left in Japan.[123] Formalizing and solidifying the trends that had already emerged in Minjŏn in the preceding years, Chongryon tied itself to the DPRK in a clear and unmistakable way in its founding declaration of May 26, 1955, which concluded as follows:

> From now on, we will more tightly bind the entirety of our 600,000 compatriots in Japan to the government of our proud ancestral land, the Democratic People's Republic of Korea, and the leadership of our Dear Leader Kim Il Sung. And in order to realize the peaceful unified independence of our ancestral land, we will firmly struggle against the invasion of Korea by the American imperialists and against Syngman Rhee and his treacherous traitors.
>
> We will strengthen the unity and solidarity of our 600,000 compatriots in Japan, preserve—as citizens of the Democratic People's Republic of Korea—our various democratic rights and democratic national education, secure our proper livelihood, and strengthen the laudable custom of reciprocal aid among compatriots in Japan.[124]

With this declaration, Chongryon linked itself directly to the North Korean state and explicitly situated the Korean residents that it represented as citizens of the DPRK. Even more importantly, perhaps, Chongryon's founding bylaws declared that the group "joined the Democratic Front for the Unification of the Ancestral Land" (Choguk T'ongil Minjujuŭi Chŏnsŏn).[125] Since the Democratic Front was an official organ of the DPRK state, this professed a formal affiliation between Chongryon and the North Korean government in Pyongyang.

This was not simply a matter of words. The establishment of Chongryon as an explicitly DPRK-linked entity elicited the August 1955 dispatch of the first of many official delegations sent by the organization to meet with Kim Il Sung and other officials in Pyongyang.[126] It also initiated the incorporation of resident Koreans into the formal organizational life of the DPRK: in 1957, at the second meeting of the Democratic Front for the Unification of the Ancestral Land in Pyongyang, the Chongryon leader, Han Tŏksu, was appointed one of seven chairmen of the Central Council alongside Kim Il Sung, Hong Myŏnghŭi, Kim Ch'ŏnhae, Hong Kihwang, Kim Tarhyŏn, and Ri Yŏng, and two other Chongryon members, Ri Simch'ŏl and Hwang Ponggu, were likewise appointed to the Central Council;[127] in the same year, three Chongryon writers—Hŏ Namgi, Nam Siu, and Kim Min—were appointed members of the Korean Writers' Alliance, the primary state-sponsored literary organization in the DPRK.[128]

In tandem, the establishment of Chongryon also opened up an unprecedented material flow from the DPRK to Japan. In April 1957, the DPRK state began funding Chongryon's network of Korean schools in Japan in British pounds,[129] soon expanding this aid to Chongryon's Korea University (Chosŏn Taehak) in Tokyo, which had been established the previous year.[130] This financial support facilitated tremendous growth in this network of schools, and it elicited a tremendous amount of goodwill toward the DPRK on the part of resident Koreans in Japan, for whom Korean schools were, as Sayaka Chatani has put it, a "key ethnic symbol," "*the* place within the place of the [Korean neighborhood]."[131] It also worked hand in hand with an extensive influx of North Korean publications. As educational materials flowed into Japan, so did a range of other types of texts, and in 1958, Kuwŏl Sŏbang, the bookstore mentioned above, moved into a newly constructed, multifloor location. It also came to house the Research Institute on the Korean Problem.[132]

With the establishment of Chongryon, therefore, the Korean Left in Japan turned its gaze away from the center of power in Japan. No longer collaborating with the Japanese Communist Party in challenging the domestic power structure in Japan, the resident Korean activist community instead looked toward Pyongyang and reimagined its identity in terms of ethnic solidarity and patriotism. This did not mean, however, that Chongryon ignored its position in Japan. On the contrary, what the group's realignment enabled was not only a formal tethering to the DPRK but also a new project of engagement with nonrevolutionary compatriots in Japan. In turn, this enabled new connections to compatriots in South Korea: new connections that, in time, would transform both the Chongryon and North Korean cultural spheres.

NEW SOLIDARITIES

In a New Year's Day 1956 statement published in the *Haebang sinmun*—now an official organ of Chongryon—Ri Ch'anŭi, the chief of the group's culture and propaganda division, reinforced the transformational importance of the "change of direction" (*rosŏn chŏnhwan*) embodied in the founding of Chongryon. In the years before 1955, Ri argued, the community had "deviated from the fundamental line of the Korean people."[133] "Overly preoccupied," he wrote, "with the particular situation of 'residing in Japan' [*chae Ilbon*]," the movement had taken up the cause of Japan's "democratic national revolution" under the "attractive appearance of proletarian internationalism."[134] Yet this cause and its positioning of the Korean resident community as a "minority ethnicity" (*sosu minjok*), Ri continued, had been nothing more than a misguided "cosmopolitanism" that had undercut the possibility of fostering the resident community's connections to its "national culture" (*minjok munhwa*).[135] For Ri, therefore, the establishment of Chongryon was a corrective action that refocused the community's attention and activism around its Korean identity, and it was a corrective action whose full development could only be achieved by "arming oneself on an everyday basis with patriotic ideology and dedicating oneself fully to the transmission and development of national culture while engaging in deep study of the writings of the Leader Kim Il Sung and [other] publications from our ancestral land."[136]

The "change of direction" embodied by Chongryon was thus a turn from proletarian internationalism to ethnonationalism, and this had a wide range of implications. Even while tethering itself formally to the DPRK state and to Kim Il Sung, Chongryon—with this new ethnonational vision—also presented itself as an organization for all resident Koreans regardless of politics or ideology. Therefore, the group's founding bylaws stipulated that Chongryon was a "national front representing the purpose and benefit of all of our compatriots made up of all groups and individuals from our compatriots in Japan who support our declaration, principles, and bylaws without regard for ideology, political authority, faith, or social position."[137] Unlike Minjŏn, which had listed resident Korean organizations from the political Right among its enemies,[138] Chongryon here positioned itself as a nationalist entity willing to cross political and ideological lines.

The goal here was co-option of the broader resident Korean population, and in practice, this entailed a number of new strategic initiatives. Among these was a turn toward engagement with and co-option of those outside Chongryon: in particular, so-called "neutralists" and members of the Korean Residents Union in Japan (Kr. Chae Ilbon Taehan Min'guk Mindan; Jp. Zai Nihon Daikan Minkoku Mindan; hereafter, Mindan), the ROK-aligned organization of Korean residents in Japan. Instead of excluding such individuals as reactionary, bourgeois influences, mid-1956 saw Chongryon organizing joint Liberation Day celebrations with Mindan members as well as facilitating ongoing "contact and exchange" (*chŏpch'ok kwa kyoryu*) with them, especially through the activities of women's groups and the adult education that they offered. Such activities were described as stepping stones for "serious collaborative action that would remove the thirty-eighth parallel between compatriots,"[139] and they reemerged regularly across the late 1950s and beyond.[140]

During this period, moreover, Chongryon also turned toward making contact with the South. This turn was closely linked to the contemporary one in the North mentioned above. In 1955, the Chongryon press reported prominently on the prelude to the formation of the Northern Council for the Promotion of Peaceful Unification: a message to compatriots in the South from An Chaehong and other leaders in the North of "southern origin."[141] And the following year, when the council came into being, it likewise received great attention from the Chongryon press.[142] In tandem, the Chongryon press also began echoing its DPRK allies in calling for new activities of co-optive engagement with those in the South: both ordinary citizens and writers. In Japan, however, the ability to carry out such activities was quite different than in the North. The existence of ongoing commercial, postal, and transportation links between Japan and South Korea meant that actions of "liaison" (*ryŏn'gye*) were far more workable for Chongryon members than their colleagues in the North, and they took action accordingly. In February 1956, for example, Chongryon members in Toyoma Prefecture reported making contact with South Korean sailors landing at the harbor by ship.[143]

Something similar happened in the literary domain. As noted above, by the time of the Second Congress of Korean Writers in 1956, North Korean perspectives on South Korean literature had already shifted toward recognizing the presence of "writers of conscience" to be engaged with. Like the formation of the Northern Council for the Promotion of Peaceful Unification, the meeting of the Second Congress of Korean Writers was reported on in the Chongryon press and some Chongryon members also listened to it in its entirety via radio broadcast from Pyongyang.[144] In tandem, they also began calling for greater activities of "liaison" with South Korean writers. Yet the way in which they did this was once again different than their colleagues in the North—or rather its temporality was. Indeed, instead of shifting, first, to new ways of describing South Korean literature and then, in subsequent years, to reprinting, Chongryon writers in Japan went directly to this second step, leading the way in a practice that subsequently crossed the sea to the North.

In 1955, Hŏ Namgi, who would become the foremost Chongryon poet, published a new anthology of modern Korean poetry in Japanese translation.[145] Split into three parts focusing on the colonial era, the immediate post-Liberation era, and the era since the outbreak of the Korean War, this anthology was a landmark one that, as we will see in chapter 3, was soon imported to South Korea, where it was seized because its latter two sections focused on work by writers affiliated with the North. The colonial-era section, however, was somewhat surprising in its makeup. To be sure, this section of the anthology included its fair share of poems by those who had gone North or been taken North after 1945, including Pak Seyŏng, Pak P'aryang, Cho Pyŏgam, Rim Haksu, Kim Kirim, and Chŏng Chiyong. Yet it also included poems by a range of writers who did not fall into this category: that is, not only writers who died before 1945, including Pak Yongch'ŏl, Yi Sang, Yi Sanghwa, Yi Yuksa, Kim Sowŏl, Yi Changhŭi, Han Yongun, Cho Myŏnghŭi, and Yun Tongju, but also writers who had lived beyond the end of colonial rule and stayed in the South, such as Yang Chudong, O Sangsun, Kim Sangyong, Sin Sŏkchŏng, Yu Ch'ihwan, and O Ildo. In fact, many of these latter writers had not only stayed in the South but become central figures in the growth and development of South Korean poetry, and Hŏ's inclusion of their colonial-era work in his anthology thus departed substantially from practices in the North at the time. With this anthology Hŏ suggested that there were contemporary South Korean writers whose work—albeit from the colonial era—could be integrated into a progressive vision of modern Korean literature, a position that had not yet emerged in the North.

Published by the Japanese company Aoki Shoten, this anthology was not an official Chongryon publication. Yet Hŏ's influential position within the Chongryon literary world at the time nevertheless makes it significant, and something similar can be said in relation to the journal *Pulssi*.[146] A bilingual coterie poetry magazine founded in 1957 and published in three issues that year, *Pulssi*, as Song Hyewŏn has made clear, was loosely affiliated with Chongryon.[147] Moreover, the most well-known poet affiliated with the journal was Kang Sun, one of the most prominent poets in Chongryon at the time, who contributed poems to *Pulssi* under his own name as well as under a pseudonym, Ri Sŏngha.[148]

Within this context, the journal's engagement with South Korean literature is striking. In November 1957, the third issue of the journal carried translations of twelve postcolonial South Korean poems: Pak Tujin's "Sun" ("Hae"), Yi Hanjik's "Inundation" ("Pŏmnam"), Kim Sangwŏn's "Egret" ("Paengno"), Kim Sangok's "Cave" ("Tonggul"), Pak Kiwŏn's "Dying Words" ("Yuŏn"), Han Haun's "Midautumn" ("Chungch'u"), Kim Ch'unsu's "Flower" ("Kkot"), Kim Yunsŏng's "Almanac" ("Ch'aengnyŏk"), Kim Kyudong's "The Butterfly and the Square" ("Nabi wa kwangjang"), Yi Tongju's "Ritual for Rain" ("Kiuje"), Yi Hyŏnggi's "Cosmos" ("K'osŭmosŭ"), and Pak Yanggyun's "Window" ("Ch'ang"). The first seven of these poems were translated by Kang Sun while the subsequent five were translated by Kim Yun, a wartime transplant from South Korea[149] who was credited as this issue of the journal's publisher and editor via the pseudonym Kim Tongil,[150] and as a group, the poems brought together many of the most influential poets then active in the South Korean literary sphere. They also brought Chongryon into contact with South Korean literature in a way that went far beyond what was then occurring in the North, where Kim Song's short story "Green Frog" had been the only piece of South Korean literature republished before 1960.

This was not, moreover, a onetime occurrence. In 1960, at the time of the April Revolution, when South Korean literature emerged as a significant presence in official Chongryon publications, it did so in a way that preceded—and set the stage for—the emergence of a similar presence in North Korean publications. This began, in particular, in relation to works by South Korean students and youths themselves. As noted at the beginning of this chapter, on May 16, 1960, soon after the April Revolution, the *Chosŏn minbo* newspaper republished "Why My Older Brothers and Sisters Bled" ("Oppa wa ŏnni ka wae p'i hŭllyŏnŭnji"), a poem by a young South Korean student named Kang Myŏnghŭi, which had originally appeared in the Seoul-based *Chosŏn ilbo* newspaper on April 23.[151] In fact, lines from the poem had already appeared in Japanese translation as a photo caption a week earlier in Chongryon's Japanese-language newspaper, *Chōsen sōren*.[152] Yet this was the first time that the organization had republished the poem in its entirety, and it set a precedent that would soon be repeated. After appearing in Korean in the *Chosŏn minbo*, the poem appeared in its entirety in Japanese translation in the Chongryon-affiliated Japanese-language journal *Atarashii sedai* in July 1960 and in the Chongryon-edited book *An April of Blood: The Southern Korean People's Uprising* in August 1960.[153]

Furthermore, when Kang's poem appeared in the latter two publications, it did so together with other works from South Korea. When the poem appeared in *Atarashii sedai*, it did so on the heels of Yu Sŏnjun's "Flag" ("Ki"), which had appeared in the journal the previous month, and it appeared side by side with two other poems from the South: Sim Chaesin's "Embarrassed" ("Pukkŭroum") and Kim Yosŏp's "Masses" ("Kunjung").[154] Such works continued to appear in the journal in subsequent issues. For example, to commemorate the first anniversary of the April Revolution, *Atarashii sedai* published two South Korean poems—Ko Yangsun's "At My Younger Brother's Funerary Altar" ("Au ŭi yŏngjŏn e")[155] and Yi Wŏnsu's "Song of a Younger Sister" ("Au ŭi norae")[156]—alongside a cluster of other related texts: a journal of the events of the uprising written by a student from Korea University in Seoul, a parting letter from a Seoul National University student to his mother before leaving for the protests, and another parting letter, this time by a mother.

The August 1960 republication of Kang's "Why My Older Brothers and Sisters Bled" in *An April of Blood: The Southern Korean People's Uprising* was also one that positioned the poem side by side with other works from the South. Although Kang's poem appeared on its own on the book's first three pages, subsequent sections of the monograph included a variety of South Korean poems and testimonials. Like the April 1961 issue of *Atarashii sedai*, this cluster of texts included Ko Yangsun's "At My Younger Brother's Funerary Altar"[157] and Yi Wŏnsu's "Song of a Younger Sister," complementing these poems with five others: Yun Kwŏnt'ae's "Funerary Song" ("Chinhon'ga"), Han Kyŏngja's "Younger Sister's Song" ("Yŏdongsaeng ŭi norae"), Kim Sŏnhyŏn's "A Father's Song" ("Pu ŭi norae"), Ch'oe Okcha's "A Mother's Wish" ("Mo ŭi sowŏn"). Additionally, side by side with the mother's letter included in the April 1961 issue of *Atarashii sedai*, the book also included the famous parting note left by the young protester Chin Yŏngsuk for her mother before her death, as well as a variety of other testimonials by student protesters and texts by family members.[158]

Many of these texts would continue to circulate throughout the Chongryon press across subsequent years. Indeed, Kang Myŏnghŭi's poem reappeared repeatedly in both newspapers and journals—for example, in the Chongryon literary journal *Munhak yesul* in 1963[159] and in the *Chosŏn sinbo* newspaper in 1973[160]—and such poems by students, youths, and other nonprofessionals were soon joined with poems by well-known South Korean poets. The first such poem—Kim Yosŏp's "Masses" ("Kunjung")—appeared in *Atarashii sedai* in July 1960, and their numbers increased in subsequent years. As noted earlier, Yi Insŏk's "A Human Has the Right to Live" ("In'gan ŭn sara issŭl kwŏlli ka itta") and Ku Chungsŏ's "Come Smash the Altar" ("Wasŏ chedan ŭl pusura") appeared in the *Chosŏn sinbo* in 1963. Likewise, in 1965, the *Chosŏn sinbo* republished Cho Pyŏnghwa's "Open, Unification" ("T'ongil iyŏ! Yŏllyŏra"), Yi Kŭnbae's "On 4.19" ("4.19 e puch'yŏ"), and Pak Tujin's "Ah Ancestral Land" ("A choguk"), the last of which appeared again in the paper in 1973 and 1975.[161]

As noted previously, this practice of republication of South Korean texts not only interacted with a parallel practice in the North but also preceded and shaped it in important ways. The post-April Revolution wave of republications of South Korean poetry began—in the case of both professional and amateur poets—in the Chongryon press and was then picked up in North Korea. This was the case with Kang Myŏnghŭi's poem, which had been republished in the North's *Adong munhak* after appearing in the Chongryon press in Japan. And it was likewise the case for a range of other poems by both professional and amateur poets, including Ko Yangsun's "At My Younger Brother's Funerary Altar" (August 1960 in Japan;

October 1960 in North Korea), Yi Wŏnsu's "Song of a Younger Sister" (August 1960 in Japan; October 1960 in North Korea) and Ku Chungsŏ's "Come Smash the Altar" (April 1963 in Japan; June 1963 in North Korea). Chongryon's engagements with South Korean literature were thus pathbreaking. They were not simply influenced by the North but also influential toward the DPRK, and in fact, this was the case in relation not only to republication but also to practices of creative composition.

CROSS-BORDER WRITING

On April 12, 1960, as the series of protests that would eventually be known as the April Revolution unfolded in South Korea, the front page of the North's *Munhak sinmun* newspaper, the official organ of the Korean Writers' Alliance, featured a poem called "Blaze" ("Pulkil") about these events by the Chongryon-affiliated poet Kang Sun, one of the central figures in the journal *Pulssi*, mentioned above.[162] This was by no means the first time that a work by a Chongryon writer had been carried in a North Korean publication. In fact, Chongryon-affiliated literature had appeared in publications in the North since the mid-1950s, and Chongryon publications, proud of these connections, had even reprinted North Korean reviews of Chongryon literature that had appeared in the North.

The appearance of "Blaze" in the *Munhak sinmun* newspaper was nevertheless significant. Although North Korean publications, by this time, had already started focusing significant attention on the transformational protests emerging the South, writers had not yet translated this interest into works of heroization or support. That is, although North Korean writers had previously written a range of fiction and poetry about the South, they had not yet reacted to the events of the April Revolution in their creative work. This changed with "Blaze," which appears to have been the first literary text about the April Revolution to be published in the North. Once again, therefore, Chongryon writers and publications led the way in reimagination links to South Korea, and indeed, in the days, weeks, months, and years after April 12, 1960, a tremendous amount of poetry, fiction, drama, and more would be published about the April Revolution by writers in the North.

In this way, "Blaze" was pivotal in the formation of what would become a recurring topic and theme in North Korean literature—the events of the April Revolution—and it was also pivotal in pioneering a new form of literary practice. "Blaze" frames the student protesters in the South as individuals who sympathized with the North and listened to DPRK broadcasts—their "lamp of hope"—in secret at night, and it thus departs centrally from the concrete details of events in the South. At the same time, Kang's text also contains elements that engage quite concretely with developments from below the thirty-eighth parallel. Directly following its reference to the consumption of radio broadcasts from Pyongyang, the poem includes a stanza that relays five of the protesters' slogans and/or demands:

> "Do not make students into political tools!"
> "Give schools freedom!"
> "We reject 'campaign' activities in schools!"
> "Do not suppress our words!"
> "Do not compel subscriptions to the *Sŏul sinmun*!"[163]

Appearing within quotation marks, these demands are, of course, emphasized as words voiced by the protesters themselves. Yet they are also in quotation marks because they are, themselves, drawn from another text—or rather, another set of texts—that Kang had access to.

In its opening lines, "Blaze" emphasizes the nationwide scope of the uprisings in the South, noting their spread—as an "unextinguishable blaze"—from Taegu "To Seoul's Kwanghwamun intersection / To Suwŏn, to Taejŏn, to Pusan, to Chŏnju / To Masan."[164] With these words, the poem paints a picture of common outrage and indignation shared by students across the country. In reality, however, the set of demands quoted in the stanza reproduced above was a set of demands presented by students at a specific protest in a specific city: a protest held on March 8, 1960, in the city of Taejŏn that had been reported on with great fanfare in Chongryon's *Chosŏn minbo* newspaper on March 16.[165] This was twelve days before the original version of Kang Sun's poem appeared in this same newspaper,[166] and the article in question was one that not only paraphrased reporting on the protest from the Seoul-based *Tonga ilbo* but also reproduced images of this day's morning and evening issues of the newspaper prominently next to its text.[167]

Kang's poem, in other words, was not simply about the April Revolution. It was a poem about the April Revolution that, while representing South Korean protesters as in touch with North Korean media, drew directly upon South Korean reporting. It thus enacted a novel form of literary engagement: that is, cross-border writing that both imagined and performed inter-Korean media links. As we will see, this was a practice that North Korean writers soon took in much more robust directions. Yet it was a practice pioneered in Japan—a practice that, like the republication of South Korean literature, migrated across the East Sea and transformed the North Korean textual domain. And it was a practice, in fact, whose origins even predated the April Revolution and Kang's imagination of it.

Once again, Chongryon-affiliated poetry led the way in beginning to imagine new ways of engaging with South Korean journalism. Published in the journal *Chosŏn munye*, Chŏn Hwagwang's "South Korean News" ("Han'guk nyusŭ") narrates an encounter with a South Korean newsreel.[168] Opening with a description of scenes of women, children, and the elderly confined behind wire fences, the poem nevertheless focuses not merely upon the tragic reality depicted in the newsreel but also on the response that it occasions in the speaker who views them. For the speaker, the individuals on the screen are not figures of distance but rather closeness:

> There, a girl of about ten,
> Wipes her rain-soaked face,
> And the expression she sends this way
> Is just like my daughter's
> When filled with sorrow.
> Grasping the folds of the girl's skirt,
> A young child, just old enough to walk,
> Waddles forward, pink and naked.
> Ah, they were orphans . . .
> The next moment, my eyes open widely again
> And I catch my breath.
> The face of the old woman, over sixty,
> Is so similar to that of my mother, whose fate I do not know.
> I am surprised.
> I rise from my seat
> And yell, "Mother . . ."[169]

For the speaker in Chŏn's poem, the images of the South appearing on the screen are not simply harrowing but close to home. They are images that produce a bodily response—images that draw the viewer's voice into the newsreel, at which point a convoy of American trucks and jeeps appears:

> One, two, three, four
> Trucks and jeeps appear.
> The corpses and injured soldiers they carried
> There in the mud and melted snow.
> The clamoring masses cry, "Wangk..."
> And raise their hands and murmur,
> As if cheering.
> No, it is not a cheer but a scream.
> Chaos as if having shaken a beehive.
> And amid it, "Aigu!"
> The ear-shattering voice of a women rings out.
> But it is a sound only I heard.
> The newsreel is a silent film.[170]

The boundary between the viewer and image here collapses, and this is not only because the viewer identifies with those in the newsreel but also because the viewer has begun supplementing their images and actions with his or her own voice and imagination.

In Chŏn's poem, the precise set of images being described is left unclear. Yet other poems from this period pinpointed their references in clear and unambiguous ways. On June 8, 1957, the *Chosŏn minbo* published "We Cannot Bear It Anymore" ("Tŏ nŭn ch'amŭl su ŏpta"), a recent poem by a devoted reader named Kim Hongsik.[171] Like many other works from this period, Kim's poem decried the devastating conditions that compatriots in South Korea, and especially in the author's home region of Chŏlla Province, had to deal with: exploitation and expropriation; the despair of scavenging for food; the transformation of spring, as the poem put it, into "A sad season / When the belly's skin bloats."[172] Although Kim's poem was meant to pull at the heartstrings of its readers, it was not meant to surprise them; after all, such representations were commonplace in Chongryon publications at the time.

At the same time, the exact source of the familiar image of the South that Kim's poem invoked was nevertheless notable. Like its title, the first line of the poem was a direct quote from an article that had been published in the newspaper two months earlier.[173] Titled "Mom, Please Give Me Some Food" ("Ŏmma pap chom chuso"), the article had indeed described recent devastation in a flood-ridden part of South Korea's Chŏlla Province. Yet it had been neither an original product of the *Chosŏn minbo* nor a reprint drawn from a North Korean or Japanese source. On the contrary, it had been reprinted, in edited and truncated form, from Seoul's *Tonga ilbo* newspaper, and it was thus a South Korean text—one drawn not only from across the East Sea but also from across the political divide of the Cold War order—that Kim was responding to in his poem.

At the time, Kim occupied a particular space. As the *Chosŏn minbo* noted in its presentation of Kim's text, the author was a member of the Ōmura Korean Literature Association, the literary group organized by those imprisoned at the Ōmura Detention Center, where Koreans judged to have violated Japan's immigration laws were kept before being deported.[174] Imprisoned in a liminal space at the margins between Japan and Korea, Kim developed a practice of cross-border writing with unique mediating power. Yet such practices soon moved outward from the liminal, marginal space: both to other parts of Japan and across the East Sea. On March 4, 1964, the *Chosŏn sinbo* published a recent work by Kang Sun, the poet mentioned above, under the title "Leaving Words Like a Last Testament" ("Yusŏ kat'ŭn mal ŭl namgigo").[175] Like many other poems by Chongryon writers, the poem, which dealt with conditions in a Seoul "slum lined with shacks," painted a harrowing portrait of life on the southern side of the thirty-eighth parallel divide. Yet Kang's poem was not simply an imaginative vision; it was also a response to a concrete text from the South that the author had recently encountered.

Subtitled "Upon Reading the January 26th Issue of the *Chosŏn ilbo*," Kang's poem began with a quotation: "Today, too, dad bought us bread. Why doesn't mom come? I miss her. Because the baby keeps crying."[176] Reproduced from the issue of the *Chosŏn ilbo* mentioned in the poem's subtitle, the quotation was a line from a diary written by a nine-year-old boy who was one of three siblings killed by their father amid the desperations of poverty, and an image of this diary entry had appeared side by side with a substantial article reporting on this tragic series of events that had transpired in the Namgajwa neighborhood of Seoul's Sŏdaemun District.[177] Kang's poem, in fact, returned to the words of this diary entry repeatedly throughout its development, weaving them together with information from the *Chosŏn ilbo* report and words of emotional response from the poem's speaker, who beckoned the nine-year-old boy and his siblings to return as "swallowtail butterflies" (*horang nabi*) and "eagles" when the "bright spring" of revolution finally allowed the "ice of the Han River to melt" and "the larks of Ch'anggyŏng Zoo to fly up into the sky."[178]

Kang's poem thus engaged with multiple layers of South Korean texts, funneling them, gently but concertedly, toward a vision of potential revolutionary transformation in the South. And like the practice of reprinting post–April Revolution South Korean literature, this was a practice that would soon emerge in North Korea. In May 1966, the journal *Chosŏn nyŏsŏng* published a reportage-style narrative focusing on the struggles of young, female bus and taxi attendants working in Seoul.[179] Appearing under the title "Women Who Resist" ("Hanggŏ hanŭn nyŏsŏngdŭl"), this work by Ch'ae Kyusang followed the plight of a young attendant, Sunhŭi, struggling to support her sick father while dealing with an injured throat and resisting the undue pressure being exerted on her by her manager, an undercover police officer seeking to root out activist-minded "troublemakers" like Sunhŭi's friend, Yŏngok, another one of the company's attendants.

As we might expect, the narrative culminates in Sunhŭi, Yŏngok, and the other attendants banding together to send the manager, nicknamed "Raccoon," scurrying away in fear. His threat to fire both Sunhŭi and Yŏngok is thus inverted, and he is the one who must leave. Yet this turn of events is also something of a surprise considering the original inspiration for the text. Ch'ae's narrative includes neither a reference nor a genre label, but it is clearly based on real events in the South. In March 1964, the South Korean newspaper *Chosŏn ilbo* reported on the recent suicide of a young attendant named Yŏngok, who struggled to support her sick father despite an injury to her throat, only to be unjustly fired by her manager.[180] Amid broader controversies surrounding the treatment of young female attendants, this reporting was then picked up by the *Rodong sinmun* in the North in 1965,[181] and it clearly served as the basis for Ch'ae's narrative, which reversed Sunhŭi and Yŏngok's characters and redirected the original story's destitution toward empowerment.

In this way, Ch'ae's text does not simply draw upon and dramatize the South Korean newspaper report. Drawing upon the practice of creative engagement developed by Chongryon writers, it rewrites it by revolutionizing its protagonists. Yet just as Chongryon publications were never simple copies of North Korean ones, North Korean publications did not simply reproduce what their colleagues in Japan had already done. On the contrary, what North Korean writers developed—alongside their reception of practices from Japan—was a novel form of creative rewriting of South Korean literature.

EXPLOSIVE WORDS

On the evening of April 20, 1960, writers gathered in a Pyongyang theater for a "Poets' Evening"[182] where the poet Pak Seyŏng offered a reading of a new poem that included the following words:

> Shaken by resentment, building up and building up, the southern land
> Has erupted like a ridge of volcanoes! Following the flames in Masan
> In Seoul, Pusan, Taegu, and Kwangju,
> Students and citizens, the blood they inherited from their righteous ancestors boiling
> Have issued a fiery decree against Syngman Rhee's rule of fascist terror!
> . . .
> Seoul, you were no longer like my hometown! [But] you have risen again!
> In Kwanghwamun, where I walked so often, and on all streets,
> Ranks surge, spouting flames of rage, and
> Resentment, building up like Samgak Mountain, explodes![183]

Published in the following morning's *Rodong sinmun* newspaper, Pak's poem historicized the ongoing events of the April Revolution in dual temporalities: first, it placed it within a longer historical trajectory; second, and more importantly, it described it as the outcome of rage and resentment built up over years, deploying the trope of volcanic eruption.

In picking up this trope of the volcano, Pak's poem not only anchored its vision in temporal depth but also in a broader spatial domain: in particular, that of South Korean representations. In South Korea, literary responses to the April Revolution varied noticeably according to age. While many older writers reacted in awe, their young colleagues noted that the April Revolution did not appear out of nowhere. For such writers, the uprising of April 1960 had to be seen as the product of a series of latent transformations, and this was most canonically represented with reference to the image of a volcano. Dormancy, this image implied, was not the same as passivity; it was, instead, the invisible, subterranean gathering of an even larger reaction.

The image of the volcano appeared in South Korean reporting on student protests as early as March 18, when the *Han'guk ilbo* likened the emergence of the March 15 uprising in Masan to the opening of a "volcanic crater" (*punhwagu*).[184] This image, moreover, was subsequently taken up by poets the following month. Yi Hanjik's portion of a jointly authored poem published in *Saebyŏk* in mid-April was likely the first to do so. In Yi's prose-poem, the speaker recalls an unusual dream in which he is aboard an American "Apache" helicopter searching for underground natural resources. What surprises the American pilot the most, the speaker relates, is "the fact that actively living volcanic ranges were spread deeply across the land like a spider's web."[185] "This is trouble; these are volcanoes that could erupt at any moment," the pilot then says, to which the narrator responds, "Trouble? Aren't those irreplaceably precious underground resources? ... They are irreplaceably precious treasures for the attainment of democracy."[186]

For Yi, then, the silent surface of the Korean landscape—like the sleeping mind—hides an active subterranean world out of which the explosive demand for democracy emerges. It does not come from above—or from economic power—but rather from below, and this was a conviction that many other poets echoed. Kim Yongho's "Each Year When April Comes" ("Haemada 4-wŏl i omyŏn"), published on April 28, 1960, thus proclaimed:

> A volcano erupted. Flames blasted into the sky.
> The suppressed subterranean heat of rage exploded
> At once. March 15! The alert rang out

In my hometown.
The angry waves of the southern sea were the signals.[187]

As in Yi Hanjik's poem, pent up rage has produced an explosion in the name of democracy—an explosion that, after emerging in Masan, has spread across the country. Indeed, the image of the volcano soon became tethered to the broader set of events culminating on April 19, as Hwang Kŭmch'an's "Young Mountain Ridges" ("Chŏlmŭn sanmaektŭl"), for example, made clear:

> In the April 19 collision with the heavens, when a generation
>   erupted like a volcano,
> I saw the movements of life.
>
> They are exploding, young mountain ridges, flag-bearers of
>   justice,
> The last fortresses of democracy,
> Symbols of life.[188]

Spewing rage and resentment, this eruption, Hwang implied, was also life-giving. And this meant that April, as Pak Hwamok put it, was a "month of resurrection" when "living things that had seemed to exist in silence / almost as if dead / shot up fiercely, fiercely like an eruption."[189]

The power and prevalence of this symbol of the volcano in South Korean representations of the April Revolution made it a prime focus for North Korean writers. In search of a means for literary engagement with their colleagues across the border, they took it up with zeal, deploying it as a means of participating in the ongoing literary dialogue on revolutionary possibilities then occurring in the South. At the same time, however, they also provided it with new nuances and dimensions. On April 14, the *Rodong Sinmun* carried a poem by Yun Ch'angju underneath a photo of Masan citizens heading for a police station with clubs in hand. Titled "Masan Has Raised the Signal Fire" ("Masan ŭn ponghwa rŭl ch'uk'yŏ tŭrŏtta"), Yun's poem began with the following words:

> People! Masan has raised the signal fire.
> Enraged, Taegu and Pusan bolt up.

In Seoul, too, flames of rage burn and spread—
Fifteen years of fraud, day and night
The southern land, having shed blood innocently on the penal rack,
Is now spewing fire like an erupting volcano.[190]

For Yun, as for others, the flames engulfing the South were flames of rage, of resentment, and of revenge: those hidden deep underground until ready to explode. Yet he also described them as "signal fires" (*ponghwa*), an invocation of the Chosŏn (1392–1910) dynasty's military communication system, which relied upon mountaintop signal fires to relay messages across the peninsula. In Yun's imagination, therefore, revolution was not merely a conjuring forth of latent possibilities; it was also an act of communication, an attempt to signal the North and articulate solidarity.

In this way, Yun's poem constructed cross-border reciprocity. Engaging with texts from the South, it rewrote them to include attempts at communication with the North, and this was drawn out further in the work of the veteran novelist and playwright Song Yŏng, who published the play *The Volcano of Rage Has Erupted* (*Punno ŭi hwasan ŭn t'ŏjyŏtta*) in the June 1960 issue of *Chosŏn munhak*. Performed for the first time at the National Drama Theater on June 3,[191] *Volcano* begins with the stage set as follows: "The curtain opens with the grand sound of a chorus.... An active volcano is visible with smoke rising from its peak. As the sound of the chorus gets louder, the volcano erupts with the sound of an explosion. The fierce flames continue to grow."[192] The play then travels to the city of Masan to tell a fictionalized account of the family of Kim Chuyŏl, a student killed by the police during the protests of March 1960, and its transformation in the wake of his death: not only its eye-opening effect on his aunt and uncle but also its mobilization of his cousin, a student in Seoul, who realizes that the necessary task is creating a "new way of life, a new politics, a new system."[193]

For the cousin, Sŭngwŏn, this task ultimately means leading a group of armed youth in a fatal confrontation with the ROK military—a confrontation that is energized, at a crucial moment, by a message of solidarity broadcast via radio from North. What happens here, however, is not one-way co-option. Already in the second-to-last scene, protestors themselves have become forces of communication, as the scene's staging makes clear:

A map of the darkness of southern Korea (in a color that expresses darkness) appears. Above it, signal fires flare up here and there. As the signal fires pervade southern Korea, the flames grow larger. Masan, Chinhae, Chinju, Pusan, Ulsan, P'ohang, Kimhae, Seoul, Inch'ŏn, Suwŏn, Taegu, Taejŏn, Kimch'ŏn, Kwangju, Chŏnju, Kunsan, Mokp'o, Ch'ŏngju, Ch'unch'ŏn, etc.

As the flames continue to grow, southern Korea in its entirety becomes a signal fire.[194]

At this moment, the volcanic eruption that began the play becomes a "signal fire," and this turns the North Korean broadcast in the subsequent scene into a dialogic response.

Of course, the April Revolution in the South did not proceed as many in the North might have hoped. Although Syngman Rhee and his Liberal Party were pushed out of power, the events of April 1960 neither overthrew the ROK state nor led to widespread expressions of solidarity with the North. Nevertheless, writers in the North did not abandon the visions of eruptive possibilities that they had developed during this period. Instead, in the years after April 1960, North Korean writers shifted their focus from deploying tropes from South Korean literature as way of reimagining the April Revolution as a cross-border, communicative event to reworking and rewriting specific works of South Korean literature in order to transform them into revolutionary texts at the border between North and South Korean authorship.

Such practices of rewriting South Korean literary texts, in fact, began with North Korean publications' practices of republishing them. While some texts were republished in their entirety, others were shortened and excerpted. Ku Inhwan's "In the Shadow of Shacks" ("P'anjajip kŭnŭl"), for example, was abridged by excising the part of the text dealing with the Korean War. In the original text, which deals with slum demolition projects in Seoul, the critique of South Korean state and society that emerges through the hardships of the poor protagonist who loses his home is paired quite explicitly with a parallel invocation of the threat of the North Korean state from the wartime-era past.[195] In the North Korean reprint, however, this middle section is edited out, and the text becomes a unidimensional critique of South Korean state and society.[196] Similarly, Kim Suyŏng's poem "Go, Get Out" ("Kadao nagadao"), republished in the North Korean magazine *Chosŏn hwabo* and then again in the *Rodongja sinmun* newspaper, was edited to voice its demand to "get out" solely to Americans rather than to both Americans and Soviets.[197]

It was not only via strategic excision, however, that South Korean works of literature were reshaped. In March 1965, the South Korean magazine *Yŏwŏn* published a text-and-photo essay on a young woman named Kwŏn Pyŏngsun, then making a living in Seoul as a shoeshiner.[198] A native of Ch'ungch'ŏng Province, Kwŏn had come to Seoul seeking work after the death of her father, and after a series of jobs, she had taken up the task of shining shoes in front of Seoul Station. For Kwŏn, whose goal was to make enough money to reunite her family, the task was exhausting. Yet she channeled its challenges into art—in particular, into a series of poems titled "Shoeshining," "Thoughts of My Hometown," and "The Flower Seen in My Dreams." Like the other texts mentioned above, the first two of these poems were picked up by North Korean publications and reprinted in a variety of forms. For example, the July 1965 reprint in *Chosŏn nyŏsŏng* printed the poems and the accompanying explanatory text in more or less the same form as the original in *Yŏwŏn*,[199] and the June 1965 reprint in the popular magazine *Ch'ŏllima* did something similar with minor paraphrasing in the explanatory text.[200]

In contrast, the youth magazine *Sonyŏndan* took a noticeably different approach by dramatizing Kwŏn Pyŏngsun's character in a reportage-style piece that included portions of "Shoeshining" embedded in the text as words written by Pyŏngsun the character. Written by Pak Myŏngch'ŏl, this dramatization was a reshaped version of the one introduced in *Yŏwŏn*. Yet it placed Pyŏngsun in a South Korean context marked not only by economic deprivation but also by state oppression and American colonization:

> Pyŏngsun, who had been shining shoes in the street, was dragged to the police station.
> "Who told you to come out into the streets in this sorry state, huh?!" The police bastard screamed and hit the desk with a crash.
> "Then what am I supposed to do? If I don't earn money, I can't eat."
> "Is that our problem, huh? Since you kids stream out onto the streets looking like beggars, the streets are dirty. Huh? Do you know who is coming here to Seoul Station today?

"..."

"The president, who was just on a tour of the provinces, is coming with an American visitor."²⁰¹

Framed in this way, Pak's dramatization departed significantly from the original essay, and it ended accordingly: with the flashing up, in Pyŏngsun's eyes, of "limitless hatred for the American imperialists and traitor Park Chung Hee [Pak Chŏnghŭi]."²⁰²

At stake here, to be sure, was an attempt to radicalize "Shoeshining" and its author by recontextualizing them in a narrative that developed in revolutionary directions. At the same time, what such practices of recontextualization performed was a hybridization of literary voices. By inserting words of South Korean poetry into a narrative rewritten via North Korean words and perspectives, the text wove together North and South Korean authorship in a way perhaps most strongly seen in *Chosŏn nyŏsŏng*'s 1966 republication of selections of Chŏn Ponggu's 1965 memoir, *With My Life on My Back* (*Nae insaeng nae chige e chigo*).²⁰³ In this republication, the order of sections of the memoir was significantly rearranged, and they were presented in a hybrid, textual mode that mixed quoted reproduction in the first person, which was drawn directly from the South Korean text, with North Korean paraphrasing of the original text in the third person. What emerged here was something like a hybrid, cross-border text: one that demonstrated the subtle and complex ways in which practices of cross-border reading and textual reproduction gradually bled into transformed modes of North Korean writing.

Not all attempts at rewriting South Korean literature, however, included direct quotations from or citations of the original works. One of the most unique and interesting experiments in cross-border writing was Ryu Tohŭi's short story "The Article that Could Not Be Published" ("Palp'yo toeji mothan kisa"), which appeared in the *Munhak sinmun* in April of 1961.²⁰⁴ Ryu's text tells the story of a South Korean journalist, Tŏkchun, who has been sent to P'anmunjŏm to cover the most recent set of inter-Korean talks, and it thus takes up the call for a new literature dealing with unification. More importantly, however, it is also a quite explicit attempt at rewriting a contemporary South Korean story: Yi Hoch'ŏl's "P'anmunjŏm," which was published in the March 1961 issue of

Sasanggye and earned Yi the *Hyŏndae munhak* New Writer's Prize for that year.[205]

Like Ryu's, Yi's text tells the story of a South Korean reporter sent to P'anmunjŏm, and its narrative focuses on the relationship that this reporter, Chinsu, establishes with a female reporter from the North. Although there is a mutual curiosity and desire for connection between Chinsu and his counterpart, the relationship that arises between them—as between their colleagues—is not a naturally harmonious one but rather a conflicted and competitive one. Marked simultaneously by the desire for attachment, the desire for recognition, and the feeling of derision, their interaction soon reaches an impasse; there can be no mutual comprehension in the realm of politics, and the subsequent shift into the personal domain both offers new possibilities and shuts them down via Chinsu's patriarchal vision of gender relations.[206] As a result, the only way the text can imagine overcoming the "feeling of estrangement" (*iyŏkkam*) that pervades P'anmunjŏm is to turn its perspective inside out: to move, via Chinsu's half-awake, half-asleep meanderings, into an imagined future vision in which the history of P'anmunjŏm is rewritten retrospectively from an outside perspective (that of a historian from "a certain African republic").

Ryu's rewriting, on the other hand, takes a quite different approach. As he appears in the beginning of the text, Tŏkchun is neither an especially political person nor someone with a close personal connection to the North; he is visiting P'anmunjŏm for the first time and he has neither relatives nor friends above the thirty-eighth parallel. Nevertheless, his journey fills him with a powerful mix of both curiosity and excitement:

> What excited him uncontrollably was not simply the curiosity of wanting to visit Panmunjom, a place both known around the world and at the center of the attention and interest of all Korean people; nor was it simply the strong, accompanying urge that he felt, as journalist, to go there and write an article. What excited him most of all was the expectation of being able to meet northern Korean [*Pukchosŏn*] reporters and talk with them.
>
> (The first northern Koreans he had seen in about ten years!)
>
> His heart raced. He had no relatives or close friends in northern Korea. But for some reason, his heart pounded as if he were going to meet a close family member, and he was unable to sleep the whole night.[207]

In this scene, Tŏkchun's emotions run far ahead of his physical body. His journey, however, is not an altogether joyful one. In preparing for the trip, Tŏkchun and his colleagues have been briefed by an American intelligence officer who has warned them not to interact with the Northern journalists who will be there. This warning leaves Tŏkchun with an unsavory feeling that is only heightened when he finally arrives at P'anmunjŏm. Observing that the boundary line is guarded on the northern side by a Korean soldier but on the southern side by an American, he feels "national indignation" (*minjokchŏk ŭibun*) and gazes at the flock of doves across the valley, flying freely above.

With this image in mind, Tŏkchun enters the reporters' lounge, where he observes the Northern and Southern journalists sitting in their respective groups. Soon, however, the space between the two groups breaks down when one reporter from the North unexpectedly encounters his younger brother in the group of reporters from the South. As the two embrace, the entire room is "filled with a strong but indescribable stream of emotion" and Tŏkchun finds himself crying as all those present burst into spontaneous applause.[208] It is an encounter that shakes the entire room and affects them all as if the brothers were members of their own family, yet it is interrupted as an American MP enters the room and separates the Southern reporter from his older brother.

The entire room looks at the MP with eyes of "sharp hatred" and Tŏkchun's fist tightens spontaneously, but the MP disregards this and drags the younger brother outside. The result, at once, is the separation of the brothers and the suturing of Tŏkchun's emotions to that of the older brother:

"Doglike bastards! Are you trying to divide brothers' blood? You can't divide it! You can't!"

The elder brother shouted at the back of the American with his fists clenched and his voice trembling with resentment. His eyes gleamed with a furious light. Looking at his face, Tŏkchun's heart felt so sore that it seemed as if it would burst.... Tŏkchun felt as if all the blood in his body were shooting up to the top of his head at once. His body shook and he gnashed his teeth. He barely restrained himself from going after that American bastard, grabbing him by the throat, and smashing him.[209]

Returning home that night, Tŏkchun recalls everything that happened that day: the image of the Korean soldiers on one side and Americans on the other, the contrast between the "dignified" reporters on the Northern side and the "unnatural" ones on the Southern side, the unexpected meeting between the brothers, and its hateful interruption by the American MP. Tŏkchun realizes that all of these things are connected and that tracing the line connecting them will produce a shattering, powerful news article.

In this way, Ryu's story once again revolutionizes its South Korean protagonist and transform's Yi's original story into one of a revolutionary coming to consciousness. In doing so, however, it also adds an additional dimension. Tŏkchun knows that such a news article could never be published in the South due to censorship. He thus takes up his pen not to write a report for his newspaper but rather to write an entry for his journal:

> He took up his pen. The face of the American intelligence officer and the lanky figure of MP appeared, by turns, on the paper, at the end of his running pen. Yet, he . . . wrote as his heart directed him, following the cry of his conscience.
>
> "No one can divide the Korean people's blood. The American robbers should leave Korea immediately!"
>
> He wrote dozens of pages through the night. At the end of his text, with his face flushed and his shoulders shaking, he wrote:
>
> "I am writing this absurd story, this righteous cry of conscience, not for the newspaper but in my diary. But this story must be published and the day when it will be published will come. The battle starts now!"
>
> . . .
>
> The refreshing dawn air penetrated deeply into his excited heart. Looking at the gray sky of daybreak, he was preparing for a new struggle.[210]

With this concluding scene, Ryu's story produces a latent text in the South, and in doing so, it sets up a complex yet off-kilter relationship of mirroring vis-à-vis the latent text in the North that inspired the story: Yi's "P'anmunjŏm," which was never republished in the DPRK. By creatively rewriting Yi's story without ever mentioning it and then inserting a hidden, unpublished revolutionary text into his vision of the South, Ryu produces the two sides of the peninsula as mirroring domains of unspoken connection. And as we will see, this was not entirely untrue—although the reception in the South of literature by those who had gone North took a quite different path than the interactions outlined above.

CONCLUSION

As we have seen, the Chongryon press and its interactions with South Korean texts transformed North Korean literary practices. Drawing upon Chongryon writers' literary engagements with journalistic texts from the South, writers in the North went one step further by writing South Korean literary texts themselves. And as we will see in chapter 2, this was a practice that continued to gather steam, a practice that eventually reshaped North Korean writers' visions of their own revolutionary heritage from the colonial era, and a practice that traveled back to Japan to influenced Chongryon writing.

But what of the South? In 1978, the young Seoul-based critic Yŏm Muung, surveying South Korea's fiction landscape of 1977 in an essay included in an anthology of that year's "controversial works" (*munjejak*), praised Kim Chŏnghan's short story "Letters from Okinawa" ("Okkinawa esŏ on p'yŏnji") for the "strong historical consciousness" that it demonstrated in its vision of continuity and connection—although not equivalence—between the situation of young women sent to Okinawa as cheap agricultural laborers for sugarcane fields in the 1970s and the situation of young women sent to Okinawa as sexual slaves ("comfort women") during the late Japanese colonial era. "Through the simple form [of letters sent by a young woman back to her mother in Korea]," Yŏm wrote, "the past exploitation and labor expropriation of Japanese imperialism, the shape of those traitors to the nation who collaborated with the Japanese Empire, and the post-Liberation reality in which these contradictions have not only not been overcome but have actually been strengthened are movingly paid witness to."[211]

At the same time, what Yŏm leaves out here—or perhaps, was not in a position to know at the time—is another set of links that appear to stand behind the ones explicitly drawn out in Kim's story. On April 19, 1977, on the seventeenth anniversary of the April Revolution and only months before Kim's story appeared in the South Korean journal *Munye chungang*, Chongryon's *Chosŏn sinbo* began serializing a report on the plight of South Korean workers in sugarcane fields and sugar factories in Okinawa. Outlining the exploitative contracts that brought these workers to Okinawa as well as the lack of food, sexual violence, and physical abuse they experienced there, the report was immediately followed, on the next day and in the same location in the paper, with a report about Pae Ponggi, an elderly Korean woman living in Okinawa who had been brought there as a sexual slave in 1944.[212]

This report on Pae, which preceded interviews with survivors in South Korea by many years, was extremely important in its own right for the way in which it gave voice to her story. Yet it was also important for the link that its publication produced between her story and the stories of young sugarcane field workers from South Korea in contemporary Okinawa. This was precisely the link that Kim Chŏnghan—unlike anyone else in the South at the time, it appears—would make in his story a few months later, and it thus served as a point of connection not only between two historical periods but also between two media domains: the South Korean literary domain and the Chongryon journalistic domain in Japan, which were not permitted to cross. Therefore, just as the Chongryon press came to influence North Korean literature and the North Korean imagination so too did it come to influence the South Korean literary imagination, as we will continue to see in subsequent chapters.

TABLE 1.1 South Korean publications referenced in the *Rodong sinmun*, 1940s–1960s

Type	Publication	Year of First Observed Citation
Seoul daily	*Chosŏn ilbo*	1947
	Chungoe sinbo	1947
	Hansŏng ilbo	1947
	Minjung ilbo	1947
	Taedong sinmun	1947
	Uri sinmun	1947
	Chayu sinmun	1949
	Chosŏn chungang ilbo	1949
	Minju ilbo	1949
	P'yŏnghwa sinmun	1949
	Segye ilbo	1949
	Sŏul sinmun	1949
	Yŏnhap sinmun	1952
	Han'guk ilbo	1954
	Minju sinbo	1954
	Tonga ilbo	1954
	Sanŏp kyongje sinmun	1955
Regional daily	*Kukche sinmun*	1949
	Inch'ŏn ilbo	1954
	Pusan ilbo	1956
	Yŏngnam ilbo	1957
	Chŏnnam ilbo	1958
	Taegu maeil sinmun	1959
	Kukche sinbo	1960
	Taegu ilbo	1961
	Kyŏnggi maeil sinmun	1963
	Chŏnnam maeil sinmun	1964
	Ch'ungch'ŏng ilbo	1964

Type	Publication	Year of First Observed Citation
	Masan ilbo	1964
	Mokp'o ilbo	1964
	Taejŏn ilbo	1964
Popular magazine	Hŭimang	1954
	Sinch'ŏnji	1954
	Sint'aeyang	1954
	Ch'ŏngch'un	1955
	Yŏsŏnggye	1955
	Han'guk hwabo	1956
	Sirhwa	1959
	Sedae	1963
	Yŏwŏn	1964
Specialist journal	Han'guk ŭnhaeng chosa wŏlbo	1954
	Kosi wa chŏnhyŏng	1954
	Munye	1954
	Chaejŏng	1957
	Kyŏngje yŏn'gam	1957
	Saebyŏk	1959
	Sasanggye	1958
	Chayu munhak	1962
	Han'guk kyŏngje	1963
	Hyŏndae munhak	1963
	Kyoyuk p'yŏngnon	1963
	Sinsajo	1963
	Sinsegye	1964

Note: This is a partial list whose entries are not meant to be exhaustive.

TABLE 1.2 South Korean literature reprinted in North Korean publications, mid-1950s–mid-1960s

Author	Genre	South Korean Original	North Korean Reprint 1
An Tongnim	Fiction	"Hŭimang" [Hope], *Hyŏndae munhak* 9, no. 3 (March 1963): 60–71.	"Hŭimang" [Hope], *Choguk t'ongil*, February 3–February 6, 1965, 4.
Anonymous	Poetry	"Tasi torawa pogo kara" [Come Back Again and Look], *Pusan ilbo*, April 19, 1963, 3.	"Tasi torawa pogo kara" [Come Back Again and Look], *Minju ch'ŏngnyŏn*, May 9, 1963, 3.
Anonymous	Poetry	Collective "spontaneous poem" performed by female students during hunger strike. Relayed in "Uri nŭn pae kop'ŭji ant'a" [We're Not Hungry], *Chosŏn ilbo*, June 2, 1964, 8.	"Na to karyŏnda" [I Will Go Too], *Sae sedae* 117 (October 1964): 130.
Chang Habo	Poetry	"Yŏgi nŭn amu to oji malla" [No One Come Here], *Pusan ilbo*, May 19, 1960, 1.	"Uri nŭn kkŭnnaenae chik'irira" [We Will Protect Until the End], *Rodong sinmun*, February 16, 1964, 4.
Cho Chihun	Poetry	"Uri nŭn tto tasi noye il su ŏpta" [We Cannot Be Slaves Again], *Sasanggye* 149 (July 1965): 17–19.	"Uri nŭn tto tasi noye il su ŏpta" [We Cannot Be Slaves Again], *Munhak sinmun*, November 16, 1965, 4.
Cho Pyŏnghwa	Poetry	Source listed as *Chŏnnam ilbo*. Full reference unavailable.	"T'ongil iyŏ! Yŏllyŏra—1965-nyŏn ach'im e" [Unification! Open up—Morning, 1965], *Rodong sinmun*, January 14, 1965, 3.
Chŏn Ponggu	Memoir	*Nae insaeng nae chige e chigo* [With My Life on My Back] (Seoul: Taedong munhwasa, 1965).	"Nae insaeng nae chige e chigo" [With My Life on My Back], *Chosŏn nyŏsŏng* 222–224 (April 1966–June 1966): 70–75; 85–88; 84–88.

North Korean Reprint 2	North Korean Reprint 3	North Korean Reprint 4	North Korean Reprint 5
"Hŭimang" [Hope], *Samch'ŏlli* 9 (April 1965): 117–21.			
			"Uri nŭn kkŭnnaenae chik'irira" [We Will Protect Until the End], *Chosŏn nyŏsŏng* 198 (April 1964): 40.
			"Oejŏk ŭl mullich'ija" [Let's Repel the Foreign Bandits], *Rodong sinmun*, December 8, 1965, 3.
			"T'ongil iyŏ! Yŏllyŏra—1965-nyŏn ach'im e" [Unification! Open up—Morning, 1965], *Munhak sinmun*, January 15, 1965, 4.

(continued)

TABLE 1.2 (*continued*)

Author	Genre	South Korean Original	North Korean Reprint 1
Chŏn Chaeil	Poetry	"Ŏnje tasi sae hanŭl i" [When Will a New Sky (Be Visible) Again?], in Kim Yongho, ed., *Hangjaeng ŭi kwangjang* (Seoul: Sinhŭng ch'ulp'ansa, 1960), 189–191. Originally published in *Minju sinbo*.	"Ŏnje tasi sae hanŭl i" [When Will a New Sky (Be Visible) Again?], *Munhak sinmun*, October 4, 1960, 4.
Chŏng Kongch'ae	Poetry	"Mi-p'al-gun ŭi ch'a" [U.S. Eighth Army Car], *Hyŏndae munhak* 9, no. 12 (December 1963): 145–175.	"Mi-p'al-gun ŭi ch'a" [U.S. Eighth Army Car], *Rodong sinmun*, February 29, 1964, 6.
Ha Chaedŏk	Poetry	Source listed as *Kukche sinbo*, January 2, 1964. Full reference unavailable.	"Nunmul i p'inŭn iyagi" [A Tear-Blooming Story], *Sae sedae* 112 (May 1964): 88–89.
Han Muhak	Poetry	"Innae ŭi haeje ka taga onŭn nal" [The Day a Release to Our Forbearance Approaches], *Hyŏndae munhak* 9, no. 8 (August 1963): 222–223.	"Innae ŭi haeje ka taga onŭn nal" [The Day a Release to Our Forbearance Approaches], *Munhak sinmun*, February 26, 1965, 4.
Im Suil	Fiction	"Paegŭi ŭi sugi" [Record of White Clothes], *Hyŏndae munhak* 7, no. 5 (May 1961): 49–65.	"Paegŭi ŭi sugi (1–2)" [Record of White Clothes (1–2)], *Munhak sinmun*, 17 August 17–August 24, 1962, 4.
Kang Myŏnghŭi	Poetry	"Oppa wa ŏnni ka wae p'i rŭl hŭllyŏnnŭnji" [Why My Brothers and Sisters Shed Blood], *Chosŏn ilbo*, April 23, 1960, 3.	"Oppa wa ŏnni rŭl ttarŭryŏmnida" [We Will Follow Our Brothers and Sisters], *Adong munhak* 93 (August 1960): 78–79.
Kim Chaewŏn	Poetry	"Tangbun'gan" [For the Time Being], *Kyŏnghyang sinmun*, April 19, 1963, 3.	"Tangbun'gan" [For the Time Being], *Choguk t'ongil*, May 8, 1963, 2.

North Korean Reprint 2	North Korean Reprint 3	North Korean Reprint 4	North Korean Reprint 5
"Ŏnje tasi sae hanŭl i" [When Will a New Sky (Be Visible) Again?], *Rodong sinmun*, June 8, 1964, 4.	"Ŏnje tasi sae hanŭl i" [When Will a New Sky (Be Visible) Again?], *Sae sedae* 114 (July 1964): 84.		
"Nunmul i p'inŭn iyagi" [A Tear-Blooming Story], *Sonyŏndan* 176 (June 1964): 28–29.			
"Uri nŭn oppa wa ŏnnidŭl ŭi twi rŭl ttarŭryŏmnida" [We Will Follow Our Brothers and Sisters], *Sonyŏndan* 174 (April 1964): 19.	"Uri nŭn oppa wa ŏnnidŭl ŭi twi rŭl ttarŭryŏmnida" [We Will Follow Our Brothers and Sisters], *Rodong sinmun*, April 19, 1966, 3.		
"Tangbun'gan" [For the Time Being], *Minju ch'ŏngnyŏn*, May 9, 1963, 3.	"Tangbun'gan" [For the Time Being], *Sae sedae* 101 (June 1963): 19	"Tangbun'gan" [For the Time Being], *Munhak sinmun*, 1 June 1, 1965, 4.	

(continued)

TABLE 1.2 *(continued)*

Author	Genre	South Korean Original	North Korean Reprint 1
Kim Chiha	Poetry	"Ojŏk" [Five Bandits], *Sasanggye* 205 (May 1970): 231–248.	"Ojŏk" [Five Bandits], *Ch'ŏllima* 148 (May 1971): 106–111.
Kim Chunghŭi	Fiction	"Hoesin" [Ashes], *Munhak ch'unch'u* 2, no. 3 (March 1965): 52–68.	"Hoesin (1–2)" [Ashes (1–2)], *Munhak sinmun*, 18 May 18—May 28, 1965, 3–4.
Kim Sangwŏn	Poetry	"Choguk t'ongil" [Unification of the Ancestral Land], *Kyŏnghyang sinmun*, November 2, 1964, 7.	"Choguk t'ongil" [Unification of the Ancestral Land], *Rodongja sinmun*, November 21, 1964, 3.
Kim Song	Fiction	"Ch'ŏnggaeguri" [Green Frog], *Munhak yesul* 3, no. 6 (June 1956): 27–41.	"Ch'ŏnggaeguri" [Green Frog], *Chosŏn munhak* 118 (June 1957): 50–59.
Kim Suyŏng	Poetry	"Kadao nagadao" [Go, Get Out], *Hyŏndae munhak* 7, no. 1 (January 1961): 33.	"Kadao nagadao" [Go, Get Out], *Chosŏn hwabo* 90 (January 1964): n.p.
Kim Taehong	Poetry	"Choguk iyŏ!" [Ancestral Land!], *Pusan ilbo*, April 24, 1960, 3.	"Choguk iyŏ!" [Ancestral Land!], *Sae sedae* 120 (January 1965): 58–59.
Ko Yangsun	Poetry	"Au ŭi yŏngjŏn e" [At My Brother's Funerary Altar], *Han'guk ilbo*, April 25, 1960, 4.	"Au ŭi yŏngjŏn e" [At My Brother's Funerary Altar], *Munhak sinmun*, October 4, 1960, 4.
Ku Chungsŏ	Poetry	"Wasŏ chedan pusura" [Come and Smash the Altar], *Han'guk ilbo*, April 18, 1963, 5.	"Wasŏ chedan pusura" [Come and Smash the Altar], *Choguk t'ongil*, June 12, 1963, 4.
Ku Inhwan	Fiction	"P'anjajip kŭnŭl" [In the Shadow of Shacks], *Hyŏndae munhak* 7, no. 8 (August 1961): 94–113.	"P'anjajip kŭnŭl (1–2)" [In the Shadow of Shacks (1–2)], *Munhak sinmun*, December 11—December 25, 1962, 4.

North Korean Reprint 2	North Korean Reprint 3	North Korean Reprint 4	North Korean Reprint 5
"Choguk t'ongil" [Unification of the Ancestral Land], *Choguk t'ongil*, November 21, 1964, 2.	"Choguk t'ongil" [Unification of the Ancestral Land], *Chosŏn nyŏsŏng* 208 (February 1965): 28.		
"Kadao nagadao" [Go, Get Out], *Rodongja sinmun*, April 19, 1964, 4.			
"Au ŭi yŏngjŏn e" [At My Brother's Funerary Altar], *Adong munhak* 101 (April 1961): 49.	"Au ŭi yŏngjŏn e" [At My Brother's Funerary Altar], *Chosŏn nyŏsŏng* 198 (April 1964): 40.		
"Wasŏ chedan pusura" [Come and Smash the Altar], *Munhak sinmun*, April 16, 1965, 4.			

(continued)

TABLE 1.2 *(continued)*

Author	Genre	South Korean Original	North Korean Reprint 1
Kwŏn Pyŏngsun	Poetry	"Kudu takki sonyŏ ŭi si" [The Poems of a Shoeshine Girl], *Yŏwŏn* 11, no. 3 (March 1965): n.p.	"Han kudu takki sonyŏ ka purŭn norae" [The Song Sung by a Shoeshine Girl], *Ch'ŏllima* 81 (June 1965): 112.
Nam Chŏnghyŏn	Literary essay	"Puhwal hanŭn saramdŭl" [The Resurrected], *Chayu munhak* 7, no. 1 (March 1962): 182–184.	"Puhwal hanŭn saramdŭl" [The Resurrected], *Munhak sinmun*, May 11, 1962, 3.
Nam Chŏnghyŏn	Fiction	"Pujujŏn sangsŏ" [Letter to Father], *Sasanggye* 135 (June 1964): 358–375.	"Pujujŏn sangsŏ" [Letter to Father], *Choguk t'ongil*, September 19, 1964, 4
Nam Chŏnghyŏn	Fiction	"Punji" [Land of Excrement], *Hyŏndae munhak* 11, no. 3 (March 1965): 62–81.	"Punji" [Land of Excrement], *Choguk t'ongil*, May 8, 1965, 4.
O Yŏngsu	Fiction	"Anna ŭi yusŏ" [Anna's Will], *Hyŏndae munhak* 9, no. 4 (April 1963): 55–91.	"Anna ŭi yusŏ" [Anna's Will], *Chosŏn nyŏsŏng* 211–213 (May 1965–July 1965): 126–130; 131–134; 126–130.
Pak Kyŏngsu	Fiction	"Sok—Aegukcha" [The Patriot—Continued], *Sasanggye* 138 (September 1964): 348–369.	"Sok—Aegukcha (1–4)" [The Patriot—Continued (1–4)], *Choguk t'ongil*, 16 December 16–December 26, 1964, 4.

North Korean Reprint 2	North Korean Reprint 3	North Korean Reprint 4	North Korean Reprint 5
"Kudu takki sonyŏ ŭi si" [The Poems of a Shoeshine Girl], *Chosŏn nyŏsŏng* 212 (July 1965): n.p.	Reprinted within: Pak Myŏngch'ŏl, "Kudu takki sonyŏ" [Shoeshine Girl], *Sonyŏndan* 189 (July 1965): 36–38.		
"Sigan i omyŏn küttae nŭn amurŏn yaksok to ŏpsi t'ŏjil kŏsida" [When the Time Comes, It Will Explode Without Warning], *Rodong sinmun*, May 30, 1962, 3.			
"Pujujŏn sangsŏ" [Letter to Father], *Munhak sinmun*, September 18, 1964, 3.	"Pyŏrak ŭn tangsin i mandŭsyŏya hamnida" [You Must Create Your Own Thunderbolt], *Rodong sinmun*, September 21, 1964, 3.		

(continued)

TABLE 1.2 *(continued)*

Author	Genre	South Korean Original	North Korean Reprint 1
Pak Yŏngil (Zainichi author)	Fiction	"Kŭm panji" [Gold Ring], *Hyŏndae munhak* 10, no. 1 (January 1964): 210–218.	"Kŭm panji" [Gold Ring], *Chosŏn nyŏsŏng* 210 (April 1965): 104–107.
Pak Yongjin	Poetry	"4-wŏl ŭi punno" [The Rage of April], in Kim Yongho, ed., *Hangjaeng ŭi kwangjang* (Seoul: Sinhŭng ch'ulp'ansa, 1960), 142–144. Originally published in *Taegu ilbo*.	"4-wŏl ŭi punno" [The Rage of April], *Munhak sinmun*, October 4, 1960, 4.
Pak Tujin	Poetry	"Kyŏnggo, T'onggok, Kyŏrŭi" [Warning, Wailing, Determination], *Tonga ilbo*, August 16, 1960, 4.	"Kyŏnggo, T'onggok, Kyŏrŭi" [Warning, Wailing, Determination], *Rodong sinmun*, April 21, 1965, 6.
Pak Tujin	Poetry	"Tto hanbŏn manse rŭl" [Manse Once Again], *Tonga ilbo*, March 2, 1962, 4.	"Tto hanbŏn manse rŭl" [Manse Once Again], *Munhak sinmun*, July 27, 1962, 4.
Pak Tujin	Poetry	"Uridŭl ŭi kippal ŭn naerin kŏt i anida" [Our Flag Has Not Been Lowered], *Sasanggye* 83 (June 1960): 344–347.	"Uridŭl ŭi kippal ŭn naerin kŏt i anida" [Our Flag Has Not Been Lowered], *Rodongja sinmun*, November 3, 1963, 3.
Pak Tujin	Poetry	"Uri nŭn tto tasi noye il su ŏpta" [We Cannot Be Slaves Again], *Sasanggye* 149 (July 1965): 10–15.	"Uri nŭn tto tasi noye il su ŏpta" [We Cannot Be Slaves Again], *Munhak sinmun*, November 16, 1965, 4.
Pak Tujin	Poetry	"I pun'gyŏk ŏttŏk'e ch'amŭri: Haebang 20-chunyŏn e" [How Can this Fury Be Contained? On the Twentieth Anniversary of Liberation], *Chosŏn ilbo*, August 15, 1965, 9.	"I pun'gyŏk ŏttŏk'e ch'amŭri: Haebang 20-chunyŏn e" [How Can this Fury Be Contained? On the Twentieth Anniversary of Liberation], *Rodong sinmun*, August 26, 1965, 3.

North Korean Reprint 2	North Korean Reprint 3	North Korean Reprint 4	North Korean Reprint 5
"Kyŏnggo, T'onggok, Kyŏrŭi" [Warning, Wailing, Determination], *Samch'ŏlli* 9 (April 1965): 65.			
"Uridŭl ŭi kippal ŭn naerin kŏt i anida" [Our Flag Has Not Been Lowered], *Choguk t'ongil*, February 22, 1964, 4.	"Uridŭl ŭi kippal ŭn naerin kŏt i anida" [Our Flag Has Not Been Lowered], *Sae sedae* 123 (April 1965): 44–45.		
"I pun'gyŏk ŏttŏk'e ch'amŭri: Haebang 20-chunyŏn e" [How Can this Fury Be Contained? On the Twentieth Anniversary of Liberation], *Samch'ŏlli* 14 (September 1965): 37.	"I pun'gyŏk ŏttŏk'e ch'amŭri: Haebang 20-chunyŏn e" [How Can this Fury Be Contained? On the Twentieth Anniversary of Liberation], *Munhak sinmun*, October 19, 1965, 4.		

(continued)

TABLE 1.2 *(continued)*

Author	Genre	South Korean Original	North Korean Reprint 1
Ryu Sŭnggyu	Fiction	"Senongdŭl" [Petty Farmers], *Chayu munhak* 6, no. 10 (November 1961): 60–73.	"Senongdŭl (1–3)" [Petty Farmers (13)], *Munhak sinmun*, March 5—March 12, 1965, 4.
Sin Hyŏndŭk	Poetry	"I iyagi rŭl haji ank'o nŭn kyŏndil su ka ŏpkuna" [Without Telling this Story, I Cannot Survive], *Koguryŏ ŭi ai: Sin Hyŏndŭk che-2 tongsijip* [The Child of Koguryŏ: Sin Hyŏndŭk's Second Children's Poetry Collection] (Taegu: Hyŏngsŏl ch'ulp'ansa, 1964). Originally published in *Taegu maeil sinmun*.	"I iyagi rŭl ank'o nŭn kyŏndil su ka ŏpkuna" [Without Telling this Story, I Cannot Survive], *Rodong sinmun*, April 1, 1964, 6.
Sin Tongmun	Poetry	"Aa nae choguk" [O, My Ancestral Land], *Sasanggye* 120 (April 1963): 397–399.	"Aa nae choguk" [O, My Ancestral Land], *Minju ch'ŏngnyŏn*, May 16, 1963, 3.
Sin Tongmun	Poetry	"A! Sinhwa kach'i Tabidegundŭl" [Ah! Masses of Davids as in a Myth], *Sasanggye* 83 (June 1960): 353–357.	"A! Sinhwa kach'i Tabidegundŭl [Ah! Masses of Davids as in a Myth], *Munhak sinmun*, April 16, 1965, 4.
Sin Tongmun	Poetry	Appears within Sin Tongmun, "Kim Satkat ttara (11): Kim Chuyŏl pudu" [Following Kim Satkat (11): Kim Chuyŏl's Pier], *Tonga ilbo*, March 23, 1964, 3.	"Kŭ ch'ongal i mipchi anŭn'ga" [Aren't those Bullets Hateful?], *Rodong sinmun*, June 8, 1964, 4.
Sin Tongmun	Poetry	"Pando Hot'el P'och'wi" [Pando Hotel Porch], *Sedae* 1, no. 2 (July 1963).	"Pando Hot'el P'och'wi" [Pando Hotel Porch], *Munhak sinmun*, September 10, 1965, 3.

North Korean Reprint 2	North Korean Reprint 3	North Korean Reprint 4	North Korean Reprint 5
"I iyagi rŭl ank'o nŭn kyŏndil su ka ŏpkuna" [Without Telling this Story, I Cannot Survive], *Sae sedae* 113 (June 1964): 139.			
"Aa nae choguk" [O, My Ancestral Land], *Choguk t'ongil*, May 18, 1963, 3.	"Aa nae choguk" [O, My Ancestral Land], *Rodongja sinmun*, May 19, 1963, 3.	"Aa nae choguk" [O, My Ancestral Land], *Munhak sinmun*, August 3, 1965, 4.	"Aa nae choguk" [O, My Ancestral Land], *Samch'ŏlli* 16–17 (November–December 1965): 53.

(continued)

TABLE 1.2 *(continued)*

Author	Genre	South Korean Original	North Korean Reprint 1
Sin Yŏngch'ŏl	Poetry	"Mujigae rŭl omgyŏra" [Move the Rainbow], *Kyoyuk p'yŏngnon* 63 (January 1964): 92.	"Mujigae rŭl omgyŏda" [Move the Rainbow], *Adong munhak* 138 (May 1964): 49.
Sŏ Tongwŏn	Poetry	"Kiwŏn e ŭi mukto" [Silent Prayer for Wishes], in Kim Yongho, ed., *Hangjaeng ŭi kwangjang* (Seoul: Sinhŭng ch'ulp'ansa, 1960), 150–152. Originally published in *Chŏnnam ilbo*.	"Kiwŏn e ŭi mukto" [Silent Prayer for Wishes], *Ch'ŏngnyŏn munhak* 60 (April 1961): 48.
Unknown Author	Poetry	Source listed as *Yŏngnam ilbo*, May 13, 1961. Full reference unavailable.	"T'ongil ŭi kiun ŭn t'ŭinŭn'ga" [Is the Force of Unification Opening?], *Munhak sinmun*, March 16, 1965, 4.
Unknown Author	Poetry	Original source unclear.	"Mullŏgara, iri tte yŏ!" [Get Out, You Pack of Wolves!], *Sae sedae* 108 (January 1964): 144.
Unknown Author	Poetry	Source listed as *Kukche sinbo*, April 10, 1963. Full reference unavailable.	"Chŏlmŭn 4-wŏl" [Young April], *Sae sedae* 123 (April 1965): 44–45.
Unknown Author	Poetry	Original source unclear.	"Choguk ŭro uri hana ka toeja" [Let's Unite as One Ancestral Land], *Rodong sinmun*, May 14, 1966, 3.
Yi Hanjik	Poetry	"4-wŏl ŭi ki nŭn" [The Flag of April], *Saebyŏk* 7, no. 8 (August 1960): 10–11.	"4-wŏl ŭi ki nŭn" [The Flag of April], *Rodong sinmun*, June 8, 1964, 4.
Yi Insŏk	Poetry	"Tari" [Bridge], *Chayu munhak* 6, no. 9 (September 1961): 171.	"Tari" [Bridge], *Munhak sinmun*, July 27, 1962, 4.

North Korean Reprint 2	North Korean Reprint 3	North Korean Reprint 4	North Korean Reprint 5
"Tari" [Bridge], *Choguk t'ongil*, January 22, 1964, 4.	"Tari" [Bridge], *Sae sedae* 110 (March 1964): 64–65.		

(*continued*)

TABLE 1.2 *(continued)*

Author	Genre	South Korean Original	North Korean Reprint 1
Yi Insŏk	Poetry	"In'gan ŭn sara issŭl kwŏlli ga itta" [A Human Has the Right to Live], *Sasanggye* 118 (March 1963): 370–371.	"In'gan ŭn sara issŭl kwŏlli ga itta" [A Human Has the Right to Live], *Choguk t'ongil,* April 27, 1963, 3.
Yi Kŭnsam	Drama	"Kŏrukhan chigŏp" [Respectable Profession], *Hyŏndae munhak* 8, no. 6 (June 1962): 91–105.	"Kŏrukhan chigŏp (1–4)" [Respectable Profession (1–4)], *Munhak sinmun,* July 31–August 14, 1962, 4.
Yi Pongun	Poetry	"Ŏmŏni" [Mother], *Tonga ilbo,* April 30, 1960, 4.	"Ŏmŏni" [Mother], *Munhak sinmun,* October 4, 1960, 4.
Yi Wŏnsu	Poetry	"Au ŭi norae" [Song of a Younger Sister], *Tonga ilbo,* May 1, 1960, 4.	"Tongsaeng ŭi norae" [Song of a Younger Brother], *Munhak sinmun,* March 17, 1961, 4.**
Yi Yunhwa	Poetry	"Parik'eit'ŭ" [Barricade], in Yi Sangno, ed., *P'i ŏrin sawŏl ŭi chŭngŏn* [Testimony of a Bloody April] (Seoul: Yŏnhaksa, 1960), 30.	"Parik'et'ŭ" [Barricade], *Rodong sinmun,* June 8, 1964, 4.
Yu Ch'ihwan	Poetry	"Kŭraesŏ nŏ nŭn si rŭl ssŭnda?!" [And So You Write Poetry?!], *Sasanggye* 128 (December 1963): 222–223.	"Kŭraesŏ nŏ nŭn si rŭl ssŭnda?!" [And So You Write Poetry?!], *Rodong sinmun,* March 8, 1964, 4.
Yun Kwŏnt'ae	Poetry	"Chinhon'ga" [Requiem], *Han'guk ilbo,* April 17, 1960, 1.	"Chinhon'ga" [Requiem], *Sae sedae* 122 (March 1965): 58.

** This republication identified in Yi Sunuk, "Nambuk munhak e nat'anan Masan ŭigŏ ŭi silchŭngjŏk yŏn'gu" [An Empirical Study of the Masan Uprising as Depicted in North and South Korean Literature], *Yŏngju ŏmun* 12 (2006): 289.

Note: This is a partial list whose entries are not meant to be exhaustive.

North Korean Reprint 2	North Korean Reprint 3	North Korean Reprint 4	North Korean Reprint 5
"In'gan ŭn sara issŭl kwŏlli ga itta" [A Human Has the Right to Live], *Munhak sinmun*, December 11, 1964, 4.			
	"Ŏmŏni" [Mother], *Ch'ŏngnyŏn munhak* 60 (April 1961): 47.		
	"Tongsaeng ŭi norae" [Song of a Younger Brother], *Adong munhak* 101 (April 1961): 48.		
	"Parik'et'ŭ" [Barricade], *Sae sedae* 114 (July 1964): 88.		
		"Kŭraesŏ nŏ nŭn si rŭl ssŭnda?!" [And So You Write Poetry?!], *Choguk t'ongil*, February 22, 1964, 4.	

2

MOTHER(S) OF THE SOUTH

Figures of Revolution and Fracture Between the
1960s–1970s Koreas and Japan

In April 1963, the poet Chŏn Tongu published a poem titled "Go Forward Carrying that Rage!" ("Kŭ punno rŭl anko naa kasira") in North Korea's *Munhak sinmun* newspaper. Addressed, as its subtitle stated, "to a southern Korean mother," the poem began with an expression of sympathy:

> That day, like any other, you
> Helped your daughter with her bag, and
> Followed her out the door, with that one phrase
> That you were always in the habit of repeating:
> Be careful of the cars as you walk.
>
> . . .
>
> Your daughter, on that day, on that April night of towering
>   shouts,
> Never returned home.
> When you ran out, shouting your daughter's name,
> Those desolate night streets, without lights, only
> Greeted you with dizzying gunshots.
>
> . . .

You didn't cry.
In front of the book bag stained with blood!
But when you unfolded the last testament with your two hands,
Silent tears, dropping on the paper,
Fell and fell.[1]

With this invocation of a "last testament" (*yusŏ*) left by a young female protester for her mother, Chŏn's poem connected its vision to a specific text that had appeared in the North Korean press three years earlier: the poignant final note that Chin Yŏngsuk, a middle school student in Seoul, had left for her mother before taking part in the April Revolution of 1960, where she was martyred. By addressing itself to this text, which had been published in the South's *Chosŏn ilbo* newspaper in May 1960 before being republished in the North in October of that same year,[2] the poem drew upon two of the cross-border writing practices discussed in chapter 1. First, it drew upon the practice of responding in literary form to current events-related texts from the South that had first been developed by the Korean leftist community in Japan and then imported to North Korea. Second, by subsequently turning from sympathy to exhortation, calling upon Chin's mother in the South to "Put on your daughter's school bag and go out! Go out with the volcano-like rage of your ancestral land!"[3] the poem also drew upon North Korean strategies of literary adaptation, which took up the trope of the volcano from South Korean poetry's response to the April Revolution and reshaped it in revolutionary ways.

Furthermore, Chŏn's poem also presaged some of the central developments of the mid- to late 1960s that will be discussed in detail in this chapter. In particular, by foregrounding the figure of the mother and calling upon her to "shout what's left / of that which your daughter shouted until she could no more" and "seek the freedom / called for by your daughter, whose hair had not yet grown long,"[4] Chŏn's poem offered an initial vision of a figure who would reverberate not only through North Korean literature and culture but also through the literature and culture of the Korean leftist population in Japan. As we will see, this was a figure who first emerged in North Korean rewritings of South Korean texts, then filtered into other forms of North Korean literature and culture, and finally traveled in the direction opposite to the one discussed in chapter 1: that is, toward Japan, Chongryon literature and culture, and even beyond.

This chapter tells the story of this complex set of encounters, transits, and transformations. Focusing on Kim Myŏngsu's 1965 play, *Mother of the South* (*Namnyŏk ŭi ŏmŏni*), the first section of this chapter charts the emergence of a particular vision of the militant mother as it emerged in a North Korean cultural domain that was in ongoing dialogue with contemporary writing in the South. This chapter then shows how this imaginary of the militant mother who takes up her son's unfinished revolutionary tasks migrated: first, from representations of the South to representations of the North's own colonial-era revolutionary history; and second, across the East Sea as this vision of the revolutionary mother was taken up and adapted to fit the Chongryon context in the writer Hŏ Namgi's script for the 1968 film *We Have An Ancestral Land* (*Uri ege nŭn choguk i itta*). Finally, this chapter shows how the particular contours of the Chongryon version of the militant mother—a militant mother who defers repatriation to the North as a sign of her commitment—eventually spawned a range of critical visions by writers who had left the Chongryon organization and sought out new connections with South Korean literature. Overall, this chapter demonstrates how the emergence and transformation of the figure of the militant mother allows us to trace literary connections from South Korea to North Korea to the Korean diaspora in Japan and back.

MOTHER OF KOREA, MOTHER OF THE SOUTH

In mid-1967, the actress Ra Sŭngim submitted a "directing proposal" (*yŏnch'ul an*) for the five-act play *Mother of the South* to the North Korean magazine *Chosŏn yesul*.[5] First performed two years earlier, Kim Myŏngsu's *Mother of the South* was, once again, a work focused on the April Revolution in the South. Yet it was also written with a keen awareness of subsequent events across the border in the ROK. After spending its first half focused on the April 1960 activism and eventual martyrdom of a South Korean university student named Inho, the play's latter acts turned to post-1960 developments: in particular, to the story of Inho's mother, a formerly depoliticized woman named Sunnyŏ, taking up her son's banner of struggle and stepping out onto the front lines of anti-government struggle during the second round of large-scale, student-led protests that emerged in 1964 and 1965 in opposition to the Park Chung Hee regime's pursuit of diplomatic ties with Japan.

In Ra's interpretation, Sunnyŏ was a "true mother of Korea."[6] She was a figure who, "like all Korean mothers," Ra said, possessed "a firm and resolute spirit, a high humanity, and a noble character and way of life."[7] This made her firm and determined, but it also made her eminently relatable; it made her an everywoman whose movements and presence were "soft and familiar."[8] Where did this sense of familiarity originate? As Eunsung Cho, Immanuel Kim, and Suzy Kim have all noted, the figure of the mother has played a pivotal role in the social, cultural, and political life of the DPRK since its inception. One central reason for this was the heritage of the colonial era. As Suzy Kim has argued following Partha Chatterjee, in colonial contexts, "domestic and feminine spaces were deemed outside of the colonial purview, offering safe havens with greater potential for subversion"; as such, "anticolonial nationalisms placed special weight on the 'inner' realm" as the "sovereign territory that gave birth to the nation as an imagined community."[9] Similarly, in North Korea, the experience of the colonial era, which "enabled the inscription of metaphors of the family in reference to the nation-state," allowed for the "redeployment of motherhood as the vehicle that encompassed both traditional gender roles and the new revolutionary subject. Mothers became the ideal selfless public servant, a model for all members of the nation to follow in the performance of their social duty as citizens of a new country."[10]

The colonial heritage thus played a central role in giving birth to the figure of the revolutionary mother in postcolonial North Korea. And indeed, as Immanuel Kim has discussed in detail, the figures of two mothers in particular—Kang Pansŏk, Kim Il Sung's mother, and Kim Chŏngsuk, Kim Il Sung's wife—would soon become canonized as "metonym[s] that describe absolute loyalty from individuals,"[11] paragons of motherhood at once "elevated to a political status beyond the reach of any mortal" and meant to serve as models "that all North Koreans are supposed to emulate."[12] Yet what has not received sufficient attention is the way in which this colonial heritage also facilitated a particular way of representing South Korea in postcolonial North Korean culture. If spaces of family and domesticity had emerged during the colonial era as spaces of national legitimacy in opposition to those of imperial domination and collaboration outside the home, then they were also ideally positioned to be identified as spaces of national legitimacy within the context of South Korea, which was understood in North Korea as an American colony. And indeed, in North Korea, this is precisely what happened; figures of national legitimacy in the South were frequently located within the space of the home rather than the space of comprador state and society, and in particular, North Korean publications focused on figures of South Korean mothers as targets for solidarity.

This, then, was the reason that the figure of Sunnyŏ seemed so familiar to Ra. At the time, South Korean mothers had already emerged as focal points for North Korean calls for solidarity, and in fact, in articulating its vision of Sunnyŏ, Kim's play drew upon an array of specific textual precedents that had passed through the pages of North Korean publications: not only the South Korean novelist An Tongnim's short story "Hope" ("Hŭimang"), which had recently been republished in the North, but also a range of reports, again originating in the South and picked up in the North,[13] about the activities of Yi Kyedan, the mother of one of the South Korean martyrs of 1960 who had subsequently banded together with student demonstrators.

In addition to focusing on the revolution itself, South Korean literature in the wake of April 1960 also came to place emphasis on the effect of martyred students' sacrifices on their surviving family members. In particular, as Han Sunmi has discussed,[14] the image of the widowed mother now left alone after the death of her child in the April Revolution protests became a recurring trope, and it was first popularized in works by students themselves: for example, in Yi Pongun's "Mother" ("Ŏmŏni"),[15] likewise republished in the North,[16] which, like Chin Yŏngsuk's parting message, urged its speaker's mother to stand proud of her child's sacrifice rather than mourn it.

This figure also became a staple of fictional representations by professional writers. For example, An's "Hope" tells the story of an April 1960 student's internal conflict in relation to the effects of his actions on his mother. The two protagonists of the story, Yŏngsŏp and Hun, are students involved in the planning of demonstrations against the Rhee regime. Hun lives alone, having come South alone during the Korean War, but Yŏngsŏp lives together with his mother, a widow whose world centers around him.

Although he is dedicated to the cause, Yŏngsŏp thus finds himself questioning his ability to follow through in joining the demonstrations—a hesitation he eventually overcomes.

Like "Mother," An's "Hope" was subsequently republished in the North and discussed as evidence of "progressive literature" in the South. More importantly, it also sparked creative action, inspiring North Korean writers to take up their pens toward the goal of literary coproduction. This is most evident in Kim Myŏngsu's *Mother of the South*.[17] Kim's play begins with the immediate post-Liberation period and the process of waiting for Sunnyŏ's husband to return home from Japan. Although initially hopeful, Sunnyŏ and her son, Inho, soon learn from a neighbor that her husband died in a mine accident just before Liberation. The play then jumps to the year 1960. Now a university student, Inho has been involved in the planning of protests against the Rhee regime, and this has attracted scrutiny from the university administration, from sinister ROK officials, and from their American backers, who offer scholarships to the families of poor students in exchange for information.

Dedicated to her son's education, Sunnyŏ is initially attracted to the offer, and this produces an internal conflict for Inho. He does not consider providing information, but he does think twice about what effect his participation in the April 1960 demonstrations will have on his mother. "What would you do," Inho asks his close friend, Yŏngman, "if your mother were by your side, relying solely upon you?"[18] Yŏngman's response is pointed and direct. "You idiot!" he exclaims, saying, "It's not just you. There are countless mothers who have sons. Every night, I mean, they lie awake anxiously. But who is the one keeping those mothers awake? You or me? No. It is the old ghost [Syngman Rhee] lurking at Kyŏngmudae who made them that way." Yŏngman's plea, in other words, is for Inho to join him in ending this state of affairs. After all, as he puts it, "we cannot live like our mothers, can we?"[19]

In staging Inho's hesitation and Yŏngman's response in this way, *Mother* draws directly upon An Tongnim's "Hope." As noted above, "Hope" tells the story of Hun and his friend Yŏngsŏp, whose concern for his mother leads him to question whether he can take part in the upcoming demonstrations he has been helping to plan. Speaking with Hun after one of the group's secret meetings, he uses the exact same words as Inho, asking, "What would you do if your mother were by your side, relying solely upon you?"[20] Yŏngsŏp, in other words, is torn between filial duty to a mother for whom his life and future are everything, and a duty to nation, justice, and friendship—values that, to Hun, seem clearly paramount. And the response he receives, therefore, again echoes the one that Yŏngman provides in *Mother of the South*: "You are not the only one who is a son. Even tonight, there must be a mother lying awake anxiously, thinking of her son. But no son wants to live like his mother, does he?"[21] Like Inho, therefore, Yŏngsŏp ultimately chooses not to hold back from taking part in the protests despite his worries and concerns. Surprising Hun by showing up on the front lines, he ends up sacrificing his life to the cause of the April Revolution, staining the ROK flag that he carries with him red with his blood.

Implicit in the conclusion to An's story is the assumption that Yŏngsŏp was correct in his understanding of his mother. "My mother," he says to Hun at one point, "does not love humanity.... She loves her son, only her son"[22] In Kim's play, however, Sunnyŏ is present rather than absent, and the voicing of Inho's posthumous message spurs a dramatic transformation in her character. After Inho's death, Sunnyŏ spends the next three years taking care of his comrades as her new "sons and daughters." Yet she also goes beyond this, eventually pushing back against the bounds that the youths place upon her. As conflicts over the ROK-Japan normalization treaty heat up and the figures responsible for her son's death reappear, Sunnyŏ returns to her son's notebook to articulate a belated reply: one that transforms her into an active subject whose origins, once again, were located in South Korean texts.

In April 1965, North Korea's *Rodong sinmun* newspaper published a half-page spread devoted to Yi Kyedan, who it described as "the mother of [Yi] Kŭnhyŏng, who, on the day that all of southern Korea was engulfed in the flames of resistance, was sacrificed while fighting heroically at the front lines of the struggle for a new politics, a new system, and a new way of life."[23] Moreover, noting that amid the student protests against the ROK-Japan normalization "[Yi] had been arrested ... while taking the place of her sacrificed son in the struggle against corruption and evil," it went on to present an ensemble of excerpts of South Korean articles about her, accompanied by photos.[24]

This was not the first time that the newspaper had reported on Yi. Just two days earlier, it had carried a four-column article by Ri Sŏngbok that demanded her release.[25] Yi, the article noted, had quite famously declared, at the time of her son's death in 1960, "Why would I cry? My son died so gloriously.... Since my son, Kŭnhyŏng, died so gloriously, this mother will not cry."[26] Considering the death of her son, who had died fighting for justice, an "honor," she had more recently taken action to fill the space he had left behind. Fasting together with hunger striking students, she had pledged "to fulfill [her] son's portion of the fight,"[27] and she had joined them in the streets, taking up a position on the front lines. Yi, the article thus demanded, "must be released,"[28] and a subsequent version of the same piece published the following month articulated a similar position.[29]

Recirculated in the North Korean press, Yi's words and actions became tools for appropriation. In April 1960, the South Korean newspaper *Han'guk ilbo* had published a note that Yi had written to her son immediately following his death. Republished in the North's *Rodong sinmun* in 1965, the note read, in part, as follows:

> "The twenty-four years I spent devoting myself to my son were not spent in vain."
>
> My virtuous child! I'm telling you now that you are departing forever. At the time of the demonstrations, I spent three or four days wandering around looking for you. Then I finally found you, but you could not reply!...
>
> I wanted to depart forever with you, but what could I do as an unfilial youngest child with sick parents? Your mother has no way of expelling the grudge buried in her heart. But since you have a strong spirit, I will rid you of your grudge so that you can rest in peace. Come to me in my dreams and reveal the grudge in your heart.[30]

Drawing upon this note, Kim's play refashions it in the words that Sunnyŏ offers to her son after returning to his notebook:

> My virtuous child! With you departing first for the benefit of the nation, the thirty years I spent devoting myself to you alone as my only family in the world were not spent in vain. I pledged not to cry in front of the spirit of one who died so gloriously, but today I teared up once again, so forgive me. But, Inho! You must know that these tears are not tears but

the thirty million flames buried in your mother's heart that cannot be extinguished. With my whole body now made of flames, I will seek vengeance on your enemies. Come to me in my dreams and reveal the grudge in your heart.[31]

Sunnyŏ here pivots from suppressing her emotions and standing on the sidelines of the struggle to expressing them and calling for justice, and she does so via words borrowed directly from Yi Kyedan.

Moreover, Sunnyŏ also mirrors her actions. Ignoring the pleas of the students to stay out of harm's way, Sunnyŏ realizes that she can no longer be content with her existing role of providing food and support to them. Instead, she replaces her buckets of food with buckets of rocks, marching arm in arm with the students. She also dons the cotton handkerchief that her husband had worn during his labor activism and her son had worn in April 1960, telling the students that it is "her turn" to take up the banner of struggle.[32] In this way, Kim's play rewrites "Hope" in light of Yi Kyedan's emergence as an alternative model of motherhood. Crossing the thirty-eighth parallel divide, it brings together disparate elements of South Korean texts, creating a revolutionary coproduction: a coproduction that, while clearly unidirectional in its power relations, nevertheless attempts to speak together with South Korean literature in a creative and transformative way.

MOTHER OF THE SOUTH, MOTHER OF KOREA

In fact, there was another dimension to the sense of familiarity that Ra located in Sunnyŏ. As noted above, Kim rewrote An's "Hope" by transforming its mother figure: in particular, by refashioning her in the image of Yi Kyedan. The outcome of this refashioning, however, was not a wholly new character who had not been seen in North Korean literature before. Of course, there is a long history of imaginations of the mother figure in revolutionary literature stretching from Maxim Gorky to Ding Ling and beyond,[33] and wartime North Korean literature had included a number of narratives of militant mothers.[34] Yet the 1960s witnessed a particularly pointed emphasis on such figures, forming the essential context and backdrop for *Mother of the South*'s vision.

Amid the events of the April Revolution, audiences in North Korea were enjoying a musical adaptation of *Mother of Korea* (*Chosŏn ŭi ŏmŏni*), a drama by the playwright Pak Hyŏk.³⁵ First performed in 1959 and then published in text form the following year, *Mother of Korea* takes place near the Manchurian border in the 1930s and follows its widowed protagonist, Han, a strong and resolute character who prioritizes revolution over personal concerns in an act of what Immanuel Kim has called, in relation to another work, "the sublation of the nuclear family."³⁶ In words that echo those later associated with Kim Il Sung's own mother, Kang Pansŏk, Han here castigates her son for the tears he sheds, saying, "Don't worry about home. Just focus on one thing [i.e., revolution],"³⁷ and she also rejects the violent extortion of the Japanese authorities. When the authorities take Han's youngest son hostage, threatening to kill him if she does not follow their orders to speak out publicly against the partisans, she resists. This is a pivotal moment that she eventually turns toward her advantage; pretending to follow the authorities' demands, she ends up offering a full-throated call to support the partisans. Yet it is also a pivotal moment in which the play makes a clear and direct reference to another work: the canonical *Sea of Blood* (*P'ibada/Hyŏrhae*).

In 1953, as Suzy Kim has noted, Kim Il Sung sent an investigative team to Manchuria to recover the historical remnants of the colonial-era partisan struggle.³⁸ *Sea of Blood* was one of the remnants identified during this trip, and it was introduced to the North Korean public, as Chŏng Chonghyŏn has discussed in detail, in multiple variants by the writers Song Yŏng and An Hamgwang.³⁹ Although these variants' depictions of the work's main character—a mother eventually dubbed Sunnyŏ—ranged from sacrificial martyr to militant fighter, the bare bones of their narratives remained constant.⁴⁰ Set in 1930s Manchuria, the story comes to its narrative climax when Sunnyŏ resists the Japanese authorities' attempts to extort information about the partisans from her by taking her youngest son hostage. *Sea of Blood*'s Sunnyŏ thus provided the model for Pak's protagonist in *Mother of Korea*, and her influence in fact spread widely, especially after the former partisan Kim Myŏnghwa—another model of revolutionary motherhood—and An Hamgwang identified *Sea of Blood* as the work of Kim Il Sung himself.⁴¹

As such, Kim Myŏngsu's Sunnyŏ was not an aberration transplanted from the South Korean literary world but rather a point of interconnection linking North and South Korean textual domains. She was also an agent of change binding them together in transformational ways. In 1966, the year after *Mother of the South* was first put on stage, the Hyesan Theater Troupe performed a new seven-scene play by Pak Hyŏk, the author of *Mother of Korea*.[42] Titled *North Star* (*Pukkŭksŏng*), the play was said, once again, to portray the "lofty internal world of a mother,"[43] and it focused, like previous narratives, on a widow from the 1930s who sends her children, one after the other, to join the partisans, taking pride in the prospect of sacrificing their lives for the nation.[44] Nevertheless, it did not end with this gesture alone. In the play's final scene, Hwang, the mother-protagonist, having decided to end her life out of grief over her son's death, finds out that her daughter and daughter-in-law, also partisans, have died in battle and cannot avenge her son's murder. She thus realizes that she, herself, must rise up, and when a messenger from Kim Il Sung appears, summoning her, she responds in turn, pledging, as the actress who played the part of Hwang put it, to "inherit the task that her ... children could not complete," to "take up the will of the General and fight in her children's place."[45]

Hwang here takes up the task of resistance from her fallen children, joining the partisans in their stead. As such, she goes beyond the model found in plays like *Mother of Korea*, mirroring, instead, that of Sunnyŏ in *Mother of the South*, who also replaces her child on the front lines. Moreover, similar transformations in representations of the 1930s revolutionary past also emerged at this time in fiction. This can be seen, for example, in Kim Subŏm's short story "Embrace" ("P'oong"),[46] based upon the life of another "mother of Korea," Chang Kilbu, the widowed mother of the colonial-era revolutionary Ma Tonghŭi, here referred to as Wangjun, Ma's childhood nickname.[47] In the story, Chang sees the Japanese arrest her son as he tries to infiltrate the village, but when she visits him in prison, she finds that he carries a misguided sense of guilt; he sees himself as an "unfilial child" who has caused her unnecessary suffering.[48] Like the mothers above, however, Chang dismisses this self-critique, seeing his dedication to the nation as a value superseding individual notions of filiality.

Furthermore, she sees this dedication as something that must be carried forward after his death, and at this point, the narrative goes far beyond accounts of Chang's life provided in early nonfiction accounts. "Couldn't

I do the work that he had done, crossing the river, in his place?," she here asks, at which point she "feels a new strength throughout her body."[49] Chang's newfound activism, taken up in place of her son, thus mirrors Sunnyŏ's declaration that it is finally "her turn" to take up the cloth handkerchief of struggle. Once again, this suggests that the cross-border encounters staged in *Mother of the South* did not remain fixed within representations of the South but rather fed back into visions of the North's own past in transformative ways.

It also suggests that interactions with South Korean texts helped shape the direction of a much broader set of canonical figures in North Korean literature. As noted above, when *Sea of Blood* was introduced to the North in 1956, its story existed in multiple variants, which portrayed the figure of the mother in significantly different ways ranging from sacrificial to militant. Before long, however, descriptions of Sunnyŏ as a martial figure who took up arms against the Japanese faded away. Instead, discussions of the play came to describe her engagement in the struggle as ending either with her resistance to divulging information,[50] or with her subsequent seeking out of the partisans in order to be reunited with her eldest son.[51] This soon changed. In 1967 and 1968, a militant vision of the mother-protagonist reappeared, with the work's conclusion now summarized as "the mother and daughter join the partisans to fight"[52] and "the mother and Kapsun [the daughter] join the partisans and fight the Japanese Empire."[53]

Of course, this was not exactly the version of Sunnyŏ canonized in the film of 1969–1970 and subsequent operatic (1971) and novelistic adaptations (1973); in the canonized version, she engages in combat with the Japanese, avenging her son's murder, but does not join the partisans herself. Nevertheless, the canonized version of her clearly bears the imprint of this swing toward the militant variant of Sunnyŏ's character—a swing that occurred in the immediate aftermath of the emergence of a partisan mother in works like *North Star* and "Embrace" and had far-reaching implications for North Korean literature and culture more broadly.

In fact, these years also witnessed the emergence of a number of other canonical figures of revolutionary motherhood in North Korea. It was, for example, the precise time at which the influential drama (1966) and film (1967) *The Rose of Sharon Handkerchief* (*Mugunghwa kkot sugŏn*) appeared and gained popularity. And even more importantly, it was also the precise time at which Kim Il Sung's own mother—alongside fictional adaptations of her—was first canonized across all forms of North Korean media. Before 1967, Kim's mother, Kang Pansŏk, had little if any presence in North Korean culture. Between 1967 and 1968, however, she emerged dramatically as a central figure for representation and emulation: a presence that she retained across subsequent decades. The emergence of the revolutionary mother as a central trope of North Korean culture thus bound representations drawn directly from an engagement with South Korean texts to a much broader cultural milieu. And this milieu was one whose bounds extended beyond the bounds of the Korean peninsula. It was one that extended to the Chongryon community in Japan, where it took on new contours and nuances in dialogue with the literature of "repatriation" (*kwiguk*).

REPATRIATION, RECALIBRATION

As we saw in chapter 1, from at least the mid-1950s on, Chongryon members imagined their relation to the South as radicalizing. More often, though, their visions focused on those already in Japan—in particular, those associated with Mindan, the ROK-affiliated Korean diasporic organization, and those living out of touch with the Korean community altogether. As a result, literary texts from this era recurred to visions of Chongryon members who brought other diasporic compatriots into the fold. Rim Kyŏngsang's 1957 short story "Mr. Song" ("Song sŏbang"),[54] for example, focuses on a manual laborer named Song and his encounter one evening with his son's teacher, who provides him with a new perspective on the possibilities open to the next generation. Song and his family live on the margins of the Chongryon organization. They are close enough to it to send their children, Chŏngnam and Chŏngsun, to a Chongryon-affiliated Korean school. Yet they are not active in the organization, and Song's concern for Chŏngnam's future goes little beyond hoping that he will be able to find a way to get by on the margins of Japanese society. For someone fated to make his way through life "bent over in the labor market," as Song puts it, "learning to write his name is enough."[55]

Teacher Kim, in contrast, sees the possibility of a much brighter future for Song's son, Chŏngnam. Well-liked by his peers, Chŏngnam has been elected class president at school. Teacher Kim, too, praises Chŏngnam for his abilities, and when he encounters Song one night at a local bar, he attempts to impress upon him the importance of providing his son with additional support and guidance at home: "Chŏngnam is a kind child. He is a kind child who will become a kind, able hand [*ilkkun*] for Korea. Therefore, our ancestral land cannot let that type of talent rot and come to nothing. You, too, should collaborate [to develop it]."[56] At first, Song sees the teacher's request as ridiculous. Behind on payments to the school and just barely able to put food on the table, Song sees little hope in pushing Chŏngnam to pursue his education more seriously. Additionally, largely uneducated himself, Song laughs at the prospect of being able to provide such support; what could he possibly offer, he asks, that would benefit his children's futures?

In response, however, Teacher Kim emphasizes the difference between Japan, where it is a struggle to survive, and "our country," where "no one is unemployed" and "everyone is able to develop their power and ability to the fullest."[57] He also tells Song about the DPRK's recent bestowal of financial support for education in Japan. Chŏngnam, he says, could even continue on to university, and all that he needs at home, he emphasizes, is simple encouragement. Song is affected by Teacher Kim's response, and he begins to see new hope for the future—in particular, via education. He thus offers the money that he has earned that night at the Pachinko parlor to Teacher Kim for his missed school payments—something which, of course, Teacher Kim says is now unnecessary thanks to DPRK financial support—and he returns home with a new dedication to supporting his children in seeking out a better future in concert with Chongryon and the DPRK. Indeed, once home, he departs from his usual routine of getting directly into bed and instead checks in on his son, pledging to join him at the school for the upcoming celebration of the DPRK's seventh anniversary.

Song here comes to understand, as Teacher Kim puts it in the 1958 republication of the story,[58] that Chŏngnam is not only his child but also the "child of the state,"[59] and this transforms his vision of the future from despair to hope, from an insular emphasis on self-preservation to a new openness toward collective engagement. Similar developments were presented in a variety of other texts from these years. "Comrade and Friend"

("Tongmu wa ch'in'gu"), a 1958 narrative essay by the novelist Yun Kwangyŏng, thus follows the development of the narrator's relationship with an old friend who has joined the Mindan organization.[60] Acquaintances from the late colonial period whose paths had subsequently grown apart, the narrative outlines the challenges presented by the two old friends' recent reencounter. Whereas the narrator is a teacher at a Chongryon school, his friend owns a bathhouse in a well-developed Japanese business district. This difference in current circumstances does not prevent the two from regularly sharing a drink and spending time together once they come back into contact, but politics soon rear their head; one night, when the narrator refers to his friend as "comrade," the friend responds by asking him if he is a "red" (*ppalkaengi*) and then cursing them and their ways.[61]

These comments produce a fracture between the two, and gradually they begin to meet less often. Yet the narrator does not abandon his friend, and the situation soon takes a turn once again. One lunar new year, the friend invites the narrator over, and they discuss their longing for Korea. Considering the friend's membership in Mindan and his comfortable economic standing, the narrator then muses that his friend must be able to visit his hometown in the South if he wishes—something that he, as a Chongryon member, cannot do. The friend's response, however, is unexpected; it is a critique of Mindan and its unkept promises, a critique of their constant request for money while failing to send their members to the South as they promised. The friend's faith in Mindan has come undone, and the narrator thus emphasizes that it is only by seeking to reunite the nation under the DPRK that true hope of returning home can be realized. The friend does not respond to this last statement, but his silence provides the narrator with hope: that is, hope that he will soon be brought into the fold of cooperative action with Chongryon; hope that he will soon become someone who the narrator could refer to proudly as both a "friend and comrade."[62]

Such visions recurred throughout subsequent years across multiple forms of writing and imagination. They also took on additional contours with the advent of the project of "repatriation" (*kwiguk*) from Japan to the North, which brought 93,340 migrants—86,603 ethnic Koreans, 6,731 Japanese spouses or dependents, and six Chinese spouses or dependents—to the DPRK between 1959 and 1984.[63] With this development, the Chongryon imagination of co-option took on a geographic component: it became an act of transformative remaking that culminated in migration to the North. This was the case, for example, in Pak Wŏnjun's story "Hwansong" (Send Off/Return), published in the *Chosŏn sinbo* newspaper between March and May of 1961.[64] Like "Comrade and Friend," "Hwansong" also looks back, in part, to an encounter in the late colonial period. In the core of the text, the story's two main characters meet in a Japanese prison, where one, a student who serves as the narrator, is being held for unnamed crimes assumed to be ideological, and another, a peddler named Sŏnggyu, is being held for the attempted murder of the Japanese leader of the local neighborhood watch (*kyŏngbangdan*) who raped his wife while he was forcibly mobilized for the war effort. The two characters then meet again on two occasions: once in 1946, after Sŏnggyu has returned from the South Pacific, where he escaped from his servitude in the Japanese military; and again in the text's present, when Sŏnggyu, about to board a repatriation ship to North Korea along with the son he raised alone after his wife's death, encounters the narrator, who is there to bid him farewell.

Like the texts mentioned above, "Hwansong" charts the transformation of one character—in this case Sŏnggyu—from a nonideological compatriot to a supporter of the DPRK and a believer in the revolutionary cause. Moreover, it does so, once again, while noting the guiding influence that a more ideologically attuned and organizationally connected acquaintance—in this case the narrator, alongside a range of other characters who appear at various points in the story—provides to him. It is through such influence that Sŏnggyu comes to consciousness with new pride and dedication. Yet the endpoint of this trajectory is not, as in the stories above, simple entry into the revolutionary community but rather—and more pointedly— embarkation for North Korea, a practice described as one of "self-liberation" (*chagi haebang*),[65] the culmination and completion of the decades-long cycle of colonization and decolonization chronicled in the story.

Repatriation thus reshaped the existing literature of co-option. It also transformed works that dealt with the despair of the resident Korean situation, as Song Hyewŏn has noted.[66] This can be seen in the novelist Kim Min's 1960 adaptation of his 1956 short story "The Sky that Does Not Clear" ("Kaeji annŭn hanŭl") as "The Eye-Opening Doll" ("Nun ttŭnŭn inhyŏng").[67] Originally published in the December 1956 issue of *Chosŏn munye*, Kim's story takes place during the Korean War and centers around a middle-aged man, Pak Yŏnghwan, who has recently snuck into Japan from South Korea. Although he is now a day laborer, Yŏnghwan had been a teacher in the South, and the story narrates his chance encounter inside a bookstore with a young girl, Yŏngja, whom he had previously taught back home. Unlike Yŏnghwan, who has come to Japan as a stowaway in order to escape persecution by the South Korean government, Yŏngja has come with her father, a South Korean official whose life in Japan is one of comfort and wealth. Indeed, despite being instructed by Syngman Rhee to return to the South, Yŏngja's father has expressed his desire to stay in Japan, where he is working with the US Eighth Army, and Yŏngja echoes her father's sentiments. "I don't want to go [back] either," she tells Yŏnghwan, as "there is nothing that you can't find in Japan."[68] And indeed, she is enjoying her wartime life abroad, where she attends an English-language American school.

The path that Yŏngja's family has followed to Japan thus stands in contrast to Yŏnghwan's, and his encounter seems to offer him a new perspective on the question that has been nagging at him—namely, whether his migration to Japan had been a cowardly form of "flight" or "desertion" (*top'i*):

> Faced with this, Pak Yŏnghwan reflected again upon himself.
> > This is not desertion. I am not a deserter. Here, too, there are those to fight right before my eyes . . .
> Crying out like this, he walked as the streaks of rain fell on him. From somewhere, he felt strength flare up and return to him.[69]

The figure of Yŏnghwan, a recent transplant from the South, is here shown to be one who holds radical potential: one who comes to grasp the mission before him and the power that he possesses to pursue it. And yet, right after this, the text pulls back and ends on a significantly more docile and despairing note as Yŏnghwan recalls his inability to put any of his discontent into words or action:

> "An American school?" he said to himself. I guess they'd like to become American [lit. change their blood], huh? How absurd. . . . I can never become like them.

He kept walking while muttering this.
But [the image of] himself, holding Yŏngja's hand and unable to say anything, gave his chest a pent-up feeling.
The moldy wind pelted him repeatedly and resolutely with rain.[70]

In the end, the story thus returns to its opening vision of the rainy season weather and the peculiar "mold smell" (*komp'aengi naemsae*) that accompanies it in Japan, pairing it with an image of a silent, passive, "pent-up" Yŏnghwan. The sky, as the text's title says, "does not clear," and the story's parting vision of its protagonist is once again despairing rather than determined.

In contrast, Kim's 1960 rewrite of this text moves in a significantly different direction. Published in the *Chosŏn minbo* in early February of 1960, "The Eye-Opening Doll" extends the narrative of "The Sky that Does Not Clear" into the repatriation-era present in order to turn the original story's Pak Yŏnghwan—previously a man of frustration, silence, and directionlessness—into a hopeful, DPRK-bound "repatriate" named Kim Yŏngsun. As in the original text, the Korean War–era section of the text presents Yŏngsun as a middle-aged former teacher who has recently entered Japan as a stowaway and is now working as a day laborer. Once again, it focuses on this former teacher's chance encounter in a bookstore with a young girl from his past in South Korea: a young girl—here named Sunja—who comes from a rich family and attends an American school in Japan.

Neither of these two figures, however, is quite the same as they were in the original text. Instead of following the lead of her father—who, in the 1960 version, is a South Korean businessman who has become a Mindan official—Sunja strafes at the isolated life that he has imposed on her and secretly travels to the bookstore on a regular basis to meet Yŏngsun, the father of her old schoolmate, whose influence is presented as radicalizing. Likewise, Yŏngsun—who offers Sunja solace and encouragement—is no longer the same man that appeared in the 1956 text. Rather than a man of silence and frustration, he is a man of solidarity who has entered the revolutionary community and begun to make good on the fleeting image of radical potential in the original story by becoming a teacher at a Chongryon school.

However, the most important way in which the rewrite presents Yŏngsun making good on his radical potential is by linking his path to repatriation. Although the majority of the text, like the 1956 original, takes place during the Korean War era, the opening and closing sections take place in 1959, at the time of the first repatriation ship's departure for the DPRK. Yŏngsun is a passenger on this ship, and among his belongings is a doll in a glass box, a gift from Sunja. In the rewrite, therefore, Yŏngsun is presented as having succeeded in expressing his revolutionary potential to the extent that he has chosen to board the ship to the DPRK, and in narrating this culmination of revolutionary transformation, the text introduces one additional dimension not present in the original: that is, an additional character who serves as narrator. The text is narrated by Pak Mansu, the activist responsible for initially bringing Yŏngsun toward the revolutionary community in the Korean War–era past. Traveling to the Niigata port to bid the first group of migrants farewell, Mansu runs into his old acquaintance Yŏngsun, who he describes as having "a smile that reaches deep into his heart,"[71] and the text is thus a testament to the wonders produced by Mansu's revolutionary intervention in the past: an intervention pointedly missing from the original.

"The Eye-Opening Doll" here comes to a quite different conclusion than "The Sky that Does Not Clear." In this story, the doll's eyes do indeed open, as Yŏngsun's revolutionary transformation is narrated as coming to full fruition with his repatriation. And yet, this transformation in the story is only possible via a displacement of the narrating perspective from Yŏngsun to Mansu, who watches his old friend board the ship to the DPRK but does not board it himself. This would become a recurring trope of repatriation literature in Japan, and it would produce, as we will see below, the peculiar mix of revolutionary solidarity and skepticism that would emerge in 1960s and 1970s resident Korean culture in Japan.

EMPTY CENTERS

When we look at Chongryon media accounts from the 1950s and 1960s, the narrative of repatriation that we get is often less than nuanced: a narrative of migration from the unending hardship of Japan to the shiny salvation of the North. We thus see images of departure in which repatriation, as a *Chosŏn minbo* reader put it, is nothing other than a "starting point for rebirth,"⁷² and we read reports in which the greatest care that repatriates seem to face in the North is the worry that they are eating so well and gaining so much weight that future repatriates will not be able to recognize them.⁷³

We might expect, therefore, that fiction of the time would present a similar image: that is, that it would portray migration to the DPRK as an unproblematic goal to be pursued almost reflexively. And yet, what we find is something quite different: a range of texts that seem noticeably hesitant to abandon the work of activism that the Korean Left in Japan had been pursuing since 1945; a range of texts that refrain from representing repatriation itself, pushing it repeatedly into a deferred future; a range of texts that, adapting a phrase from the work of Cindi Textor, reemphasize rather than remove the "particular temporality" of the resident Korean situation of "being 'in Japan' *for now*."⁷⁴

As Song Hyewŏn has discussed, the origins of this vision are in official Chongryon policy. After all, it was obvious to the organization from the beginning that if all dedicated cadres left for North Korea at once, the group would implode. As a result, while some cadres did make the journey in the early years, they were generally encouraged to stay in Japan to continue spreading the group's message to the resident Korean population while sending family members and acquaintances to North Korea.⁷⁵ What this produced, as Song has noted, was a whole new batch of separated families—a tragic mirror image of those separated by division on the Korean peninsula⁷⁶—and in cultural production, this policy gave rise to the types of narratives discussed above: narratives in which activists stayed in Japan while sending family members and acquaintances to the DPRK.

This was quite clear in the work of the Chongryon-affiliated novelist Ryu Pyŏk. For Ryu, the relationship between revolutionary center and margins was a recurring concern, even before the advent of repatriation. Published in the *Chosŏn minbo* newspaper in early 1958, Ryu's "Unfinished Self-Portrait" ("Miwansŏng ŭi chahwasang")⁷⁷ takes up this problem by narrating the story of a young man, Chongha, who is about to graduate from the normal school at Chongryon's Korea University. For Chongha, as for all of his peers, the ideal postgraduation assignment is at one of the schools in Tokyo—the more central the better and the more advanced the students' level the better.

Nevertheless, what becomes apparent is that not all of the graduates can be assigned to schools in the capital. Instead, some of them will have to go to the provinces to spread Chongryon's educational work to the most marginalized members of the Korean diaspora in Japan, and this is precisely the situation that Chongha finds himself in when his teacher calls him into his office. The teacher, Ch'oe, knows that Chongha wants an assignment in Tokyo. But other than a "skilled" comrade like Chongha, a young educator "capable of working amid any type of difficulty," who—Ch'oe asks—could be sent to the provinces for this important task of constructing a new Chongryon school?[78]

This is, of course, a rhetorical question. The answer is set—and the remainder of the story, therefore, centers on Chongha coming to terms with this change of course alongside his love interest, Sullye. Revolution, they must realize, is not just a project of transforming the world. It is also—or perhaps first and foremost—a project of remaking the self to be open to such tasks, and Chongha and Sullye thus pledge, in the text's final scene, to find a way to complete parallel self-portraits "with the fiery ink of practice" in the space of the provinces.[79] This story, then, leads away from the center of power and revolutionary practice in Tokyo. Instead, it leads toward the Japanese provinces—the margins, where revolutionary practice is most desperately needed—and this produces an interesting dynamic in Ryu's work once repatriation gets underway.

Ryu's early 1960 story "Pride" ("Charang") is an instructive example.[80] Once again, it tells the story of a university student approaching graduation, and once again, this student must choose between the task of educating compatriots in a rural province and another path tied to the urban center. In "Pride," the space of the margins is Akita Prefecture, and it is a place that the story's protagonist, Myŏnghwan, has been visiting regularly during school breaks in order to teach Korean. Unlike Chongha in "Unfinished Self-Portrait," Myŏnghwan does not have any misgivings about dedicating his time to teaching these children in the provincial margins. Instead, he is forced to choose between this path and another one that his father wants him to pursue: namely, joining him as he boards an early ship to the North. An elderly widower, Myŏnghwan's father has been able to secure a spot on one of the first ships, and he can think of nothing that he would like to do more than to return to the ancestral land and spend his silver years with his children attempting to make up for all of the time he lost during his decades living in Japan.

Myŏnghwan, however, feels that to leave at this time would be to abandon the compatriots still enduring hardship in Japan—especially those in the provinces without access to a strong Chongryon network. And indeed, when Myŏnghwan sets out to convince his father to leave for the North without him, he does so by reading him the letters, written in a mix of Korean and Japanese, that he has received from the students waiting for him in Akita. "How can I break my promise, leave them like this, and go?," he then asks his father. "Did you send me to college to make me into someone who only thinks of himself?"[81]

Framed in these terms—that is, in terms of a responsibility left unfinished—Myŏnghwan resists his father's demands to accompany him and ultimately succeeds in convincing him that he should go without his son. And when he does so, there is a ripple effect. In the text's final scene, the father tells the rest of the local Chongryon members about his son's decision—and he does so with the "pride" of the story's title, a pride that convinces all those present that his son has made the right decision. Once again, therefore, the story emphasizes the importance of activism on the margins. To live in the revolutionary center—here Pyongyang rather than Tokyo—is not disputed as ideal, but the story nevertheless frames the deferral of such a life as heroism and dedication. Indeed, the story emphasizes the value of repatriation's deferral in favor of a life on the revolutionary margins: a life in Japan, a life in the provinces.

This vision, moreover, extended beyond the initial moment of the repatriation project's emergence. In a poem published by Chi Myŏngsun in a December 1963 issue of the *Chosŏn sinbo*, the speaker, a teacher at a Korean school in Fukuoka Prefecture, addresses a friend who has already migrated to the North as follows:

> I received it with joy
> Your letter, comrade for whom I yearn.
> Bearing the scent of our ancestral land
> It makes me yearn for you even more
> And plunges me into memories of the past.
> When we were young women

> We became close through our life in the organization.
> Blood boiling
> And full of hope, we sat up nights
> With such great enjoyment.[82]

In Chi's poem, the trope of letter writing allows the speaker to conjure up memories of the past and those with whom it had been shared. Indeed, it allows the speaker to look back to the range of experiences shared in common with her friend: the hardships of life in Japan, the difficult yet rewarding struggle to establish the repatriation program, and the "incomparable" joy of seeing the first repatriation ship arrive at the docks in Niigata.

It also allows the speaker to narrate the experience of parting. In Chi's poem, the speaker finds herself—like many of those in the works fiction discussed above—in the position of bidding farewell to her repatriating comrade while deciding, herself, to remain in Japan to continue the struggle:

> You repatriated, taking the lead
> I stayed here to continue in this land of struggle
> And so we have lived to this day.
> By word of mouth, I hear of your activities
> And I, too, worked just as hard.
> ...
> The glory of teaching our script to our compatriots
> I will not forget, living each day to the fullest.
> You in our ancestral land
> And I here in Japan
> Let's go forward more powerfully.
> Until the day our mortal enemies, the American imperialists, are driven away
> Until the day we are able to meet, with a firm handshake, at the line of division.[83]

What Chi's poem narrates here is quite striking. Although the speaker clearly notes her gratitude and support for the path that her friend has taken in migrating to the North, her words are also quite clear in separating out this path from her own, which she sees as equally valuable. Moreover, it is not simply that Chi's speaker has decided to defer repatriation in the way many of the characters discussed earlier decided to do. Instead, she has decided to remain in Japan until she can return to the South, where she will greet her friend at the thirty-eighth parallel. And in the meantime, what she will pursue is an alternative path: one bound to the North but also separated from it.

Such representations continued to be produced across subsequent years. This was evident, for example, in Pak Kwanbŏm's 1979 story, "Together with My Elder Sister" ("Nuna wa hamkke").[84] Although the opening and closing frame of the story, which focuses on a middle and elementary school teacher named Tongsik, takes place in the 1970s present, the bulk of the text takes place in the 1960s past, showing how Tongsik came to occupy his current position. In particular, it focuses on how Tongsik transformed from an unengaged youth educated in a Japanese school to a beloved educator in the Korean school community—a teacher whose dedication to his students is evident in the detailed knowledge of each pupil that he displays as he is distributing gifts brought from a recent trip to North Korea.

As in other such stories, this transformation is facilitated by those around the protagonist: in this case, two family members. The first such family member is Tongsik's father, whose hometown is in the North. Tongsik's father came to Japan in 1943, leaving behind a wife and a young daughter. Like many others, he came to Japan under duress, a forced laborer mobilized to build military runways for the war effort, first in Kyūshū and then in the South Pacific. Although he had been certain that he would meet his end during the conflict, Tongsik's father had survived, only to learn, after the end of the war, that his wife had died, leaving his daughter to be raised by her uncle. Shocked by this news, Tongsik's father had never returned to Korea, instead staying in Japan to start a new family and live a life with few ties to his past.

With the beginning of repatriation, however, Tongsik's father begins to have a change of heart. He resolves to bring his new family back to his hometown and to reconnect with the daughter he had abandoned. This daughter is the "elder sister" of the story's title, a sister that Tongsik and his brother Yŏngsik never knew that they had, and in preparation for repatriating to the DPRK and meeting this sister, Tongsik and his brother begin attending a Korean school rather than a Japanese one, learning to read and write Korean. Their mother, too, begins attending adult classes in preparation for the move.

Not everything, however, goes according to plan. With his new Korean-language abilities, Tongsik begins writing to his long-lost sister, Kyŏngsuk. Although she has been hurt by their father's neglect, she is thrilled to learn that she has two younger brothers and is looking forward to meeting them. At the same time, having been raised with a "proper" DPRK education, she also knows that she cannot put her personal desires before the needs of the revolution. Therefore, after Tongsik raises the question of staying in Japan as a teacher in a Chongryon school, she voices strong support for this idea:

> I want to meet you as soon as possible. But Chongryon's patriotic work of advancing the unification of the ancestral land is more important. . . . We are still young. We will have many opportunities to meet.
> I am very proud to have a brother with such outstanding thoughts. I fully support your admirable idea to stay in Japan and contribute to national education.[85]

Inspired, this is what Tongsik decides to do, and rather than join the rest of his family in departing for North Korea, he stays in Japan, graduating from a Korean school's education program in Tokyo and then volunteering for an assignment in the provinces.

The story's title, "Together with My Elder Sister," is thus a curious one, as the text ends not with togetherness but rather the type of parallel paths seen above. Indeed, in the letter that Tongsik receives at the very end of the story, his sister writes: "I am now enjoying the happiness of living together with my parents and siblings, but I am most proud to have someone like you, who has taken up the Great Leader's teachings and remained in Japan alone to dedicate himself to Chongryon's patriotic work. My dear brother, we are now separated by the sea, but let's work as the same type of able hands, loyal to the Leader in devoting all of our energy to the peaceful unification of the ancestral land."[86] Once again, the most revolutionary of paths is the one that chooses not to travel to the revolutionary center—the DPRK—choosing instead to remain on the front lines of the struggle in Japan.

Likely the most influential vision of this type, however, was not a work of literature but rather a film. In early 1968, North Korea's Korean Art Film Production Studio (Chosŏn Yesul Yŏnghwa Ch'waryŏngso) released *We Have An Ancestral Land* (*Uri ege nŭn choguk i itta*), a film based upon a script written by Hŏ Namgi, one of the most influential Chongryon writers and critics, about the experience of Koreans in Japan.[87] A landmark work in Chongryon-North Korean artistic collaboration, *We Have An Ancestral Land* clearly drew upon this trope of repatriation deferral. Yet it did so in a way that signaled the complex trajectories of exchange produced by North Korea's adaptation of South Korean literature. After all, in depicting its hero as a mother who, following the death of her son, takes up a position on the front lines of struggle in the Chongryon organization and thus decides not to repatriate, the film linked narratives of repatriation deferral to the trope of the activist mother that North Korean literature had developed in its reimagination of South Korean texts. That is, the film, as we will see in more detail below, demonstrated the nuanced ways in which Chongryon cultural production situated itself vis-à-vis inter-Korean exchanges.

BANDITS ACROSS THE SEA

In May 1970, the South Korean journal *Sasanggye* published an extended narrative poem by the young writer Kim Chiha, a figure who would soon become one of the most famous symbols of the South Korean movement for democracy. Titled "Five Bandits" ("Ojŏk"), the poem was a parodic critique of the South Korean state and its business allies that compared them to the so-called five bandits who signed the 1905 treaty that turned Korea into a protectorate of the Japanese Empire.[88] Soon after, on June 3, Kim Chiha was arrested for violating South Korea's National Security Law and *Sasanggye* was shut down, producing a major outcry, not only domestically in South Korea but also abroad. In tandem, the poem itself also spread abroad, most importantly in Japan, where "Five Bandits" soon appeared in Japanese translation in a range of publications in mid-1970: the *Shūkan asahi*, *Koria hyōron*, and *Shin Nihon bungaku*.[89]

Even before the poem appeared in translation in any of these publications, however, it had already been republished by the Chongryon press. In fact, the day after Kim's arrest, the text of "Five Bandits" appeared in the pages of Chongryon's newspaper, the *Chosŏn sinbo*, picking up on the existing practice of republication mentioned in chapter 1.[90] Furthermore, writers within Chongryon also began engaging with "Five Bandits" creatively not only by referencing it in poems of their own but also by rewriting it in ways that mirrored the North Korean practice discussed earlier.[91]

Pak Kwangt'aek published one such work of rewriting in Chongryon's literary journal, *Munhak yesul*, in August 1970.[92] Kim's original poem uses a frame narrative structure. Instead of simply telling the story of the five bandits and their destruction, it does so via the voice of an itinerant poet, who speaks self-reflexively at the beginning and the end of the text in a manner adapted, as Youngju Ryu has written, from the oral genre of *p'ansori*.[93] The poem thus presents its reader with not just a story but also a storytelling scene that contextualizes the delivery of its main narrative.

What Pak's rewriting does with this frame narrative structure is peculiar yet interesting. Labeled at its head as a specific kind of musical performance done by itinerant peddler-minstrels (*changt'aryŏng*), Pak's rewriting—which mixes verbatim quotation from the original with creative adaptation—preserves the original poem's frame narrative structure while adding an additional layer to it. While it still includes the voice of the itinerant poet who speaks self-referentially before relaying the story of the five bandits, it prefaces the appearance of this itinerant poet's voice with its own additional storytelling frame:

> Ehe—
>
> Now listen, a certain southern Korean poet wrote a text called "Five Bandits" exposing the crimes of Park Chung Hee and they imposed death, life imprisonment, and fabricated crimes, producing uproar in the puppet National Assembly, uproar everywhere—*p'umba, p'umba*, those five bandits,
>
> Huh? What did he write in that text to make Park Chung Hee frame another innocent person? It is really something. To tell you what he wrote (clearing throat) . . . [94]

Pak's rewriting here begins with an itinerant minstrel's retelling of the story of Kim Chiha's persecution by the South Korean state before turning, in subsequent lines, to the original poem and its own opening frame narration.

Pak's rewriting, in other words, presents the story of the five bandits, and then two layers of framing: the voice of the original poem's itinerant poet; and the voice of the rewrite's itinerant minstrel, who speaks via the very outer layers of the texts. Yet what is significant about this complex structure is that it gradually gets confused over the course of the poem—such that, by the end, the reader can no longer tell the difference between these two voices and these two levels of framing, which blend together. Both the perspective and the position of the Japan-situated voice of critique and the South Korea-situated voice of critique become conflated, and the text thus attempts to co-opt South Korean critique toward Chongryon's vision of revolutionary solidarity with the North. This is an attempt at co-option that is only made clearer at the end of the text, which describes the "southern compatriots' fierce flames of struggle, which have burst forth like a volcano on the path toward reunification," as flames that have been ignited by Kim Il Sung, "the great sun of the forty million Korean people."[95]

This, however, is not the only move made in the rewrite. In the original poem, the story of the five bandits includes two characters other than the five villains: the first is the police chief (*p'odo taejang*) who initially attempts to catch the villains and then decides to join them; and the simple country man, Kkwesu, who has come to Seoul to make a living but is ultimately the one accused of the five bandits' crimes and sent to jail in their place. Kkwesu is the sympathetic center of the text. He is the representative of the downtrodden who are just struggling to get by amid the corruption and wealth of those who abuse their power, and it is not a coincidence, therefore, that when he is finally put in jail at the end of the poem, the villains responsible for his fate are struck down by unexplained forces of heavenly retribution. This figure of Kkwesu—and other figures like him—would be central for the imagination of "the people" or *minjung* associated with Kim Chiha's work. However, Pak's rewriting eliminates him from the text altogether, likewise erasing the heavenly retribution that his imprisonment produces in the original. The result is a more strenuous call for revolution: a call transform the entire system.

What the text does, therefore, is engage in practices of rewriting that parallel those developed in North Korea by inserting its own context, audience, and vision into the South Korean poem, producing commonality and overlap. Texts like Pak's, however, were not the only ones that drew upon North Korean practices of rewriting South Korean literature. As we have seen, the figure of the militant mother developed by *Mother of the South* via engagements with South Korean texts did not remain immobile within this singular work. Instead, this figure traveled outward across North Korean literature, finding itself in works like "Embrace" and *North Star*, which implanted the figure of the militant mother into literature of the North's own colonial-era revolutionary heritage. This figure's itinerary of transit, however, in fact extended further, making its way to cultural production in Japan. This occurred via Hŏ Namgi's script for *We Have An Ancestral Land*, the film mentioned above, albeit with important transformations that implanted this figure into Chongryon's own context of literary production.

On New Year's Day 1965, North Korea's *Rodong sinmun* newspaper carried a report on a new play then being performed at the Pyongyang Theater. Directed by Pak Chaeok and Kang Pongwŏn with a script by Han Sangun, this new play, *I Have An Ancestral Land* (*Na ege nŭn choguk i itta*), was part of a line of new works, produced in North Korea, about the repatriation of resident Koreans from Japan.[96] *I Have An Ancestral Land* is the story of a water scientist, Kim Tongnyŏl, who has come of age in Japan. Experiencing discrimination and contempt from Japanese society, Kim is determined to succeed in inventing a new water filter in order to "spread the glory of Koreans." However, the director of his research institute conspires with "Japanese imperial capitalists" to steal his invention, so Kim destroys his plans and decides to migrate to the North, where the "path of free scientific inquiry" provided by the "warm bosom of the Party" allows him to recreate his invention, bringing greater access to clean water to the nation.[97]

On its own, this play is largely unremarkable. Placed next to *We Have An Ancestral Land*, however, it takes on new significance. The *Rodong sinmun*'s report on this play was republished, in edited form, in Chongryon's *Chosŏn sinbo* on January 25, 1965,[98] and it is clear that this play was the inspiration for the film's title. It is also clear that the significant gap between these works speaks to important processes of transformation that occurred between the play's production in North Korea in 1964 and the film script's composition in Japan a few years later. Indeed, what sets the film script apart from the play is its transformation of the main character into a militant mother of the kind developed in *Mother of the South* as well as its transformation of her trajectory into one that converges with existing literary forms then being produced in Japan: in particular, those of the deferring repatriate.

Unlike the main character of *I Have An Ancestral Land*, the protagonist of *We Have An Ancestral Land* is a mother, Oksun, whose story of revolutionary growth forms the backbone of the work. At the beginning of the narrative, Oksun is an "ordinary farm girl,"[99] as critics said at the time, who knows little about politics. However, once she migrates from then-colonial Korea to Japan in search of her husband, who has been mobilized to work at a coal mine, she gradually begins to gain consciousness. This begins when Such'ŏl, whom she meets on the ship to Japan, tells her about General Kim Il Sung, and it continues once she reunites with her husband, an activist who teaches her to read and write Korean. Oksun's transformation, however, is far from complete at this point. Indeed, even after Liberation, when her husband, whose health rapidly deteriorated after his colonial-era imprisonment, attempts to contribute to the struggle for resident Korean rights in Japan, Oksun tries to convince him to prioritize his physical well-being, earning a strong rebuke from him for her priorities.

Oksun's transformation is thus incomplete, and it only reaches its higher stages once her husband and one of her sons die in succession. Coming right at the close of what, in at least one printing,[100] is marked as the end of the first half of the scenario, this latter set of events is especially significant. After losing her husband at the time of the American occupation's forced closing of Korean schools in 1949, Oksun devotes herself to work in order to support her family. When the Korean War breaks out in 1950, therefore, her response is muted; she listens to Kim Il Sung's speech on the radio but makes no concrete plans for action. Her two sons, however, respond differently, taking it upon themselves to act. Along with friends, they begin printing handbills criticizing American war efforts in Korea, something that Oksun decides to help with. And when one of her sons is subsequently shot by an American soldier for distributing the handbills at a military installation, her involvement deepens. In the following scene, she is instead the one running the handbill press, receiving help from others.

In this way, Oksun's loss of her son, whose tasks she then takes up, becomes a pivotal moment of transformation in which she comes to mirror Sunnyŏ in *Mother of the South*. From this time on she becomes increasingly radicalized, and when Chongryon is established in 1955, she becomes a leader of the women's division of her local branch, emerging as a paragon of militant motherhood. This new image sets her apart from her former self, as do some actions that she takes with regard to her surviving sons. In an intriguing yet underdeveloped scene in the latter half of the narrative, Oksun's oldest son, Munho, attends a rally at his Chongryon-run school in support of the organization of a public education corps (*kyoyang sŏnjŏndae*) that will send students to remote areas to educate members of the Korean community. Although present at this rally, which ends with echoing applause and shouts of excitement, Munho is "lost in different [*namdarŭn*] thoughts."[101] Indeed, as his subsequent conversation with a classmate suggests, he is not only hesitant to join the corps but also planning, it seems, to quit school and get a job instead. In his brief conversation with this classmate right after the rally, he thus states, "Of course, I know that my mother did not send me to school for her own benefit [*rak ŭl pojago*]. However, as a son, I want to allow her to live more comfortably now."[102] When she finds out about this, Oksun is livid:

> OKSUN: So, your studies have all been for nothing! Spending sleepless nights (without giving it a thought), I worked until my fingers were worn thin, and you were having such thoughts. When I received contempt and abuse from those bastards, I clenched my teeth and endured it, thinking that you would dispel my grudging rage by attending school and becoming an outstanding young person, but you . . .
>
> . . .
>
> OKSUN: Do you think I sent you to school in order to live a comfortable life supported by you? Everyone else is clamoring to join the public education corps for the good of the country, but you are simply thinking about the upkeep of our life in this warped shack? Do you know how your father died and who killed your younger brother? Huh?[103]

Oksun's anger here consolidates the audience's understanding of her transformation. Just as her husband once castigated her for being focused on the material well-being of her family rather than the broader community's needs, she is now castigating her son for a similar failing.

Additionally, however, Oksun's anger here is also significant because it points back to Sunnyŏ in *Mother of the South*. In the first scene of Kim's play, after Sunnyŏ mentions the scholarship money that the villain, Yang Kwŏnmo, has offered, Inho threatens to quit school and go to work in a factory. Hearing this, Sunnyŏ is enraged:

> SUNNYŎ: Do you think I've gone through all of this hardship for my own benefit [*rak ŭl parago*]? Do you think I've been groveling in front of others subserviently because I enjoy it? If you want to see your mother's heart in pain, then sure, quit school . . .
>
> SUNNYŎ: The way your father, abused by others, could not live like a human being and ultimately met an unjust death is imprinted in my bosom. I wanted to die having seen you live like a human being. But now you say you want to quit school?[104]

To be sure, the cause of Sunnyŏ's anger here is different than the cause of Oksun's. In the play, after all, this scene comes before the protagonist's transformation, when she is still family-focused rather than revolution-focused. Yet the overlap between these two scenes is nevertheless telling, showing how Hŏ's script draws upon and adapts narrative elements formed in *Mother of the South* and its engagement with South Korean literature.

And indeed, what Hŏ's script does is not simply replicate existing narrative elements but transform them by placing them in dialogue with existing forms of narrative developed in Chongryon literature in Japan. As noted above, *We Have An Ancestral Land* focuses on the transformation of an "ordinary farm girl" into a militant mother who takes up a task left unfinished by her husband and son, a transformation that echoes those seen in the North. Nevertheless, the endpoint of Oksun's transformation is unique to the Chongryon situation and its vision of revolutionary commitment. By the end of the narrative, Oksun has become a leader in her local Chongryon chapter, and she greets the advent of repatriation to the DPRK with active exuberance. Yet once again, this does not mean that she herself leaves for the North. On the contrary, what she does is send her son, Munho, deciding herself to stay in Japan to continue her activism, saying, "You go to our ancestral land and study to your heart's content, and I will work with Chongryon here to expel the American bastards. When our ancestral land is reunified, let's meet in our hometown!"[105] Munho thus sails away, eventually becoming a scientist like the protagonist of *I Have An Ancestral Land*, while Oksun stays in Japan and continues her activism, standing at the front lines of struggle "shoulder to shoulder with young people."[106]

What brings Oksun's activism and militancy to its greatest height is here her deferral of repatriation, her commitment to living the hard life of struggle in Japan rather than migrating to the North for a life of ease and opportunity in the revolutionary center. As such, the conclusion of the narrative brings *We Have An Ancestral Land* firmly in line with Chongryon writing of the 1960s, engineering convergence between this line of representation and the tropes borrowed from North Korean literature's engagement with the South. Moreover, such visions of the militant mother who remains in Japan reverberated through Chongryon literature in subsequent years.

In April 1969, for example, Hŏ Ongnyŏ published a poem titled "They Cannot Block Our Advance" ("Uri ŭi chihyang ŭl magŭl su ŏpta") in the *Chosŏn sinbo*. Written from the perspective of a mother, the poem begins with an invocation of the joy, yearning, and tears brought forth by the arrival of a letter in the mail. The letter, the reader learns, is from the speaker's children, who have migrated to the North without her, and she is thus left to learn of their lives—and the lives of her young grandchildren, who have been born in the DPRK—via mail. Conjuring up their "happy and hopeful image" in her mind's eye, she assures them that, despite the physical distance between them, they are together in spirit:

> My dear children!
> How warm is the soft bosom of our ancestral land, and
> How beautiful
> Are the mountains and rivers of spring in our ancestral land.
> Distant as I am in this foreign country,
> My heart races toward the ancestral land
> And resides in the soft bosom of the Leader.[107]

The poem's speaker thus tells her children not to despair at the physical distance separating them, and she then proceeds to reiterate the vision of parallel paths:

> My dear children,
> You will be in our ancestral land
> Following the call of the Leader
> Vigorously spurring on the movement of the *Ch'ŏllima*
> For the complete success of socialism, for the reunion of our motherland, and
>
> We will be here
> Inscribing the instructions of the Leader in our hearts and
> Shoring up
> Our Chongryon organization.[108]

To be sure, the poem—published in 1969, in the gap between the initial repatriation program's conclusion in 1967 and its reinstatement in 1971[109]—blames this distance on the United States and Japan, who it accuses of blocking the continuation of the repatriation project. Yet by emphasizing the committed activism of the mother in Japan, who pledges, "Today, too, I will stand at the front lines of the struggle,"[110] the poem nevertheless reproduces the image of the dedicated revolutionary as the one who remains in Japan.

What can we make of the recurrence of this image and figure across multiple years and forms of expression? On the one hand, as noted above, the call for activists to defer repatriation was one that Chongryon itself promoted. At the same time, the reverberation and appeal of this call also appears to have drawn upon other tendencies within the Chongryon community: that is, subtle hesitancy in relation to the project of repatriation. As the Osaka-based novelist and teacher Cho Namdu acknowledged in a 1961 essay in the *Chosŏn sinbo*, "In relation to the repatriation issue, there are still many in the young generation who hesitate psychologically and express implicit unease . . . those who think about repatriation in terms of cost-benefit analysis, those who place Japan and our ancestral land on a scale and calculate accordingly, those who hesitate because they are unable to forget their hometowns."[111] For such individuals, Cho suggested, repatriation remained an open question, and such questions only became more prevalent over time.

Beginning in the latter half of the 1960s, after knowledge of the tragic fate of many repatriates become known in Japan, and after North Korean culture, for its part, became more and more fixated on the cult of the Kim family, Chongryon experienced internal upheaval, with many influential figures leaving the organization. Chongryon thus faced a new round of critiques, and in these works, too, the figure of the mother who has remained in Japan once again occupied a crucial place. Yet in such cases, this figure—rather than a Chongryon hero—became a sorrowful, frustrated one pointing to the necessity of a new approach.

POINTS OF DEPARTURE

Although the post-1959 literature of repatriation focused on the movement—as well as deferred movement—of the living, this was not exclusively the case. This was evident, for example, in Kim Sŏkpŏm's short story "Spirit" ("Honbaek"), which was published in the October 1962 issue of Chongryon's *Munhak yesul*.[112] "Spirit" is the story of a factory worker and Chongryon activist whose mother has recently died, and its central question—pondered as the narrator travels to the send-off party of one of his mother's friends, who is repatriating to the DPRK—is whether he should send her remains across the sea together with her. For the narrator, this question is one that emerges unexpectedly, as his relationship with his mother had not been close: he had not visited her frequently in the hospital; he had not cried at her funeral; and he had not thought about her especially frequently in the time since her death. With her friend's departure for the North, however, something in his emotions shifts: he sheds tears; he finds himself visiting the hospital where she had been a patient before she died; and he eventually asks himself whether he should send his mother's remains together to the North with her friend.

In the end, however, he changes his mind, deciding that this would not be the best course of action. And while this decision is not clearly explained in the story, it seems to be linked to the particular location of the family's hometown. Like the friend who is repatriating, the narrator's mother is from Cheju, an island off the southern coast of the Korean peninsula. Sending his mother's remains to the North, therefore, would not mean returning her to the place of her birth. The narrator thus reconsiders his plan; he defers the repatriation of her remains, just as he has deferred his own, with the implication that he will continue his activism in Japan until a revolutionary return to the South is possible, at which time he will take his mother's remains to their proper resting place on the island of her birth.

Understood in this way, "Spirit" fits within the overall trend of deferred repatriation narratives mentioned above. Yet the lack of clarity and explanation in its conclusion also raises questions about this fit, and indeed, "Spirit" is one of the works of his Chongryon era that Kim rewrote after his split with the group. Published in Japanese in 1973, more than ten years after the Korean-language original, the revised version of "Spirit" is titled "Night" ("Yoru") and it resembles the original in many of its basic elements.[113] Like the original, "Night" focuses on a narrator whose mother has recently died, and it likewise emphasizes the change in his relationship to her. As in the original, he did not cry at her funeral, had not visited her frequently in the hospital, and has not thought of her frequently since her death. Yet this suddenly changes, and on his way to a send-off for his mother's friend, who is again migrating to the North, he finds his body unconsciously seeking out the hospital where she had stayed, seeing her image in front of him and hearing her voice.

From this point, however, the story moves in a different direction. In "Night," there is no question of the repatriation of the mother's remains and no discussion, likewise, of the narrator's own plans with respect to leaving Japan; these repatriations are entirely unconsidered rather than deferred. Instead, the issue of deferred repatriation enters the text through an additional character—another mother—who is not in the original. This new character is Rannyŏ, the wife of the owner of the small factory where the narrator works. Like the narrator's mother and her friend, Rannyŏ is from Cheju, and she fled the island during the 4.3 Uprising, when her entire family was killed. Because of the horrors she witnessed, she has no desire to return to Cheju—or to the South, for that matter. Yet her current life in Japan is also painful, as the proximity of her home to a crematorium where bodies—including the narrator's mother's—are burned gives her continued traumatic flashbacks to her experiences in Cheju. As a result, she yearns to join the repatriation movement to the North, but her husband, whose mother is still alive in the South, refuses to go, prompting recurring fights between the couple.

For Rannyŏ, therefore, repatriation must be deferred indefinitely. And in this case, deferral—rather than a revolutionary choice to continue the struggle—is a passive outcome of an unworkable set of countervailing demands. Rannyŏ here emerges as a tragic figure, and the sense of tragedy that the text produces is heightened by the conclusion. At the end of the story, the narrator encounters Rannyŏ and her children as they all head to the repatriation send-off party. In the conversation that ensues, Rannyŏ repeats her determination to never go to the South, and at this point, one of her young sons chimes in, telling the narrator that going to the South is impossible because of the presence of "American imperialists," who are "murderers."[114] Surprised at hearing such words from a young child, the narrator looks into the child's eyes and sees a reflection of the "cruelty that his mother had brought from Cheju."[115] He further senses that what now connects the mother and child is not blood but rather the "desire for revenge," something that is being facilitated by the Chongryon education that the children are receiving in Japan.[116] In Kim's story, therefore, Rannyŏ's deferral of repatriation is far from heroic; instead, it coincides with her inability to escape the trauma of the past, and it coincides, moreover, with the reproduction of the effects of this past trauma in her children.

Kim was not the only writer to present this type of vision. In January 1972, the novelist Ko Samyŏng published an essay, "Encounter with My 'Hometown'" ("'Furusato' to no kaikō"), in the Japanese journal *Tenbō*.[117] In the essay, Ko narrated a recent visit to the village on a small island near Shimonoseki where he had been born, asking whether this place—or in fact, any place—could properly be considered his "hometown" (*furusato*). On the one hand, Ko noted, his ever-present consciousness of being Korean pointed to the fact that he was located in a Japan to which he could never fully belong. And yet, as a second-generation resident Korean who had spent his entire life in Japan, this "ancestral land" (*sogoku*) existed for him more as an abstract entity than a real, lived experience. Where, then, did he fit? Where was his "home"? Did he have one? These were the questions that Ko's essay addressed in its chronicle of his return to his "hometown" after more than twenty years, and they were also the questions that stood at the center of "Encounter" ("Kaikō"), the short story based on this essay that he wrote three years later.

"Encounter" was published in August 1975 in *Kikan sanzenri* (Kr. *Kyegan samch'ŏlli*), a Japanese-language journal founded by Kim Sŏkpŏm and a number of other former members of Chongryon, including Kim Talsu, Kang Chaeŏn, and Ri Chinhŭi.[118] Although Ko himself had not personally broken away from Chongryon—instead, he had left the Japanese Communist Party in the 1950s—this work was published in a journal associated with this position. "Encounter" follows its protagonist, Ha Kut'ae, as he returns to the village of his birth, asking whether he, as someone who identifies as Korean, can see this place as his "hometown." As in the essay, it has been more than twenty years since the protagonist has visited the village, but in the novel, what occasions this return is the death of his mother, which has made him think deeply about origins and identity. Suddenly, therefore, the thought of this place from the past, which has been buried deeply in his memory and consciousness, has come to the fore.

As expected, Kut'ae finds that much has changed in the village. Once quite poor, it is now dotted with sturdy, well-built homes. The old school is gone, and so, too, is the place where the Korean residents used to live, which is now a park. There are, however, some people left whom Kut'ae hopes to visit—in particular, his old friend, Munsik, who is also Korean and has stayed in the village his whole life. Like the village, much has changed in the appearance of these two friends. Yet they are still able to reconnect, speak of the past, and understand each other. Despite the differences in their present situations and the different experiences that they have had as adults, they also realize that they share another thing in common: the fact that they have both considered repatriation to the DPRK. Some of the residents of the village, Munsik tells Kut'ae, have indeed migrated to the North, and Kut'ae reports that he, too, had considered it because his closest friend in Osaka, where he has spent most of his life, decided to go. Yet he ultimately abandoned the idea, and Munsik notes that he had a similar experience. Although he had considered it, his father, who is originally from Pusan in the South, rejected the idea, and he has thus stayed in the village with his wife, who is Japanese, and his children.

Munsik has, however, visited the South. Since his father is from Pusan, he accompanied him on a trip, changing his citizenship to South Korean. Yet his experience, he says, was not at all what he expected. It felt, as he relays to Kut'ae, "like he had gone to a foreign country," and it completely destroyed the sense of "longing" (*okogare*) that he had felt for it as his father's place of birth.[119] What he realized, therefore, was that it was here, in this village in Japan, where he belonged. It was at this time, he says, that he began to feel that this village was his "hometown,"[120] and this is the same realization that Kut'ae eventually comes to by the end of his visit. In the last section of the text, Kut'ae accompanies Munsik to visit the oldest surviving Korean villager, an old woman who had worked side by side with Kut'ae's mother when they were young. Hearing her speak of a past shared with his mother—in words rendered entirely in *katakana* and thus presumed to be in Korean[121]—Kut'ae comes to see that there is no conflict between his Korean identity and an understanding of this village as his hometown. After all, it was here, in this Korean neighborhood, where he developed his sense of Koreanness, and it was here that his identity in its many complexities was formed.

As in Kim's "Night," the protagonist's loss of his mother is here complemented by the emergence in the text of an additional mother figure, one who speaks not of hope or the future but rather of the past and the futility of the present; after all, while desperately yearning to return to her hometown in Korea before her death, the mother in "Encounter" is resigned to this wish's impossibility. Like Rannyŏ in "Night," therefore, the elderly mother in "Encounter" stands in contrast to the militant, hopeful mother of *We Have An Ancestral Land*, and she also produces a contrasting movement of identification. In *We Have An Ancestral Land*, as in the other Chongryon works discussed earlier, the deferral of repatriation is a symbol of the strength of one's commitment to DPRK-aligned revolution; the protagonists in such works stay in Japan in order to continue to work for this cause rather than give up their frontline struggles.

In "Encounter," something quite different happens. Unlike the mother in Chongryon texts, whose position in Japan was a product of her decision to continue the fight on the front lines rather than take the supposedly comfortable route of migration to the North, the mother in both of these texts is one whose position in Japan is the product of her resignation to a pitiable fate: the impossibility and/or unworkability of repatriation in the current political context, something that leaves her hopelessly tethered to the past rather than open to a new, hopeful future. Moreover, in

Ko's story, the encounter with this figure of the mother produces a transformation in the self-consciousness of the male protagonist, who comes to understand his position in contrast to hers: that is, in terms of his rootedness in Japan. This is, clearly, the opposite movement that Chongryon stories were intended to produce; they were, instead, meant to intensify pride in the strength of the Chongryon movement's dedication to the DPRK.

At the same time, "Encounter" does not ultimately reject a connection to Korea altogether. On the contrary, at the end of the story, hearing the elderly mother's plea for reunification of the Korean peninsula—"No matter what, Korea must be unified. No matter what. It must be unified!"[122]—Kut'ae pledges that he will work toward this end, using his connection to this land to extend beyond it: "Once I, as a Korean, have tightly embraced this land with both hands, my footsteps will begin.... Yes, grandmother, Pak's grandmother, as a Korean, I will head toward unification.... Tightly embracing this land, I will walk... and walking... walking I will cross the sea. If, walking, I can cross the sea, I will look up at the shining stars in the sky over Korea. I will embrace the countless stars with these two hands. As a Korean, that is, and with my own feet... I will walk. Into that wide universe."[123] By the end of the story, then, the Korean voice of the elderly mother has produced dual movements within Kut'ae. First, there is the movement of disidentification in which Kut'ae realizes that his understanding of "home" is different from hers. Second, however, Kut'ae—freed from the question of repatriation and the question of "choosing sides" that comes with it—is able to embrace her plea for reunification, pledging to work toward it from a nonstate vantage point of critique: one that finds its critical potential in the undivided sky that not only links the two Koreas but also oversteps the borders of the broader planetary (nation-state) system.

This final moment of the text is essential because it marks the specific contours of the vision that would emerge, like "Encounter," in the pages of the journal *Kikan sanzenri*. This journal—formed, as noted above, by a group of former Chongryon members—not only distanced itself from both Korean states and their representatives in Japan but also attempted to produce a new, active, critical relationship to Korea. As such, the journal would in large part replicate the dual motions of disidentification and suturing seen in Ko's story—and a primary motive force in forming this position would be one drawn from critical reserves present in the contemporary South.

POETIC PIVOTS

As noted above, Ko's "Encounter" was published in the fall 1975 issue of *Kikan sanzenri*, a journal that Kim Sŏkpŏm, alongside others, had played an important role in founding. Kim was also a frequent contributor to the journal, and the issue immediately preceding the one that carried "Encounter" in fact carried a story called "Cloudburst" ("Shūu") by Kim.[124] "Cloudburst" tells the story of Chang, a middle-aged owner of a *yakiniku* restaurant in Tokyo. Born on Cheju Island and an activist in his youth, Chang came to Japan, we learn, in the early postcolonial era to flee political persecution by the Syngman Rhee regime. In Japan, he has retained "Chosŏn" nationality and is a regular subscriber to Chongryon's *Chosŏn sinbo*, which signals his connection to the political Left and to the organization.

At the same time, he no longer identifies himself as an activist, and familial concerns have recently driven him even further from the organization. Three years prior, when his mother-in-law—living back in Cheju—passed away, his wife had traveled there by changing her nationality to South Korean. And now that his mother-in-law's three-year memorial ceremony is approaching, he is considering making the trip himself, something that will also allow him to tend to his own parents' gravesite, which has apparently fallen into neglect. He has thus changed the sign in front of his restaurant, removing the phrase "Korean food" because of its use of the term for "Korea" associated with the DPRK ("Chosŏn"). It now simply advertises *yakiniku* without specifying a particular political position in relation to national division in Korea.

Moreover, he has started strafing at the "organization" and its behavior. In the story, Chang attends the funeral-in-exile for a friend's mother, who has likewise passed away in Cheju. As someone who still considers himself an activist, this friend, Chin, cannot travel to Cheju to attend the funeral in person. Yet his relationship with Chongryon is also strained.

When he phones Chang to tell him of the news, he asks him to bring recent copies of Chongryon's *Chosŏn sinbo* with him to the funeral, confessing that his subscription has been interrupted by the organization due to a squabble. This is a spiteful move by the organization that Chang cannot help but see as childish and petty, and the text's critique of Chongryon is only heightened when Chang sees the telegraph that Chin received notifying him of his mother's death. Addressed to a fabricated Japanese identity that Chin has created in order to receive communications from his family without risking their safety, the message appears tragic to Chang as a symbol of the way in which Chin's unwavering dedication to the organization has undercut rather than strengthened his Korean identity.

The story, however, is not only critical of Chongryon but also of Mindan, the South Korea-affiliated diasporic organization in Japan. After an encounter with a Mindan official, Chang learns that he will not have to change his citizenship in order to be able to travel to Cheju; visit permits, the official tells him, are available "with no strings attached."[125] Yet Chang knows that this offer is nothing more than a means of psychological warfare aimed at co-opting those affiliated with Chongryon, and as a result, Chang is unable to see the organization as anything other than manipulative, applying pressure and making use of individuals' personal pain for political gain. Sandwiched between these two manipulative state actors, Chang feels frustrated, isolated, and unsure of what to do, and the story thus presents a dual critique of both state actors in Japan: that is, both Chongryon and Mindan.

Like "Encounter," however, the story does not ultimately turn away from Korea altogether. This is evident in the final scene of the text, in which Chang is walking home from the funeral. Throughout the story, the political pressure that Chang feels is linked to the oppressive weather of the summer months immediately preceding the rainy season. It is a tense atmosphere that produces a feeling of being bottled up. In the final section of the story, however, the long-awaited rain finally comes, falling intensely as Chang walks home from Chin's house. This is the "cloudburst" of the story's title, which "removes a pent-up knot inside [his] body."[126] Yet it does so in an unexpected way: by removing the petals from the line of cherry blossom trees on the side of the road and putting them in motion in the air and in the stream flowing nearby.

With cherry blossom petals landing on his torso and flowing fantastically in front of him, Chang begins to "unconsciously" mumble, *saogi*, the word for cherry blossom in Cheju dialect. He realizes that he has forgotten neither this "affectionate" word nor the place where he grew up, which, he says, is the true origin of such cherry blossoms despite Japan's reimportation of them as its own imperial symbol during the colonial era.[127] In this moment, then, Chang is returned to his Cheju past and his Cheju identity, which have been dormant within him. Yet this identification is only momentary. After repeating *saogi* over and over again himself, he begins to hear it whispered outside his body as well. In tandem, he also begins to hear the voices of the Chongryon and Mindan representatives: "Those who will make revolution should go," the Chongryon representative says; "Go, no strings attached. You should visit your ancestral land and hometown," the Mindan representative then says.[128] Hearing these two voices, both of which are attempting to manipulate his relationship to his hometown, the whispering of *saogi* no longer seems addressed to him, and the emergence of this feeling of disconnection makes it clear that the representatives of the two states are the ones who are isolating and estranging Chang from his Cheju heritage and identity.

It also allows Chang to rethink his relationship to the world around him in Japan. Earlier in the text, while discussing petty squabbles between the Japanese parents in the local middle school parent-teacher association, Chang notes that he feels like an onlooker or spectator in the "stands" (*kankyakuseki*). This, he says, is primarily because he is a resident Korean living in "their land," and it once again highlights Chang's position of isolation and estrangement in the text.[129] It is not surprising, therefore, that when the Chongryon and Mindan voices return in the final scene to push back against his identification with the words of Cheju dialect, he is also reminded of his position as onlooker vis-à-vis the Japanese individuals around him, who return in his imagination and begin laughing uncontrollably as he watches from the sidelines. "You are in the stands," one of them tells him as he continues to hear the estranged sounds of *saogi*, and he feels the desire to want to laugh with them.

And this, in a way, he is soon able to do, as he realizes that his balding head, which resembles the cherry blossom trees around him that have lost their leaves in the cloudburst, is quite humorous. At this moment, Chang simultaneously reasserts his connection to Cheju and takes up a position of laughter together with his Japanese colleagues, and the sky, he notes, becomes "clear for the first time in a while."[130] The end of the story thus finds Chang taking a subtle yet significant turn: a turn away from the two Korean states and their representatives and toward both Cheju and Japan. Here, Chang simultaneously reasserts his Korean identity in a nonstatist, locally emplaced way and reinforces the importance of his position in Japan, and the link between these movements and locations is further emphasized by one more element in the text: its use of *katakana*.

As Cindi Textor has shown, linguistic play between Japanese and Korean is central to Kim's literary vision. By inserting the sounds, vocabulary, and expressions of Korean into his Japanese-language works, he creates "moments of unresolvable dissonance," and this allows him, Textor argues, to represent "radical, productive" forms of difference without devolving into essentialism.[131] In "Cloudburst," Kim does something similar, but the "radical, productive" difference produced in the text is oriented toward the two Korean states, and it emerges not so much via dissonance as via unexpected overlaps: in this case, between Cheju dialect and Japanese. Indeed, in the text, Kim not only uses *katakana* to render the Cheju dialect (the word *saogi*) but also to render a Japanese phrase that Chang hears in the subway and then repeats to himself throughout the story: "When I take the train, I feel lonely [*sabishii*]."[132]

This phrase, originally delivered by a Japanese man to his friend, is important to Chang because this invocation of loneliness speaks to a feeling that mirrors his own sense of isolation and estrangement. Yet it also intrigues Chang because the phrase's speaker, who says that he feels lonely when he takes the train because he is now usually the oldest person on the train, is not actually the oldest person on the train. There is, in fact, an elderly man returning from a wedding, and the speaker's feeling of loneliness, as such, seems misguided. Therefore, when Chang returns to this statement throughout the text, he is also returning to the question of whether his feeling of isolation and estrangement is also misguided. And when he returns to this statement in the final scene of the text, placing its *katakana* rendering side by side with the *katakana* rendering of *saogi*, he seems to answer this question in the affirmative, emphasizing dual modes of connection—to Cheju, to Japan—over disconnection.

Like "Encounter," therefore, Kim's "Cloudburst" produces a vision that emphasizes links to both Japan and Korea, and this complex position was broadly representative of that which was developed in the journal *Kikan sanzenri*, which sought to use its position in Japan to seek an alternative to both Korean states. And in practice, what this most often meant was using its position in Japan to voice critiques of both states and, in tandem, to amplify critical voices in Korea that operated outside them. These critical voices came from South Korea, and the most important of them during these years was the poet Kim Chiha. As An Chŏnghwa has noted, *Kikan sanzenri* published twenty-three texts related to Kim Chiha (including some of his own writing and an appeal written by his mother) in its first three years of publication alone,[133] and this was not only, as An has put it, because the journal located in Kim and his cause a vital means "to express its will for democratization and unification" but also because many of those closely involved with the journal had already been engaging in activism and writing relating to Kim for multiple years.[134]

Already arrested twice previously for his poetry, in 1974, Kim Chiha was sentenced to death as part of the so-called National Federation of Democratic Youth and Students case fabricated by the Korean Central Intelligence Agency.[135] Even before this sentence was officially pronounced, however, as Wada Haruki subsequently chronicled in the pages of *Kikan sanzenri*,[136] colleagues in Japan banded together to form the Committee to Assist Kim Chiha and Associates (Kim Chiha-ra o Tasukeru Kai), a group that built upon the experience of similar ones formed in 1972, at the time of Kim's previous arrest.[137] On July 10, the day after the news arrived that the ROK was seeking the death penalty against Kim, the group held a press conference, where it read a statement of protest drafted by Tsurumi Shunsuke and signed by the group's members—who included Kim Talsu, Kim Sŏkpŏm, and Ri Chinhŭi, all involved with *Kikan sanzenri*—alongside Howard Zinn, Noam Chomsky, Jean-Paul Sartre, and Simone de Beauvoir.[138]

The group also took a range of other types of action, from staging demonstrations to holding solidarity events to engaging in hunger strikes. On July 13, the day that Kim's death sentence was announced, the writer Matsugi Nobuhiko proposed staging a hunger strike on Kim's behalf. Joined by Kim Sŏkpŏm, Kim Sijong, Ri Kaisei, and Nanbō Yoshimichi, Matsugi began his hunger strike on July 16 in Tokyo's Sukiyabashi Park.[139] The hunger strike ended after three days, but it was followed by a second one lasting from July 27 to July 30 that included Kim Talsu, Ri

Chinhŭi, Tsurumi Shunsuke, and Hariu Ichirō. A few weeks later, on August 8, a group of Japanese members of the movement traveled to South Korea to deliver a petition on Kim's behalf with 17,000 signatures.[140] Alongside their Japanese colleagues, therefore, the group of ex-Chongryon, resident Korean writers who established *Kikan sanzenri* had been involved in activism in support of Kim for multiple years already.

They were also already involved in publishing about him. As early as 1970, Kim Talsu had already written about Kim, and by 1974, so had both Kim Sŏkpŏm and Ko Samyŏng, among others.[141] The profusion of texts about Kim Chiha in the early issues of *Kikan sanzenri* was thus embedded in a longer history of both activism and writing related to Kim Chiha, and what all of these writings and activities seemed to agree upon was that Kim represented the critical voice of "the people" (Kr. *minjung*, Jp. *minshū*): that is, those marginalized from state power as well as the social and economic power that flowed from it. For the writers at *Kikan sanzenri*, who were looking for their equivalent of the dialect voice in "Cloudburst," the figure of Kim Chiha was therefore pivotal. And what the extended engagement with him and his allies did was link the journal's critical vision to the South—although not its state—in new and important ways.

CONCLUSION

There were, of course, some differences in how the writers associated with *Kikan sanzenri* engaged with Kim Chiha as dissident hero and writer. As noted above, those involved in the journal, as a group, saw in Kim's writing and activism the true critical potential of "the people"; he spoke on behalf of the marginalized and on behalf of justice, and he mobilized the critical power found at the depths of despair and at the limits of the human condition.[142] Some writers also located other significant dimensions in Kim's writing. This was the case, for example, for Kim Talsu. Kim was likely the earliest of the *Kikan sanzenri* writers to take up Kim Chiha's writing, and when he discussed him at the time, what he saw in Kim—in particular, in "Five Bandits"—was a form of critical imagination that had strong connections to Korean tradition: more specifically, the critical heritage of "satire" (Jp. *fūshi*, Kr. *p'ungja*) as it had been practiced by Kim Rip (also known as Kim Satkat), Pak Chiwǒn, and others.[143] In Kim Chiha's writing, therefore, Kim Talsu found a link to the critical reserves of the past, and this was significant because Kim Talsu was, himself, engaging in a similar turn in his own writing practice.

Kim, often referred to as the "father" of resident Korean literature,[144] had been the most influential writer in the Korean leftist community in Japan for many years: that is, from the 1940s until he left Chongryon in the late 1960s. When he broke with the group—formalized with his purge in 1972[145]—Kim also reoriented his writing from the present to historical work dealing with the past: in particular, the tracing of the heritage of migrants from the Korean peninsula in ancient Japan. Kim's first writings in this historical project were published in 1970—the same year that he encountered and wrote about Kim Chiha for the first time—and the two Kims' relations to the past as critical reserve were thus tied together in a way that set the stage for future developments. Indeed, as we will see in detail in chapter 4, Kim Talsu's historical writings from 1970 onward served as a fundamental inspiration for a transformational work of historical fiction produced in South Korea: Ch'oe Inho's *The Lost Kingdom* (*Irhǒbǒrin wangguk*, 1985–1988).

3

CRITICAL CONNECTIONS AND CRITICAL LIMITS IN 1950s SOUTH KOREA

The Human and Nonhuman Across the
Cold War and East Sea Divides

Still centered at its wartime outpost in Samdŏk-tong, Taegu, the popular magazine *Sint'aeyang* closed out the year 1952 with an unorthodox Christmas message. As part of its continuing focus on contemporary film culture, the magazine's November 1952 issue had begun a new recurring feature called "Introduction to Famous Actors and Actresses of the World" ("Segye myŏngpaeu sogae"), in which full-page photographs of Hollywood stars—Marilyn Monroe, Ann Blyth, Victor Mature, and others—graced its opening pages. The December 1952 issue continued this feature with a portrait of Esther Williams [see figure 3.1], then appearing in the military recruitment film, *Skirts Ahoy!* Yet it used this portrait in a surprising way. Under a banner reading, "Merry Xmas," Williams's smiling face was flanked by a text box, written in Korean, which offered the following message to *Sint'aeyang*'s readers:

> I send my Christmas greetings to each of you, the 30 million Korean citizens who are fighting bravely in this war to repel communism. Here in Hollywood, the film world is abuzz with Christmas presents, and this Christmas I have decided to send my lover a copy of the world-famous author [C. Virgil] Gheorghiu's masterwork, *The Twenty-fifth Hour*. This is because he has not been able to read it yet. I encourage all of you to join me in offering each of your parents, siblings, friends, and lovers a copy of *The Twenty-fifth Hour*. Well, see you in the new year. Goodbye, my friends![1]

FIGURE 3.1 An advertisement for the Korean translation of C. Virgil Gheorghiu's *The Twenty-fifth Hour* featuring Esther Williams.

Sint'aeyang 1, no. 5 (December 1952): n.p. prefatory images.

Fabricated by the magazine's editors, this hybrid image was peculiar in a number of ways. First, it was peculiar in its form, which integrated an advertisement for the Korean translation of *The Twenty-fifth Hour*—just released in a second printing by the magazine's sister company, Tonga Munhwasa—into a part of its feature material.

More importantly, however, it was also peculiar in its content, which juxtaposed a stock invocation of anti-communist solidarity with a counter-discourse of quite different meaning. Originally composed in Romanian but first published in French translation in 1949, *The Twenty-Fifth Hour* is set during the years surrounding the Second World War and it tells the story of a simple young man from the Romanian countryside as he is persecuted by various forms of "Western technological society" (*la société technique occidentale*), including representatives of both the United States and the Soviet Union. First translated into Korean in early 1952 by the novelist and playwright Kim Song, the novel quickly attracted widespread attention in South Korea, with this dual critique of both sides of the Cold War divide playing a key role. An October 1952 advertisement also published in *Sint'aeyang* thus sold the text in terms of its relevance to the contemporary conflict in Korea, writing, "The writer's [depiction] of the suffering and fate of weak nations [*yakso minjok*] moaning between the two camps of the United States and the Soviet Union is precisely shared in common with us."[2]

Counterintuitively, therefore, the *Sint'aeyang* image deployed a glamorous icon of American popular culture to sell a text whose perspective was quite critical of this culture as a kind of pathological "other half" of Soviet-style communism. And the irony of the image, in fact, went significantly deeper. Although the *Sint'aeyang* advertisement linked the novel to American popular culture, it had in fact been introduced to South Korea, as we will see below, via Japan. Kim's translation of the novel, therefore, was closely linked to a wartime influx of Japanese texts that, officially banned, tested the bounds of the South Korean state's authority, and it thus highlighted, implicitly, the third dimension of the novel's critical vision. In Gheorghiu's novel, the critique of "Western technological society" is not directed at the Soviet Union and the United States alone but also at Nazi Germany and its allies in Romania. The novel's critique, in other words, is triple rather than double, taking up the domestic state alongside its set of foreign antagonists.

The irony of the Esther Williams advertisement, therefore, pertained both to the United States and to the South Korean state, and it also pertained to the role of Christianity in 1950s South Korea. Although Christianity played a pivotal role in South Korean anti-communism across these years and throughout subsequent decades, it was also through Christianity—or more specifically, through Christian existential thought—that elements of Marxism were reintroduced to South Korean discourse. The advertisement's Christmas wishes thus pointed, once again, in a surprising direction: not toward the importance of the "war to repel communism" but rather toward the nuanced ways in which writers and thinkers in South Korea during these years sought to undo the Cold War divide and challenge the bounds of acceptable discourse in the Republic of Korea.

Such challenges are the focus of this chapter and the one that follows. In this chapter, I focus on the wartime era and the postwar 1950s to show how the outbreak of the war—in addition to deepening and solidifying division and hostilities in Korea—also opened up new opportunities for their contestation in a variety of creative ways. First, I demonstrate how wartime South Korean literature and criticism, influenced in part by texts entering the country through Japan, developed a vision of dual critique voiced toward both sides of the "two worlds" conflict. I then show how this dual critique—which eventually came to be voiced in terms of dual forces of "mechanism" as opposed to "humanism"—was gradually transformed into a triple critique that, turning inward toward the multiple forms of the South Korean self, not only conflated the South Korean state with the antagonists of the "two worlds" conflict but also set the stage for a subsequent challenge to the domestic state's regime of anti-communist censorship.

To make this latter point, I turn to the forgotten history of the United Nations Korean Reconstruction Agency's Foreign Book Retail Store project, which South Korean intellectuals used to order significant amounts of Japanese Marxist texts, including ones that attempted to bridge the gap between Marxism and Christian existentialism. Demonstrating how a similar reengagement with Marxism emerged in mid-1950s South Korean thought via Christian existentialism, I show how the critical "humanism" of the Korean War era took up a Marxist perspective that had not been possible before. I then conclude by returning to the literary domain to show how fiction writers likewise challenged the censorship regime of the South Korean state. After taking up a position that, like Christian existentialism, questioned the bounds of the human, writers gradually opened up a space that allowed for a critical breakthrough: the reclaiming of banned works from the colonial era by writers who had gone North after 1945. Chapter 4 then turns to subsequent decades to show how this space of cross-border interactions was further widened and developed.

TOWARD MOBILIZATION

With the establishment of the Republic of Korea in August 1948, the deepening structures of division became formalized and institutionalized. They also took on new modes of legal enforcement. In December 1948, the National Security Law, which had been a topic of debate for months in the National Assembly, took effect as the tenth new law promulgated by the ROK. The law had a variety of targets, including: "those who form groups or associations for the purposes of violating the constitution by calling themselves a government or . . . overthrowing the state"; "those who form groups or associations . . . for the purposes of committing crimes such as murder, arson, or the destruction of transportation, communication facilities, or other critical infrastructure"; and "those who propagandize the purposes mentioned above or conspire to incite, by the directive of such groups, the carrying out of their purposes."[3]

The promulgation of the law signaled the dramatic opening of a new era in the crackdown on the postcolonial Left: in the following five months alone, approximately 89,700 individuals were arrested;[4] and in 1949 as a whole, approximately 118,621 were arrested.[5] At the same time, it also gestured back in time. As Chŏn Sangsuk has noted, echoing critics at the time, the National Security Law drew upon the colonial-era precedent of the Peace Preservation Laws of 1925, 1928, and 1941 by outlawing the formation of groups with proscribed purposes and the propagandization of those purposes rather than acts carried out by such groups toward such purposes.[6] This link, moreover, only gained strength over time. The law's 1949 amendment added penalties for "those who form groups or associations with the purpose of supporting groups [with the previously described purpose of overthrowing the government],"⁷ and the Anticommunist Law of 1961, which was subsequently incorporated into the National Security Law in 1980, included a clause outlawing "acts benefiting an antistate organization by praising [it or its members], encouraging [it or its members], sympathizing with the praise or encouragement of [it or its members], or other means."⁸

These legal developments had profound consequences for the literary domain as they did for other domains. As noted above, the original version of the National Security Law criminalized "propagandizing" for proscribed purposes. In its 1958 revision, the law introduced penalties for "collecting information about the nation's politics, economics, society, culture, and military with the purpose of benefiting the enemy" as well as for "producing, copying, or distributing" or "storing, handling, transporting, or carrying texts, records, images, or other forms of expression [in order to propagandize that which is a purpose of a proscribed group, association, or organization]."⁹ And the Anticommunist Law of 1961 again went one step further with the criminalization of "producing, importing, copying, storing, transporting, distributing, selling, or handling texts, records, images, or other forms of expression for the purposes of [benefiting an antistate organization]."¹⁰ This meant that the bounds of acceptable discourse were rigidly policed by the South Korean state in increasingly restrictive ways. Yet it did not mean that there were no gray areas—or that challenging these bounds was not possible—and indeed, this is precisely what an array of writers pursued across the Cold War decades.

In Korea, the debates of the immediate post-Liberation period between 1945 and 1948 produced a cultural and intellectual field structured around the problem of political engagement. For the Left, thought and culture could not be separated from the political demands of the present without sacrificing their historical and creative value. For those in the center and on the Right, on the other hand, cultural and intellectual production could under no circumstances be dictated by the demands of a specific program. This position was strenuously distinguished from the individual-centered approach of "art for art's sake" (*yesuljisangjuŭi*), but its basic premise was compatible with it: namely, that the ultimate ends of thought and literature were fundamentally apolitical. This was the vision formulated by Kim Tongni and his associates as "pure literature" (*sunsu munhak*), and it stood at the heart of "South Korean literature" (*Han'guk munhak*) as it was constructed in the postcolonial late 1940s.[11]

However, the outbreak of the Korean War in June 1950 essentially fractured this framework. Amid the combat, writers could no longer remain detached from the surrounding political reality, and many of the most influential figures thus began organizing their action immediately following the June 25 invasion. On the following morning, cultural leaders met at the offices of the journal *Munye* in order to begin organizing their own communications offensive, and they established the Emergency Citizens' Propaganda Brigade (Pisang Kungmin Sŏnjŏndae) on the following day, June 27. The activities of such leaders initially focused on radio broadcasts aimed at the general populace. Yet as the Northern army pushed south and the ROK government abandoned Seoul, the many writers who followed the state southward reorganized their work in a new group, the National Federation of Cultural Organizations' National Salvation Brigade (Munch'ong Kuguktae), which focused on the dispatch of so-called "embedded writers" (*chonggun chakka*) to the front lines with ROK troops.[12]

Over the following three years, many of the writers who remained in the South took part in such government-sponsored reporting from the front lines, and cultural organizations with their own publications were likewise established in association with the various branches of the ROK military, including the ROK Army, Air Force, and Navy.[13] Drawing upon a history stretching back to the Pacific War,[14] this mobilization fundamentally changed the shape of cultural and intellectual discourse in South Korea. In this wartime context, the ideal of apolitical "purity" (*sunsuham*) was no longer tenable, and the cultural field reorganized in support of an ethic of mobilization, a new "war literature" (*chŏnjaeng munhak*), and the slogan, "intellectuals, too, to the battle lines."[15] As the ROK military's cultural liaison put it, war demanded "an epochal reformation of literature,"[16] and many writers responded to this call in kind. The soldier-cum-poet Kim Chongmun thus called on fellow writers to take up the project of propaganda as "a cutting-edge weapon no less [powerful] than the atomic bomb in modern warfare,"[17] and the novelist Ch'oe Tokkyŏn likewise proclaimed that the proper role of the writer during this period was to take up her pen as "a hand grenade, field artillery, and flamethrower," as the "new weapon of the atomic hydrogen bomb."[18]

Such calls for mobilization were calls to resist the enemy from the North. More importantly, however, they were oriented toward a second target within the South Korean cultural and intellectual field: in particular, those who were understood to have sought a neutral position in the ongoing conflict by remaining in Seoul during the North Korean occupation between June and September 1950. Writing in opposition to such opportunistic "grayism" (*hoesaekchuŭi*), Kim Song, the novelist, playwright, and translator mentioned above, thus wrote, "this is not an age in which we can seek an artistry-centered literature of seclusion,"[19] and he further critiqued the "self-intoxication" (*chagi toch'wi*) and "de-colorism" (*t'alsaekchuŭi*) of "writers who—even while breathing smell of gunpowder and hearing the sound of gunshots—grope for dreams [in] the ivory tower of art as if they have no relationship to historical reality, politics, or society."[20] Also writing in 1952, Pak Kijun similarly critiqued "the writers who, hiding behind the sophistry of 'pure literature,' had attempted to camouflage their lack of 'the real' [*rial*]" and argued for the necessity of "bravely casting off the 'husk of purity' [*sunsu ŭi kkŏpchil*] in order to deal with the literary task offered by the war."[21] The project of "pure literature" here receded into the background in a clear and decisive way. Yet the vision of engagement that replaced it contained a number of heterogeneous trajectories—some of which guided the new "war literature" in directions orthogonal to that which we might expect.

SIGHTS/SITES OF MISRECOGNITION

For some, the war meant something predictable: that is, "choosing one or the other" (*yangcha t'aegil*) in the ongoing conflict. The Protestant theologian and cultural critic Kim Chaejun, for example, expressed this position quite clearly when he wrote: "The entire universe and all of history are divided into 'this or that.' There is no perspective that is neither this nor that. [We must] say 'either cold or hot.' Lukewarm [water] is fated to be purged.... The bat that pretends to be a bird and also a rat has no courage to fly into the light. It is 'yes' or 'no'; there is no position that is neither 'yes' nor 'no'... We can no longer avoid war. That is because everything is [now] war."[22] For others, however, the problem of choice and engagement was not quite so simple. In a 1952 essay on the wartime proliferation of identification cards of all sorts, the writer Pak Hwamok noted: "Whatever we think of them, they are extremely dear to us. We cannot ignore them. We cannot think of them lightly. Today, our identification cards are akin to one of the valuable bodily organs directly connected to our survival."[23] For Pak, the war did not produce clarity of "this or that." On the contrary, what it produced was unending confusion, and it was for this reason that identification cards had become so important. In this war, friend and foe were constantly in danger of being conflated, and this was a topic dealt with frequently by literary texts of the time, which recurred to problems of misidentification in order to emphasize the blurring of boundaries and binaries—rather than the clarification of them—produced by the conflict.

In particular, one of the most powerful ways that texts addressed this type of concern was through the depiction of refugees who found themselves under bodily threat from both sides of the conflict as a result of misrecognition. Yu Chuhyŏn's "Mountain Pass" ("Yŏng," 嶺) is a representative example of this kind of vision.[24] A young writer who had debuted in the magazine *Paengmin* in 1948, Yu rose to prominence during the wartime period as an embedded writer with the ROK Air Force, an editor of its literary journal, *Ch'anggong*, and an editor of the popular magazine *Sint'aeyang*. "Mountain Pass" was published in *Ch'anggong* in 1952, yet its content is surprising. The story follows a mother, Yŏngsuk, as she travels by foot with her daughter, Kyŏngja, to Taegu to rejoin her husband, a writer who left Seoul with the military as an "embedded" writer. In particular, it focuses on the pair as they cross a snow-covered mountain pass near Suwŏn, and it frames this space of passage as pointedly indeterminate: a space of blinding snow, ice, and rain; a space in which they have "no way of knowing whether the sun has set or not"; a space, as in all of the stories discussed below, centered around the ambiguous border zone of a mountain.[25]

Yet the primary dangers encountered here are not natural but man-made. They are told that the Chinese People's Volunteer Army is advancing, so they must hurry; they may even have already fallen behind enemy lines. Soon after, they hear gunfire and artillery in the mountains around them and a group of US-UN jet planes then appears and begins to fire back, circling around them left and right. The mother and daughter freeze and hide while the combat continues, and then they continue on their path, where they find a succession of gruesome sights:

> There, collapsed on the ground, was the dead body of the old man who had told them to discard their possessions at the bottom of the pass. And on the corpse's face sat two crows, pecking at its skin and neck with the sound, "Kok, kok, kok." Its two eyeballs were already missing. Dug open, its nose, mouth, and throat were all bright red. . . . Then, only a few steps ahead, Yŏngsuk saw an even more cruel sight. There, too, laid the family that had sympathized with them at the bottom of the pass—the old woman, the man, the young woman, and the two children—all together in a row, having received the plane's baptism of fire. The old woman was missing an arm. Draped across the chest of the young woman was one of the man's arms, which had fallen [off his body]. Next to them was a pot hanging over a hole in the ground where the remains of a fire were still smoldering. . . . The entire family, having set a fire to cook without thinking of the planes above, seemed to have been misrecognized [*oin*] as an enemy [contingent] and been annihilated.[26]

In this scene, the text sets up a complex series of crossings. Fleeing the advancing Chinese forces, the refugees lying dead in this scene have been misrecognized by the warplanes above as enemy soldiers. Their bodies have been mutilated, with parts of one intermingled with parts of another, and their pitiful fate moves Yŏngsuk to imagine that she is the one there on the ground.

This line of crossing, moreover, gains additional intensity as the text reaches its conclusion. After Yŏngsuk and Kyŏngja flee this scene, they encounter refugees retracing their steps on the path ahead. "You cannot go this way," a man tells her, adding, "A young woman cannot go [this way]," and she soon gets a similar warning from a middle-aged woman, who says, "Let's go back a different way! Since you're a young woman . . ."[27] Dumbfounded and then dispirited, Yŏngsuk understands these warnings to mean that women have been raped by unidentified assailants in the area down below, and she thus stands motionless in place, unable to decide which way to go. Just then, from up above Yŏngsuk hears the sound of yelling in Chinese, followed by sounds of gunshots, screams, and shrieking crows, and she realizes that some of the refugees who had told her to turn back as they passed by must have been seized—and probably killed—by Chinese soldiers back in the same spot that the planes shot down the refugee family. At this moment, her body—now shrouded in "complete darkness"—moves instinctively down the hill.[28] She does not know who she will encounter at the foot of the hill, but it scarcely seems to matter now.

In this way, Yu's text fundamentally blurs the binary structure of the Korean War by framing it, instead, in terms of a set of conflations. Insofar as US-UN planes misrecognize refugees as enemy combatants—that is, confuse friends and foes—their status as friends likewise becomes unclear. Indeed, by attacking refugees, they turn into foes whose violence overlaps with that of the antagonists they are fighting. And indeed, at the end of the text, the exact identity of the threat that stands at the bottom of the mountain no longer seems important. For refugees, the foreign forces on both sides of the conflict are sources of danger, and this leaves them with nothing but mountain after mountain—that is, trial after trial—in front of them.

In placing a woman and her daughter at the center of this tragic vision, Yu's story draws upon a history of gendered representations. As Kwŏn Myŏnga has discussed in detail, already in the immediate post-Liberation period, writers like Hwang Sunwŏn had produced influential and enduring modes of representation linking narratives of women's bodies under threat from outside—that is, narratives of sexual violence and exploitation—to narratives of a nation under threat from outside.[29] In such visions, which, Kwŏn further notes, gained additional power during the Korean War era, women—in particular mothers—were made to stand in for and embody an originary purity and innocence of the nation increasingly threatened by a "history of misfortunes" (*sunansa*) imposed by external forces and phenomena.[30]

This was, of course, the depoliticized representation that *Mother of the South*, the 1965 North Korean drama discussed in chapter 2, sought to contest in its militant rewriting of the mother figure in An Tongnim's "Hope." Yet it was not only in the North—and not only in the 1960s—that writers pushed in this direction. In fact, wartime literature in the South likewise challenged the representation of women as innocent victims of foreign aggression and thus surrogates for the natural, ahistorical purity of the nation. Yet it did so not by reimagining the figure of the mother but rather by reimagining the figure of the daughter in terms of strategic intervention.

In his 1951 story, "Mountain Demons" ("San tokkaebi"), the veteran writer Yŏm Sangsŏp likewise told the story of a group of female refugees traveling amid the dual threats of US-UN aerial warfare and Chinese and North Korean ground soldiers—all coded as foreign.[31] In Yŏm's text, Yŏngi's mother and her two daughters have decided to return to Seoul in order to wait out the end of the war in their family home. In doing so, they are presented with two options: travel by day or travel by night. At first, they assume that it will be safer to travel during the day, when Chinese soldiers are supposedly in hiding from US-UN bombing campaigns. Yet their calculus soon changes. Walking on foot, the ominous silence that has enveloped the landscape around them is soon broken by the sounds of crows shrieking and beating their wings up ahead of them. As in Yu's story above, what they soon encounter are "piles of corpses" (*songjang ŭi mudŏgi*)—including civilians—shot down by US-UN planes, and seeking refuge in a nearby village, they narrowly escape being caught in a house that has been destroyed by planes that have mistaken an old woman in a yellow blanket for a Chinese soldier.

Once again, the issue at stake here is the misrecognition of the refugee as an enemy, and it is likewise paired, once again, with a vision of parallel threats from the two antagonists. Already traumatized by the war, these events do not seem to shock them. Yet they do prompt them to alter their plan and travel at night. The group thus continues on in the dark, and as they make their way closer and closer to Seoul, the children's "eyes brighten and [their bodies] become lighter." As they pass by a mountainside, however, a set of voices calls out to them from the darkness and they "come to a halt as if their throats are being grasped firmly by a black, unseen hand, and their entire bodies quake as if electric waves are running through them."[32] These people "without shadows"— who are presumably North Korean soldiers, since they speak Korean—are the "mountain demons" of the story's title, and the threat that they pose is once again an unstated yet clearly understood threat of sexual violence. Yet whereas the protagonist in Yu's "Mountain Pass" is ultimately left with no choice but to walk toward this threat, the family in Yŏm's text is able to flee when US-UN planes enter the area, forcing the soldiers to hide.

Or rather, they are able to flee when the family's youngest daughter allows them to take advantage of the threat that the planes pose. The planes flying above are B-29 bombers; a child of the wartime era, she knows this well. She also knows that this means that they are not the threat that everyone else assumes. "Those are B-29s, so it doesn't matter," she subsequently tells her family; "they don't strafe with artillery."[33] Yet she does not do so until the soldiers have fled, allowing them (the soldiers) to mistake the type of challenge passing overhead. The story's resolution is thus deceptively simple. While it does indeed end upon a note of gratitude vis-à-vis the planes flying above, its more important intervention lies in the way in which the young Yŏngi appropriates the problem of misrecognition. Whereas Yu's text ends with an intensified powerlessness, "Mountain Demons" moves in the opposite direction. The decision between night and day is ultimately useless. What is necessary, instead, is a means of taking advantage of blurred identifications for one's own use.

In this sense, Yŏm's story stakes out new ground by attempting to open up a limited space for refugee agency. Yet for other writers, the type of strategic maneuver that it imagined could not offer anything other than temporary respite. This was, for example, a recurring point in the work of Kang Sinjae, one of the most important female novelists of this period. This was evident in her short and enigmatic "Fighter Plane" ("Chŏnt'ugi," 1952), a story about a middle school-aged South Korean soldier who, after being wounded in a battle that leaves his uniform covered in mud, is misrecognized by members of the North's Korean People's Army (KPA) as one of their own. Playing along, the protagonist is nursed back to health by the KPA soldiers, only to be killed by US-UN planes above.[34] This was also a central motif in "Foot of the Mountain" ("San kisŭk").[35] Written in 1952 and published in 1954, "Foot of the Mountain" tells the story of a young "daughter of the bourgeoisie" and her relationship with a North Korean military officer. The story takes place in the days surrounding the September 1950 retaking of Seoul by UN-ROK forces and it follows a young woman named Rein who flees the city with the Northern military officer who has fallen in love with her. The military officer, the text explains, was part of a group that took over Rein's family home during the occupation, and she pretended to be a communist sympathizer and allowed him to fall in love with her in order to protect her brother and father.

Kang's protagonist here makes strategic use of the possibilities of misrecognition. Yet this only produces a momentary reprieve, and problems soon arise. Now that the UN-ROK forces are pushing northward, the KPA and its sympathizers have begun to retreat, and the North Korean officer expects Rein to join him. If she tells the officer now that everything was an act, she believes that he will surely kill her, so she ends up with no choice but to keep up the act by changing into a KPA military uniform and following him. Rein's strategic use of misidentification here overflows its intended boundaries, and it also gradually comes to influence her own understanding of their relationship. Although her feelings toward the officer and his fellow retreating comrades are initially framed in terms of her position as an "outsider," they take a turn as the pair's path moves from the mountainside to the valley and into a timeless natural space:

A small spring was gurgling, "pung-pung-pung-pung."
    The officer cupped his hands together and drank some water. Then, standing with his head tilted to the side, he began to adjust the bandage on his arm.
    Rein felt what could be called the sympathy of humans who have placed themselves in the same danger. Or perhaps it was compassion directed at the attachment that the officer—a person with no family, no ties of human love—had felt toward her.
    (If that person were not a KPA soldier and if this weren't wartime . . .)
    Rein thought for a moment. Was it only fear which that rifle pointed at her heart last night had brought with it . . . ?
    Finding three or four late-season wild strawberries in the woods nearby the spring, Rein put them in her hand and held out the bright red, marble-like things to the officer. Taking them from her, the officer seemed to blush slightly for some reason.[36]

In this nonideological space where both of their watches have stopped, Rein's emotions move gradually from sympathy to attachment.

This is, for a moment, a hopeful point in the text that gestures toward possibilities for North-South reconciliation. Yet it is soon undercut as misguided. While the officer is away, two young KPA soldiers come down the mountain. One wants to abandon his position and go south; the other tries to stop him, eventually taking aim with his gun. When the defector turns to go anyway, his friend hesitates. Yet the officer returns to the scene at this precise moment; understanding the situation and acting without hesitation, he acts "mechanically" and kills the young soldier trying to flee. Rein is devastated and runs out onto the path at the foot of the mountain. At that moment, a US-UN warplane appears above and shoots her down in her KPA uniform:

> She felt a sense that the officer was following her. And at the same time, she saw the plane soar up with its body rising diagonally above the mountain peak.
>
> Its humongous wings barreled toward her. But she neither stopped walking nor tried to take cover on the ground.
>
> A terrifying sound enveloped the world.
>
> Rein collapsed.
>
> She felt the shock of a moving body splitting in half. (Me, of all people . . .)
>
> The world traced a semicircle and spun in front of her eyes. The slanted mountains, the fields and paddies that looked like they would spill over sideways, the deep blue sky that was flowing like a waterfall.[37]

The two sides of the conflict here descend upon Rein at once. They come at her from both sides, and the result is the fracture of her body into two pieces: a deathly reinscription of the binary structure of the Korean War and the Cold War, more broadly.

In Kang's text, therefore, the strategic use of misrecognition is powerful yet ultimately unworkable as a means to evade the violence of the conflict—and so, too, is the retreat to nature and its organic powers of mediation. Yet the story nevertheless gestures toward new critical possibilities. In "Foot of the Mountain," the deathly threats that descend upon Rein are not simply dual; they are both framed, in varying ways, as mechanical. And in this regard, the text intersects with a parallel set of visions and critiques then emerging in the South Korean literary and intellectual spheres as they engaged with texts and discussions from abroad.

MECHANISM, HUMANISM, AND THE TWO WORLDS CRITIQUE

For many writers during this period, the problem of engaged literature had to be seen in terms of global links and a global context—that is, a global literary project—and it was here that C. Virgil Gheorghiu's *The Twenty-fifth Hour* appeared on the scene in South Korea. First published in Korean translation in 1952, Gheorghiu's novel tells the story of a young Romanian farmer as he and his family are persecuted, manipulated, and abused by all of the combatants of the Second World War: the United States and Soviet Union alongside Nazis and their Romanian allies. In so doing, it argues—through the voice of Traian, a character in the text who is also writing a novel called *The Twenty-fifth Hour*—that in all of these forms of "Western Technological Civilization," the human is no longer dominant; rising up against its creator, the "technological slave" has "dehumanized" and "proletarianized" the human, who is now subject to the laws of the machine (automatism, uniformity, anonymity). As a result, "Western civilization" has now reached a point of assured destruction. It is now in its "twenty-fifth hour," which means that the time of potential salvation has already passed.[38]

As noted above, when Gheorghiu's novel appeared in South Korea in 1952, it gained widespread popularity. It went through three printings before the end of the war and six printings by 1955, and this popularity was linked, in part, to the novel's perceived contemporary relevance. The October 1952 advertisement quoted in the introduction to this chapter thus praised the text for its depiction of a suffering "precisely shared in common with us."[39] And indeed, in wartime South Korea, many readers saw in the novel a parallel vision of what domestic literature was depicting in the types of stories mentioned above: that is, stories of "friendly fire" and the dual threats of both sides of the "two worlds" conflict.

Gheorghiu's text, however, was not the only foreign novel being consumed in this way in wartime South Korea. In October 1951, the critic Cho Yŏnhyŏn published an extended review of George Orwell's *Nineteen Eighty-Four*, which had just been translated into Korean.[40] Framing the threats faced by the characters in Orwell's novel as problems of "mechanism" (*mek'anijŭm*) shared by Koreans in the contemporary wartime situation, Cho wrote as follows: "This kind of 'mechanism' necessarily means that the two powerful sides of the modern spirit, communism and highly developed mechanical civilization, result in the corruption of humanness [in'gansŏng]. That is, 'mechanism' takes the place of humanity. This is precisely the direction that communism, which places limits on human thought, and the mechanical civilization of modernity, which is heading toward a radical division of labor, are pulling the human . . ."[41] Although Cho did not explicitly name the "second side of the modern spirit" that he invoked here as capitalism, his description of a "mechanical civilization" that is "heading toward a radical division of labor" made the implicit reference here clear, and he thus suggested that the "two worlds" of the contemporary world were suffering from a common sickness that robbed the human of its proper nature.

This vision served as the foundation for the subsequent reception of Gheorghiu's text. The following year, Cho linked Orwell's novel to *The Twenty-Fifth Hour*, writing, "If contemporary despair in *The Twenty-fifth Hour* lies in the collective, total technocracy that does not accept the existence of the individual and the administrative technocracy that does not pay attention to the real truth but only places value on facts found on forms, then in *Nineteen Eighty-Four* it lies in the . . . rule-by-power in which the human is nothing more than a slave."[42] He then continued this comparison, noting that both texts shared "the conclusion that contemporary despair lies in the human's submission to an enslaved position in relation to the various forms of mechanism in contemporary civilization."[43]

This was a formulation echoed by many other critics. The critic Paek Ch'ŏl, Cho's longtime colleague-cum-antagonist, agreed that "Just as the crisis of the modern human is found in mechanism, so too are we seeing mechanism in communist society,"[44] and in another article from the same year, he wrote:

> The crisis of culture that has emerged today as we enter the second half of the twentieth century [should be] understood as something raised in the context of . . . the maturation and deepening of the historical conditions under which modern mechanism has shackled the human. . . . The author of *The Twenty-fifth Hour* experimented with [portraying] this human crisis in the particular situation of the POW, and that which the

protagonist encounters in the Germans, in the Soviet Russians, and later when he is taken prisoner by the U.S. military is [a form of] mechanism that abuses and ignores humanness.[45]

Similarly, critics like Im Kŭngjae also wrote of Gheorghiu's novel, discussing "mechanism" and a contemporary world in which "the existence of the human is surrendered to [a] total, collective mechanism and the individual—enslaved to machines and concepts—cannot express its value of existence."[46] For all of these writers, the contemporary age was not the age of ideological conflict but rather the age of the human's last stand. It was the age of a global struggle against the degradation of the human at the hands of "mechanism," and the conflict in Korea was thus world-defining.

Implicit in these discussions was the notion that the crisis of the contemporary age—insofar as it was defined by the threat of "mechanism"—called for a new form of "humanism" (*hyumŏnijŭm*). Indeed, for critics like Kwak Chongwŏn, the wartime age was, as he wrote in 1951, one in which the "counterweights to the brutalization and impoverishment of the human" had collapsed, and it was therefore one that necessitated a search for a "new human" and a "new humanism."[47] Renaissance humanism, Kwak argued, had performed a heroic deed in "breaking the religious oppression of the past" and allowing "the original nature of the human ... and its various desires to express themselves freely," and the humanism of the Romantic era, too, had fought valiantly against the "abstraction of modern European culture," which had undermined the "vitality" (*pallal*) and "soundness" (*kŏnsil*) of the human.[48] Yet in the contemporary age, Kwak said, these struggles to free human nature from its confines had unleashed a danger latent within them—the turn toward an inhuman "barbarism" (*yaman*)—and what was necessary was thus a new vision that moved beyond these centuries-old models of humanism.[49]

For Kwak, the proper meaning of humanism "varied according to time and place," and what was necessary for the Korean present was a humanism—and humanist literature—that emphasized social action rather than the expression or cultivation of human individuality. In this respect, his writing returned to the critiques of "pure literature" mentioned above, yet it also went beyond them by offering a specific model for such practice. Looking back to the 1930s, Kwak wrote that "what is desperately needed today in our literary world is the 'active humanism' [*haengdongjŏk hyumŏnijŭm*] that swept across the French literary world twenty years ago," and this meant that ". . . what must be depicted is the kind of human who, like the more than ten main characters who appear in André Malraux's *The Human Condition*, devotes her life to her task."[50]

For Kwak, the call for a return to Malraux's 1930s model of "active humanism" was a recurring theme across the wartime years, and its goal was the creation of a "new human type" whose strong and courageous will allowed her to translate her thoughts and ideals into direct action. Indeed, what Kwak located in Malraux was a model both for engaged writing and for a literature of engaged action in opposition to contemporary forces of dehumanization. The next year, he wrote, for example:

> The fact that France's André Malraux, during the Second World War, went to battle as a soldier and wrote manuscripts both on planes suffused by the sound of propellers and in the basements of buildings being destroyed by bombing [means] that he is a living model of "active humanism." And in the . . . action of the many characters who appear in his works *The Conquerors* and *The Human Condition*, hesitation and wavering are unable to be found no matter how hard one looks. The functions of consciousness and action have been instantaneously unified and interlockingly combined.[51]

For Kwak, then, the importance of Malraux's model was its emphasis on resolute action rather than opportunistic wavering, and he thus called upon Korean writers to take up this vision in order to both "resist barbarism and violence" and produce the type of "urgent faith" (*chŏlbakhan sinjo*) that the country needed to overcome the spiritual chaos of the war.[52]

Certainly, the point of invoking the World War II–era *Résistance* was to tie communism together with fascism as dual forms of "totalitarianism." This was a common trope frequently used in anti-communist discourse in South Korea as in other contemporary locations.[53] Yet the decision to tie the wartime call for engagement to André Malraux in particular was also peculiar because he had been the figurehead—despite his later association with Charles de Gaulle—of "fellow-traveler" cooperation with the Soviet Union and the communist movement more broadly. The reappropriation of the 1930s Malraux heritage in wartime South Korea was thus ambiguous and overdetermined: on the one hand, it linked the current struggle against communism to an earlier one against fascism, conflating the two; and on the other hand, it linked the ongoing struggle to a long-standing skepticism toward capitalism.

This tension was most evident in the work of the poet and critic Yang Pyŏngsik. Like Kwak Chongwŏn, Yang also looked back to 1930s France to call for a "new humanism" and to distinguish it from older ones. For Yang, writing in 1952, the present was "an age of transformation," "an age full of contradictions," and an age in which "the human [found itself] trifled with [nongnak] by irrationality and paradox."[54] As such, it was an age that "demanded the establishment of a new understanding and ideology of humanness and the ideal of the human."[55] For Yang, however, the essential core of humanism was "the spirit of liberation and the spirit of resistance," and the new humanism that he sought for the present was, like Kwak's, one that emphasized social action rather than inward-looking freedom. Looking back to Louis Aragon's assertion, he said, that "culture could not be separated from the human of reality," Yang argued that "social action is the concrete expression of the truest human."[56] The new humanism that Yang sought, therefore, was "active humanism," and it was, once again, a form of humanism traceable not simply to France in general but more specifically to writers like Malraux.[57]

For Yang, however, this link to Malraux and his colleagues—like his reference to Aragon—also meant that the call for a new "active humanism" was more complex than a call for simple anti-communist mobilization. In a late 1951 essay, Yang thus wrote of André Malraux's more recent activities:

> When the first general meeting of the UNESCO cultural division opened at the Sorbonne in Paris in 1948 [sic., November 1946], Malraux's lecture produced great international reverberations.... There he said, "What today are the values of the West? We have seen enough of rationalism and progress to know that these are not [them].... The first European value is the will to conscience; the second, the will to discovery." As always, he took up the position of defending "humanism," and he extolled, to the end, the values of Western civilization in opposition to the two "materialisms" [maetŏriarijŭm] of both Soviet "communism" and American "capitalism."[58]

Similarly, in a subsequent section of the essay dealing with the threat of nuclear annihilation, Yang noted that a wide range of European intellectuals, in reflections on trips to both the United States and the Soviet Union, had all voiced resistance to "uniform[ism]" (*hoegilchuŭi*) and to the forces that "ossify [*kyŏnghwa*] and dehumanize the human" that they had found in both of these societies,[59] and he further argued that European intellectuals were now in a position in which it had become necessary to "confront the political, scientific, and technological civilizations of the two worlds."[60] For Yang, moreover, the same applied to "us" in East Asia, and he thus called upon his colleagues to "travel together" (*pyŏngjin*) with European intellectuals in "confronting the two worlds" and preventing the human from being "subordinated" (*chongsok*), through them, to the "machine" (*kigye*).[61]

Although Yang was careful here to distinguish his position from "neutrality" (*chungnipsŏng*) in the current conflict—which, he said, was "no longer possible"[62]—he nevertheless approached a kind of "third way" or "third force" position vis-à-vis the broader Cold War binary. This was, at the time, a politically risky position. Yet it was also one that attracted significant interest in South Korea. Indeed, writing in 1953, the critic Kim Yongsŏng noted, "the term 'third force' [*che-sam seryŏk*] has become a catchphrase drifting through the streets. You can hear it in universities and, at the same time, in tea rooms."[63] Faced with the catastrophic effects of the Cold War conflict, "third way" imaginations gained deep relevance in South Korea. They also provided links to colleagues across borders.

As Su Lin Lewis has noted, "The idea of creating a 'Third Force' to counter the excesses of communism and capitalism emerged in the postwar era, both in Europe... and in Asia."[64] Such a position emerged in France,[65] and it was also promoted, as Lewis has further discussed, by the "radical wing of the post-war British Labour Party" as well as by a range of socialists in Asia: by Ram Manohar Lohia and U Kyaw Nyein, from India and Burma, respectively, and by the left wing of the Socialist Party of Japan, which split into its own party (the Left Socialist Party) in October 1951.[66] It was this last organization that played a particularly important role in the emergence of the above discussions in South Korea, and this was a result, as we will see below, of the particular exigencies of the wartime situation as well as of a particular set of intellectual links going back to the colonial period.

THIRD POSITIONS

The outbreak of the Korean War transformed the relationship between South Korea and Japan. As Jeong Min Kim has discussed in detail, "Within the first two months of the war, a triangular supply channel that connected the U.S., Japan, and South Korea had been established.... After the basic facilities were established in Korea, many perishable items and high-delivery cost supplies were procured from Japanese providers throughout the war. As the [General Headquarters Far Eastern Command] put it straightforwardly, *'Japan is our major supply base for Korea.'*"[67] This meant that regular flows of goods linked South Korea and Japan throughout the wartime era, and people, too, likewise circulated in both directions in this circuit as US military personnel arrived in Korea and departed Korea via Japan, where they also took "R&R" leaves.[68] Moreover, it was not only Americans and their wartime procurements that crossed these borders. The wartime crisis sent a significant number of writers and intellectuals from South Korea—and even some POWs from the North[69]—to Japan as newspaper journalists, translators, and personnel in the UN Command's psychological warfare unit, and this greatly expanded the flow of Japanese texts into South Korea.[70] It also made possible new forms of cross-border interaction.

Despite Yang's assertions, the project of a new humanism that rejected both communism and capitalism as rival forms of "materialism" was, in fact, not André Malraux's at all. Instead, this interpretation of Malraux came from a January 1951 article on Malraux's recent three-volume work, *La Psychologie de l'Art*, by the Japanese critic Komatsu Kiyoshi,[71] who here claimed, in terms taken virtually verbatim by Yang, that Malraux "extolled, to the end, the values of Western civilization in opposition to the politics and civilization of the two materialisms of Soviet communism and American capitalism."[72] For critics in Korea, Komatsu Kiyoshi would have been a well-known name from the colonial era. Komatsu had lived in France between 1921 and 1931, during which time he had befriended Malraux. Through his connection to Malraux, Komatsu had become the "Far Eastern Correspondent"[73] for the *Nouvelle Revue Française* upon his return to Japan in 1931, and after founding the journal *Kōdō* in 1933, he had focused his writing on introducing contemporary French literary and cultural trends to Japan.

In his writings for *Kōdō*, Komatsu focused on the emergence of what he called, by turns, a new French movement of "active humanism" (*kōdōteki na hyūmanizumu*) and "actionism" (*kōdō shugi*), first introducing these ideas in a 1934 text that began with a discussion of Ramon Fernandez's "Open Letter" in relation to the Comité de Vigilance des Intellectuels Antifascistes and then concluded with the following statement: "Today, with [Andre] Gide, Alain [Emile-August Chartier], [Jean-Richard] Bloch, [Jean] Guéhenno as its pioneers and [Ramon] Fernandez, [Louis] Aragon, [Pierre] Drieu La Rochelle, and [André] Malraux as its vanguards, the movement for a revolutionary, active humanism (in Fernandez's words) is the leading, representative [force of] a new French literary spirit."[74]

Komatsu here pointed to Fernandez as the originator of the term, despite the fact that he only appears to have used it once: in the title of a four-page contribution to the 1926 Les Cahiers du Mois collection *Examen de Conscience*, a text that was not, at all, about revolutionary tendencies but rather about reconstituting the totality of the individual.[75] However, in his 1935 monograph on the topic, Komatsu most forcefully linked this term to his friend André Malraux, to whom the book was dedicated,[76] and this association soon traveled to colonial Korea, where it was picked up by critics like Kim Osŏng.[77] When Kwak Chongwŏn and Yang Pyŏngsik called for a new "active humanism" modeled on Malraux, they were thus looking back to this 1930s history and heritage.

Yet this was not all that was happening, as Yang's implicit quotation of Komatsu's 1951 text on Malraux makes clear. In addition to looking back to the colonial past, writers like Yang were also looking to contemporary Japan: in particular, to its political domain, where Komatsu occupied a specific position. A contributor to the Left Socialist Party's journal, *Shakai shichō*, Komatsu Kiyoshi was one of the supporters of the "third force" position mentioned above. In a March 1951 roundtable published in *Shakai shichō*, Komatsu thus rejected the common wisdom that the world was already split into two and asserted that ". . . the force that is not subordinated to Soviet force yet does not follow what America says—this force is not weak but rather quite strong."[78] Describing the unity of this "third force" (*daisan seiryoku*) as a "problem of will" rather than formal political alliances, he further declared:

The thirteen countries of Asia—and in particular Nehru—are struggling desperately [on behalf of this program] at the UN in relation to the Korea problem [*Chōsen no mondai*]. . . . This is an issue of the weak nations [*jakushō minzoku*] resisting war for their mutual benefit and their survival. That is to say, this is resistance against American power and resistance against an inclination toward the Soviets. If this resistance collapses and the world splits into two as at Sekigahara, then I think this will be the beginning of the [next] war.[79]

For Komatsu, then, pursuit of a "third force" was not a question of detached neutrality but rather engaged resistance to both sides of the Cold War. It was likewise, he said, the only way to keep the current war in Korea from developing into a third world war; as in France, it served as a necessary "buffer zone" (*kanshō chitai*) between the two antagonists.

Komatsu also linked this position to the heritage of European anti-fascism of the 1930s–1940s. In a July 1950 article in *Sekai*, he looked back to the influence of the First International Congress of Writers for the Defense of Culture held in Paris in 1935, arguing that this event had provided essential momentum and inspiration for the formation of subsequent anti-fascist mobilization in Europe, including the French *Résistance*. Claiming that the reverberations of this conference continued to shape the words and actions of European intellectuals, he wrote: "Among the writers who, in the magazines of today, amid an international situation that continues [to produce] uncontrollable tension, are courageously speaking on behalf of French and European history and culture, humanism and democracy, and autonomy and neutrality, there are many who are still carrying this spirit in their bodies."[80]

Komatsu offered a similar vision in another article published the following month in *Risō*. In this article, "The Tradition of the Intellectuals' Front: On the Case of France," Komatsu once again reinforced the central importance of the 1935 Paris writers' conference as precedent, reproducing the statement quoted above from his *Sekai* article.[81] He then moved on to discuss the place of communist and noncommunist actors in the organization of the *Résistance* in France before turning to the post-1945 era. In contemporary France, Komatsu asserted, there were two movements that warranted particular attention. The first, associated with Jean-Paul Sartre and David Rousset, was the Rassemblement Démocratique

Révolutionnaire (Revolutionary Democratic Assembly), while the second, associated with Emmanuel Mounier and Gabriel Marcel, was the Personalist movement. And what connected the two, according to Komatsu, was their formation of a kind of "third force" (*daisan seiryoku*).[82] This was not the "third force" of contemporary party politics in France—it had a much stronger "revolutionary tendency,"[83] Komatsu argued—but it was perhaps the type of "third force" that Komatsu called for in Japan.

Komatsu was far from the only Japanese writer of these years to present this type of vision. This was evident, for example, in the work of the British literature scholar Nakahashi Kazuo. In his writing of these years, Nakahashi described Japan, as he wrote in May 1950, as "adjoining the border between the two worlds, in the same position as Germany and Belgium—or in fact, the countries of the West more broadly."[84] He thus sought cross-border collaboration, and by the time the Korean War had begun, he had likewise begun calling for the establishment of a "third position" (*daisan no tachiba*) in the ongoing Cold War conflict. In a March 1951 article, Nakahashi explained that intellectuals who sought such a position did not reject the ideology of communism but rather supported its ideals. What they rejected, he said, was the way in which these ideals were being pursued in the Soviet Union,[85] and he argued that "most intellectuals in the West and in Asia maintain a third position or something close to it."[86]

He then provided a set of examples, including the French Catholic novelist and *Résistance* veteran François Mauriac. As Nakahashi had discussed in an article from May 1950, Mauriac had recently made waves by writing, in *Le Figaro*: "It is not what separates the U.S.S.R. from the U.S.A. that should scare us, but rather what is common to them. Their ideological oppositions may be less daunting for us than their agreement concerning the scale of human values. These two technocracies that we believe to be antagonists pull humanity down in the sense of the same 'dehumanization.'"[87] This dual critique of technocratic dehumanization, Nakahashi argued, constituted a "third position" of the type he was calling for, and he pointed, likewise, to contemporary works of literature. In fact, the very first example that he invoked—even before mentioning George Orwell's bestseller, *Nineteen Eighty-Four*, which he discussed repeatedly during these years—was C. Virgil Gheorghiu's *The Twenty-fifth Hour*, which had appeared in a 1950 translation by Kawamori Yoshizō. Gheorghiu's text,

Nakahashi said, articulated a broad-based critique of "inhuman, Western technological society,"[88] and it thus fit his vision of a "third position."

The link between South Korean discussions of "humanism" and contemporary Japanese discussions of a "third force" or "third position" here circled back to Gheorghiu's novel, and given the context, this was far from surprising. As Yi Haengsŏn has noted, Kim's translation was not a direct one produced from the novel's original French publication but rather a "mediated" one (*chungnyŏk*) produced via Kawamori's 1950 Japanese-language translation.[89] This was acknowledged, at least implicitly, in the use of the term "supervising translator" (*ch'aegim pŏnyŏk*) next to Kim's name on the text's cover and publicity materials. It was also gestured to implicitly by contemporary critics like Paek Ch'ŏl, who questioned the appropriateness of the use of such a term for Kim in a late 1953 article published in the journal *Munye* regarding recent translated fiction.[90]

Moreover, it was not only the novel that was imported via Japan; critical discussion of it likewise entered South Korea from across the East Sea. This was most clearly demonstrated by the interview with Gheorghiu carried in the December 1952 issue of *Sint'aeyang*.[91] Although the interviewer was not listed, it was in fact conducted by Hirabayashi Taiko during her recent trip to Paris and published in the Japanese newspaper the *Yomiuri shimbun*.[92] This was intentionally obscured by the editors of the journal, who changed selected phrases. For example, the sentence in which Hirabayashi describes the great interest in *The Twenty-Fifth Hour* in Japan was changed, in the Korean version, to say "in Korea" rather than "in Japan." However, not all links to the novel's critical reception in Japan were so easily obscured, and what they would soon facilitate, as we will see below, was the emergence of a vision of triple critique: one in which the South Korean state was itself implicated; one that would finally produce, through its critical turn inward, the possibility of re-engaging with the "other side" of the Cold War order.

TRIPLE CRITIQUE AND THE TURN INWARD

For writers like Nakahashi, Gheorghiu's novel was a forceful call to reject both Soviet-style communism and American-style capitalism and reclaim the mediating ethos of Western "humanism." Yet the book also produced interest in those who sought a way forward through the crisis of the present that looked beyond the simple reconstitution of Western modes of thought, governance, and practice. Indeed, while the novel pronounced that it was too late to save "Western civilization," it did hold out hope for "the East." As Traian, the novel-writing son, states:

> This great light will probably come from the East, from Asia. But not from Russia. The Russians have bowed down and worshiped the electric light of the West and will suffer the same fate as the West. It is the Orient that, at length, will conquer this technocracy of ours and will keep electricity for lighting streets and houses instead of building altars to it and bowing down before it as Western society, in its barbarism, is doing today. The men from the East will not try to floodlight the hidden ways of life and the soul by means of neon tubes. They will subdue and control the machines of Technological Civilization by the power of their own spirit and genius, as a conductor controls his orchestra by means of an instinctive sense of musical harmony.[93]

Such a vision sparked interest, for example, in philosophers like Nishitani Keiji, who was associated with the Kyoto School and its long-term attempt to articulate a theory of subjectivity, knowledge, and experience that differentiated itself from and "overcame" a Western frame. This vision had become central to the fascist imaginary of wartime Japan, and it did not disappear in 1945. In a 1950 article focusing on Gheorghiu's novel, Nishitani thus took up the vision from the passage above, linking it to a "third perspective"[94] (*daisan no manako*) that went beyond American and Soviet critiques of each other's systems to identify an alternative to the "technological society of the West": that is, an alternative to that which bound them together.[95]

In his article, Nishitani compared Gheorghiu's despairing vision, in which "the human ruled by mechanism [*mekanizumu*] is considered a being who is no longer left with the 'human' strength to transform itself," to the hopeful vision of Henri Bergson, who saw in the "mysticism" of religion the power for the "human ruled by mechanism to transform itself into a human that rules mechanism."[96] He then critiqued both, locating an alternative in "the openness of the heart of those in the East to [that which] has been called 'void' [*kyo*] and 'space' [*kara*]." For Nishitani, this openness served as the basis for a form of "subjectivity" (*shutaisei*) that "could not be mechanized," and it likewise served as a resource for the ability to restart "even after the end of the twenty-fifth hour."[97]

Nishitani, however, was not the only Japanese thinker to take up Gheorghiu's hopeful vision of "the East" at this time. Despite occupying a very different political space, Takeuchi Yoshimi, a Chinese literature scholar and theorist who would soon develop a close link with Maoism, also displayed an interest in the novel and its vision of the human transformed, in Western civilization, into "nothing more than a single card in a humongous mechanism [*mekanizumu*]."[98] In Takeuchi's eyes, the way in which the novel had been taken up by Japanese anti-communists and Japanese "Asianists" (*tōyō shugisha*) like Nishitani was "laughable" (*kokkei da*).[99] At the same time, he was also critical of the interpretation of the text offered by the French philosopher Gabriel Marcel, who had championed the novel in France and written a preface for it. Marcel's preface, Takeuchi argued, had seized on the reference to Noah's Ark in the dying words of one of the text's main characters, Father Koruga, and used it to interpret the novel's message as one that was critical of Western civilization but still held out a glimmer of hope for its survival. This interpretive direction, Takeuchi wrote, was misguided, as the text located hope not in the West but rather in "the East."[100]

For this reason, Takeuchi continued, the text pinned its last glimmers of hope on the ordinary, "Ah Q-like" figure of Johann, the Romanian farmer who stands at the center of the novel and at the eastern edge of Europe,[101] and the words of Father Koruga, he likewise argued, resembled Judaism, animism, and even "Lao Tzu's descriptions of a primitive, communist, ideal society."[102] Takeuchi here attempted to reposition Gheorghiu's text both geographically and politically, and indeed, he was skeptical of the common, flatly anti-communist reading of the novel. The strong rejection of the Soviet Union displayed in the text, Takeuchi here argued, was influenced by the USSR's "family relationship" (*shinseki kankei*) with Romania, which produced an exaggerated sense of betrayal.[103] This linked the text, as Takeuchi argued in another October 1950 essay, to the contemporary experiences of those in the Eastern European people's republics,[104] and it suggested that its political position could perhaps be rethought.

As Takeuchi made clear in these essays, the exact contours of Gheorghiu's vision of "the East" were vague, and this allowed both for creative interpretation and a range of supplemental questions. The shorter of these two October 1950 essays by Takeuchi was published as part of a feature on the novel published in the journal *Tenbō*. The other essays in the feature were written by Takeda Kiyoko and Iizuka Kōji, and despite significant differences in perspective, they were structured around a similar question: What time is it in "the East"? This was the question that Takeda Kiyoko noted that she could not help but consider as she read the novel, and it was a question that she adapted as the title of her essay. If the West, as Gheorghiu's novel suggested, had already reached the twenty-fifth hour, then did this mean that the East had too? Or was the East living in an altogether different time? Alternatively, could the East be living in multiple times simultaneously: the twenty-fifth hour in the dimensions of its culture and society modeled on the West and another time—even "the first hour of a new 'human'"[105]—in its other dimensions?

In this essay, Takeda presented many more questions than answers. Yet these questions clearly linked her writing to that of her colleague in the feature, Iizuka Kōji, who was likewise concerned with the proper location of "our time" (*wareware no jikoku*). For Iizuka, the question of time—central, he suggested, to the novel's vision as a whole—was not as complex as it had been for Takeda; Japan's clock had stopped, he said, "around noon," at a point before the establishment of "the citizen."[106] Yet his vision nevertheless echoed and drew out Takeda's gesture toward imagining multiple times and temporalities. It also helped highlight, alongside Takeda's essay, the emergence of similar lines of questioning in wartime South Korea. In a three-part article serialized in in the *Sŏul sinmun* newspaper in early 1952, the novelist Yi Ponggu introduced his discussion of Gheorghiu's text by pointing to its robust reception in both France and Japan.[107] He also implicitly drew upon the Japanese discussions mentioned above regarding the current "time" in Asia, arguing that the local time in Korea was different than it was in the West. Yet whereas Iizuka located Japan in a time far less advanced than that of the West, Yi moved in the opposite temporal direction: that is, forward rather than backward.

Leveraging the Christian dialectical logic of death toward rebirth, Yi argued that wartime Korea had the potential to give rise to new hope and a new "gospel" (*pogŭm*) because its current time was more advanced—that is, its situation was more desperate—than anywhere else. "Compared to the tragedy of this land [i.e., Korea]," Yi thus wrote, "the suffering and tragedy of the Romanian people depicted in *The Twenty-Fifth Hour* is nothing. It is like the crying of a child."[108] He then continued, "This land, which is walking in silent submission amid indescribable sadness, pain, and despair that seem to be the first and last of their kind in human history, has gone beyond the twenty-fifth hour and is now struggling to survive in the holy land of the twenty-sixth hour."[109] Yi here pivoted in a different direction than his peers. Even as he preserved the vision of non-Western possibility presented in Gheorghiu's novel and its reception in Japan, he did so in a way that leveraged the crisis of the historical present rather than Korea's removal from it.

This vision allowed Yi to elude the rigid binaries of East and West presented in the discussions mentioned above, and it also allowed him to present a new vision of writerly practice. In the beginning of the article, Yi described writers as voices of "conscience" (*yangsim*) denigrated and mistreated by contemporary society, noting that "suffering necessarily comes to those who take up their pens and attempt to live uprightly."[110] On this basis, he further likened the figure of the writer to the figure of Jesus who had experienced "agony over the sins of humanity in the garden of Gethsemane," writing, "If the Gospels are a 'mirror' of humanity's conscience and atonement [*sokchoe*], the struggling that emerges from writers' sense of justice [*chŏngŭigam*] must be this sad land's gospel for the rebirth of the spirit."[111]

In subsequent sections of the article, however, Yi went on to suggest that the figure of the writer was not as self-righteous as this opening image suggested. In the wartime present, Yi wrote, the nation had experienced all-encompassing suffering. Yet this suffering also produced new possibilities and opportunities:

> To the extent that, in this moment today, we are living at the pinnacle of a tragedy in which there is no home without sadness, true love for our ancestral land springs forth to a degree that surprises ourselves. We can say that it is a good time and historical moment for the ancestral land, with its warm hand, to help us understand what true love is.
>
> "Do you hate your ancestral land?"

"Do you love your ancestral land?"

"Am I wandering around on the sidelines [literally, in the rear, *paehu*] of my ancestral land?"

"Am I loving my ancestral land, writhing so much that tears pour out?"

This continued self-questioning is an expression of... the fact that, touching the tree branches that grow on this ruined land and listening to the cries of crows amid such bitter—no, such intense—[word illegible] sadness, we are loving our ancestral land through silence and resignation. I am trying to learn... silence and resignation from this intense feeling of loving the ancestral land. This is because silence is always the path of accord with nature. It is also because it is always the path that, coming face to face with ruins, gives rise to a new gospel. And it is because it is the path that, amid the spirit of expectation for rebirth that overcomes economy, tries to listen to the gospel of the twenty-sixth hour.[112]

For Yi, the essential sprouts of love for the nation emerged spontaneously from suffering and hardship. Yet in order to develop them, one had to engage in this process of self-questioning. This was a continuous process that transformed silence and resignation into the words of a new gospel—and it was a process that writers like Yi had to learn.

Indeed, for Yi, self-questioning would be a long-term endeavor. In subsequent years, he would become known for a peculiar form of self-reflexive writing in which a fictional version of Yi himself appeared alongside the writer's real-life friends and acquaintances, often in tandem with quotations from their work, and in 1959, he would also adapt elements of the essay above into a short story called "Weeds" ("Chapch'o"), focusing on the visit of a Gheorghiu-quoting visitor from France who arrives in wartime Seoul searching for rebirth amid ruins.[113] Yet even before this time, other writers would also take up Yi's focus on self-questioning and self-critique, pushing it in challenging new directions via a familiar trope: wartime "friendly fire."

This was evident, for example, in a 1955 short story called "Roadblock" ("Ch'adan") by the young writer Kim Chunghŭi. "Roadblock" tells the story of a family's attempt to escape People's Army-occupied Seoul under the cover of night.[114] The story takes place during the days between the Inch'ŏn landing on September 18–19 and the retaking of Seoul by the UN forces on September 28, and the family's path out of the city thus takes them through a war zone structured by roadblocks. As in wartime stories, the threats that the family faces are necessarily dual: not only the threat of being discovered by soldiers and partisans loyal to the North but also the threat of being mistaken for the enemy by UN artillery and bombing campaigns. And indeed, while hiding from "enemy" foot patrols, the family accidentally enters the space between the KPA barricades and the UN forces: a space where, taking refuge in a foxhole, they are hit by a napalm shell from the UN forces that severely burns their two-month-old daughter, Yŏngok.

Up until this point, the story follows the model set by earlier stories of "friendly fire," but it soon diverges. Devastated by what has happened to Yŏngok, her mother, Hyeok, holds her tight. In contrast, her father, Chunho, attempts to convince her to abandon the baby and make a run for it. Before the war, Chunho worked as a newspaper reporter, and the text thus takes a turn here toward a third line of critique: an internal critique oriented toward the self-interested nature of the South Korean writer. Moreover, the opening up of this third dimension of critique and the link that it establishes between the two opposing military forces and the writerly self is further highlighted by the final sequence of the text. As the couple fights over what to do, they hear footsteps approach. They are soon discovered by a KPA patrol whose "vicious shadow" appears "in close up" and then begins to descend up on them, but at that moment, "a cluster of artillery fire completely obliterate[s] the existence of the bunker . . ."[115]

With this explosion, the text's presentation of dual and dueling threats from outside is once again highlighted; when the KPA patrol descends on the family, so too do UN artillery shells. At the same time, this concluding sequence also doubles down on the text's critique of the writerly self. Although the "existence of the bunker" is obliterated by the artillery shells, not all of those present die. At the very end of the narrative, a baby's crying can be heard from the ruins of the bunker and the reader learns that the young child, alone, has survived. This seemingly miraculous survival reinforces the text's critique of Chunho, who had wanted to abandon her to save himself, and this serves as the narrative's closing vision—one oriented not so much outside but rather within.

Such turns toward self-critique were not only visible in texts about writers but also, and perhaps most importantly, in texts focused on the other types of South Korean selves. For example, Han Yŏnghwan's "Return" ("Pokkwi"), also published in 1955, takes up a similar perspective while applying it to an ROK soldier.[116] Han's text once again begins with a familiar narrative frame. Having been separated from his unit, an ROK soldier travels alone through a region whose position he cannot determine. Soon, however, he discovers that he has fallen behind enemy lines, and he decides to take cover to avoid the gaze of the KPA soldiers who soon enter the area. Moreover, he soon learns that the KPA soldiers are not the only threat. Above his head, he observes the rhythmic action of US-UN warplanes, which begin circling around in preparation for an attack. Watching them, the protagonist's trust in his allies turns into "uneasiness" and he is "seized by the impulse to waive a white handkerchief,"[117] wondering whether he will be "misrecognized" (*oin*) as an enemy, as he has been before.

Once again, however, the story's critique is not merely dual. As he lays on the ground in hiding, the protagonist encounters a young counterpart from the KPA, with whom he develops a sympathetic bond of a particular sort: one that, as it turns from curiosity to care and care to "love," produces a sense of self-loathing. Watching this young KPA soldier, the protagonist sees that he is sitting beside a wounded comrade. Not too long ago, he too had found himself in a similar situation, but instead of caring for his friend, he abandoned him to save himself and complete his military mission. With his emotions reawakened by the KPA soldier before him, the protagonist now feels a deep sense of guilt. His critical gaze, that is, turns inward toward his own act of betrayal, and he is driven to make amends via his interactions with the young KPA soldier in front of him.

From early on, the protagonist has held his fire not simply because of his growing connection to the young KPA soldier but also because he knows that if he were to shoot him, he would end up alerting the soldier's comrades to his presence and become their target of attack. Eventually, however, the young soldier's sobs begin to sound like screams of the "devil," and this pushes him to cast aside his hesitation. At this moment, the protagonist accepts the full weight of his guilt, shooting the KPA soldier and bringing a hailstorm of fire upon himself from all sides. Having failed to follow through with his pledge to his South Korean friend to die side by side, he instead dies together with the North Korean soldier, undercutting the distinction between friend and foe, the South Korean self and the North Korean other.

In Han's story, therefore, the critical turn inward toward the self takes on increasingly challenging forms. By setting its sights on the figure of the ROK soldier, the South Korean state—of which the soldier is a representative—comes into critical focus in a powerful way. South Korean discussions of *The Twenty-Fifth Hour* here came full circle, drawing out the local implications of the text's critique of the Romanian authorities and their Nazi allies alongside the forces of the United States and the Soviet Union. They also extend beyond, as Han's story allows the North Korean other to emerge as a target for engagement, understanding, and affective suturing.

This had dramatic implications, and they were once more linked to contemporary developments in the critical domain. This is evident if we return to the critic Yang Pyŏngsik. In an August 1953 essay published in the journal *Sudo p'yŏngnon*, for example, Yang continued his assault on those who saw the role of the intellectual as standing on the sidelines of history, calling again for a new spirit of "active humanism" modeled after Malraux as well as after Sartre, Camus, and Gide. Yang here reprised his call for introspection among intellectuals—his call, that is, for intellectuals to turn their critical gaze inward toward their own mode of behavior—yet the content of this vision now took on additional contours. "Today," Yang wrote, "we must humanize and make subject to humanness the directionless 'capitalist,' who has become a machine of the system, and at the same time, we must impart a high humanness to the fanatical 'Marxist' as well."[118] Yang's vision here toward the possibility of ideological mediation and reengagement across the Cold War divide, and this was something that would only gain steam over the course of subsequent years. In order to make this possible, however, it would be necessary to draw on additional sources as moderating influences: not just the nonreligious existentialist writers referenced in Yang's article but also, and increasingly, their Christian colleagues.

THE TWO SIDES OF "EXTENSIVE CULTIVATION"

On December 3, 1956, Marie-Louise Abeille, then serving as Chief of the Education Projects Section at the United Nations Korean Reconstruction Agency (UNKRA) in Seoul, wrote to Ko Kwangman, the ROK's Vice-Minister of Education, to lodge a complaint against the Foreign Book Retail Store (FBRS), a private corporation established in Seoul a few years earlier with the joint support of UNKRA and the ROK Ministry of Education.[119] In late November of the same year, UNKRA's Supply Division had received three parcels of books for which the organization was unable to find "any trace of such an order,"[120] and what this shipment contained, Abeille and her colleagues thus surmised, was an "irregular" order by the FBRS "utilising illegally the name of UNKRA."[121] It was far from the first time that UNKRA had attempted to reign in the FBRS' use of the UNKRA acronym in its name, advertising, and correspondence.[122] Yet there was also something unique about this latest order that may have led Abeille to think that her colleagues in the South Korean state might finally take action. The three parcels in question had been sent by the Japanese Publications Trading Company in Tokyo, suggesting that the FBRS was using the UNKRA name—that is, strategically misidentifying itself—in order to do something that the ROK state had itself begun cracking down upon two years earlier: the procurement of Japanese texts, whose ideological character had come under an increasing amount of scrutiny.

The importation of Japanese texts had not always been seen by the South Korean state as inherently problematic; on the contrary, it had been integral to the project's original design. On September 19, 1952, the prominent Korean educator, official, and diplomat O Ch'ŏnsŏk wrote to the Pusan headquarters of the United Nations Korean Reconstruction Agency from Tokyo, where he was then serving as an advisor to the Psychological Warfare Section of the United States Army. Addressed to UNKRA Program Director Donald K. Faris, the letter requested support for a seemingly unlikely project:

> I am writing this letter to you [on] behalf of [the] Federation of Educational Associations of Korea ... [which] has been requested by its

members and schools throughout the country to purchase for them books on various subjects written in Japanese. Since the end of the war few new Japanese books were available to Korean teachers, and much of whatever books that had been left over from the Japanese days were either destroyed or lost during the current war. There have come some English books to our schools but not many of our teachers or students could read them.... I am wondering if your organization would view this matter with favor and buy the books for us in Japan and ship them over to Korea. The Federation will be glad to pay for them in Pusan or Seoul. A list of books they need will be furnished by the Federation.[123]

A proven and trusted ally of the American presence in Korea, O's appeal soon bore fruit. Stewarded by Paek Nakchun (outgoing ROK minister of education) and Ch'oe Kyunam (president of Seoul National University), UNKRA's Foreign Book Retail Store program was signed into being in late 1952 and early 1953. Allowing teachers, students, and medical professionals to use public procurement and currency networks to request and purchase foreign—primarily Japanese—books, it served the basic purposes outlined in O's letter via a slightly different set of institutional arrangements.

Although funding for FBRS imports ultimately came from UNKRA, the plans for the program itself originated in a peculiar wartime space of intergovernmental negotiation. Beginning in October 1951, representatives from the ROK Ministry of Education, the United Nations Civil Assistance Command, Korea's Civil Information and Education Section, the United States Information Service, and the United States Embassy gathered each week at the office of Paek Nakchun, the ROK minister of education, for the meeting of the Education Advisory Committee (EAC). A graduate of Princeton and Yale, Paek was one of the most important and respected US allies in the Korean educational field. An internal memo from the Committee for a Free Asia—the CIA-funded nonprofit organization later called the Asia Foundation—thus wrote, for example, "We believe Paik [Paek] to be the outstanding cultural and educational leader in Korea today and as such worth extensive cultivation by CFA."[124]

He was also an adept diplomatic navigator. At the EAC meetings, the plan for the FBRS was called "UNKRA Project 17F," and it was discussed for the first time around February 1952.[125] The project was given an initial budget of $50,000 and it was designed as a three-way joint venture between UNKRA, the ROK Ministry of Education, and three private educational associations. Under the agreement finalized in March 1953, eligible consumers would submit book requests to the Ministry of Education, which would vet them, collate them, and submit them to UNKRA. After being approved, they would be sent out for procurement from private sources in US dollars. The books would then be sent in bulk to UNKRA in Korea and forwarded to Seoul for sale in the FBRS, a private entity jointly incorporated by the three educational associations. The store, located in T'ongin-dong (and later Ogin-dong), Seoul, would sell the books for purchase in hwan, with prices calculated based on the costs of procurement plus shipping, and then send 80 percent of the proceeds back to UNKRA; the remaining 20 percent would be kept by the store to cover its operating expenses.[126]

The first shipment of books ordered for the FBRS arrived in Pusan between May and June 1953, via a Japanese merchant ship called the *Yurishima Maru*.[127] The second shipment arrived on the *Kaishin Maru* in July, and together these two shipments brought at least 8,893 Japanese-language texts to Korea.[128] These texts ranged across a wide array of genres, disciplines, and audiences: reference works, pedagogical texts, general interest monographs, scholarly monographs. This complex mix, moreover, was deepened after the first two shipments of texts; subsequent orders, which arrived in Korea in late 1953 and early 1954, continued these trends in Japanese-language procurement while complementing them with English, French, German, and Russian-language texts. For example, orders submitted in August and September 1953 called for 900 Japanese books, 700 English books, 400 French books, and a small assortment of German and Russian texts alongside film and office equipment.[129]

As this brief description suggests, the program was flexible enough to be useful to a wide range of scholars; in 1954, it was thus given an additional $31,000, which allowed the program to remain in operation until 1956.[130] Yet what is significant here is that the program's expansive and flexible scope also caused problems. In April 1954, government fears of "seditious" texts entering the country through Japan provoked new crackdown measures and a series of confiscations whose scope exceeded those of previous years.[131] And while it is hard to know whether the stores targeted at this time were, in fact, in possession of leftist texts, the FBRS, for its part, had a good many. Surprisingly enough, the lists of books requested—and delivered—to the FBRS included a much wider range of texts than one might think, including its fair share of Marxist and socialist texts, which formed the other side of the project's "extensive cultivation."

These texts were present from the beginning. The first two shipments of books that arrived on the *Yurishima Maru* and the *Kaishin Maru* thus included: thirty out of thirty-three volumes of the Japanese translation of the *Selected Works of Marx and Engels*, edited by the Marxist-Leninist Research Center; Sakizaka Itsurō's five-volume translation of Marx's *Capital*; Friedrich Engels's *Ludwig Feuerbach and the End of Classical German Philosophy*, translated by Ide Takashi and Fujikawa Satoru; Leon Trotsky's three-volume *History of the Russian Revolution*, translated by Tsushima Tadayuki; and eleven out of the thirteen volumes of the *Complete Works of Joseph Stalin*.[132] The program also ordered the five-volume translation of the *Selected Works of Mao Zedong*, which was listed by the publisher as out of stock and therefore not delivered.[133] These shipments also included an array of works by recent and contemporary Japanese Marxists and socialists: Kawakami Hajime, Sakizaka Itsurō, Umemoto Katsumi, Kobayashi Ryōsei, Tsushima Tadayuki, Uehara Senroku, Ōtsuka Hisao, Aihara Shigeru, Miki Kiyoshi, Hani Gorō, Uno Kōzō, and others.[134]

In both of these shipments—as in later orders—Marxist and socialist works amounted to a small portion of the total requests. Yet such requests continued, and by mid-1954 the numbers of copies requested for such texts were increasing. Among other items, then, requisition PS 17 of April 8, 1954, called for ten copies of Uno Kōzō's *Theory of Crisis* (*Kyōkōron*), twenty copies of Hani Gorō's *Citiens Have a Right to Know* (*Kokumin wa shiru kenri ga aru*), twenty copies of Yamada Sakaji's *Freedom and Necessity* (*Jiyū to hitsuzen*), thirty copies of Yamada Sakaji's *Ideology and Practice* (*Shisō to jissen*), thirty copies of Komatsu Setsurō's *A Critique of German Idealism* (*Doitsu kannenron hihan*), thirty copies of Amakasu Sekisuke's *A Critique of Contemporary Philosophy* (*Gendai tetsugaku hihan*), and one hundred copies of Takakuwa Sumio's *On Individuality* (*Kosei ni tsuite*).[135] Although we cannot be certain, these numbers are the likely reason that this order, in particular, was "turned down by the ROK Office of Planning because of the Japanese books" and all Japanese-language procurement through the program subsequently ceased.[136]

They are also likely the reason why the ROK Office of Planning, as Abeille subsequently put it, "was not very keen on the continuation of the Store through UNKRA."[137]

To be sure, many of these texts were likely used to produce anti-communist critiques. This was the case, for example, in the political scientist Yang Homin's landmark 1956 monograph, *The Theory and History of Communism: A Critique of Marxism-Leninism* (*Kongsanjuŭi ŭi iron kwa yŏksa: Marksŭ-Reninjuŭi ŭi pip'an*).[138] Yang's study was one of first academic accounts of the history and theory of communism published in South Korea, and it relied heavily upon Japanese translations of Marxism as well as on works of Japanese Marxism in order to ground its critiques. Yet the double-digit requests in the April 1954 order strongly suggest that interest in these texts was more widespread than we might think, and the fact that the importation of Japanese texts through the FBRS was shut down by the ROK state demonstrates that the influx of these texts was perceived as a threat rather than a part of the normal functioning of an anti-communist polity. Of course, this does not mean that those who requested these texts "crossed the line" of the Cold War ideological conflict. Instead, what it suggests is that they were attempting to undermine its stability. And indeed, if we focus on the text requested in the largest numbers—Takakuwa Sumio's *On Individuality*—we can get a sense of what this may have meant.

One of the protagonists in the Japanese "subjectivity" (*shutaisei*) debates of the late 1940s and early 1950s, Takakuwa was a Marxist philosopher with training and expertise in the Christian philosophy of medieval and early modern Europe.[139] Although these two elements of his thought may appear contradictory, his project was, in many ways, aimed at bridging the gap between them by framing central features of Marxist revolutionary thought—including its "socialist humanism" or "people's humanism"—as reformulations of developments in earlier Christian thought. He thus argued, for example, that the philosophy of Thomas More was responsible for transforming humanism into a social project[140] and that Martin Luther, for his part, had transformed the project of human freedom into a historical rather than natural one.[141]

Most importantly, however, Takakuwa used Blaise Pascal to argue that a proper vision of the "subject" in revolutionary Marxism also had to be understood in terms of the visions of the social self and of community developed in Christian existentialist thought.[142] As J. Victor Koschmann has noted:

> According to Takakuwa, there were two great traditions in European ideas of death: the Greek, which included Lucretius and Montaigne, and the Christian, which included Pascal. It was the Christian view that implied a subjective (*shutaiteki*) approach to death. For example, Pascal admitted that he felt no personal connection to the death of the Spartans, but he did feel strongly linked to the martyrs' deaths. That is, he belonged to their same body, and thus felt that "their resolve (*ketsui*) is our resolve." As Takakuwa explained in other essays, the religious subjectivity of Christianity was premised on common membership in a "sacred society," understandable as the body of Christ . . .
>
> . . .
>
> However, Takakuwa is not content to stop with Christian *shutaisei*, precisely because the "body of Christ" is an invisible, that is to say ideal, society rather than a "real" one. Therefore, his third philosophical approach to death, and by extension, to *shutaisei* is formed from the materialists' recognition of real connections between "individual subjects" and the social subject in the form of class consciousness and common interests.[143]

For Takakuwa, the Christian heritage of Pascal—that is, his existential analysis of the Christian subject and its death-bound limit—served as an essential springboard for the social solidarity and collective subjectivity of Marxism. The line linking Christianity and Marxism here led through Pascal and through the heritage of Christian existentialism's analytic of the bounds of human existence, and this was a path that would soon take on new importance in South Korea.

As noted above, the one hundred copies of Takakuwa's *On Individuality* were never delivered to South Korea; this request was terminated by the ROK state as part of the ban on Japanese-language imports that it implemented in 1954. Yet the fact that they were ordered demonstrates a demand for Takakuwa's particular brand of philosophy—that is, his attempt to link Marxism and religious existentialism—and Korean critics soon made this link without him. Indeed, by 1956, when the South Korean journal *Sasanggye* published an article by one of these thinkers, Paul Tillich, calling for a synthesis of Kierkegaard, Nietzsche, and Marx in order to combat "depersonalization in a technical society," it followed this with the publication of related calls by Korean philosophers and critics, as we will see below.

A NEW SET OF MIRRORS

Existentialism was by no means new to Korean readers and writers in the 1950s. During the colonial period, when Koreans were educated in a Japan-centered academic context, existential philosophy from the Germanic-language world—in particular, the work of Martin Heidegger, Karl Jaspers, Herbert Marcuse, and Søren Kierkegaard—had been extensively discussed and debated. Likewise, Jean-Paul Sartre's fiction and criticism had been introduced in the immediate post-Liberation 1940s, when it was largely dismissed for being overly speculative and individual focused.

During the Korean War, however, the situation changed. Given the wartime discussions of the French *Résistance* mentioned previously, writers in South Korea looking for creative inspirations from abroad took up with new interest the work of French existentialists who had participated in this movement. And they did so, once again, within the context of the wartime critique of "mechanism." In the above-mentioned 1952 article by the critic Paek Ch'ŏl, for example, the problem of "mechanism" had appeared not only in relation to Gheorghiu but also in relation to other contemporary writers. The broader context for the statement quoted above thus read:

> Wherever it goes, the human has already lost the ability to escape the devilish hand of such mechanism and cannot help but run into a dead-end wall. Early on, Sartre's "The Wall" symbolized this crisis of the human. The author of *The Twenty-fifth Hour* experimented with [portraying] this human crisis in the particular situation of the POW, and that which the protagonist encounters in the Germans, in the Soviet Russians, and later when he is taken prisoner by the U.S. military is [a form of] mechanism that abuses and ignores humanness. The critics of the new year propagating this despair are Camus and Gheorghiu.[144]

Paek here linked Gheorghiu, Sartre, and Camus under the banner of the threat of modern "mechanism," and indeed, similar statements had been written about Camus at this time. In 1952, Camus's *The Plague* was published in installments in *Sasang*, the precursor to *Sasanggye*. Translated by Yang Pyŏngsik, the poet and critic previously mentioned, this serialization was interrupted before its completion, with a full translation by Yi Ch'obu appearing the next year. Yet these initial installments of Yang's translation were nevertheless significant, and they overlapped with another work, the poet and critic Cho Hyang's "Artistic Trends of the Twentieth Century," serialized in the same journal.

A wide-ranging work, Cho's essay closed its narrative with a discussion of existentialism, which he contextualized in relation to Gheorghiu's *The Twenty-fifth Hour*. Gheorghiu's novel, Cho wrote, clung to hope despite its portrayal of "modern mechanism's arrival at a dead-end time where salvation was no longer possible,"[145] and he then turned to Sartre and Camus, noting, in relation to the latter writer, the "psychological anarchism" of *The Stranger*, its depiction of "resistance to the mechanism of society that seeks to deal, via the vulgar arithmetic of ethics and inference, with the incalculable and unknowable psychological state deep within the individual."[146]

During the war, therefore, Korean writers reengaged with the critical and creative possibilities offered by French existentialist writers like Camus and Sartre, and they also paid new attention to French existential philosophers of the Christian sort. As Korean writers were no doubt aware, Gheorghiu's novel had become popular in France with the assistance of a laudatory preface by the Catholic philosopher Gabriel Marcel. And indeed, when *The Twenty-Fifth Hour* entered South Korea, its Christian content was hardly ignored; such content, voiced by the character of Father Koruga and reinforced by the novel's praise by Marcel, was central to its reception, for example, by the novelist Yi Ponggu, mentioned above.

Wartime interest in French existentialism was thus not confined to the literary or secular domains—and neither was it confined to contemporary writers. Looking back to the origins of existentialist thought, writers and critics in the South also directed new attention toward Blaise Pascal. This was evident in the work of the historian Yi Haenam. Writing in the *Kyŏnghyang sinmun* newspaper in 1954, Yi described the contemporary age as a "deformed" period of "contradictions" in which a humanism that promised to "liberate the human, render human reason all powerful, and expressed unlimited optimism regarding the autonomous ethicalness of human practice" emerged side by side with "collectivist apparatuses of production" and their process of "limitless, mass-production" that "transformed the individual into a composite part and enslaved the human."[147] This made the contemporary age an "unfortunate" era of crisis.

For Yi, however, the goal could not simply be to resolve this contradiction. After all, as Yi noted in an article on Pascal also published in the *Kyŏnghyang sinmun* in 1954, the human was a tragic being because she was a being whose existential "riddle" could not be solved via human reason or human self-actualization: "Historians often record the 'liberation of the human,' philosophers often perceive [the attainment of] 'complete individuality,' and 'new humanisms' often declare a 'new humanness.' But the human nevertheless remains incomprehensible to itself."[148] The "riddle" of the human was unsolvable, a reality that pointed to the limited, imperfect nature of human power and understanding. This could be a source of unending uncertainty, anxiety, and despair. But it could also make possible a new approach to religious faith. Because of the limited nature of human power and understanding, Yi explained, Pascal understood that there was no way that certainty regarding God's existence could be obtained. Yet a "wager" of faith was still possible—and such a wager, Yi emphasized following Pascal, was the only workable path forward for the contradictory nature of human existence.

Via Pascal, Yi here gave voice to a new critical potential offered by religious existentialism: that is, the critique of the human and an emphasis on the limits of its power and ability. The bounded, limited nature of the human here came into critical focus, and what it offered was not merely new philosophical opportunities but new political ones as well. The literary critic Yi Hwan thus began his 1954 essay on Pascal as follows:

> His nostalgia-filled gaze is directed toward the sky. At times, it reaches even beyond the sky, fathoming the limits of the star-engraved heavens. Pascal, riding a marvelous light and ascending into the far, far distance.
> But the more he does so, the more he is with us. His wounded, menaced spirit produces ripples in our hearts. This does not happen in the world of logic or form. These waves vibrate forth from the heartstrings

of simple life. They are waves of life like the trembling of the naked proletariat in the empty space where logic has deteriorated and form has collapsed. This means that in the beginning, the flow of the pure heart throbbing with the breath of God was a wave snaking around invisible corners of human history.[149]

Yi here linked Pascal's mode of Christian existential thought to both the social and the historical: that is, to both the bare life communality of the proletariat and the transformative nature of human history. He also emphasized that Pascal's critique of Cartesian rationalism was not one that indulged in the "endless mockery of speculation" or "meandered in metaphysics."[150] In his focus on the heart, Pascal sought out "you and me, living humans rather than metaphysical beings," and he was thus not, Yi wrote, one of the "bourgeois who removes himself from the flow of things and reposes in serene contemplation."[151]

In this way, taking up Pascal's critique of humanism was not premised upon a retreat from social engagement. Neither did it preclude creative connections with other forms of contemporary thought. In the article on Pascal mentioned above, Yi Haenam had explained the "wager" of faith as one that had a seemingly contradictory relationship with human reason, and indeed, for Pascal, human reason was limited and imperfect, leaving it unable to achieve any certainty regarding the existence or nonexistence of God. Given this uncertainty, however, it was nevertheless possible to rationally assess the potential gains and losses of both belief and disbelief. If God did not exist, then whether one believed or not, one's fate would remain the same. Yet if God did exist, there would be a great deal of difference between the fate of a believer and a nonbeliever. Therefore, the only rational choice, Pascal suggested, was to believe despite one's lack of certainty, and this allowed him to counter the position of anti-religious rationalists in a new way. Although many rationalists had rejected faith because the existence of God could not be proven, Pascal here turned the tables, arguing, Yi said, that the only "rational" (*isŏngjŏk*) path was that of faith. Given the "wager" analysis outlined above, rejecting faith was itself "irrational" (*pi isŏngjŏk*)—a useless attempt at stubborn "heroism" (*yŏngungjuŭi*)—and the result was an ironic situation in which many of those who "threw off the 'yoke of religion' and liberated humanness . . .

suffered this 'liberated humanness' so much that they had no choice but to drag their old and tired bodies back to religion's door."¹⁵²

In Yi's account of Pascal, rationalist resistance to religion was fated not only to collapse but also to lead—paradoxically enough, via reason itself—back to religion, and this vision of atheist resistance transmuting into religious acceptance became a recurring feature of discussion of existentialist thought during these years. Writing in *Hyŏndae kongnon* in 1953, for example, the critic and translator Im Ch'un'gap, a frequent commentator on Kierkegaard, suggested that the atheistic and theistic forms of existentialism were closely linked, with the atheistic leading toward the religious: something he referred to as the affirmation of God "through negation." "This is how I see the theory of salvation uniting existentialist writers," he wrote, continuing, "Only when the human takes her absurdity and anxiety upon herself as truly her own can she give herself up."¹⁵³

Im here drew upon Kierkegaard's vision of the dialectical and ultimately paradoxical nature of Christian faith, and other contemporaries likewise applied this vision to the internal structure of existentialism as a philosophical movement. In a 1955 discussion of Franz Kafka, the critic Hong Sajung thus wrote:

> The words of Emmanuel Mounier, who said that existentialism (whether Christian or atheist) signifies the return of the religious, may indeed be going too far. However, it is an undeniable fact that the trajectory of existentialism, after passing from religion through agnosticism and atheism, is pulled back toward religion. The stream [of thought] that, in the space where God is negated, opens up the limits of human action for God's restoration and attempts to find God in the direct intersection with reality by taking up the will ... to pierce through [existential] anxiety—this can be called the spiritual domain of the 20th century.¹⁵⁴

For Hong, religious and atheistic existentialism were not two separate streams of thought. Instead, one led in its development to the other, and a similar point was echoed by philosophers like Kim Hyŏngsŏk, who saw in existentialist thought not only the possibility of bringing philosophy back into consonance with religion in "worldview unity"¹⁵⁵ but also the possibility of "overcoming"¹⁵⁶ humanism and the forgetting of the dual nature of the human as both material and spirit that had led, among other things, to the rise of "mechanism."

At the same time, linking atheistic thought to the religious in this way did not always produce expected outcomes, and this became most evident, perhaps paradoxically, in the theological domain. In 1950s Korea, discussion of religious existentialism did not end with Christian philosophers like Pascal, Kierkegaard, and their followers. On the contrary, influential commentators on this philosophical trend included theologians like Kim Hat'ae, who published in specialized theological journals as well as general intellectual ones like *Sasanggye*, and his work further linked the philosophical and theological domains by defining neoorthodox Protestantism—the Protestantism of Karl Barth, Emil Brunner, Reinhold Niebuhr, Paul Tillich, and others, whose revelation-centered rejection of the secularizing tendencies of previous decades drew heavily upon Kierkegaard to emphasize the unbridgeable gap between the "wholly depraved" nature of the human and the "wholly Other" nature of the divine—as "theistic existentialism."[157]

Like many of those mentioned above, neoorthodox theologians identified humanism as the root cause of the crisis of the present. For example, the theologian Chi Tongsik, a frequent contributor to *Sasanggye* who was strongly influenced by the thought of Karl Barth, thus proclaimed: "If we look into the origins of the [forces of] mechanical civilization, class conflict, and strong state power that have planted the seeds for the crisis of the contemporary age, we find that all of these things come from human freedom, or in other words, from humanitarianism [*indojuŭi*]. Therefore, in order for the human to regain a proper humanness, a perspective that overcomes the humanitarianism of humanism [*in'ganjuŭi*] is necessary."[158] More forcefully, he emphasized that the human desire to break away from God and assert its independence was not simply a historical mistake but rather a facet of human sinfulness. Writing in the inaugural issue of *Sasanggye*, Chi therefore argued that a proper understanding of the nature of the human had to begin from its existence as a "being tethered to evil" (*ak e maeyŏ tallin chonjae*), a "sick being" (*pyŏngjŏk chonjae*) bound by nature to sin.[159]

At the same time, neoorthodox theologians could also be quite expansive in the range of thinkers and influences that they brought into their writing, and this was especially the case with Paul Tillich. A strong influence on Kim Hat'ae, Tillich's work was regularly discussed in both general intellectual and specialist theological publications during these years. Korean publications also reprinted his work in Korean translation. This included a 1953 article published in translation in *Sasanggye* in March 1956,[160] in which Tillich looked back to existentialism as a movement of "rebel[lion] in the name of personality against the depersonalizing forces of technical society."[161] For Tillich, this rebellion was still very much a relevant and necessary one, and he saw it, as a result, as a project to which contemporary Christianity was called to contribute in a leading fashion.

At the same time, in looking back to existentialism for inspiration, Tillich by no means privileged the theistic heritage of Kierkegaard alone. Side by side with Kierkegaard's essential contributions, Tillich also looked to Nietzsche, emphasizing his vision of the "creative power of life"—and he likewise looked to Marx, who he here presented as an "existentialist": "Marx saw much more clearly than Kierkegaard that it is not a system of thought, but the reality of modern society which is responsible for the reduction of the person to a commodity. His famous descriptions of the dehumanizing effects of economy in the industrial age center around the proletariat, but they are meant for all groups of society. Everyone, insofar as he is drawn into the all-embracing mechanism of production and consumption, is enslaved to it, loses his character as person and becomes a thing."[162] For Tillich, the problem of the "technical society" was not simply a problem of life, faith, and belief. It was also a problem of material structure and its transformation of human character, and it thus allowed him to reach back to his own Marxist heritage to expand the bounds of existential thought.

In tandem, Tillich's vision of syncretic interconnections between different forms of thought took on a substantially more generous form than it did in the visions mentioned above. "Looking back at the three great movements of protest against dehumanization in the technical society," Tillich wrote, referring to Kierkegaard, Marx, and Nietzsche, "we can say that he who fights today for the person has to become an heir of all three of them."[163] In Tillich's thought, therefore, the religious critique of contemporary technological society did not operate alone. One needed Kierkegaard and his Christian existential thought, but one also needed his atheistic colleagues: Nietzsche, Marx, and their followers. Under the banner of existentialism and its critique of the technical society, Tillich here linked Christianity and Marxism in a way that not only recalled the work of thinkers like Takakuwa Sumio but also intersected with the work of writers active in South Korea.

The March 1956 issue of *Sasanggye* that included Tillich's essay also included a piece by An Pyŏnguk, a philosopher who was one of Korea's earliest experts on Kierkegaard and would soon become one of the editors at the journal. An had translated work by Reinhold Niebuhr and others for *Sasanggye* in 1954, and the following year, he had published an introduction to existentialism that drew on the work of two Japanese philosophers: the Kyoto School philosopher Kōsaka Masaaki; and the Marxist philosopher Akizawa Shūji.[164] An adaptation of this 1955 article on existentialism, An's contribution to the March 1956 issue of *Sasanggye* was one installment of an ongoing serialization of "lectures" on contemporary thought, and its goal was not only to introduce the main currents in recent philosophical debates but also to seek out a way of dealing with the crisis of the present. In one of the concluding installments of the lectures series, An thus quoted Marx's famous dictum, "The philosophers have hitherto only interpreted the world in various ways; the point, however, is to change it," setting the stage for an unexpected form of anticapitalist critique.[165]

Like many of those mentioned above, An called for a "new worldview" that would push back against the transformation of "human control of machines" (*in'gan ŭi kigye chibae*) into "machine control of humans" (*kigye ŭi in'gan chibae*).[166] According to An, science and technology—created as tools for human use and convenience—had become uncontrollable "giants"[167] whose power, automaticity, and mass productivity were threats to both the freedom and existence of the human. The threat of the technological, An wrote, was the threat of the human's "extinction by the power of the civilization that it had created itself."[168] There could be nothing more tragic than this, An argued, and he called for a new approach to technology that neither rejected it entirely nor accepted it uncritically. Technology once again had to be subjected to human flourishing and benefit—and toward the project, following the apostle Paul, of transforming the "old human" into a "new human."[169]

A new approach to technology, however, was only one aspect of An's project of a new worldview. For An, the tragedy of the present world was also the "tragedy of Mammonism."[170] "You cannot serve God and Mammon," the Gospel of Matthew had noted, and for An, a proper form of human society could not coexist with the worship of money, as such Mammonism, An noted, inevitably demanded the sacrifice of "personality" and "conscience." It led to dehumanization through "the commodification of the human,"[171] and the new worldview that An sought thus had to be one that "overcame the tragedy of Mammonism." More broadly, it had to "overcome the capitalist spirit, which stands upon Mammonism."[172] In turning toward a Christian-inspired critique of Mammonism, An's thought here also turned toward anti-capitalist critique, and this link between anti-capitalism and Christianity was reinforced by his vision of an alternative society. Envisioning a new worldview based upon love, cooperation, and Kropotkin-inspired "mutual aid,"[173] An called for a cosmopolitan society exceeding the bounds of nation and ethnicity where the only divisions, as in the thought of the Christian socialist Henri de Saint-Simon, would be between those who contributed to the collective and those who did not.[174]

With this reference to Saint-Simon's Christian socialism, An here leaned into the religious grounding of his thought while circling back toward the anti-capitalist implications of his opening invocation of Marx. This circling back to Marx, moreover, recurred and took on additional dimensions in An's subsequent work. In the April 1957 issue of *Sasanggye*, An published a follow up to his call for a "new worldview" that once again quoted Marx's thesis that philosophy should change the world rather than simply interpret it,[175] and this article likewise identified capitalism, the state, and mechanical civilization as the "three large systems that, despite being made by and for humans, had become shackles oppressing them."[176] Then, in October 1957, he concluded another essay published in the journal with the provocative admission that his critique of the "human's transformation into a slave of money and materiality" overlapped not only with Hegel's vision of the "loss of ethics" but also with Marx's vision "human self-alienation."[177]

By engaging with the content of Marx's critique of capitalism more directly, An's vision moved toward the types of formulations offered by Takakuwa Sumio and Paul Tillich. It also played with the boundaries between them and the more common attempts to link existentialism and Marxism: that is, nonreligious ones. In these 1957 articles, the religious dimension of An's work was noticeably de-emphasized, and this brought his writing into much closer dialogue with another philosopher contributing to *Sasanggye* at the time: Ha Kirak. In March 1957, Ha published an article in the journal that attempted to synethesize a Marx-inspired account of the human as "object" (*kaekch'e*) to an existentialist account of her position as "subject" (*chuch'e*). Locating a form of "humanism" in Marx's critique of the alienated position of the worker under industrial capitalism, Ha called for the integration of this critique of the material conditions of human alienation with Karl Jaspers's vision of the possibility of the human to overcome her contextual limits as subjective being.[178]

Ha's philosophy was undoubtedly more secular than An's. However, he understood Jaspers as a thinker who brought together influences from both theistic and atheistic existentialism, and this meant that he stood at the line of the religious in a mediating fashion. Undoing the binary between the religious and the atheistic, Jaspers's thought here opened up new possibilities for connection. These were connections to Marx—in particular, the supposedly "humanist" dimension of his thought—and they were also connections to the past. Indeed, the attempt to formulate a "new humanism" by linking a Marxist account of the human's place as "object" to an existentialist account of the human's place as "subject" was not new. It had been proposed by numerous thinkers abroad as well as by a particular philosopher in colonial-era Korea: Kim Osŏng, an activist in the syncretic new religion Ch'ŏndogyo (Religion of the Heavenly Way) who rose to prominence in the 1930s by translating his religious call for a "new humanism" into secular, literary, and intellectual terms, including those of Komatsu Kiyoshi's "active humanism."[179] Since Kim had gone North after 1945, his philosophy could not be invoked directly, but Ha here reformulated it, setting the stage for similar testings of political and temporal boundaries in the literary domain.

BORDER LINES

As discussed in chapter 1, the Chongryon writer and critic Hŏ Namgi compiled a pivotal, border-crossing anthology of modern Korean poetry for the Japanese publisher Aoki Shoten in 1955. Bringing together the work of colonial-era South Korean writers with the work of those in the North, the anthology served as a pivotal inspiration for cross-border literary connections in North Korea. It also made its way to the South. In 1957, Hŏ's anthology was seized from booksellers by the South Korean state as one of more than seventy different titles—comprising more than a thousand (and perhaps up to five thousand) individual copies—suspected of being "seditious" (*puron*).¹⁸⁰ It was also among more than ten of these titles that were ultimately identified as pro-communist propaganda, and as a result, the proprietors of five book companies, including Pak Chongt'ae, who later became an important antiauthoritarian politician, were arrested and charged with violation of the National Security Law.¹⁸¹ This chapter in the illicit availability of North Korean literature in the South thus ended abruptly, but in fact, other avenues of access were already opening up. As we will see below, the colonial-era literature of those who had gone North was already being incorporated into South Korean literature at this time, and once again, critical challenges to the human and its bounds played a pivotal role.

Indeed, it was not only in the philosophical and theological domains that the critique of the human gained traction—as well as malleability—during these years. In the literary domain, too, a range of writers likewise began looking beyond the human realm to speak critically back toward it, and such visions, while perhaps influenced by religious discourse, rarely invoked it directly. This began during the wartime era with stories like Kim Kwangju's "Expression: A Puppy's Monologue" ("P'yojŏng: Kangaji ŭi monorogŭ"). Published in the journal *Sinjo* in June 1951, "Expression" is narrated from the perspective of a puppy that has been passed from owner to owner, in this case witnessing repeated relations of infidelity among couples in the refugee space of Pusan. It is also a story in which this nonhuman narrator develops a critique of the humans around it, asking, "If this continues, won't all of the people in the Republic of Korea go crazy?"¹⁸² and "If this continues, won't going crazy be the only way that the people of the Republic of Korea will be able to endure?"¹⁸³ Paired with its critique of the North Korean and Chinese troops who, during their occupation of Seoul, rounded up all of the dogs and turned them into soup, the narrator here voices pointed skepticism toward the South

Korean citizens around it, pointing, in addition to their infidelity, to the way in which they sit around all day in tea houses, addicted to coffee as though it were "opium."

An alternative version of this type of vision likewise emerged in Kim Sŏnghan's "The Protestation of a Cactus" ("Sŏninjang ŭi hangŭi"). Published in the journal *Munhwa segye* in 1954, "Protestation" is a fictional account of the life of Adolf Hitler's mother, Rosa, in the last days of the Second World War.[184] More specifically, it is the story of her turn from an admiring mother and unfailing supporter of the Nazi Reich to an apostate who calls on her country's troops to surrender. The groundwork for this transformation, as critics at the time emphasized, begins with her witnessing of a public execution outside her window: the execution of a "Jewish" traitor for having collected the propaganda leaflets dropped overhead by American planes. Yet the treatment of this woman in the manner of a "thing" (*mulgŏn*) does not produce any lasting effect on Rosa. The lives of ordinary people—and especially "traitors"—must of course be sacrificed in service of her son's mission.[185]

The event that transforms her vision, therefore, is not the execution but rather that which follows it: her semifantastic interaction with the cactus in her room. Confronting Rosa, the cactus asks, "Who do you think you are?," and then proceeds to lay out the yawning gap in power between its own position as a vulnerable being, "a being that cannot move one inch, a being who will snap if snapped and be flattened if stepped upon," and Rosa, the "privileged and powerful" mother of the Fuhrer, who, "without lifting a finger," nevertheless "eat[s] well and spend[s] well, with rolls of fat rippling across [her] stomach."[186] In the story, the exact reason why this confrontational monologue from the cactus spurs transformation in Rosa is left ambiguous. But what is clear, nevertheless, is the origin of this moral transformation outside the human.

Similarly, the following year, at roughly the same time that An Pyŏnguk was emerging as a frequent contributor to *Sasanggye*, the journal published a short story called "Twenty-Four Hours of Flux" ("Yujŏn 24-si") by Yu Chuhyŏn, the author of "Mountain Pass," one of the wartime stories mentioned above. Narrated from the perspective of a 100-hwan bill, "Twenty-Four Hours of Flux" is an unusual story that endows money not only with language but also with self-consciousness, emotions, and sociality. The narrator thus muses, in the opening section of the story:

> This morning, I finally came out to the teller. It had been a boring three months that I had waited in full dress.
>
> I am now sitting on the teller's desk, looking out from the window. It is in order to observe this world outside the window that I have the power of thought. The reason that I accept my own value of existence is likewise because there is this outside world. If I have hopes and aspirations, they are hopes and aspirations related to this outside world.
>
> My name is bill and my number is 7.[187]

Through this narrative perspective, the story functions, on one level, as a parody of the fetishism of money that picks up on a wide array of precedents from early proletarian texts from the 1920s to Korean War–era indictments of the camptown and black-market economies and their grounding in the all-consuming power of (usually American) cash.[188]

Moreover, the story is not only critical of contemporary visions of money but also contemporary uses of it. The text begins with the narrator's emergence from a "special warehouse surrounded by a wall of steel five *p'un* thick and stone half a *cha* long," and its guarded transit, alongside "countless colleagues," to a bank, where it enters circulation for the first time.[189] The story then follows its narrator from hand to hand, pocket to pocket, wallet to wallet, outlining in the process the relationships of corruption and mutual exploitation affecting all levels of contemporary South Korean society. From ordinary citizens seeking educational and employment opportunities for their family members to government officials seeking job security amid workplace shake-ups to marginalized workers at a crematorium seeking means of momentary relief from their harrowing job, all those whose hands and pockets the narrating bill passes through are shown to be embedded in an interconnected network of manipulation, bribery, and betrayal: one in which survival only appears to be possible through the endless reproduction of such relationships via the exchange of cash like the narrator and its colleagues.

The story, however, is much more than a critique of contemporary South Korean society and its use and vision of money. The series of transactions that circulate the narrator are, in various ways, bribes, but none of the bribe recipients actually seem to follow through on the relevant action requested by the individual who provided the money. Seeing this, the narrator despairs:

I am clearly living as a traitor.

I am betraying the various people who have been my owners up to the present.

But this is something that I can do nothing about, so I have no choice but to [simply] observe my fate.

I came to realize that it is my fate to be unable to be loyal to any of my individual owners.

And I finally realized both that these betraying acts are not my intentional actions and that they are unavoidable things that cannot be resisted with my strength [alone].[190]

Although the corrupt and manipulative interactions presented in the text are all mediated by the exchange of money, the narrating consciousness of the 100-hwan bill is marked by a moral conscience that appears to exceed the one found in the human beings that exchange it. In Yu's story, it is people themselves who are corrupt and manipulative, while the money that they exchange is an unwilling tool or medium. As such, the primary target of Yu's text is the human not the monetary, and this links it to the line of stories from the wartime and immediate postwar era mentioned above.

At the same time, the story also serves as a turning point in this line of critique. In 1956, Yu published a sequel to the text, "People Who Incinerate Life" ("Insaeng ŭl pul sarŭnŭn saramdŭl"), in the journal *Munhak yesul*. At the end of "Twenty-Four Hours of Flux," the 100-hwan bill travels to a crematorium, where the workers responsible for processing the corpses of loved ones and the Buddhist monk responsible for assisting mourners in sending them off take the opportunity to extort money out of the grieving. Yu's sequel begins its narrative at this crematorium, where the previous text left off, and it reframes the narrative center of the text around one of the workers, moving away from the 100-hwan bill narrative device. It also details a peculiar transformation in the character of its protagonist, a crematorium worker named Tŏkpae. In this story, Tŏkpae's long-ill wife passes away, and, acting as if there is nothing different about this cremation than others, the tearless Tŏkpae takes up the task of grinding her bones himself, prompting his friends and colleagues to refer to him as a "machine rather than a human."[191] Indeed, unfazed and emotionally unmoved, Tŏkpae here acts "mechanically," even wondering himself whether he has become nothing more than a "machine like the kind of children's toy whose arms and legs move when one winds it up."[192]

In narrating this development, the story's turn is peculiar. On the one hand, "People Who Incinerate Life" continues the critique presented in "Twenty-Four Hours of Flux" by depicting the intense depravity of the human—a depravity only heightened as it comes into the domain of mourning and death typically associated with the sacred. At the same time, the text frames this heightening and deepening of human depravity as mechanization—that is, the loss of humanity. Moreover, the text furthers this tangling in its conclusion. Once he has finished tending to his wife's body at the crematorium, Tŏkpae turns to his closest colleague, Sunman, urging him to join him in drinking at a local establishment they frequent. He then looks to the waitress from the establishment, who is there paying her respects. Tŏkpae has developed a relationship with this waitress over an extended period of time, and when he looks at her in this moment, she thus looks back at him with a gaze that he interprets as flirtatious.

In this moment, Tŏkpae's depravity—and by extension, his mechanical inhumanity—appears to reach its highest apex. Simultaneously, however, it also begins to crumble. When the waitress looks back at Tŏkpae, her gaze makes him nauseous and strikes him as distasteful. Moral consciousness returns to his body, and he begins to cry, suggesting that emotion has reemerged as well. On the one hand, the emergence of moral consciousness at the moment that Tŏkpae's mechanical inhumanity reaches its apex fits with the text's existing critique of the human: that is, its location of morality outside the bounds of the human. At the same time, the way in which the text pairs the return of moral consciousness with the return of emotion undercuts this link, and so does the text's subsequent suggestion that the two extremes of Tŏkpae's behavior—his profane "desire to drink" alongside the waitress and his "sudden tears of distaste"—may have been "the same things."[193]

What the text's final scene performs, in other words, is a deconstruction of the boundary between the human and the nonhuman, the moral and the immoral—a deconstruction of the binary logic that had grounded "Twenty-Four Hours of Flux" and similar texts that had located morality outside the human. By focusing on the space of the crematorium and those who work there—a space, in the text's vision, that stands between life and death, as do the workers themselves—the story tangles up and then unravels this binary schema. And this allows it, moreover, to offer one final intervention. In Yu's story, the space where these workers operate is not only described as that between life and death but also compared to the "buffer zone" (*wanch'ung chidae*) between North and South:

> "Are we living in the world of people? Or are we living in the world of corpses?"
> These, too, were Sunman's words. At the time, an employee from the office happened to be next to them, so Tŏkpae asked him,
> "Which side are we actually living on?"
> . . .
> "We're living in the buffer zone [*wanch'ung jidae*]!"
> "What's a buffer zone?"
> "You know, there's a buffer zone at the thirty-eighth parallel. While it's neither Northern land nor Southern land, it's also an ambiguous zone that can be Northern land and Southern land."
> "Do people live there?"
> "Of course they live there. And they probably get mixed up from time to time. Are they living in the North? Or are they living in the South? Each side is [sitting there] facing them."[194]

In this moment—and at the border between life and death—what becomes possible is not only a deconstruction of the boundary between the human and the nonhuman, morality and immorality but also the boundary between the two Koreas. This is a political boundary, and its contestation via the laboring body of a worker is significant. It signals, if implicitly, the possibility of workers' resistance to the Cold War system's binaries and boundaries.

BOOKS OF THE DEAD

To be sure, despite challenging the boundary between life and death, North and South, Yu's story does not actually cross the thirty-eighth parallel divide in its imagination. Yet other writers active at the same time pushed in this precise direction. As we have seen, the National Security Law and the Anticommunist Law placed clear bounds upon the ability to engage with texts from across the border. Furthermore, these were not the only laws and restrictions that enforced literary division. As Kim Sŏngsu has noted, in 1951 and 1957, ROK authorities released a series of restrictions outlawing the publication and sale of works by writers who had gone North, and these restrictions applied not only to that which they had written after 1945 but also anything that they had written in the past.[195] These policies not only erased a wide swath of Korea's colonial-era literary history but they also compelled South Korean writers to censor their own memories of and connections to this past. Yet not all writers complied, and indeed, works by writers who had gone North soon began reappearing a variety of guises.

In September 1953, the journal *Munhwa segye* published a short story by the novelist Yi Ponggu titled "Spring" ("Saem"). Republished with minor edits in 1959 under the title "Like a Deer" ("Sasŭm ch'ŏrŏm"),[196] the story, set during the Korean War, is an exploration of refugee life, following its Seoul-dwelling narrator as he moves between Taegu and his hometown, Ansŏng, during the era of the "1.4 Retreat" (Il-sa Hut'oe). It is also about the encounters that he has along the way: the friendship that he develops with the youths at his boarding house in Taegu, whom he entertains with "lectures" about Dazai Osamu's *Setting Sun* (*Shayō*); and his reconnection with faces from his past, including a close friend's widow in Taegu and a childhood classmate, terminally wounded in the war, in Ansŏng.

The most important presences that emerge from the past in the narrative, however, are not people but rather texts. When the narrator first arrives in his hometown, he encounters a place that exists at the border between life and death, human and nonhuman. The space of the hometown, the reader learns, has been reduced to "half ruins" in the conflict, and when he encounters residents in their traditional garb walking down a newly built road "as though mute," the narrator describes them as "about to burst into tears like young calves."[197] Placing these villagers at the border of the human and nonhuman, the narrator then offers three lines of verse:

> You're crying, wronged in your clear, pure heart!
> You're crying, cautiously restraining
> A single, instinctual scream![198]

These lines of verse are poignant, pointing to the loss and suffering that the war has brought to the narrator's hometown. What is most striking about them, however, is their origin. Although the text simply attributes them to "a certain poet," they are adapted from a 1941 poem called "Child from the Countryside" ("Ch'on esŏ on ai") by the poet Paek Sŏk.[199] And since Paek had gone North after 1945, his works were banned at the time in South Korea. In looking back to the wartime era, Yi's text thus takes up an unexpected task. Rather than reinforcing division, it challenges it by reclaiming forbidden words from the past and rearticulating them through the South Korean narrator's own voice.

The text's intervention, moreover, does not stop with these three lines. After reciting these lines of verse, the narrator of the story turns his thoughts from the villagers he sees on the road to his own family members, and at this moment, the text breaks from its existing mode of narration to directly reproduce an entire poem: Paek Sŏk's "There Is a White Partition Wall" ("Hŭin parambyŏk i issŏ"), also published in 1941.[200] Yi's story here goes significantly beyond its initial, rather subtle testing of the bounds of acceptable discourse, performing an explicit, unmistakable reclaiming of the work of a living colleague in the North. And it concludes its vision, following the death of the childhood classmate whom the narrator has just visited, by reinforcing this transgressive act. At the very end of the story, the narrator seeks out a natural spring that he used to visit with this childhood classmate, and when he finds it, he experiences a moment of healing. Repeating a line from "There Is a White Partition Wall," the narrator comes to the realization that this spring is his small "oasis" during the chaos of the war, and, taking a cue from the title of Paek Sŏk's famous debut anthology, *Deer* (*Sasŭm*), he describes himself drinking at the spring and waiting for fall "like a deer," which is also the title given to the story's 1959 republication.[201]

By seeking out border zones between life and death, the human and the nonhuman, Yi's story opens up a space for reengagement with banned texts by those who went North. This was a tactic, moreover, that Yi's work would continue to use in subsequent years—and it was one that he would link to visions of the colonial-era past in order to carve out a safe space for increasingly strident challenges to the ROK state's censorship regime. In March 1956, Yi published a short story titled "Yi Sang" in the literary journal *Hyŏndae munhak*. Narrated by a friend of Yi Sang, the transformational experimental poet and novelist of the colonial era, the story takes place during the period between the last days of Yi Sang's teahouse, Chebi, which closed in 1935, and his death in Japan in 1937. The narrative opens with a visit to Chebi, and from the outset, it is clear that the teahouse is not doing well. Not only is Yi Sang himself absent, but so too are customers. "Even when spring comes and the flowers bloom," the text thus begins, "nothing but a desolate wind blows through the Chebi teahouse,"[202] and it goes on to describe an establishment on the verge of bankruptcy.

The telephone, we learn, has been repossessed, the gramophone has been sold, and rent is overdue, which is why Yi Sang himself keeps his distance. Likewise, the beverages available are by no means as elaborate as they used to be. Indeed, when the narrator enters the teahouse and attempts to order, the text relays the following humorous exchange with Suyŏng, the waitress who looks after the establishment alone:

> "What can I get you?"
> "I'll have a Calpis."
> "That's not available right now."
> "Not available. . . . Then I'll have a soda water."
> "That's not available, either."
> "You don't have that, either? Then what is available?"
> "We have black tea and coffee."[203]

This is not the Chebi of previous times, which had even sold drinks such as ginseng tea, and indeed, as the story subsequently relates, it soon closes its doors, only to be followed by a series of establishments owned by Yi Sang that become similarly "desolate" and meet similar fates.

The text, in other words, chronicles a series of business ventures pursued by Yi Sang that each turn into desolate, lonely, lifeless spaces on the verge of collapse, and in the aftermath of these failures, their owner, too, comes to live, as the story puts it, "amid ennui and self-deprecation, as if trying to test himself to see whether he will live or die."[204] Living in despair at the boundary between life and death, Yi Sang seems to mirror his business establishments, and indeed, as the text narrates, he soon leaves for Tokyo, where he lives a lonely existence that ends with his premature death after being arrested by the Japanese police. Concluding with an account of the sadness felt by Yi Sang's acquaintances as a result of his lonely death alone in Tokyo—a death both tragic and somehow fitting for Yi Sang's life—the story looks back with yearning toward a lost friend.

The target of this longing, however, is not Yi Sang alone. In fact, although Yi Sang is the only lost friend mentioned in the text by name, he is not the only lost friend invoked because the story is, quite explicitly, a rewritten version of a short narrative sketch about Yi Sang's teahouse Chebi written by Pak T'aewŏn in 1939. Known as one of Yi Sang's closest friends and collaborators, Pak was a modernist novelist who had gone North after 1945, and his work was thus banned. Yet Yi's story reproduces this work in key ways, re-presenting it to 1950s South Korean readers. Indeed, the link between the two texts goes far beyond an overlap in general content or descriptive phrases. Instead, it replays specific scenes, reproducing content in an unmistakably direct way.

This is evident, for example, in the comic exchange quoted above. In Pak's original version, the text, after describing the current state of the teahouse by noting, once again, that the telephone has been repossessed and the gramophone sold, relates an example of what happens when a rare visitor or two find their way into the establishment and are waited upon by Suyŏng:

> "What can I get you?"
> "I'll have a port lap. You'll have a Calpis?"
> "That's not available right now. Perhaps something else?"
> "Not available? Then I'll have a soda water."
> "That's not available, either."
> "You don't have that, either? Then what is available?"
> Without batting an eyelash, Suyŏng responds naturally.
> "We have black tea and coffee."[205]

This dialogue is clearly the same one that Yi has taken up and adapted ever so slightly, and something similar can be said about a subsequent scene.

Since Chebi is about to close its doors, Yi Sang is planning to purchase a bar to run instead. In Yi Ponggu's story, the narrator and Yi Sang visit this bar together, presenting themselves as ordinary customers to the three waitresses, who they engage in conversation:

CRITICAL CONNECTIONS AND CRITICAL LIMITS 201

"Why is this place so desolate?"
When I make this useless comment to the waitress sitting on the opposite side, [she responds,]
"There are no customers at all these days. They say the owner will change any day. So there's that reason, and the girls have also left for other places."
Picking up on the words of the girl with particularly red cheeks, the girl sitting next to me with crooked teeth [adds],
"They say that if the owner changes the indoor devices will all be changed as well, so it will be better than now. But this place never lasts long."
As she carelessly says these words which should be avoided in front of customers, the lanky girl they call "Yoshiko" enters with a bottle of alcohol [and says],
"Exactly. Even if the owner changes, it won't make a difference. Of all the places to choose, why buy this place? I'd like to see the face of this new owner . . ."
Turning to look at Yi Sang, [she continued,]
"In any case, I don't know who this person is, but what kind of business do they want to do buying this place?"
Pulling out his nose hairs and listening silently up until this point, Yi Sang [said],
"What kind of person? A senseless one."
I joined in, too.
"Senseless! He must be crazy, no?"[206]

Like the scene discussed above, this one, too, is taken directly from Pak's "Chebi." In fact, Yi Ponggu's story reproduces this entire passage verbatim with only two exceptions. The first is a change in the word used for "face" in Yoshiko's comment, and the second comes right at the end of the passage. In Pak's original story, Yi Sang, after calling the new owner—himself—"senseless," asks his friend Kubo—that is, Pak—what he thinks, which prompts the concluding comment.[207] Yi Ponggu's story, however, omits this invitation to join in, and with it, the text covers the origins of the scene enough in order to be able to reproduce it.

By narrating the past and taking up the story of those on the border between life and death, Yi Ponggu set the groundwork a new type of literary space where banned texts could once again become audible. And he continued to do this in subsequent works from this same period that reclaimed the work of O Changhwan, a hometown friend who went North and attained a high position in the DPRK before his premature death in 1951. However, because O, due to his position, was so beyond the pale, Yi here opened up a space for engagement in a multistep process: one that first looked to the borders between life and death and then moved toward narrating the colonial past.

In July 1956, Yi published a story called "Nostalgia" ("Nosŭt'arŭji") in the journal *Hyŏndae munhak*. A familiar topic for Yi's work, the story follows its narrator, a writer from Seoul, as he visits his hometown in the countryside. Not surprisingly, therefore, the text quickly turns to nostalgia, the work's title, drawing out the nostalgic pull of the hometown. Yet it also includes a significant number of unexpected moments, the first of which occurs on the bus from Seoul. The narrator strikes up a conversation with another passenger on the bus—someone he gets to know quite well when the bus breaks down before reaching its destination—and he learns that this acquaintance's hometown is in the North. The new friend here wonders whether he will ever be able to "step foot in his hometown again,"[208] and this gives the narrator a new perspective on his trip; what was, initially, perhaps a perfunctory visit becomes endowed with new emotional meaning.

This meaning further grows as the narrator arrives in his hometown and goes to visit Ilsŏk, his closest childhood friend. Ilsŏk, we learn, lives alone with no family, passing each day in the dark, in bed, in futile despair. He is a ruined man, someone on the path, as he acknowledges himself, to becoming a "living corpse" (*san songjang*).[209] From the text's perspective, however, Ilsŏk's liminal position—removed from society and seemingly approaching the border between life and death—is also an opportunity, and what this makes possible is the brief yet significant speaking of a forbidden past. In order to help him escape from his despair, the narrator encourages his friend to get married and then move to Seoul. Ilsŏk, however, insists that it is too late to marry, telling the narrator that he has missed "the last train, as in our old friend's poem."[210]

This is a reference to O Changhwan's "The Last Train," a poem that had appeared in his 1939 anthology, *Dedication* (*Hŏnsa*).[211] Through the voice of the friend, who occupies a borderline space between life and death, society and its exterior, the title of a forbidden poem returns, and this situation appears again in a subsequent story published two years later: Yi's "Book of the Dead" ("Saja ŭi sŏ," 1958).[212] Also published in *Hyŏndae munhak*, "Book of the Dead" is narrated by a dead person laying in a grave, and it opens with this narrator, who previously lived a life of poverty, hardship, and a desire to escape abroad, comparing the crying of the insects in the grass surrounding the grave to the crying of a shaman performing a ritual for the dead.

The narrator, the reader learns, has always been drawn to shaman performances. Even as a youth, the narrator, despite feeling fear, could not help but listen to such performances. In them, the shaman gave voice to the spirits of the dead, speaking on behalf of them, voicing their worries, and calming them, and the narrator sees this act as a beautiful one. Moreover, he implicitly compares it to love, which, he explains, is premised—like life's inexorable development toward death—on parting, pain, and loss. Here the narrator reflects on his own history of love and separation, and when he thinks of those who he has loved and parted with in the past, he again invokes O Changwhan's "The Last Train," comparing these people from the past to those in the poem waiting to board their trains.

Speaking from the grave—in the ground yet still within earshot of the world of the living—the narrator here steps into a role resembling that of the shaman. Giving voice to those from the past whose words have been lost and forbidden, the narrator acts to ease the pain of parting and separation. Those with whom we've parted, the text suggests, are still bound up with our love and our memory, and it thus excavates the past of those who have gone North, reclaiming them, implicitly, as targets of love and affection. In these texts of Yi's, the boundary between life and death not only serves as an insulation mechanism for the radical act of reengaging with O's work but also turns such texts into similar mechanisms for other engagements with O's work that emerged at the same time.

This was the case, for example, in Yi's "Yŏnghoe" (詠懷), which he first published in September 1956, between "Nostalgia" and "Book of the Dead." Written with these characters, the title literally means, "poetic expression of sentiments held inside," and within the context of the story, it accrues a range of meanings, from the parodic to the poignant. The story, which takes place during the colonial period, contains two separate anecdotes held together by a shared concern: the relationship between "poetic expression" in a linguistic sense (the poet's literary activity) and "poetic expression" in a bodily sense (the poet's urination). The first anecdote centers around a young Korean poet who eventually sets off for Manchuria because he is "[u]nable to bear the fate of the Korean language under the oppression of Japanese rule" and because his life in Korea forces him to suppress his frequent need to urinate, something that he does not have to do in Manchuria, where he is "able to urinate as his heart desires."[213] In contrast, the second anecdote focuses on a Japanese Dadaist poet—likely modeled after Takahashi Shinkichi—who is likewise traveling to Manchuria but doing so as a function of the fame of his freewheeling, experimental writing rather than his desire for escape from censorship. Likewise, he feels—and has—no need to control or restrict his urination. In fact, on the night that he stays at the boarding house where the story takes place, not knowing where to find the toilet or how to use a chamber pot, he simply urinates in the bed.

By the end of the story, therefore, it becomes clear that colonial difference adheres not only to linguistic autonomy but also to bodily autonomy, and this allows the reader to return to the text's opening lines with a new perspective. The story begins as follows:

> Urinating in the boarding house alleyway,
> Youth, wither!
> Love, depart!
> To your desolate hometown!
> I hummed this song.
> Even if a passerby scowled,
> "Just urinating wherever!"
> I discharged urine as though an excretion of resistance,
> "What? I can't even urinate as I please?"[214]

Understood in relation to the subsequent development of the narrative, the "resistance" invoked in this opening scene is a declaration of bodily autonomy voiced not simply toward potential passersby but also toward the colonial state whose differentiations of subject positions restrict or allow expressions of bodily needs. Likewise, the narrative's subsequent development, in which bodily autonomy and linguistic autonomy are linked, also prompts a reconsideration of the "song" that accompanies this opening act of excretory resistance. In such a reconsideration, it becomes clear that the narrator's act of "humming"—that is, voicing these words at the boundary of the audible and/or semantically intelligible—speaks to the text's vision of the colonial era as one in which the possibilities of linguistic expression are constrained and in question.

At the same time, the origin of these words, which also appear in quotation marks in the closing lines of the text, pushes the narrative into more transgressive territory. With the exception of one word,[215] these lines of song are drawn directly from another poem by O Changhwan. Titled "Dedication Artemis" ("Hŏnsa Artemis"), the poem in question was also published in O's 1939 anthology, *Dedication*, and this collection, which also included another poem called "Yŏnghoe" (the same title as Yi's story), followed an earlier collection, *Castle Wall* (*Sŏngbyŏk*, 1937), containing a poem, "Ocean Beast" ("Haesu"), that figured a similar scene of alleyway urination.[216] Yet all of these works were banned in South Korea. As such, the story's anti-colonial critique is more expansive than it seems. The "excretion of resistance" that it figures in this opening scene and returns to in the story's conclusion is also an implicit critique of the postcolonial South Korean state, which, rather than fully decolonizing and removing restrictions on the "expression of that which is held inside" (*yŏnghoe*), has instead simply reproduced them, interrupting the ability to speak of the past and voice "dedications" (*hŏnsa*) to lost friends.

CONCLUSION

In 1950s South Korea, the devastating experience of the Korean War served as an essential touchpoint for continued mobilization against the North and against leftist politics more broadly. At the same time, the violence perpetrated by all combatants in the conflict as well as the oppression carried on in the postwar era by the domestic state and its American allies ensured that the binary of "us" vs. "them" could not be accepted transparently and that—to the contrary—the *overlaps* between the two sides of the Cold War—"this side" and "that side"—would continue to be highlighted. In order to do this, writers and critics in the South drew upon a range of literary and critical resources, including ones that, like the conflict itself, exceeded the bounds of the Korean peninsula. Looking to Japan for inspiration as well as for access to texts and ideas from Euro-America, South Korean writers and critics not only challenged the binary structure of Cold War division but also developed creative ways of reengaging with a "humanist" Marx and the banned work of colleagues who had gone to the North through carefully devised literary "buffer zone[s]." This would set the stage for more widespread and penetrating challenges in subsequent years, especially after the April Revolution of 1960 pushed the Syngman Rhee regime from power.

4

TRAGIC RETURNS

Writing Border-Crossing Pasts in
1960s–1980s South Korea

In early 1967, the young critic Im Chungbin published a short, introductory essay on methodology in the study of historical literature in *Sŏngdae munhak*, a journal published at Sungkyunkwan University, where he was then a fourth-year student.[1] Opening with a discussion of literature as inescapably historical—that is, always a "product of history" (*yŏksajŏk sanmul*)—Im then turned to defining the more specific type of literature that his article sought to interrogate: "historical literature" (*yŏksa munhak*).[2] For Im, the category of historical literature could, on the one hand, be defined by the types of material that it included, and he here asserted that both popular folklore and mythology (*sŏrhwa munhak*) as well as narratives contained in elite textual records (*sŏsa munhak*) should be understood as types of historical literature. He also emphasized, however, that historical literature had to be understood in terms of its character and its relationship to history, writing that proper historical literature should be seen as literature that expressed the "true artistic form of [its] concrete historical age."[3]

At the time, readers may or may not have been familiar with this last phrase. Yet it was a quotation taken from the work of the Hungarian Marxist literary scholar and theorist György Lukács, something that Im made clear by placing this phrase in quotation marks and citing a Japanese translation of the original text. Further, drawing upon Lukács to argue that historical literature constituted a "basic genre of realist aesthetics that, through a historical theme, creates an epic yet dramatic character and, at the same time, allows its readers to confirm as reality the lives of ordinary people,"[4] Im here demonstrated that the influence of Marxist thought mediated via Japan continued to be powerful beyond the 1950s years discussed in chapter 3. He also pointed to the ways in which writers in the post-1950s years went significantly further in challenging the bounds of acceptable discourse in Cold War South Korea.

In subsequent sections of the essay, Im turned to a discussion of historical literature in Korea. Returning to his opening argument concerning the importance of including popular folklore and mythology (sŏrhwa munhak) in the general category of historical literature, Im noted that in the Korean context, too, the "fundamental origin [of such folklore and mythology] was contemporaneous with the historical origin of the [textual traditions of the] 'Korean humanities' [Chosŏn inmun],"[5] and he then transitioned into a discussion of specific examples from the Korean past, including the Tan'gun myth, which, he noted, had been the topic of recent scholarly discussion.[6] Once again, what was important here was not the content of Im's claims but rather their sourcing. In reference to the first claim about contemporaneous origins, Im cited the work of Kim T'aejun, an influential scholar of Korean language and literature who had been executed by the South Korean state in 1949–1950 for his role in the Southern Korean Workers' Party (Namnodang), and in reference to recent scholarship on Tan'gun, he cited a recent essay from the journal Chosŏn munhak, the most influential literary publication in North Korea. Both of these texts were banned in the South, and Im's use and citation of them points to the extent to which writers in the South were, by the mid-1960s, engaged in expanding the bounds of that which could be said, read, and discussed. It also points to the central role that visions of the past—both recent and distant—would serve in this endeavor across these and subsequent years.

Of course, Im's essay, published in a university journal while he was a student, had a limited audience, and Im himself would soon be arrested by the ROK state for his activities on two separate occasions in 1968 and 1970, having an unmistakably chilling effect on such acts. Yet the practices that he engaged in in this essay would soon ripple through the broader South Korean literary and cultural sphere. This chapter narrates these developments, focusing on the 1960s, 1970s, and 1980s. In particular, it shows how the turn toward the past allowed writers in South Korea to engage with pre-1945 as well as contemporary works by those in (or formerly in, prior to their death) the North. First, this chapter returns to chapter 3's discussion of the novelist Yi Ponggu to show how he was able to pivot, as a result of the border-crossing controversy surrounding the Japanese novelist Matsumoto Seichō's 1962–1963 novel about the Korean poet and critic Rim Hwa,[7] to reclaiming banned works from the immediate post-1945 context.

Next, this chapter turns to the 1970s and 1980s to show how writers of the younger generation—those who did not have the colonial-era personal connections of the older generation—reclaimed banned texts from the past via an alternative practice that moved in the opposite temporal direction: that is, by engaging in literary historical dialogue with them regarding precolonial eras of further and further remove. This chapter argues that new ways of contesting the contemporary structures of Cold War censorship emerged here, and it then concludes by showing how this turn toward deeper pasts allowed 1980s novelists like Ch'oe Inho to pivot sideways across the East Sea, where an engagement with a group of former Chongryon figures allowed for new modes of dialogue between texts from North Korea, South Korea, and Japan.

"TRAGIC" RETURNS

In December 1962, the novelist Ch'oe T'aeŭng began serializing a series of articles on a group of writers who had gone North: Chŏng Chiyong, Ri T'aejun, Rim Hwa, Sŏl Chŏngsik, Ri Kiyŏng, and Han Sŏrya.[8] Published in seven installments in the journal *Sasanggye*, this series of articles came on the heels of a landmark, three-part feature on North Korean literature in which Ch'oe, writing in the journal *Sinsajo*, had offered one of the first in-depth critiques of the first ten years of North Korean literary production to be published in the South. Compared to this earlier feature on North Korean literature, however, the tone of this series on writers who had gone North was notably conflicted. The title of the series framed these writers' northward trajectories as "tragedies" (*pigŭk*)—a characterization that would recur throughout the series—and indeed, although its vision was, in general, strongly critical of this group's behavior as "puppets" (*koeroe*) of nefarious communist forces, it also offered notable statements of sympathy toward them as targets of manipulation and, in many cases, unjust punishment and persecution.

The shift in Ch'oe's tone was most evident in the sections of the serialization that dealt with the experiences of these individuals after going North. While critical, for example, of Chŏng Chiyong's interactions with the Left while in Seoul, the text then narrated—with palpable sympathy and sorrow—the translation tasks that, it said, Chŏng had been compelled to perform in the North:

> Long or short, each time a flier was complete, they brought in a recording device and had him read it, shouting with feeling (?).
>
> We do not know whether his reading was smooth or not. But it was a lamentable shout made through tears.
>
> Perhaps they heard this old, frail poet's shaking voice, projected as if his heart were being torn, as possessing "feeling."⁹

Such statements were clearly meant to produce sympathy for Chŏng, the "main character of the tragedy" in this installment,¹⁰ and similar presentations recurred throughout, often paired uncomfortably with critiques of these same characters for the way in which they engaged with the political forces of the revolutionary Left. This, for example, could be seen in the section on the poet and critic Rim Hwa, one of the most influential figures of the colonial-era proletarian literature movement and its immediate post-1945 revival.

In the text, much of Ch'oe's discussion of Rim is far from sympathetic. At the same time, when the narrative shifts to its discussion of his experience after going North, the tone changes, portraying him as a victim of internecine political fractures in Pyongyang. Rim, Ch'oe notes, was actually quite hesitant to go North, and when he did, he found himself—like others who made the same transit—"unable to avoid tasting the fear and threat of being ripped apart, kicked, and beaten by the true puppets of the Soviet faction and the jealous northern natives."¹¹ After presenting the fate of Rim and others who went North in this way, Ch'oe suggests that he can "sense"—and by implication, understand—the feelings of those who, having gone North, returned to Seoul during the war as part of the occupation. And in relation to Rim Hwa in particular, he describes these postmigration years as ones that produced "shock and despair more dizzying and vexing than that from any other experience."[12]

The most important part of Ch'oe's discussion of Rim, however, is that which deals with his trial and execution alongside Sŏl Chŏngsik, another "tragic" figure in the series, and others. In 1953, Rim and a group of others including Sŏl were put on trial for being American spies. Convicted of these outlandish charges—which the text clearly labels as false and manufactured—they were executed the same year, and in his feature, Ch'oe uses these events as an essential pivot point for the production of sympathy. Noting, for example, that reports claim that Rim confessed to these crimes, the text emphasizes the "brutality" that would be necessary to force such a confession, describing the "shivers and sympathy" that such thoughts produce.[13] It likewise describes the scene of the trial and sentencing by invoking the "lamentable position" (aedalp'ŭn chase) in which Rim, already reduced to a "half corpse" (pansi sangt'ae) by the time of the trail, received his sentence.[14] Clearly, the goal here is to emphasize the brutal means and manipulations of the North Korean state and its leadership. This vision, however, is produced alongside a transformation of Rim into a victim, a transformation that calls upon the reader's sympathy.

In presenting this vision, Ch'oe was not working in isolation. On the contrary, as Ch'oe noted in his article, there were two inspirations for this serialization that came from abroad. In the text's opening installment, Ch'oe noted that this "tragedies" series was first inspired by a eulogy for the poet Sŏl Chŏngsik written by Tibor Méray, a Hungarian journalist who, after spending much of the Korean War in the North as a reporter for *Szabad Nép*, had participated in the Hungarian Revolution of 1956 and defected from the communist cause. This eulogy, provided to *Sasanggye* via the CIA-funded Congress for Cultural Freedom,[15] had been published in Korean translation in the September 1962 issue of *Sasanggye*,[16] and Ch'oe noted that its vision of Sŏl as a victim of the "tragedy" of the show trial that he shared with Im convinced him that the "tragedy" and "misfortune" (purhaeng) of those who had gone North could not simply be ignored as "someone else's" issue.[17]

Perhaps more important, however, was the second influence—this time from Japan—that Ch'oe discussed robustly across multiple installments of the series.[18] In January 1962, the Japanese mystery writer Matsumoto

Seichō began serializing a novel in the journal *Chūō kōron* about Rim Hwa. Written in a semireportage mode, this novel, *Poet of the North* (*Kita no shijin*), narrated the events of Rim's life between 1945 and 1948, concluding with his execution in North Korea in 1953 for being an American spy,[19] and it was based upon Japanese translations of Rim's writings by the resident Korean writer Kim Talsu and others as well as Japanese translations of the records of Rim's trial in the North, which had been published in 1954.[20] It was also surely influenced by the ongoing association between Matsumoto and the Chongryon organization, whose Japanese-language publications Matsumoto contributed to during these years.[21]

Not surprisingly, therefore, Matsumoto's novel did not question the official North Korean narrative of Rim's life and activities but rather dramatized it. It likewise presented a severely critical vision of life below the thirty-eighth parallel between 1945 and 1948, reproducing the official North Korean position regarding the post-1945 American presence and its Korean associates. Because of this latter presentation, in particular, the novel produced great controversy in South Korea across the latter half of 1962, 1963, and 1964. Moreover, its appropriation of the names and events of immediate post-Liberation Korean history was seen resentfully as a remnant of colonial hubris. This spurred numerous writers in the South to take up their own pens in response, and the result was a cross-border debate spanning the East Sea.

As Yi Pongbŏm has also noted,[22] this debate began with a critique of the story by Cho Chaech'ŏn, a former ROK minister of justice, which was read on the air at the Seoul International Radio Station on November 24, 1962, in a thirty-minute broadcast directed at Japan,[23] and it was then published in the inaugural, December 1962 issue of *Tonga ch'unch'u*.[24] Cho then followed this critique with an open letter to *Chūō kōron*, the Japanese journal publishing the novel, in the *Han'guk ilbo* newspaper.[25] In Japan, the journal *Shūkan yomiuri* then published a report on this critique and an assortment of responses to it, including one by Kim Talsu.[26] This text was then republished in Korean translation in *Tonga ch'unch'u*,[27] which had continued to present Korean critiques of the novel.[28] Focusing primarily on factual inaccuracies and distortions in Matsumoto's representation of officials and official actions in the southern occupation zone, this set of South Korean critiques was itself less than remarkable. What was significant, instead, was its outcome: the unexpected way in which the critique of Matsumoto's North Korean–inspired account of the actions of officials below the thirty-eighth parallel became tethered to the critique of Matsumoto's North Korean–inspired account of Rim's supposed behavior.

Pushing back against Matsumoto's "distorted" representation of Korean officials in Seoul, writers in the South ended up occupying a new position of sympathy in relation to the other target of Matsumoto's critical gaze: Rim Hwa. This, as we have seen, was the position that Ch'oe T'aeŭng took up in his "tragedies" series of 1962–1963, and it was a position that others occupied as well. Between 1963 and 1965, for example, Yi Ch'ŏlju, a writer and former editor of the North's *Minju ch'ŏngnyŏn* who had defected to the South in 1957, published a text that offered the longest and most exhaustive account of 1950s purges in the North. Serialized in *Sasanggye* and then reprinted in monograph form, it began with a discussion of Matsumoto's novel, noting that the impetus to share the details of Rim Hwa's "sad death" came from the novel and the great interest that it had produced.[29] Yi's goal, he said, was not to argue "against" Matsumoto; *Poet of the North* was a "subjective" (*chugwanjŏk*) and "dogmatic" (*toktanjŏk*) distortion, but that was the fiction writer's "freedom."[30] Nevertheless, the vision of Rim that he offered was substantially different from Matsumoto's—both in its understanding of the cause of his tragic death (Kim Il Sung's liquidation of his political rivals) and in the sense of "sympathy" that he felt for him as someone who had lived "under the same sky."[31]

In the South, visions of writers like Rim thus changed, and so too did the approachability of their literary work. On March 29, 1963, the *Kyŏnghyang sinmun* newspaper carried a large-format advertisement for the upcoming issue of *Tonga ch'unch'u*. Established in late 1962, *Tonga ch'unch'u* was still a young journal.[32] Yet the March 1963 advertisement would have been striking for readers at the time not because of the new names that it featured but rather because of the old ones that it placed at its head: Rim Hwa, Pak T'aewŏn, Ri T'aejun, Kim Kirim, and Chŏng Chiyong. As previously noted, all of these figures were prominent writers whose trajectories had taken them North between 1945 and 1950,[33] and the publication of their work—both pre-1945 and post-1945—was banned in South Korea after 1951. Yet after a decade or more of excision under the censor's pen, they had suddenly returned, and selected pieces of their colonial-era work—accompanied by critical reflections by South

Korean writers—were gathered together in a special feature [see figure 4.1] dedicated to so-called *wŏlbuk chakka* (writers who had gone North).

Published by Hŭimangsa, a company specializing in magazines for a popular readership, *Tonga ch'unch'u* was not a radical journal but rather one that was responding to the shifting cultural and political context around it. In their introduction to the feature, the editors stated this quite explicitly, writing:

> The direct motivation for compiling this special feature was the large controversy produced by the *Poet of the North* incident. Although it is abominable the way in which the Japanese author used a poet wandering like a reed as his protagonist and reduced his entire life to large political forces in the background, the insincere way in which Rim Hwa [Im Hwa] and others, not knowing their proper position, became caught up like falling leaves in the tide of a lacking "ism" must also be rejected. No, they have already been rejected. However, now that time has passed, they have become wandering spirits in the graves they dug for themselves, and they have no place to rest. The demise of traitors! That it is, but it is also the tragedy of people of culture, so we are tracing their footsteps so that this does not happen again.[34]

Presenting these writers, by turns, as both traitors and as tragic figures, the editors of the journal compared them to the protagonist, Nora, of Henrik Ibsen's *A Doll's House*. Whereas Nora was ultimately faced with two paths—return home or become a "fallen" woman—the writers who went North were left without any options. "Their return path was closed and the path of the prostitute was in no way permitted.... In the end, they ... had no choice but to flail about in their own pitiful fates."[35]

This type of presentation continued in the body of the feature. From the five writers included, the publication carried a range of pre-1945 texts: the poem "The Strait of Korea" ("Hyŏnhaet'an") by Rim Hwa; the short story "The Real Estate Office" ("Poktŏkpang") and the essay "For Whom to Write?" ("Nugu rŭl wihae ssŭl kŏt in'ga") by Ri T'aejun; the short story "The Girl Next Door" ("Yŏpchip saeksi") by Pak T'aewŏn; the poems "Paengnoktam" and "Orchid" ("Nanch'o") by Chŏng Chiyong; and the poem "Customs of the Sun" ("T'aeyang ŭi p'ungsok") and the essay "Travel" ("Yŏhaeng") by Kim Kirim.[36] It also carried works of criticism about

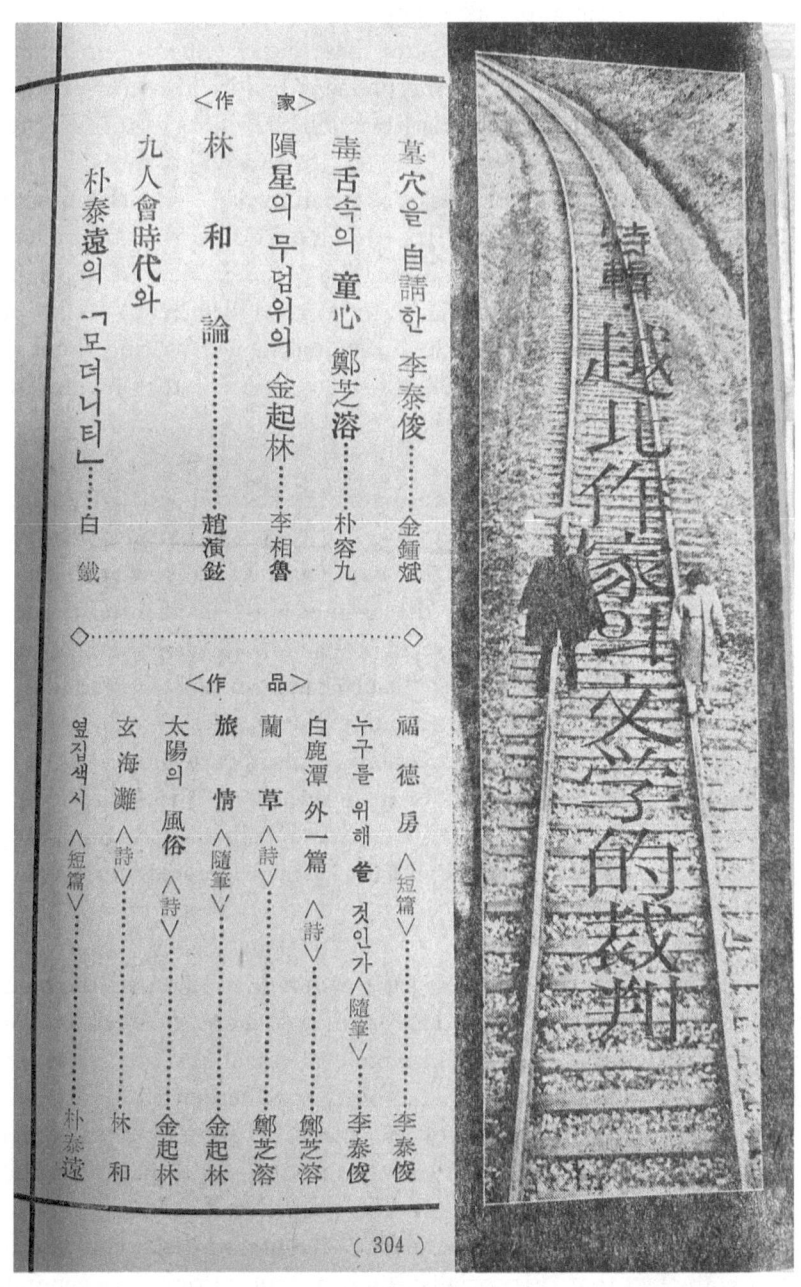

FIGURE 4.1 A special feature on writers who went North in the South Korean journal *Tonga Ch'unch'u*.

Tonga ch'unch'u 2, no. 4 (April 1963): 304.

each author by Yi Sangno, Pak Yonggu, Paek Ch'ŏl, Cho Yŏnhyŏn, and others, all then in the South. Most of these pieces were unremarkable. They focused, for example, on the pre-1945 historical contexts of the works, emphasizing the modernist tradition that most of these writers were working in at the time.

Yet others brought out and developed the irony of the situation in striking ways. This was particularly true in Cho Yŏnhyŏn's essay on Rim Hwa, which was titled, notably, "Rim Hwa, Who Swallowed Myth and Tragedy" ("Sinhwa wa pigŭk ŭl samk'in Im Hwa [Rim Hwa]"). Cho was the most conservative critic of the group, and he was writing about the most radical of the writers, yet his essay was surprisingly glowing. Cho began with the following memory:

> I once met Rim Hwa [Im Hwa] during the late colonial period. He said at that time that he was going to live like a scholar from the Middle Ages. What that meant, I thought, was that he was not going to collaborate with the present reality (the Japanese Empire) and instead stick to his convictions. Whether the set of convictions he was referring to at the time was the socialist ideology that he had possessed since the early days or the direction of pure literature [sunsu munhak]—in which, beginning at that time, he had occasionally taken up the critical pen—was not clear, but I was deeply affected by his resolve. This was because, whatever his ideological or literary character or path may have been, his one resolution to not collaborate with the Japanese Empire was precious in the society of that time.[37]

What is notable here is not simply the way in which Cho uses the memory of colonial oppression to produce an image of nonideological, nationalist bonding but also the way in which he essentially neutralizes the significance of ideological conflict altogether. Whether Rim's resistance to colonial domination came out of his socialist beliefs or his dedication to "pure literature" is ultimately irrelevant for Cho, and this is a position that he returned to multiple times in the article.

Essential to Rim's outstanding place in the literary field, Cho continued, was the fact that "his socialist, literary conceptions were generally tethered to national sentiments [minjok kamjŏng]. Therefore, there are many cases in which Rim's [Im's] poetry and criticism have been received positively even by those who opposed the direction of KAPF [Korea Artista Proletaria Federatio, the foremost proletarian arts organization of the colonial era]."[38] Regarding the poem "Suni at the Crossroads" ("Negŏri ŭi Suni"), for example, Cho noted: "Even beyond political and ideological issues, the image of our nation's trials under the Japanese Empire are more visible before our eyes. In particular, the anguishes and desires of the Korean youth under the Japanese Empire are truthfully exposed. The feeling that [the poem] is directly connected with national sentiments more than political and ideological issues is not absent."[39] Cho here attempted to draw Rim's literary heritage out from the shadows of its close association with Marxism, framing its central character as nationalist. And this carried over to Cho's account of Rim's post-1945 activities as well. After Liberation, Cho noted, Rim had attempted to stake out a nationalist, united front position, earning attacks from writers on both the Left and the Right. And although this had, Cho noted, been a strategic approach taken in coordination with the communist leadership, it had nevertheless placed Rim and his leadership in the political center—one that, of course, had become increasingly untenable as division hardened. Once again, Rim emerged as a "tragic" figure, sacrificed at the altar of post-1945 Cold War politics.

OLD FRIENDS, NEW TIMES

As we saw in chapter 3, the novelist Yi Ponggu had already begun testing the bounds of acceptable discourse in the South in the 1950s by referencing and quoting the pre-1945 work of those who had gone North. By and large, these challenges had been voiced in Yi's stories by characters inhabiting the boundary between life and death. That is, by depicting characters who had either recently died or existed near the border between life and death, Yi had punctured the boundary of the articulable as well, bringing words from banned poets like Paek Sŏk and O Changhwan back into the field of South Korean literature. Moreover, in stories like "Yŏnghoe" and "Yi Sang," he had also used temporality as a pivot point, moving into the colonial-era past, when such references would not have been transgressive, to situate his narrative. In subsequent years, however,

Yi would push into significantly more daring territory, and his first step in this direction was closely related to opportunities offered by the evolving political climate: in particular, the advent of the student-led April Revolution of 1960.

As seen in chapter 1, the April Revolution produced pivotal transformations in the literatures of Chongryon and North Korea and their relationships to the South. The April Revolution, however, was most transformative for South Korean literary practice, as the Rhee-era state that had initiated the National Security Law and subsequent crackdowns on distribution of the work of those who had gone North was no longer in power. Within this context, calls for peaceful, nonaligned reunification gained new levels of support and urgency, and so did discussions of textual engagement with those across the border in the North. In May 1960, the UN command in the ROK began soliciting letters and messages to be broadcast to family members and friends in the North,[40] and in subsequent months, South Korean students moved to take this function into their own hands by collecting letters to those in the North and attempting to deliver them to P'anmunjŏm.[41]

Professional writers like Yi Ponggu also saw new possibilities for engagement during this time. Between September 1960 and June 1961, Yi serialized an extended essay called "A Literary Stroll" ("Munhakchŏk sanbo") in the journal *Hyŏndae munhak*. Separated into a series of subsections focused on different writers, Yi used the essay as a forum to look back to the colonial-era past and reminisce about writers from that time. In doing so, Yi once again brought back into print the words of those whose writing had been banned; except this time, he used their names, something that had not been possible in the 1950s, and he placed his reminiscences in the 1960s present rather than the colonial-era past.

This began in the second installment of the essay, published in November 1960, in which Yi, reminiscing about the colonial-era novelist Kim Yujŏng, reproduced a set of writings—including a full-page elegy—by Kim's closest friend, the novelist An Hoenam, who had gone North after 1945.[42] Yi's most important challenges to the existing bounds of acceptable discourse, however, came in later installments of the essay. The fifth installment, published in March 1961, focused entirely on Chŏng Chiyong, another poet whose works were banned at the time in South Korea. Yi nevertheless took up his memory and that of his work, beginning this installment with a clear invocation of this memory within the context of the colonial present: "The 'Eliza' Tearoom of the past is the site of today's 'Mona Lisa' Tearoom in Myŏngdong. When exchanging drinks at the 'Ŭnsŏng' bar across the street, my dear [friend] Cho Yŏngsuk, her face flushed, sings Chŏng Chiyong's 'Hometown' ['Kohyang'] and makes me think of the era of the 'Eliza' Tearoom and Chŏng Chiyong."[43] After these opening words, the essay reproduced Chŏng's "Hometown" in its entirety, and this was only one of multiple works by the poet—all banned—that this installment presented to its readers. Indeed, interspersed with reminiscences of nights spent together with the poet, the essay went on to reproduce the entirety of Chŏng's "Another Sun" ("Tto hana tarŭn t'aeyang"), the majority of his "The Path Home" ("Kwiro"), and extended portions of two 1939 works of criticism that, together, covered approximately three full pages of the essay.

This installment of Yi's essay was thus much more than a reminiscence. It was also a reclamation, and Yi extended this treatment to a range of other writers as well. Already in the fourth installment of his essay, published in February 1961, Yi had reproduced short texts by the banned writers Kim Kirim and Pak T'aewŏn.[44] In his June 1961 installment, Yi expanded his treatment of Pak in dramatic fashion. A modernist pathbreaker whose 1934 novella, *A Day in the Life of Kubo the Novelist* (*Sosŏlga Kubo-ssi ŭi iril*), Yi compared to James Joyce's *Ulysses*,[45] Pak had also gone North after 1945, rendering this pivotal work of the colonial era off limits for readers in South Korea. In this installment of his essay, however, Yi directly undercut that prohibition. After reproducing almost a full page of a critical text that Pak had written after the publication of *Kubo*[46]—one of two quoted at length in the essay—Yi then offered his reader the full text of the first installment of the novella, noting, without any vagaries, that this is what he was doing.[47]

He then continued on to a discussion of Pak's next major work, *Scenes from Ch'ŏnggye Stream* (*Ch'ŏnbyŏn p'unggyŏng*), which had been published between 1936 and 1937, and once again, Yi went beyond a discussion of this banned writer to reproduce his banned work as well: in this case, excerpts from the first and twelfth sections of the novel, which amounted to approximately three full pages of the essay.[48] Yi's intervention was here unmistakable. What he did for readers was reclaim this lost work and return it—albeit only in part—to legibility in Cold War South

Korea. Through Yi's essay, that is, this work—and the author in the North for whom Yi yearned—suddenly reappeared, and this occured without recourse to the strategies that Yi had used during the 1950s: the excision of authors' names; the embedding of such authors' work in fiction, some of which was set in the colonial-era past, when this work would not have been banned.

However, published immediately following Park Chung Hee's May 1961 military coup, this June 1961 installment of Yi's essay was its last, suggesting that the space for this type of reclamation had closed. Indeed, in the period immediately following the coup, Yi returned to the type of practice he had pursued before the April Revolution of 1960 by republishing "Yŏnghoe," the story discussed above, under the title "In Your Desolate Hometown" ("Ssŭlssŭrhan nŏ ŭi kohyang e") in the April 1962 issue of the journal *Chayu munhak*.[49] As in the original, the poems by O Changhwan, while present, were not attributed to him directly, and they were positioned, once again, within a fictional context of the past. Similarly, other works that Yi published during the years immediately following generally refrained from such transgressive practices of quotation and reproduction.

And yet, this retreat and recalibration was only temporary. In 1964, Yi published a short story called "Splendid Solitude" ("Hwaryŏhan kodok") that reproduced, in the voice of one of its poem-reciting characters, the entirety of Kim Kirim's "Glass Window" ("Yurich'ang"), one of the poems from his 1946 anthology, *The Sea and the Butterfly* (*Pada wa nabi*).[50] Then, the following year, he began serializing a long-form essay called *Twenty Years in Myŏngdong* (*Myŏngdong 20-nyŏn*) that, after reproducing a colonial-era poem by his old friend O Changhwan, proceeded to reproduce, in its second chapter, an extended excerpt from the same poet's "Ailing Seoul" ("Pyŏngdŭn Sŏul," 1945). Despite the fact that this poem, "read in front of a mass rally" in late 1945,[51] had become linked to O's post-1945 turn toward the revolutionary Left, Yi's text spared no praise in introducing it, noting as follows: "The deep emotion of August 15 was thrilling and moving enough to bring anyone to tears. However, that which brought forth tears by expressing this honestly in writing was O Changhwan's 'Ailing Seoul.' In the bars of Myŏngdong, 'Ailing Seoul' constantly flowed out of everyone's mouths. It was a pure song of love, the tearful shout of overwhelming emotion."[52] Yi's work here reclaimed O's poem by framing it as nationalist, the same move that Cho Yŏnhyŏn had made in relation to Rim Hwa in the essay mentioned above. It also soon pivoted, as we will see below, on the central trope of the *Poet of the North* discussions: that of the "tragic" figure, who soon appeared in force in Yi's fiction of the late 1960s and early 1970s.

An early movement in this direction was evident, for example, in Yi's 1968 work "Futile Wandering" ("Hŏmanghan paehoe").[53] "Futile Wandering" is a story of the years between 1945 and 1948, and it focuses on the involvement of its narrator, who is also an author named Yi, in the Committee for the Preparation of Korean Literature (Chosŏn Munhak Kŏnsŏl Ponbu) and its subsequent incarnation, the Korean Writers' Alliance (Chosŏn Munhakka Tongmaeng). The story begins with the hope of the days immediately following Liberation on August 15, 1945: in particular, with the promise and possibility embodied by the Committee for the Preparation of Korean Literature, which was established the day after the Japanese surrender, on August 16, 1945. With its headquarters at the Hanch'ŏng Building in Chongno, the committee is established for the purpose of a "new construction of national literature [*minjok munhak*],"[54] and its core members are familiar, trustworthy faces. When the narrator, accompanied by his friends O Changhwan and Kim Kwanggyun, becomes a regular at the committee's offices, he finds himself side by side with Ri T'aejun, Chŏng Chiyong, and Kim Kirim.[55]

The story thus begins by introducing a cast of banned-writer characters—O Changhwan, Ri T'aejun, Chŏng Chiyong, and Kim Kirim—who reappear throughout the text alongside others, including Ri Yongak, Kim Tongsŏk, Hong Kimun, and Sŏl Chŏngsik. What is significant, moreover, is the way in which these figures are represented. With the exception of O Changhwan and Yi Yongak, all of these characters are presented to the reader as figures of shared hope, understanding, and passion who, for various reasons, end up walking down the regretful path of crossing the thirty-eighth parallel. These figures, in other words, are represented as tragic ones, and the text narrates the unfolding of this tragedy in a series of steps, beginning with the merging of the Committee for the Preparation of Korean Literature with the left-wing Korean Writers' Proletarian Alliance (Chosŏn P'ŭroret'aria Munhak Tongmaeng) to form the Korean Literature Alliance (Chosŏn Munhak Tongmaeng), later renamed the Korean Writers' Alliance. In the story's vision, this process entails the takeover of the committee by KAPF, and it results in the sidelining of the trustworthy, familiar faces that had greeted the narrator at the committee offices.

This is the first tragic turn in the text's vision, and it accelerates as these trustworthy, familiar faces begin to cross the thirty-eighth parallel in response to the crackdown on the alliance and on the Left by the authorities. In the story, such decisions are not presented as betrayals, but rather as regrettable mistakes occasioned, for example, by friendship and "weakness of heart" in the case of Kim Yongjun.[56] And in fact, what the story suggests is that tragedy ended up coming not only to those who decided to go North but also to those who did not. Given the changes in the alliance, the narrator begins to distance himself from the organization. His vision of literature as art does not fit with the politics-first, "warrior" (*t'usa*) mode promoted by the new alliance's leaders, and once the alliance goes underground as a result of the establishment of the South Korean state, he discontinues all ties with it. This does not remove his name, however, from the alliance's roster. As a member of the committee, his name has automatically been transferred to the roster of writers in the alliance, and it remains there even after his association with the group ends. The South Korean state, however, does not see things this way, and once the group goes underground, the state comes to arrest and interrogate the narrator about his affiliation.

The story here takes its final tragic turn, as those who were pushed to the margins of the alliance as "grayists" (*hoesaekchuŭija*) are now being persecuted by the South Korean state for their links to this same group. The narrator, that is, becomes stuck in the middle of the political standoff, and he is not alone. After his first arrest, the narrator is told to join the Reporting League (Podo Yŏnmaeng), a state-sponsored organization for those who have "recanted" (*chŏnhyang*) their leftist beliefs. Joining this organization does not save the narrator from future arrests—later in the story, he is imprisoned again for forty days—but it does give him the opportunity to reunite with some colleagues who have also stayed in the South and entered the league: in particular, Chŏng Chiyong and Sŏl Chŏngsik, two of the banned writers mentioned above.

Caught in the tragedy of the political middle, these "moderates" (*chunggan p'a*) find themselves negatively branded, as Chŏng Chiyong says in the story, by both sides—first as "reactionaries" and now as politically suspect "recanters"—and the text thus articulates a critique of the South Korean state's ideological crackdown alongside its critique of the North, one that had not been present in such a direct form in Yi's 1950s works. It highlights this critique, moreover, by having Chŏng Chiyong recite, at this precise moment, one of his poems, "Horse 1" ("Mal 1"), which is reproduced in the text.[57] The critique of the branding of these individuals as "recanters" is here paired with a rejection of the South Korean state's constraints on the bounds of acceptable discourse, and this is done via the voice of Chŏng Chiyong himself. Yi's story, therefore, moves significantly beyond the model developed in the 1950s, and it ends, powerfully, with the narrator's realization that he no longer has an interest in the horse-drawn carriage (*mach'a*) rides through the city that he had once enjoyed with his friends. Echoing the way that it has outlawed works like Chŏng Chiyong's "Horse," the South Korean state has outlawed such carriages in central Seoul, pushing them to the margins of the city.

Drawing upon the discussions surrounding Matsumoto's *Poet of the North*, Yi's story here renarrates the events of the years between 1945 and 1948 in terms of the dual tragedies of "moderates" who stood in between the political poles established by national division. And while the work of banned literature that this text inserted into its narration was not a postcolonial one, Yi would soon add such a work into the mix of his fiction. In 1972, Yi published a story called "Turkey" ("Ch'ilmyŏnjo") in the journal *Wŏlgan munhak*.[58] "Turkey" is a complex story that takes place in the 1970s present. Yet it looks back to two earlier eras over the course of its narration: the immediate post–April Revolution era; and the immediate post-Liberation era. In the text's 1970s present, the narrator— once again a writer named Yi—encounters an old acquaintance, and the two engage in a set of dialogues about the individuals who connected them in the past: a resident Korean in Japan who had run for the National Assembly in South Korea in the first set of elections after the April Revolution; and the banned poet Ryŏ Sanghyŏn, whose post-1945 trajectory took him North.

The story's two main characters in the 1970s present are thus linked by two mutual acquaintances from the past, and these two mutual acquaintances from the past are, themselves, also linked in dual ways. The first way that they are linked is via the title of the story, "Turkey." "Turkey," as we learn in the text, is the title of a poem and a poetry anthology published by Ryŏ Sanghyŏn in 1946–1947, before he was taken to the North and separated from his acquaintances in the South, who have "no way to know whether he is alive or dead."[59] As in Yi's earlier works, the story here narrates the recitation of this satirical poem—which is reproduced in the text and which offers a critique of the American presence in postcolonial Korea, the various forms of culture that it has imported, and the opportunism of those who have adopted it—from a copy of the eponymous anthology that the nonnarrating character has on his bookshelf. The conversation then turns to the other mutual acquaintance from the past, a resident Korean in Japan named Sŭng who had himself discussed the topic of turkey with the narrator, noting his distaste for it despite its association with luxury because of its links to the opportunistic changeability of its "seven sides."[60]

Additionally, these two figures from the past are also linked together via the tragic fates that they are both said to meet. For Ryŏ Sanghyŏn, this is the "misfortune" (*purhaeng*) of having been "kidnapped to the North" (*nappuk*). Sŭng's tragic fate, on the other hand, is more complicated. Clearly based upon a real individual named Sŭng Hosŏk,[61] Sŭng is a wealthy businessman who made his money in Japan, came to South Korea after the April Revolution, and joined the election for National Assembly, a campaign that the narrator assisted him in and the other character in the 1970s present also supported him in. Because he was a political unknown from Japan, however, rumors about the source of his money and his intentions circulated, including the accusation that his campaign was a front for the Chongryon organization. After this, Sŭng lost a great deal of motivation in his campaign, ultimately failed to be elected, and returned to Japan where he spent all of his money on idealist projects that sought to end the Vietnam War, promote world peace via policies of "neutralism" (*chungnipchuŭi*) and "moderation" (*chungyong chi do*),[62] and more, eventually ending up losing his family, living alone, and making a living as a truck driver in Yokohama.

In the story, therefore, the tragedy of figures like Ryŏ Sanghyŏn, whose names and works have been silenced because, in their calls for national sovereignty and independence, they ended up on the wrong side of the political divide that fractured the cultural realm in Korea after 1945, is linked to that of figures like Sŭng, whose attempts to "contribute to his nation" and, subsequently, find ways beyond the bifurcated Cold War politics of the present are undercut by the entrenched forces of power and the popular cynicism that they have produced. By the same token, the text's recovery of Ryŏ's name and words is tethered to the call for an alternative perspective on individuals like Sŭng. In fact, although Sŭng is commonly derided in the press as a "modern-day Don Quixote,"[63] the narrator and his acquaintance in the 1970s present hope dearly—and believe—that in this changeable, "turkey-like world,"[64] Sŭng's situation will once again swing back toward good fortune. And in fact, they question "which side is the true tragedy" between Sŭng's life trajectory and those who deride him, mistaking the power of his refusal to sacrifice his principles.[65] Mirroring the *Poet of the North* discussions, the story here turns to Japan to challenge the ban on the writings of those who crossed the thirty-eighth parallel, even doing so via texts from the post-1945 era with explicit political content. It also goes farther than this, suggesting that those in Japan who seek seemingly impractical visions of "neutralism" should be embraced rather than derided or rejected.

Of course, there were still limits to the scope of Yi's transgressive practice. In particular, he refrained from referring to texts written in the North or written after the beginning of the Korean War. His focus also stuck very closely to the bounds of his own personal experiences and friendships. It was thus far from an approach that could be drawn upon and replicated by others—especially those of a young generation who had not grown up together with those who had eventually gone North. Younger writers, however, soon developed their own ways of engaging with those who had gone North, and inspiration once again flowed from the controversy surrounding *Poet of the North*—although they used it to go further back in time rather than forward.

NOVEL PASTS

The debate over *Poet of the North* continued to affect the literary and cultural scene for years after the initial publication of the novel, and this was the case not only in South Korea but also in Japan. In part, this was due to a critique of Matsumoto published in South Korea's *Sasanggye* by Hirabayashi Taiko, the Japanese novelist and critic whose interview with

C. Virgil Gheorghiu had been surreptitiously reprinted in South Korea in 1952. Critical of *Poet of the North*, Hirabayashi had suggested, in the pages of a *Sasanggye* roundtable published in August 1962, that Matsumoto was more akin to a "typewriter" than a "human," and she had likewise suggested that he employed a group of ghostwriting assistants, including "communists," in order to produce the vast amount of text that appeared under his name.[66] Not surprisingly, this comment traveled back to Japan, where it produced controversy that was linked in the press to the simultaneous debate over the content of *Poet of the North*.[67]

Another point of contention in Japan, however, dealt more directly with the figure of Rim Hwa. In 1967, as Chang Munsŏk has recently discussed, the Japanese scholar of Korean literature Ōmura Masuo published an article on Rim Hwa's post-1945 activities that sought to redirect discussions of the poet and critic from the details of his life to those of his writing, highlighting, in particular, the possibilities for a Left-Right united front that he had attempted to develop in the immediate post-Liberation era.[68] In doing so, moreover, Ōmura took up texts that had not received significant attention in these recent discussions—including ones from the North—and this approach soon moved back toward South Korea.

In mid-1971, the literary scholar and critic Kim Yunsik, then an assistant professor at Seoul National University, returned to Korea from a yearlong stay as a visiting professor at the University of Tokyo.[69] A specialist in the literary criticism of the Korea Artista Proletaria Federatio (KAPF, 1925–1935), Kim had spent the year seeking out colonial-era research materials not available in Korea in the libraries of Japanese universities.[70] Being in Japan, however, had also allowed Kim to interact with Japanese scholars of Korean literature, including Ōmura.[71] In April 1972, after returning to Korea, Kim published an article on Rim Hwa—which cited Ōmura and which Ōmura would later translate into Japanese[72]—in a journal of humanities and social science research published by Seoul National University.[73] On the one hand, Kim's article clearly drew upon the vision of the tragic as it had emerged in the 1960s in relation to Rim and other writers who had gone North. It thus framed Rim as a "sacrificial offering to history" (*yŏksa ŭi hŭisaengmul*),[74] and it noted the "tragic" end that he had met in the North: one that it acknowledged was tied to the "tragedy" of national division.[75]

At the same time, Kim, who was born in 1936, saw Rim as the symbol of a tragic condition that was neither primarily personal nor solely postcolonial. With distance from the colonial era that his older colleagues had lived through, he saw it, instead, as a condition that infected Rim's entire literary *oeuvre*, and indeed, that of many of his colonial-era colleagues as well. In his article, Kim diagnosed this condition as "Straits [Hyŏnhaet'an] Complex"—a seemingly inescapable yearning for and tethering to the straits between Korea and Japan.[76] It was no accident, Kim argued, that images of the straits between Korea and Japan recurred throughout Rim's poetry as well as that of his contemporaries, and it was also no accident, he said, that Rim's time in Japan exerted such an influence on his development as a revolutionary critic and theorist, again mirroring the experiences of many of his colleagues. And yet, the effects of this fixation on the connection to Japan, Kim argued, were self-contradictory and devastating. What they signaled was the extent to which writers like Rim, while seeking anti-imperial revolution, were entirely colonized in their literary and creative consciousnesses by the forces of empire, as their points of references, modes of thought, and forms of writing were all based upon Western ones imported through the metropole in Japan.

Kim's implantation of the tragic into Rim's *oeuvre* as a whole allowed him to engage with a much wider array of texts than the other writers and critics mentioned above. While these critics avoided engaging with or reproducing Rim's more overtly revolutionary works of the colonial era and his post-1945 works, Kim's analytic of the "Straits Complex" and its tragic double bind allowed him to access the entire swath—or as close as possible to it—of Rim's writing. Kim's article thus reproduced a wide array of quotations from Rim's poetry and critical writings, including the entirety of "The Pier of Yokohama Under the Umbrella" ("Usan padŭn Yokohama ŭi pudu," 1929), whose revolutionary, proletarian vision filled a page and a half of the article's text.[77] Kim's article also broke the 1945 divide, reproducing texts from after division in a groundbreaking and dramatic way. This began with quotations from Rim's immediate post-Liberation criticism written in Seoul and even extended into a discussion of Rim's writing in the North, including a partial reconstruction—via reverse translation from Ōmura's Japanese version—of one of the poems that Rim had published in the DPRK.[78]

Kim's approach also broke the 1945 divide in another way. Since Kim was of a different generation than those mentioned above, his goal in this text was not to reconnect with lost friends or reclaim texts remembered from the past. As a young scholar, Kim's goal was instead to rethink and rewrite Korean literary history, and he saw an engagement with Rim as central to this task. This was because, as Kim noted, Rim's central place in Korean literature was tied not simply to his work as a poet or a theorist of proletarian literature but also—in fact, first and foremost—to his pathbreaking role as a literary historian. Rim, as Kim noted, was the first critic to attempt to write a history of modern Korean literature, and this project—which, for Rim, focused on the precolonial age of the "new novel" (*sin sosŏl*), which had emerged around the turn of the twentieth century—was one that he had first turned to in 1935, after the colonial state's forced breakup of KAPF.

For the field of modern Korean literary history, Kim suggested, Rim was thus unavoidable. He was, in a way, its founding figure, and the enduring tragedy of his "Straits Complex" was not only present in this founding work but also, as a result, in all subsequent works in the field. For Rim, as Kim noted, "modern literature" (*kŭndae munhak*) was a form of "transplanted culture" (*isik munhwa*).[79] It was a foreign entity imported to Korea via Japan from the West, and it was thus fundamentally separated from earlier forms of Korean literature and culture. This meant, as Kim noted, that Rim's project of writing a modern Korean literary history made no attempt to interrogate existing forms of literature in Korea, ignoring them *in toto*. It also meant that Rim made no attempt to define the particularity of the Korean form of modern literature, instead accepting it as a transparent mirroring of the foreign.[80] As a result, Kim argued, Rim's project of looking to the past as a mode of anti-colonial critique was grounded, tragically and paradoxically, in nothing other than colonial consciousness—the search for forms of Korean culture that mirrored the foreign—and this approach likewise marred Rim's postcolonial calls for decolonizing and deimperializing Korean culture. While calling for such decolonizing and deimperializing work, Kim thus poignantly concluded, Rim did not realize that the imperial remnants were "inside himself."[81]

This was not, however, the endpoint of Kim's argument. In postcolonial South Korea, it was not uncommon for critiques of Marxism and revolutionary socialism to frame these forms of thought and organization as foreign imports that stood in opposition to a proper connection to nation and national identity. Kim's discussion of Rim, however, ran counter to such a vision by arguing that Rim's problematic approach to modern Korean literary history had been replicated in subsequent works of literary history published in the postcolonial South—in particular, the influential literary histories written in the South by the critics Paek Ch'ŏl (1949) and Cho Yŏnhyŏn (1961).[82] Critical of these works, Kim suggested that understandings of modern Korean literary history remained at an impasse because the contradictory "Straits Complex" of Rim's founding vision had not been meaningfully addressed but simply replicated in postcolonial South Korean works. In Kim's analysis of methodological precedents in modern Korean literary history, the Left-Right ideological divide thus fell away, and there emerged a direct line linking Rim Hwa, Paek Ch'ŏl, and Cho Yŏnhyŏn as targets of the same category of critique that sought, instead, a proper national consciousness and a proper account of the nation's precolonial literary past.

This had dramatic implications. At roughly the same time that he published his article on Rim Hwa, Kim was beginning to serialize his pathbreaking history of modern Korean literature that he wrote with fellow new-generation critic Kim Hyŏn. Serialized in the journal *Munhak kwa chisŏng* and then published in monograph form, this new history of modern Korean literature offered many significant interventions. Its starting point, however, was a methodological discussion of Rim Hwa's pioneering project of literary history and, once again, the extent to which postcolonial South Korean critics had replicated its problematic approach.[83] In its opening chapter, therefore, which focused on methodological considerations, it turned to the context of Korean literary history via a discussion of Rim, who it critiqued for his literary historical work's assumption that "the modern spirit [*kŭndae chŏngsin*] was a product of the era following the introduction of Western European culture [to Korea]."[84] It then continued by expanding the bounds of this critique's applicability, asserting that this assumption likewise "formed the approach of virtually all literary historians and critics who poured their interest into the modern literature and the modern spirit, leading to the critical problem of the break with tradition of the mid-1950s."[85]

Rim's work here became broadly "representative" of existing methodological approaches and the "coloniality" of their perspectives—something that, the text asserted, reached into postcolonial South Korean scholarship and criticism.[86] For example, the two authors here asserted, as Kim Yunsik had done on his own, that a "radicalized" version of Rim's opinion that "modernization = Westernization" could be found in the work of Paek Ch'ŏl,[87] and as a result, the critique of Rim and his approach once again became detached from Left-Right ideological debates. It became tethered, instead, to the search for a proper understanding of the nation's precolonial literary past, and the influence of this approach spread rapidly to other influential critics in the younger generation. In 1973, the same year that Kim Yunsik and Kim Hyŏn's literary history was published in monograph form, the critic Im Hŏnyŏng likewise traced the practice of writing modern Korean literary history back to Rim Hwa, who he understood, following Kim and Kim's lead, to represent approaches of "coloniality" and "stagnation" (*chŏngch'esŏng*)—not Marxism or materialism—in Korean literary history.[88] Writing in 1974, Yŏm Muung similarly drew upon this work by centering Rim's "theory of cultural transplantation" (*isik munhwaron*) and its replication in subsequent understandings of Korean literature in his call for a proper decolonization and a proper "liquidation" (*ch'ŏngsan*) of colonial remnants.[89]

Once again, therefore, understandings of Rim Hwa and his role in past events and literary debates took on new and complex contours over time, and at stake here was much more than the reception of Rim alone. Indeed, Kim Yunsik's successful reintegration of Rim into literary discussions in ways that exceeded anti-communist critique and connected him to—rather than separated him out from—critical production in the postcolonial South emerged alongside discussions of another banned literary historian: Kim T'aejun, whose pioneering work on premodern Korean literary history Im Chungbin referenced in the 1967 article mentioned at the outset of this chapter. Like Im Chungbin, others writing within an academic context had also referenced Kim's work around this time,[90] and in 1972, a group at Tongguk University had produced an unofficial facsimile copy of one of Kim's pivotal texts: *Chosŏn hanmunhaksa*, a 1931 study of premodern Korean literature written in classical Chinese.[91]

For a wider readership, however, Kim Yunsik and Kim Hyŏn's long-form 1972–1973 study would likely have been one of the earliest texts to include a reference to Kim's pioneering work,[92] and it was once again after this time that Kim's work began popping up in more texts outside the university realm: once again, for example, in the writing of the critic Im Hŏnyŏng.⁹³ What this demonstrates is the interconnection between the reintroduction of Rim Hwa's literary historical work and the reengagement with other banned writers' literary historical work reaching further and further back before the colonial era. And in fact, as we will see below, such developments not only transformed literary criticism and scholarship but literary production as well. For young novelists like Cho Haeil, discussed in depth below, the reintroduction of these literary historians opened up a vital space for interacting with historical literature from the past—and what it also allowed was a new approach, via such interactions, to reclaiming writers who had gone North. Such techniques, moreover, would also form the basis for additional developments of the 1970s and 1980s, when resurgent interest in a deeper past—and in particular, in ancient relations with the Japanese archipelago—would finally enable writers in South Korea to engage directly with North Korean texts.

OUTLAW TEXTS, OUTLAW WRITERS

In 1973, the young author Cho Haeil published a short story titled "Im Kkŏkchŏng" in the South Korean journal *Hyŏndae munhak*.⁹⁴ This was the first of seven such stories that he would go on to write in the 1970s and 1980s, a set subsequently published as a linked-novel in 1986. Im was a bandit leader from the Chosŏn dynasty, and he had been the subject of an array of colonial-era, postcolonial North Korean, and postcolonial South Korean cultural production ranging from novels and plays to films, television shows, and radio dramas. However, by far the most famous of these accounts of Im's life and exploits was the original work of fiction produced about him: Hong Myŏnghŭi's *Im Kkŏkchŏng*, which made extensive use of Chosŏn-era historical records, bringing them together to shape its narrative.⁹⁵ An unfinished work of the colonial-era canon, Hong's novel had originally been serialized in the *Chosŏn ilbo* newspaper between 1928 and 1939 before moving to the journal *Chogwang*, when it briefly resumed publication in 1940 before being discontinued. It had then been partially republished in Seoul after 1945 before being banned as a result of the author's division-era itinerary. Hong had not only gone North but also attained a high political position, serving as vice premier. His writing was thus far beyond the pale in South Korea, and it was not included in any of the developments mentioned above. Likewise, when writers and other artists had recreated Im narratives in the South, they had not mentioned Hong or his work directly.

Cho's Im Kkŏkchŏng series, however, took this leap, and it was able to do so because of its unique narrative conceit and form. Rather than a self-contained narrative that introduces the character Im, his life, and his exploits—the form that other Im narratives of this era took—Cho's work offers its reader a set of fragmentary anecdotes presented in nonchronological order. It functions, therefore, as a set of supplementary tales that are meant to be understood not on their own but in relation to and in dialogue with previous Im narratives. This is made explicit, for example, in the novel's second installment, originally published in 1975, which centers Hong's banned text as its primary point of reference by prefacing its narrative of Im's death with a note that this scene is missing from Hong's original novel because it was "discontinued before reaching this part of the story."[96] Cho's novel here frames its vision vis-à-vis Hong's, which, it further says in this installment, is "known to be the most outstanding of all stories about Im Kkŏkchŏng,"[97] and indeed, in a 2000 essay published with a reprint of the monograph version of the novel, Cho noted that the text had been inspired by the "good luck" (*haengun*) of having come into contact with Hong's novel, a banned text that was "a thing of legend at the time."[98]

In this way, Cho's novel points to Hong's banned text even if it cannot directly articulate its words, and it also attempts to stake out a new relationship to the text's author. Each installment of Cho's work offers its reader a new anecdote about Im's life and exploits, and it does so via a recurring conceit; it presents each of these anecdotes as knowledge gleaned from newly acquired or newly discovered sources that the narrator claims to be reproducing—with a bit of "imagination"—for the reader. The narrator of the novel, who inhabits these narrative frames, is thus a particular kind of figure—a scholarly chronicler of the past—and this allows the novel to leverage the possibilities developed by Kim Yunsik. Just as the position of Rim Hwa shifted when Kim approached him as a fellow literary historian—someone attempting to make sense of the same national past—so too does Cho's text develop a way to engage with

Hong's text, made possible once it turns its narrator into a literary historian (or rather, a literary kind of historian) who is compiling anecdotes about the same historical figure.

There is, moreover, one additional intervention in the text. Cho's novel contains seven chapters, each of which presents one anecdote that supplements the existing narrative and thus expands the dialogue with Hong's original. As noted above, these anecdotes do not follow a chronological order in relation to Im's life. Nevertheless, the narrative does ultimately have a direction, as its latter installments depict Im's transformation from an outlaw beyond the pale of society into a figure of moderation and acculturation. At first, the Im who appears in Cho's narrative is more or less the type of character the reader would expect: an unwavering and ruthless man of strength and resolve who will do whatever it takes to rebel against and destroy the structures of corruption and oppression around him. It is thus not surprising that the outcome of Im's first set of encounters with other characters end with him bending them to his will: either defeating them or convincing them to follow and support him. In the novel's latter episodes, however, this dynamic begins to change. In episode six, a scholar seeks out Im, hoping to convince him to try to be less ruthless and violent, and somewhat inexplicably, Im ultimately agrees, calling upon his men to spare human life as much as possible. And episode seven, most strikingly, features a *kisaeng* teaching Im how to read and write the Korean vernacular script, inverting the existing power relationship between the courtesan and the womanizing rebel and bringing Im into the fold of the world of texts, learning, and reciprocal exchanges.

Although Im does not lose his sense of justice or his dedication to resistance, his excesses are here moderated, and he is incorporated into society in a way not previously possible. Once a rebel on the margins of society, Im here becomes a literate man within its textual bounds, and the final pages of the novel take this transformation one step further. In these final pages, the text reproduces a piece of writing that is presented as the work of Im himself, something that he "wrote later in life" and has once again been found in the text's newly acquired sources, which were supposedly compiled by a contemporary scholar named Hŏ Sun, a character from the text's first installment.[99] At this moment, Im becomes not merely literate but also a writer, and the story ends by quoting the words of reaction that Hŏ had supposedly appended to this text: "This is nothing more than the text of someone who was once a thief, but in its discussion of the genuine [ch'amdoem], no composition by a minister of state is comparable."[100] The outlaw becomes a writer whose words are judged for their content rather than the background of their author, and the story thus ends by calling, implicitly, for a similar engagement with Hong's work.

Of course, the implicit nature of this call meant that readers of Cho's work were never quite able to engage with Hong's novel. Other forces in the cultural realm, however, took action to make this happen. In September 1985, a Kwangju-based publishing company called Sagyejŏl published a nine-volume set of Hong's original novel.[101] Since Sagyejŏl submitted a copy of the work to the ROK state as required by publication guidelines, this publication of Hong's work was clearly not meant to be a clandestine act.[102] It thus demonstrated the extent to which the bounds of acceptable discourse in South Korea had become malleable by this time, especially since, as Chang Munsŏk has noted, this republication in the South coincided with the novel's 1982–1985 republication in the North in an edited form prepared by the author's grandson, Hong Sŏkchung.[103] Yet it also demonstrated the opposite: that is, the extent to which these bounds remained present, rigid, and enforceable. Soon after the book was sent to bookstores across the country, the South Korean state decided that it was unacceptable, ordering the confiscation of all copies.[104]

In the literary sphere, this provoked a range of responses. On the one hand, publishers attempted to go around state regulation. As Chang Munsŏk has discussed in detail, beginning in September 1986, the publishing company Kiminsa began rereleasing a series of colonial-era and immediate post-Liberation fiction and poetry monographs by writers who had gone North.[105] The following year, they were joined in this endeavor by a second publishing company, Sŭlgi,[106] and what was particular about these two companies' actions, as Chang has further noted, was the fact that they labeled the works as "not for sale" (pimaep'um). They thus did not submit them to the authorities for vetting and only distributed them via certain bookshops.[107] On the other hand, some writers responded differently, moving not only much further into the past but also to the spatial context of the Japanese archipelago and the border between literature, history, and archeology. As we will see below, this approach allowed the novelist Ch'oe Inho to reengage with the work of those who had gone North in creative new ways.

AT TAKAMATSUZUKA

In 1972, an unexpected archeological discovery electrified the Korean and Japanese media domains, bringing them together—and linking the two Koreas—in new ways. In March of that year, archeologists doing excavation work at Asuka Village in Nara, Japan's ancient capital, entered the Takamatsuzuka Tumulus for the first time and discovered a set of colorful murals that appeared to resemble those previously discovered in tumuli in the ancient Korean kingdom of Koguryŏ. Speculation about the significance of this similarity spread like wildfire throughout Japan, and so, too, did it ignite burning interest in the Koreas. Coming less than a year after the groundbreaking discovery of the tomb of King Muryŏng, the twenty-fifth king of the ancient Korean kingdom of Paekche, in present-day Kongju, South Korea, the emergence of these murals further invigorated the transformation of archeology into a topic of broad cultural discussion and relevance.

It also spurred uncommon trajectories of physical movement and interaction. In October 1972, just months after the July 4 South-North Joint Communiqué had softened tensions on the Korean peninsula, North and South Korean historians and archeologists arrived in tandem in Nara to inspect the Takamatsuzuka Tumulus. This put them in the same physical space and gave them the uncommon opportunity to share their thoughts. It also gave them the chance, as an October 5, 1972, report in South Korea's *Tonga ilbo* newspaper made clear, to confirm that such interactions had already been in process via more indirect means. Printed underneath a much longer transcript of a discussion about the murals between one of the newspaper's editorial board members and Kim Wŏllyong, an eminent historian who was then director of the Seoul National University Museum, the report offered a brief account of an exchange between North and South Korean scholars under the headline, "South-North Dialogue at Asuka Village—South: 'I read your book,' North: 'I was classmates with Prof. Yu Hongnyŏl.'"[108]

In fact, what the brief transcript of this exchange made clear was that the links between North and South Korean historians and archeologists were much more symmetrical than this headline suggested. After Kim Wŏllyong told the North Korean scholar Chu Yŏnghŏn that he had read his recent book on Koguryŏ murals, the North Korean historian Kim Sŏkhyŏng reciprocated by telling the South Korean historian Yi Kibaek that he was familiar with his work.[109] The transcript, moreover, also gestured toward the trajectories that at least some of these preceding interactions had taken. Kim Wŏllyong, in fact, did not simply tell Chu that he had read his book; he did so and added that he had read it in Japanese translation—a remediation, he noted, that had rendered the photographs less than legible.[110] What this encounter made clear, therefore, was not simply that new North-South exchanges emerged in-and-via Japan in the 1970s but also that they had already taken shape in translated textual forms in previous years.

Although they did not explicitly say so during this exchange at Takamatsuzuka, it is clear that Yi Kibaek, Kim Wŏllyong, and their South Korean colleagues would also have been quite aware of Kim Sŏkhyŏng's recent work. One of the most influential and respected historians in the North, Kim had come to be known, in particular, for his "subordinate state theory" (*pun'guksŏl*). First proposed in 1963, Kim's theory was an attempt to overturn the heritage of colonial-era historiography and its vision of the ancient relationship between the Korean peninsula and the Japanese islands. During the colonial period, the imperial state—as well as the historians and archeologists who served as apologists for it—attempted to justify Japanese rule over the Korean peninsula by pointing to historical precedent. Drawing upon ancient Japanese records such as the *Nihon shoki* and the *Kojiki*, the state and its scholars asserted that Empress Jingū had conquered the southern portion of the Korean peninsula in the fourth century and established a Japanese outpost in the southeastern kingdom of Kaya (Kr. Imna Ilbonbu, Jp. Mimana Nihonfu) in order to "enforce," as E. Taylor Atkins puts it, "the continual subjugation of the Korean kings to Japanese imperial authority" for the next two centuries.[111]

Such visions of ancient Japanese control over portions of the Korean peninsula by no means disappeared after the end of colonial rule, and it was in direct opposition to such theories that Kim formulated his "subordinate state theory." Unlike other Korean scholarship from the postcolonial era, Kim's theory did not simply reject the assertions of colonial historiography. It went further by inverting them: that is, by arguing that it was in fact Korean states that had, in ancient times, established subordinate state structures on the Japanese islands. Kim first articulated this theory in a 1963 article published in the North Korean journal *Ryŏksa kwahak*.[112] Titled "On the Subordinate States of the Three Han and Three Kingdoms in the Japanese Archipelago" ("Samhan Samguk ŭi Ilbon ryŏlto nae pun'guktŭl e taehayŏ"), the article brought together a range of sources from Japan, Korea, and China to argue that many of the more than thirty small states that supposedly existed on the Japanese archipelago prior to the establishment of a centralized state in the fifth century were subordinate states tied via migrant lineages and ongoing interactions to polities on the Korean peninsula.

Furthermore, Kim then used this assertion to reinterpret the evidential basis upon which imperial historiography was formed. The states referenced in ancient Japanese records of conquest, Kim asserted, were not states that existed on the Korean peninsula. On the contrary, he wrote, they were subordinate states of these polities that existed in the Japanese archipelago.[113] What these records described, therefore, was not an early history of Japanese domination of the Korean peninsula but rather the gradual formation of a centralized state in Japan.[114] And likewise, the much-discussed institution of the so-called Japanese outpost in Imna or Mimana was thus, Kim argued, something that had existed in the subordinate state of the Korean kingdom of Imna or Kaya in the Japanese islands rather than the other side of the East Sea.[115] In Kim's work, ancient Japanese records of conquest were not rejected but reinterpreted; what they memorialized, first and foremost, was the historical power of Korean states in the Japanese archipelago prior to the fifth century.

Kim's theory, which he expanded into a full-length monograph in 1966,[116] was not the first attempt to rethink the direction of influence in East Asia. As Kim Ch'aesu has discussed in detail, Egami Namio's "Horse-Rider Theory" (*kiba minzoku setsu*) of 1948–1949 had attempted a similar inversion of the direction of influence, drawing upon earlier precedents in the 1930s work of Oka Masao.[117] Yet Kim's theory was nevertheless transformational, and its sphere of influence was not restricted to the North Korean context where it originated. South Korean scholars like Kim Sanggi were already discussing this theory as early as 1966, although they generally did not mention the author's name directly.[118] By the early 1970s, however, this reception had become far more robust, positive, and open, and indeed, as Wi Kaya has shown, the South Korean high school textbooks developed between 1974 and 1979—with entries on ancient history by the historian Kim Ch'ŏljun, who had already begun publishing about Kim's work in 1973—incorporated the theory, teaching that Paekche and Kaya had established "colonies" (*singminji*) in Japan.[119] Moreover, this reception would soon be integrated into South Korean literary production. The itinerary of this reception, however, was once again complex, and it once again operated through Japan: in particular, via the mediation of ethnic Korean writers and scholars, for whom the late 1960s and early 1970s was a time of great change.

Kim's original article from *Ryŏksa kwahak* appeared in translation in three installments in the Japanese journal *Rekishi hyōron* in 1964, just one year after its original publication.[120] The three-part translation of Kim's 1963 article was done by Chŏng Chinhwa and bears his name. However, the translation had been arranged, assigned to him, and then edited by the archeologist Ri Chinhŭi, who was then a professor at Chongryon's Korea University in Japan and Chŏng's supervisor.[121] As Ri later explained in his memoir, the goal of assigning Chŏng this task, something that he had discussed with the historian Pak Kyŏngsik, was educational; it was oriented toward Chŏng's development as a researcher.[122] However, it also fit squarely within ongoing work that Ri had already been engaged in himself since 1960: namely, "introducing the achievements of North Korean research" to a Japanese-language audience,[123] primarily via archeological journals like *Kōkogaku kenkyū* and *Kōkogaku zasshi*.

The translation of Kim's theory into Japanese was thus closely bound up with Ri's broader work of linking North Korean scholars and Japanese scholars. This work and its reception, however, were also fundamentally shaped by Ri's own idiosyncratic trajectory as a scholar and public intellectual. Ri was the son-in-law of O Kwisŏng,[124] an influential Chongryon activist who had supported the project of "repatriation" (*kwiguk*) to North Korea before turning against it and publishing a controversial monograph-length exposé that was subsequently translated into Korean and republished in South Korea.[125] In the early 1960s, when O had broken with Chongryon and written this exposé, Ri had strongly criticized his father-in-law and refused to support his dissent.[126] By the early 1970s, however, Ri's own path had taken a similar turn, and he soon had a falling out with Chongryon, resigning from his professorship at Korea University in April 1971.[127] This allowed him to reconnect with O, and it also allowed his work to be received in new domains.

In late 1972, Ri published his most influential work of scholarship, *Research on the Stele Inscription of King Kwanggaet'o* (*Kōkaido-ō ryōhi no kenkyū*), a monograph—based upon two articles published earlier that year in the Japanese journals *Shisō* and *Kōkogaku zasshi*—that was followed the next year by a closely related monograph, *The Riddle of the King Kwanggaet'o Stele* (*Kōtaiōhi no nazo*). In these texts, Ri sought, like Kim, to overturn some of the basic tenets of colonial-era historiography on ancient Korean-Japanese relations. His approach, however, was quite different. Rather than offering alternative interpretations of extant texts and evidence, Ri questioned their authenticity. In particular, his argument focused on the inscription found on an ancient stele marking the tomb of King Kwanggaet'o, the nineteenth king of the ancient Korean dynasty of Koguryŏ, whose territory extended beyond the Amnok River. Long neglected, the stele's inscription once again gained state and scholarly attention in the late nineteenth century, when the overgrowth obscuring it was removed and a variety of rubbings were produced. In particular, the stele inscription became central to the emerging narrative of Japanese colonial historiography, which claimed, as noted above, that ancient Japan had conquered and subjugated the southern half of the Korean peninsula in the fourth century. This centrality emerged from a single phrase in the inscription relating to the events of the *sinmyo* year of 391, which Japanese scholars interpreted as recording ancient Japan's subjugation of the Korean kingdoms of Silla and Paekche. And indeed, the stele inscription became one of the most frequently cited pieces of evidence in colonial historiography's narrative of ancient Japanese-Korean relations.

The meaning of this particular passage, however, was far from clear. Multiple characters were no longer legible, and the grammatical structure of the classical Chinese text, too, was open to multiple interpretations. Even before Ri Chinhŭi, therefore, Korean scholars had challenged the standard Japanese interpretation of the passage. As both Ri and Kim Sŏkhyŏng noted in their work, the South Korean scholar Chŏng Inbo had argued in the mid-1950s that this interpretation relied upon an awkward reading of the classical Chinese phrasing and that the subject of the action of subjugation was in fact Koguryŏ not Japan.[128] Chŏng, moreover, had not been alone in pursuing reinterpretations of the stele text. Others in the South had picked up this task from Chŏng, offering their own reinterpretations, and so, too, had scholars in the North. Such work, for example, had been pursued by scholars in the North like Pak Sihyŏng, who published a monograph on the stele in 1966,[129] three years after visiting the site in present-day Jilin Province in China alongside Kim Sŏkhyŏng and others as part of a joint North Korean-Chinese archeological project.[130]

In contrast, Ri's rejection of the colonial use of the inscription was based upon the claim that the versions of the inscription that these interpretations drew upon were fabricated—and in fact multiply so. Central to Ri's argument was the revelation, produced in dialogue with other scholars working in Japan at the time, that the person responsible for bringing the first reproduction of the inscription back to Japan in 1883 was a Japanese military spy named Sako Kagenobu.[131] Ri's claim, moreover, was that the version of the inscription that he brought back to Japanese military headquarters was not a rubbing of the original inscription but rather an altered one that had been manipulated via the addition of lime.[132] He further argued that the inscription had been altered with lime once again in 1899–1900 in order to prevent detection of this earlier manipulation.[133]

In making this argument, Ri marshaled a wide array of evidence: most importantly, copies of all available rubbings from different periods, as well as photos of the inscription taken at various points. And what he claimed to be able to demonstrate by comparing these images was that the relative clarity of the characters in the initial rubbings had degraded over time and that certain of these characters had eventually come to look like different ones. For Ri, this gradual degradation and transformation was the outcome of the lime that had been added breaking apart and subsequently revealing the original inscription, and it spoke to the calculated and multistage process of manipulation that, he said, the Japanese military had engaged in for the benefit of its enterprise of imperial expansion and ideological justification.[134]

Not surprisingly, Ri's claim was met with both strong backlash and heroizing exaltation, and this latter response, in particular, crossed national boundaries with speed. Before the 1970s, Ri had not been a welcome figure in South Korea. Born in South Kyŏngsang Province in 1929, he had fled the ROK in 1948 because of the South Korean state's crackdown on the Left.[135] Crossing over to Japan with the determination to "study socialist theory deeply,"[136] he had soon become associated with the Korean Left in Japan, eventually joining Chongryon and taking up his professorship at Korea University. However, with his 1971 resignation and the publication of his work on the Kwanggaet'o Stele beginning in 1972, he suddenly became a national hero in the South Korean press. No longer affiliated with a pro-DPRK organization, his work on ancient history could be represented as a vindication of long-standing Korean rejections of colonial historiography. Ri's work—while not republished in Korean translation at the time since at least some of it continued to critique "American imperialism"[137]—was thus reported on and featured in a wide range of South Korean newspapers and journals, and this enthusiastic reception meant not only that his scholarship on the Kwanggaet'o Stele was embraced but also that his other endeavors—including his prior work introducing Kim Sŏkhyŏng's "subordinate state theory" to Japan—could be similarly taken up in new ways.

This was evident, for example, in an August 1972 article published in the popular magazine *Sindonga* by the influential South Korean historian Kim Chŏngbae.[138] Kim's article focused on recent scholarly developments that were in the process of "overturning" (*twijip'ida*) the colonial-era theory of the Japanese outpost at Imna/Mimana, and it focused a large chunk of its attention on Ri's work, which, at the time, had only been published in article form in the Japanese intellectual journal *Shisō*. For Kim, Ri's research on the supposed manipulation and alteration of the Kwanggaet'o Stele was powerful and persuasive. Yet it was also, he suggested, embedded in a broader set of scholarly developments that challenged the colonial-era interpretation of the Stele inscription. Kim's article thus went back in time, and the previous scholarship that he introduced—in addition to a brief mention of Chŏng Inbo—was a set of texts by North Korean scholars who, his citations suggested, he had been keeping tabs on via Japan: Pak Sihyŏng and Kim Sŏkhyŏng.[139]

With the reception of Ri's work, that is, it became possible to look back to Kim Sŏkhyŏng's theory in new ways, and this became evident in subsequent years. Indeed, in 1973, when the historian Kim Ch'ŏljun published an article on ancient Paekche culture in the *Kyŏnghyang sinmun* newspaper, Kim Sŏkhyŏng's "subordinate state theory" was clearly a part of the article's basic framework, as it asserted that it was "clear that the Paekche had a subordinate state [*pun'guk*] in a region of Japan," which it then identified as northwest Kyūshū.[140] As noted above, it was Kim Ch'ŏljun who later wrote the ancient history sections of South Korean high school textbooks, and there was thus a direct line between this reception in 1973 and the broader dissemination of this theory in South Korean society. Therefore, as Ri Chinhŭi came in from the cold, so too did the North Korean scholars that he had written about, and something similar happened, as we will see below, in relation to other resident Korean writers that Ri had a close working relationship with: in particular, Kim Talsu, a novelist and self-trained historian then serving as editor of *Nihon no naka no Chōsen bunka* (Korean Culture in Japan), a Japanese-language journal whose editorial activities Ri became involved with in January 1972, after his departure from Chongryon's Korea University.[141]

KOREA(S) IN JAPAN

In January 1973, the popular magazine *Sindonga* published a special issue on the topic of ancient Korean-Japanese relations. This special issue included a range of works from South Korean scholars, and it demonstrated that extent to which once-niche discussions of archeology and ancient history had become topics of popular interest. It also included a work from abroad whose origins were significant, as it was not only translated from Japanese but republished from a specific Japanese-language journal: *Nihon no naka no Chōsen bunka*. Founded in 1969, *Nihon no naka no Chōsen bunka* was an independent publication financed by Chŏng Chomun, a Kyoto-based businessman.[142] According to Ri Chinhŭi, however, it operated on the margins of the Chongryon organization, and before beginning publication, Chŏng Chomun and Kim Talsu, the magazine's editor, supposedly sought permission from Chongryon.[143] Moreover, despite repeated tensions, it appears to have continued to exist within the extended Chongryon orbit until it ceased publication in 1981.

It is remarkable, therefore, that a text from this publication found its way into the January 1973 special feature in South Korea's *Sindonga*, and this text's content, too, was significant. Written by the Japanese historian Ueda Masaaki, a frequent contributor to the publication, the text was a 1971 article about the Isonokami Shrine and a particular artifact housed there: the Seven-Branched Sword (Kr. Ch'iljido, Jp. Shichishitō), an ancient product of the kingdom of Paekche supposedly given by the kingdom's ruler to a Yamato king at some point between the third and sixth centuries.[144] Like the Kwanggaet'o Stele, the Seven-Branched Sword had been (re)discovered in the late nineteenth century and had been used extensively in colonial historiography as evidence of an ancient conquest of significant swaths of the Korean peninsula by Japan; the sword, in this interpretation, was given as a gift of tribute from a subaltern ruler to a superior one.

Like the Kwanggaet'o Stele, however, the meaning—and eventually, authenticity—of the inscription on the sword had become a topic of controversy in the postcolonial decades. Indeed, Kim Sŏkhyŏng's seminal 1963 essay, discussed above, had also discussed this sword, arguing that its terminology in fact suggested that the sword was one bestowed by a superior ruler on a subservient one,[145] and this was a central point of reference that Ueda introduced in this 1971 article. Although Ueda did not believe that Kim's alternative reading had been fully substantiated, he did emphasize the importance of challenging the colonial-era perspectives and assumptions that had shaped existing interpretations of the sword and other facets of ancient relations between the Korean peninsula and the Japanese archipelago.[146] Indeed, Ueda's central argument in the article did not have to do with the Seven-Branched Sword or the Isonokami Shrine in particular. His goal, more broadly, was to articulate an indictment of the persistence of a colonial-era historiographical vision of these ancient relations, and the term he used for this persistent historiographical vision was likewise significant.

Picking up on earlier work that he had produced in the 1960s and early 1970s, Ueda associated this historiographical vision with the term "naturalized person" (Jp. *kikajin*, Kr. *kwihwain*) as it was used to refer to those who had migrated from the Korean peninsula to the Japanese archipelago in the ancient period. This was a term that he had been critical of in the past—proposing, instead, the use of the term "person who has migrated" (Jp. *toraijin*, Kr. *toraein*)—and in this project he was joined by others. In particular, he had discussed these terms and the issues associated with them in the inaugural roundtable hosted by *Nihon no naka no Chōsen bunka*, and his interlocutor during this discussion, Kim Talsu, the editor of the journal, had also written about this issue repeatedly both inside the journal and outside.[147] Not surprisingly, then, Ueda's 1971 article began by introducing the problem with the term *kikajin* via an extended quote from Kim.[148]

For readers of *Sindonga*'s translation of Ueda's article, the argument put forth in these opening paragraphs from one of Kim's articles might not have been shocking; it asserted the irrationality of referring to migrants of this period as "naturalized persons" when a unified state and culture did not yet exist (or was still inchoate) in the Japanese archipelago.[149] More surprising for *Sindonga*'s readers, instead, would have been the identity of the author of these quoted paragraphs. As discussed in chapter 2, throughout the late 1940s, 1950s, and much of the 1960s, Kim Talsu had worked as a novelist and critic, and he had been the most influential and well-known leftist writer in the ethnic Korean community in Japan. In the late 1960s, however, he had come into conflict with the Chongryon organization, and he was purged alongside the writer Ri Kaisei in 1972.[150] In tandem, Kim's attention turned toward the past, and in particular, toward the ancient history of Korean and Japanese interactions. As noted in chapter 2, this did not signal a pulling back from activism, but together, these two developments allowed his writing to appear in South Korea.

In fact, Kim's words did not only appear in the pages of Ueda's article in *Sindonga*. Readers would also have gotten access to them in the pages of *Ilbon munje*, a publication of the Research Center for the Japan Problem (Ilbon Munje Yŏn'guso). Established in 1973, *Ilbon munje* was published by the center's leader at the time, Kwŏn Il, a lawyer and colonial-era collaborator who had served as leader of the South Korea–affiliated Mindan between 1961 and 1967 before leaving Japan for South Korea, where he became a member of the National Assembly in 1971.[151] Like *Sindonga*, *Ilbon munje* carried translations of articles from *Nihon no naka no Chōsen bunka*, publishing two articles from the journal in its Summer 1973 issue.[152] Even before this, however, the journal's Spring 1973 issue had included a roundtable, originally published the year before in Japan, featuring Kim Talsu in conversation with the Japanese writer Tanigawa Ken'ichi and the Japanese archeologist Okazaki Takashi.[153]

This roundtable gave South Korean readers direct access to Kim Talsu's words for perhaps the first time. Moreover, it gave South Korean readers an introductory glimpse of—among other topics—Kim's ongoing interest in the influence of ancient Korean language on ancient Japanese language and formative ancient texts in the Japanese canon. This interest, as Kim noted, was by no means his alone. In the roundtable, he referenced Japanese scholars whose research on this topic went back decades,[154] and other writings from this period also extended the discussion to the *Man'yōshū*, the eighth-century anthology that contains the oldest extant works of Japanese poetry, and which, Kim said, appeared to contain a large number of works by migrants from the Korean peninsula, including, most notably, Yamanoue no Okura, who the Japanese scholar Susumu Nakanishi had argued was a migrant from the kingdom of Paekche.[155]

This would have been a claim that was familiar not only to Kim's Japanese interlocutors but also, and increasingly, to interested readers in the South. At roughly the same time that the above roundtable appeared in *Ilbon munje*, similar topics were being discussed in Seoul's *Tonga ilbo* newspaper. In February 1973, the newspaper reported on a recent scholarly conference held in Japan at which the South Korean scholar Kim Sayŏp, then a visiting scholar at Osaka Foreign Languages University, had made similar claims about the influence of ancient Korean on ancient Japanese language and writing, including the *Man'yōshū*, which Kim would subsequently translate.[156] Although the *Tonga ilbo* report did not give detailed information about this conference, a simultaneous report in Seoul's *Kyonghyang sinmun* did, noting that the conference was organized by the Association for the Ancient Culture of East Asia (Tongbu Asia ŭi Kodae Munhwahoe).[157] This referred to a group that had been formed the previous year in Japan, the Association for the Consideration of the Ancient Culture of East Asia (Higashi Ajia no Kodai Bunka o Kangaeru Kai), and the founders included Ri Chinhŭi and Kim Talsu alongside a number of Japanese colleagues.[158]

It can be assumed, therefore, that these two scholars participated in the conference alongside Kim Sayŏp. And indeed, in 1975, when a piece of Kim Sayŏp's writing on the *Memorabilia of the Three Kingdoms* (*Samguk yusa*) appeared in translation in the group's journal, *Higashi Ajia no kodai bunka*, it appeared side by side with work by these two former

Chongryon figures.¹⁵⁹ This was also the case for a number of South Korean scholars—including Ch'ŏn Kwanu and Chi Myŏnggwan—whose work also appeared in the journal in these years.

Moreover, this group and this journal were not the only point of intersection linking South Korean scholarship on the ancient period with Ri Chinhŭi, Kim Talsu, and the latter's interest in the influence of ancient Korean on both Japanese language and pieces of writing such as the *Man'yōshū*. In late April 1973, the *Tonga ilbo* newspaper ran an interview with the former Buddhist monk Kim Unhak, a literary scholar who had recently completed a PhD in Japan and returned to Korea to take up a teaching post at Tongguk University in Seoul.¹⁶⁰ In this interview, Kim again made similar claims about Korean influence on ancient Japanese language and writing, including the *Man'yōshū*, and this was something that he would soon expand upon in articles published in South Korea. In 1974, Kim published an article in a Tongguk University journal on the relationship between ancient Korean and Japanese verse. This article was later republished in the literary journal *Hyŏndae munhak*,¹⁶¹ yet what stood out about this initial version was its citation of a roundtable from *Nihon no naka no Chōsen bunka* that included Kim Talsu and his discussion of Korean influence on the *Man'yōshū*.¹⁶²

What this demonstrates is the extent to which the work of Ri Chinhŭi and Kim Talsu, which had previously been off-limits due to these two individuals' central place in Chongryon, became points of reference and topics of discussion in South Korea in the 1970s. Most directly, this work included Ri Chinhŭi's research on the King Kwanggaet'o Stele and Kim Talsu's extensive research into the influence of Korean migrants and their language and writing on ancient Japanese culture. But it also included the broader mediating work that the engagement with these two scholars facilitated. The reception of Ri Chinhŭi's own research beginning in 1972 came packaged together with the reception of his work introducing Kim Sŏkhyŏng's "subordinate state theory" to Japan, and in the case of Kim Talsu, too, reception of his individual work also meant the reception, more broadly, of one of the journals he edited, *Nihon no naka no Chōsen bunka*, which retained a Chongryon link even after Kim himself had left. What this meant was that the engagement with these two figures also made possible a more challenging engagement with North Korean scholars and scholarship, and indeed, as we will see in the next section, the 1980s work of the South Korean novelist Ch'oe Inho, who interacted directly with Kim and Ri, brought all of these influences together in a triangular dialogue in his epic work, *The Lost Kingdom* (*Irhŏbŏrin wangguk*, 1985–1988).

IN SEARCH OF LOST TIME

In 1981, Ri Chinhŭi and Kim Talsu visited South Korea alongside Kang Chaeŏn, a historian who collaborated with Ri and Kim in a range of endeavors, including *Kikan sanzenri*, the journal mentioned in chapter 2. The explicit goal of the trip was to push for the release of a group of ethnic Korean students from Japan who were being held on pro-DPRK espionage charges by the ROK, but a secondary intention was to further build links to writers, scholars, and readers in the South. Reports on this trip appeared widely in the South Korean press at the time, and Kim, Ri, and Kang also sat for interviews that were published for a popular readership. One such interview appeared in *Sindonga*, and it did so under a familiar title, albeit this time in Korean: "Korea/Korean Culture in Japan" ("Ilbon sok ŭi Han'guk/Han'guk munhwa"). Like the Japanese-language publication of virtually the same name, this interview focused on the heritage of ancient connections spanning the East Sea, and it included discussions of a range of issues from that of *kikajin/kwihwain* vs. *toraijin/toraein* to the linguistic influence of ancient Korean on ancient Japanese texts, issues that, as noted above, had been introduced to South Korean readers in the 1970s.[163]

It also paved the way for much longer and more significant works by these individuals to appear in the popular press. The year after this visit, Ri Chinhŭi returned to South Korea twice: once in January to give a lecture as part of a seminar held at the National Institute of Korean History (Kuksa P'yŏnch'an Wiwŏnhoe),[164] whose director at the time, Ch'oe Yŏnghŭi, he had interacted with during the previous year's visit; and once in May to illuminate the traces of "Japan in Korea" left by Japanese delegations from the historical past.[165] Ri's itinerary during this latter visit, on which he was accompanied by a group of fifteen others from Japan,[166] served as the core for a historical travelogue that he serialized around the same time in Seoul's *Kyŏnghyang sinmun*, the offices of which he had visited in his January visit.[167] This historical travelogue appeared in forty-two installments published over the course of thirteen months between May 1982 and June 1983, providing readers with ample opportunity to become acquainted with Ri's historical vision. Moreover, also in 1982, Ri's work on the King Kwanggaet'o Stele, the Seven-Branched Sword, Korean-style fortresses in Japan, and other related topics appeared in monograph form in Korean translation.[168]

Given Kim Talsu's previously canonical position within the DPRK-affiliated literary world, it took longer for his writing to appear in an extended form in South Korea. However, it soon did. Between December 1985 and March 1986, the *Chosŏn ilbo* newspaper serialized a version of Kim's long-running historical travelogue, *Nihon no naka no Chōsen bunka* (a work with the same title as the journal Kim edited), under the title "The Korea Alive in Japan" ("Ilbon e sara innŭn Han'guk"). This was a monumental development, one that solidified Kim's idiosyncratic, boundary-crossing itinerary from revolutionary author celebrated in the North to historical pioneer embraced in the South, and significant too was the crossing that it performed in the pages of the *Chosŏn ilbo* with another serialized text that also began in 1985: the novelist Ch'oe Inho's *The Lost Kingdom*.

In October 1986, after publishing the initial five hundred installments of the novel in the *Chosŏn ilbo*, Ch'oe gave an interview with the newspaper in which he discussed the origins of the work, which by this time had become quite popular. Having traveled to Japan in 1984 to take part in a dialogue with Japanese scholars, Ch'oe explained, he had had the opportunity to meet Ri Chinhŭi and Kim Talsu: "Arriving in Japan, I met the resident Korean writer Kim Talsu and the historian Ri Chinhŭi [Yi Chinhŭi], who were knowledgeable about Korean-Japanese ancient history, and I got to know in depth the traces of our culture left in Japan. Traveling together, I learned that Paekche, Silla, and Koguryŏ, which have already disappeared in our country, are still alive in Japan in the names of places, the names of buildings, and more, and I was shocked."[169] The shock and wonder of encountering this history and this remaining presence, Ch'oe said, had given him the inspiration for the novel, and this was something that he repeated in his introduction to the monograph edition of the first volume of the novel, which was published in 1986.[170]

Of course, many readers of Ch'oe's novel would clearly have perceived this influence already. The majority of the first volume of the novel centers around the series of events that Ri Chinhŭi outlined in his works of the early 1970s: the discovery of the Kwanggaet'o Stele by Sako Kagenobu, the Japanese military spy; his journey to bring back a rubbing of the Kwanggaet'o Stele inscription; its interpretation by the Japanese military; and the operation to obscure the original. It then moves on to discussions of subsequent topics of Ri's research (the Seven-Branched Sword and Korean-style fortresses in Japan) and frequent topics of Kim's writing (Korean-style fortresses, the seventh- to eighth-century Buddhist monk Gyōki, and the Korean heritage of *Man'yōshū* poets like Yamanoue no Okura). Moreover, the novel's form would also have reminded readers of both of these writers' works. Although significant portions of the novel take place in the historical past—that is, in the seventh century, at the time of the fall of the kingdom of Paekche, and the late nineteenth century, when the King Kwanggaet'o Stele and the Seven-Branched Sword were discovered and supposedly tampered with—significant portions of it also take place in the 1980s present, following its Korean narrator as he embarks on a journey across Japan to visit historical sites associated with the ancient heritage of Paekche, a kingdom whose former rulers he is descended from. It quite clearly follows the form of the historical travelogue, a genre that, as noted above, Ri Chinhŭi and Kim Talsu had already published.

The novel, however, does not stop here, and it is much more than a novelistic adaptation of Ri and Kim's work. The fundamental premise of the novel—one that is developed as the narrator moves from place to place and uncovers more and more of this forgotten history—is that the ancient imperial state in Japan, up until the reign of Emperor Tenmu, was a "subordinate state" (*pun'guk*) of Paekche. This is the reason, the novel argues, that Paekche's King Kaero, at the time that the Paekche capital at Wiryĕ/Hansŏng fell to Koguryŏ in the fifth century, sent his queen to Japan to give birth to the future monarch, King Muryŏng, who would later return to the Korean peninsula and rebuild the kingdom. Even more centrally for the novel, it is also the reason why, when Paekche finally falls to the joint Tang and Silla forces in the seventh century, the Empress Saimei mobilizes her military in support of the attempted renovation campaign led by Paekche's Prince P'ung, who was then living at the empress's court. Moreover, in the novel, this is not only because the imperial court in Japan, as a "subordinate state," sees the fallen Paekche as its "metropole" (*pon'guk*) but also because the Empress Saimei, the novel claims, is the sister of the Paekche king at the time, King Ŭija. What this makes clear is that Ch'oe's novel, while centrally influenced by the writings of Ri and Kim, is not only that. It is also deeply embedded in the "subordinate state theory" advanced by Kim Sŏkhyŏng, and it is this theory, which comes from the contemporary North and is not a central part of either Ri or Kim's own research, which serves as the backbone of the historical vision that the novel presents.

There was, at the same time, one element of the work's vision of the past whose inspiration came from much closer to home. In making the claim that Empress Saimei is the sister of Paekche's King Ŭija, the text leans upon the work of the South Korean writer Mun Chŏngch'ang. Although he was not trained as an academic historian, Mun nevertheless published widely about ancient Korean history, and he was a contributor to the January 1973 special issue of *Sindonga* mentioned above. In this article, which drew upon material already published in his 1970 monograph, Mun had made the above claim about Empress Saimei.[171] Moreover, Ch'oe also drew upon Mun in relation to another central character of the novel: Ō no Yasumaro, the supposed compiler of the *Kojiki* and the *Nihon shoki*. As we have seen, the Paekche heritage of numerous writers from the *Man'yōshū* was a topic of discussion of many scholars in both Japan and South Korea at the time. Ō no Yasumaro, however, was another story. The notion that the compiler of the *Kojiki* and the *Nihon shoki*, the most foundational texts of Japanese ancient history, was of Paekche heritage was not a common one at the time but rather one that appears, like the claim about Empress Saimei, to have been borrowed by Ch'oe from Mun Chŏngch'ang's 1970 monograph.[172]

Ch'oe's novel thus incorporates ideas from a triangular range of contemporary sources: South Korean writers, the Korean community in Japan, and North Korean scholars. And the key entity that brings these disparate voices together is the "lost kingdom" itself, Paekche. Historical interest in and research on Paekche had grown rapidly following the discovery of King Muryŏng's tomb in 1971, which provided a wealth of new resources for both scholars and the interested public. Yet this expansion did not occur in a vacuum. On the contrary, it occurred side by side with research into Silla and Koguryŏ—the other two ancient kingdoms that comprised the Three Kingdoms alongside Paekche—and these were endeavors that had developed strong political connections and connotations. As scholars such as Robert Oppenheim and Sheila Miyoshi Jager have noted, the dictatorship of Park Chung Hee, which entered its Yusin phase in 1972, placed great emphasis on the heritage of Silla, its "unification" of the peninsula, and its *hwarang* warriors in constructing a martial vision of a proper (South) Korean subjectivity (as opposed to the counterexample of subsequent kingdoms like Chosŏn).[173] As Oppenheim has discussed, this was especially evident in the pride of place given to the reconstruction of the Silla capital, Kyŏngju, as part of the Yusin state's larger transformation of the southeastern region of the country, Park's native place.[174]

In contrast, North Korean academic discussions—operating, as required, within state- and party-sanctioned channels—increasingly emphasized the heritage of Koguryŏ (as well as Parhae). This was not necessarily the case in the early years of North Korean ancient historiography. However, as Yun Sangdŏk has discussed in detail, the emergence and consolidation of Juche Ideology in the 1960s and 1970s occasioned a transformational shift in North Korean discussions of Silla: instead of a model of national unity and brilliance, Silla came to be seen as a tool of foreign (Tang) influence that failed to unify the peninsula due to the continued existence of Parhae. Instead, North Korean discussions came to focus on Koguryŏ as the proper locus of national heritage during the Three Kingdoms period, and it came to see Koguryŏ culture—if not the structures of the state—as that which eventually unified the peninsula as a coherent entity through diffusion.[175] Not surprisingly, therefore, by the 1980s, when the DPRK state turned to present ancient Korean culture heritage abroad, it did so via an exhibition of Koguryŏ culture that traveled across Japan, attempting to frame this heritage from the northern part of the peninsula as, itself, the "origin of Japanese culture."[176]

As a kingdom with close ties to the Japanese archipelago that had been invaded and driven into exile abroad by both of these forces—that is, first by Koguryŏ, which took Paekche's capital at Hansŏng/Wirye in 475, and then by Silla and the Tang in the seventh century, when they seized the capital at Puyŏ—Paekche and its heritage had been far less actively drawn upon by the postcolonial Korean states, and this turned it into a fertile ground for alternative visions of the past and its contemporary relevance. In Ch'oe's novel, therefore, what the reader encounters is not a paean to a glorious state but rather an exploration of all that is created via its disintegration. As such, when the novel does make links to the contemporary era, it does so in ways that look away from the state and instead toward forces and communities that overstep their bounds. And within this context, it is significant to note that when the novel, in its latter half, introduces the canonical *Man'yōshū* poet Yamanoue no Okura as a Paekche migrant, it simultaneously compares his work to the "people's poetry" (*minjung si*) of contemporary South Korea's "southwestern province" (*sŏnamdo*): that is, the Chŏlla region, the center of the democratization movement.[177] What this does is tether Yamanoue no Okura—and broader trends within Paekche culture to which he is linked—to contemporary voices that speak on behalf of ordinary people in opposition to state oppression.

This does not mean, however, that Ch'oe's novel ultimately looks to Paekche culture for an alternative model of heroism not beholden to either of the postcolonial states. There is, to be sure, a great amount of bravery and heroism in the novel, and Paekche culture is clearly celebrated throughout for its beauty, innovation, and influence. However, the central problematic for the narrative as a whole is how the present-day narrator can come to terms with a Paekche heritage that he is ashamed of. As noted above, the narrator of the novel is a descendant of the Paekche throne, and this heritage is a guarded family secret. The reason for this secrecy is shame; the family descends from the line of one of King Ŭija's sons, Prince Yung, who both opened the gates of the city to the joint Tang and Silla army and returned as a Tang official to fight the joint Paekche and Japanese forces seeking to revive the kingdom. Prince Yung is thus seen as a traitor, and his descendants hide their identities out of shame.

Something similar can be said about Ō no Yasumaro. In the novel, Ō no Yasumaro is the son of the final Paekche warrior to fall on the battlefield of Hwangsanbŏl, and his scholarly abilities are praised in no uncertain terms. Toward the end of the novel, however, Ō no Yasumaro bows— with notably little resistance—to the demand to distort history in the *Nihon shoki*. This turns his character decidedly gray, and it is symbolically fitting, as a result, that his grave is discovered in a nondescript, out-of-the-way location. He has lost his clear place, and, like Yung, his memory has been abandoned by his descendants and his spirit has only been tended to by a caretaker who has inherited the task.

The Paekche heritage, therefore, is a conflicted one, but it is one that the narrator comes to terms with by the end of the novel. This happens, in part, because the narator learns that Yung, despite returning on the "other side" of the war, refuses to harm his brother, the new Paekche monarch seeking to revive the kingdom, and facilitates the escape of Paekche citizens to Japan. More importantly, though, it happens via the connection that the narrator forms with Ō no Yasumaro. At the end of the novel, the head monk at the temple where Ō no Yasumaro's recently discovered relics are housed asks the narrator to stand in as head mourner in a commemoration ceremony. Since Ō no Yasumaro's spirit has no one to care for it, the narrator agrees, eventually feeling as though he were a "descendant" with the "same blood flowing through his body."[178] The the novel here reclaims the Paekche heritage in a peculiar way. The possibilities that Paekche offer are not possibilities for alternative heroism but rather for something more complicated: coming to terms with the grayness of the past; thinking connection beyond simple praise and blame; removing the shame and silence of association with the behavior of others. It is on these grounds that the novel makes new North-South connections possible—as well as new connections to Japan.

The nuance of Ch'oe's approach, however, was easily drowned out. After completing his serialization of the novel in the *Chosŏn ilbo* newspaper in 1988, Ch'oe took up the task of writing and appearing in a six-part docuseries aired on KBS in July and August of the same year. Although much of the docuseries returned to the material presented in the novel, it also included key changes. Most importantly, the narrator of the novel was removed and replaced by Ch'oe himself, who served as guide and narrator. This meant that the novel's focus on the narrator's coming to terms with his heritage also disappeared from the docuseries, as did the novel's discussion of the grayness of Ō no Yasumaro's character. In the novel, he bows—with notably little resistance—to the demand to distort history in the *Nihon shoki*, but in the docuseries he is forced to do so under the threat of death. The grayness of this character as well as the conflictedness of the narrator's connection to Prince Yung and his broader Paekche heritage thus disappear, as does the novel's nuanced vision of what the Paekche heritage might mean.

Additionally, the nuance of Ch'oe's vision of the Paekche heritage was also undone by the state's appropriation of it. The novel was hugely successful among readers, turning ancient Korean-Japanese relations—in particular, the powerful influence that migration from the Korean peninsula had exerted on the formation of Japanese culture, state, and society—into an even greater topic of public interest. Harnessing this interest, in late 1987, the ROK Ministry of Culture partnered with the *Chosŏn ilbo* to sponsor a public trip to Japan called the "Korean History in Japan Expedition" (*Ilbon sok e Han'guk yŏksa t'ambang*).[179] A second trip was organized the following year with additional support from the conglomerate Lotte,[180] and these activities, which took more than a thousand individuals to Japan to engage in the type of trip that Ch'oe—following Ri Chinhŭi and Kim Talsu—had previously taken, undercut the alternative visions of community beyond the state that the novel had sought. Its all-inclusive package structure also undercut the fundamental goal of Ch'oe's narrative, which was not simply to reclaim the history of Korean migrants in Japan but to do so—most importantly—via dialogue between North Korean, South Korean, and diasporic Korean texts.

CONCLUSION

There was, moreover, a kind of irony to the precise context in which Ch'oe finished *The Lost Kingdom*. The novel's serialization was completed in May 1988, the final installment of the monograph version of the novel was released the following month, and the TV docuseries began airing the month after that, in July 1988. It thus coincided with one of the most monumental sets of developments in South Korean literary history: the July 19, 1988, *haegŭm* proclamation that lifted the ban on the pre-1945 work of more than 120 writers who had gone North or stayed in the North after division. As Kim Yunsik noted at the time, this transformation was the product of a set of incremental developments: the granting of permission, in March 1978, for purely academic research on the colonial-era work of such writers; the expansion of such permission, in October 1987, to include the commercial publication of such scholarship; and the March 1988 release of the ban on the work of Kim Kirim and Chŏng Chiyong, supposedly "kidnapped to the North," as an initial step toward the same treatment being extended to the larger group mentioned above a few months later.[181]

These steps did not, of course, release the ban on the pre-1945 works of all authors who had gone North. Not initially included, for example, were the pre-1945 works of those who had attained high positions in the DPRK, such as Hong Myŏnghŭi, Han Sŏrya, Ri Kiyŏng, Paek Injun, and Cho Yŏnghch'ul, which were eventually authorized for republication in 1989.[182] Moreover, it did not include works published after 1945, whose status in the South Korean publishing world would remain controversial across subsequent years.[183] Nevertheless, this was a wide-ranging and extremely significant development that fundamentally reshaped the literary scene in South Korea.

And it was one that, opening up an abundant range of new opportunities, also turned attention away from the intricate, complex, and creative ways in which writers over the previous years and decades had attempted to rebuild connections across the thirty-eighth parallel divide. This, then, was the final irony of Ch'oe's *The Lost Kingdom*. After spending years producing an intricate dialogue between texts from North Korea, South Korea, and Japan—an intricate dialogue that allowed silenced voices to speak in the South—the novel's completion coincided with the moment when such intricacy no longer seemed necessary. Suddenly, a whole range of previously silenced voices were able to speak openly again, and Ch'oe's text—while remembered for what it said about Korean-Japanese relations—was easily forgotten for what it did in relation to the North and to those, in Japan, who had previously been linked to it.

EPILOGUE

The Cold War in Korea

Suspended Animation

In early 2022, while on a research fellowship at the Academy of Korean Studies near Seoul, I visited the National Institute of Korean History (Kuksa P'yŏnch'an Wiwŏnhoe; hereafter, NIKH) to view publications produced by the Chongryon organization. At the time, Korea was experiencing a new wave of COVID-19 infections as a result of the Omicron variant, and I found myself alone in the NIKH reading room, which remained eerily quiet. Nevertheless, the aspect of that day's visit that made the most enduring impression on me was not the empty state of the reading room but rather that the robust presence of the Cold War–era South Korean state and its policies. After requesting issues of Chongryon's literary journal, *Munhak yesul*, and its Korean-language daily, *Chosŏn sinbo*, the librarian specializing in "special materials" (*t'ŭksu charyo*) related to North Korea delivered the publications alongside an explanation of the NIKH's rules regarding the use of them: no photographs, no copies, and no transcription of full sentences.

Having used "special materials" at a variety of other institutions in South Korea, I was not surprised to hear that the NIKH placed limits on such materials' use. Yet the extent of the NIKH restrictions nevertheless shocked me. I had never encountered an institution that prohibited all photocopying and even the transcription of full sentences. What, then, was I supposed to do in the reading room? Read through all of the available materials and write paraphrased summaries to draw upon later? Try to memorize key sentences that I could type up later for use in quotations in my work? Neither of these seemed like workable plans, so after reading through as much of the material as I could, I decided to make a list of citations of relevant articles that I would attempt to get copies of from other institutions and sources. This I did, and in subsequent months, I received copies of the most important articles that I had read at the NIKH reading room from various colleagues in the United States and Japan.

I found myself, in other words, reproducing the types of strategies pursued by writers discussed in this book—that is, looking to Japan and other international locations to elude restrictions on media access in South Korea—and I was thus reminded of the extent to which Cold War–era state structures and policies continue to shape the mediascape in contemporary Korea. To be sure, much has changed since the late 1980s, when the democratizing South Korean state began removing restrictions on the publication of work by those who had gone North. In contemporary South Korea, one can visit a bookstore and buy an anthology of North Korean literature in the same manner that one could buy any other book. Likewise, one can access facsimile copies of North Korea's major literary journal, *Chosŏn munhak*, in the open stacks at many university libraries, and online visitors to the National Library of Korea's digital database can freely access digital scans of the North Korean materials seized during the Korean War by the US military.

This loosening of restrictions, however, has been partial and piecemeal. The anthologies that one would find for sale at a bookstore in the South are produced by South Korean publishers who are republishing North Korean works. Likewise, facsimile copies of North Korean publications held by university libraries and other institutions are produced by either South Korean or Chinese publishers, and the seized documents offered online by the National Library of Korea are digital scans of materials held by the National Archives and Records Administration in the United States. Likewise, the Chongryon publications that can be freely accessed without restrictions are those that have been republished by either non-Chongryon publishers in Japan or by South Korean publishers. In order to see actual North Korean or Chongryon materials—that is, a newspaper or journal printed in the North or by a Chongryon publisher in Japan—one must still visit a location that deals in "special materials" and follow their rules regarding access, use, reproduction, and dissemination.

Like the National Security Law—which has been amended but not abolished—Cold War–era media restrictions are thus still very much present in South Korea. They are likewise still uneven in their contours and enforcement. As we have seen over the course of this book, the extent to which the cross-border transit of texts and people was permitted fluctuated over time in relation to the political situation, and various actors tested, challenged, and transformed these boundaries in a variety of ways through their creative practice. As a result, restrictions on access to "special materials" today are a patchwork in South Korea. While institutions like the NIKH retain very strict policies on use and reproduction of "special materials," most do not. At institutions like the Information Center on North Korea, which is run by the Ministry of Unification and housed at the National Library of Korea, access is controlled but photocopies are permitted freely as long as they are logged. Moreover, while guidelines at the Center state that such photocopies must be returned after use, researchers are routinely told that this is no longer necessary.

In South Korea, that is, the Cold War lives on in an ambiguous, hard-to-define way, especially given the shift toward co-option in the ROK's broader policy in relation to the North. As we have seen, in the 1950s and 1960s, South Korean materials were made available to North Korean writers, editors, and—on a more selective basis—ordinary readers, and there was a specific geopolitical calculus standing behind this: the DPRK's understanding that it was in a position of power vis-à-vis the ROK in terms of economic strength, military strength, and political stability. The DPRK state, as a result, did not see the presence of South Korean materials as a potent threat; on the contrary, it cultivated this presence in order to show its comparative openness—and thus power—and in order to enable the development of policies and practices of co-option.

By the late 1960s and early 1970s, however, the differential of power on the Korean peninsula had begun to shift. The ROK's program of state-led, export-oriented, rapid industrialization had begun transforming the economy, Park Chung Hee and his allies had consolidated their grasp of the reins of power, and the militarization of the South Korean state and society had entered a new, more robust phase. No longer in a clear position of power vis-à-vis the South, the DPRK state gradually restricted the previous space given to South Korean publications, and in the aftermath of the collapse of the Soviet Union and the "end" of the Cold War, the North Korean state increasingly closed itself off from transnational media flows more broadly, becoming increasingly insular. In contrast, the South Korean state began funding unification programs in newly—and increasingly—robust ways. North Korea- and communist bloc–focused think tanks and research institutes gained a new presence in the South,[1] and this entailed expanded access to banned texts from the North and from Japan.

It also gave rise to expanded reporting on the North in the South Korean media, a phenomenon that only continued to expand over time. As a result, unification-themed television shows, for example, are now a fixture of the South Korean media domain, and this demonstrates the extent to which unification policy in the now far-more-powerful South has changed over time. Yet in certain respects, it also suggests the ways in which the South's unification policies have come to mirror the early Cold War policy of the North Korean state. Indeed, it is not entirely correct to say that the current openness toward engagement with the North—albeit partial, as noted above—is a product of the post–Cold War. On the contrary, it can also be understood, on one level, as the turning of the wheel of the Cold War's balance of power from DPRK strength to overwhelming ROK strength.

A similar set of questions can be posed in relation to the DPRK's current insularity. Of course, the North is not as closed off from the rest of the world—or from South Korea—as it is often said to be. As Youna Kim has recently discussed in detail, "Since the late 1990s, the transnational spread of South Korean media, known as the Korean Wave or Hallyu, has filtered into North Korea through smuggling and black markets,"[2] and according to interviews conducted by Sonny Yoon with 140 North Korean defectors in 2011, "56% had viewed South Korean media while in North Korea and 40% viewed South Korean media whenever they wanted."[3] It is clear, therefore, that South Korean media and other types of foreign media, which enter the DPRK "through portable media devices such as Notels (the combined "notebook" and "television" multimedia players), MP3 players, mobile phones, DVDs and CDs, as well as easily concealable USB drives and micro SD cards,"[4] is accessible to a range of North Korean citizens, undercutting the prevailing image of the "hermit kingdom."

At the same time, this illicit availability, while certainly significant, is vastly different than the type of access that the North Korean writers in this book enjoyed. As we have seen, this was state-approved and state-sponsored access, and it thus stands in direct contrast to the current phenomenon of illicit access, showing just how much has changed in the ensuing decades. However, whether this turn from state-sponsored engagement to state-enforced restriction is a Cold War–era phenomenon or a post–Cold War phenomenon is a more complex question. On the one hand, consolidated by the fall of the Soviet Union and the collapse of the communist bloc, the insularity of North Korea's official media sphere and state-sponsored cultural domain is, in a way, a product of the end of the Cold War and its system of alliances. And yet, in terms of access to South Korean publications, this turning inward had already begun decades earlier with the rise of the South as a powerful entity, and the way in which the contemporary DPRK state restricts the flow of cross-border media from the South partially resembles the practices of the Cold War–era South Korean state.

As a result, while the situation on the Korean peninsula has, on one level, been fundamentally transformed by the "end" of the Cold War, it has also, on another level, simply been inverted by it, leaving its basic structures intact. This leaves inter-Korean relations in an ambiguous position. Has progress been made toward reunification? What would such progress look like? This book does not have answers to these questions, but it offers a historical framework for rethinking the nature of inter-Korean relations during the early Cold War era—with the hope that, at some point, this history may be useful for addressing the persistence of division in the present.

It has now been almost eight decades since the division of the Korean peninsula by the triumphant Allies of the Second World War. With the ever-accelerating divergence between the societies, economies, and cultures of the two Koreas and the passing of the generation with personal memories of a unified national community, the entrenchment of national division is perhaps more pronounced than ever. Within this context, it becomes even more valuable to recall and document the shifting and porous nature of division in previous decades. As this book has demonstrated, the division system never functioned as a stable structure of mutual isolation. On the contrary it produced constant comparisons and, with them, attempts at connection whose nature changed and shifted over time. This suggests that division, despite its long-term persistence, is not a set or settled affair but rather something subject to adjustment and contestation. It is, in other words, a malleable structure that is open to transformation in the present as well.

NOTES

INTRODUCTION

1. See note on names, spelling, and transliteration for more on the conventions used in this book.
2. Kim P'albong [Kim Kijin], "Pungnyŏk edo pom i onŭnde: Yi Kiyŏng [Ri Kiyŏng] ege" [Spring Comes to the North as Well: To Ri Kiyŏng], *Pukhan* 1, no. 2 (February 1972): 103.
3. Kim P'albong, "Pungnyŏk edo pom i onŭnde," 103.
4. Kim P'albong, "Pungnyŏk edo pom i onŭnde," 103.
5. Kim P'albong, "Pungnyŏk edo pom i onŭnde," 103.
6. Kim P'albong, "Pungnyŏk edo pom i onŭnde," 103.
7. Kim Talsu, ed., Kim Pyŏngwŏn, trans., "Ri Kiei [Ri Kiyŏng] no shōgai to chosaku" [The Life and Works of Ri Kiyŏng], *Shin Nihon bungaku* 10, no. 8 (August 1955): 131–39.
8. Christina Yi, *Colonizing Language: Cultural Production and Language Politics in Modern Japan and Korea* (New York: Columbia University Press, 2018), 96.
9. "National Accounts Estimates of Main Aggregates: Per Capita GDP at Current Prices—US Dollars," United Nations Statistics Division, accessed November 30, 2024, https://data.un.org/Data.aspx?d=SNAAMA&f=grID%3A101%3BcurrID%3AUSD%3BpcFlag%3A1.
10. Kim P'albong, "Pungnyŏk edo pom i onŭnde," 103.
11. Yun Namhŭi, "Pukhaenggi," *T'aep'ung* 18 (February 1949), 66–69.
12. Yun Namhŭi, "Pukhaenggi," 69–70.
13. Mark Salter, "Theory of the /: The Suture and Critical Border Studies," *Geopolitics* 17, no. 4 (November 2012): 734–55.
14. Thomas Nail, *Theory of the Border* (New York: Cambridge University Press, 2012), 1–18.

15. Michael Robinson, *Cultural Nationalism in Korea, 1920–1925* (Seattle: University of Washington Press, 1988), 5–8.
16. Monica Kim, *Interrogation Rooms of the Korean War* (Princeton, NJ: Princeton University Press, 2019), 43–44.
17. Monica Kim, *Interrogation Rooms of the Korean War*, 44.
18. Monica Kim, *Interrogation Rooms of the Korean War*, 53–62.
19. For more on these reforms, see Cheehyung Harrison Kim, *Heroes and Toilers: Work as Life in Postwar North Korea, 1953–1961* (New York: Columbia University Press, 2018), 23–24.
20. Chŏng Pyŏngjun, "1945–1948 Mi-So ŭi 38-sŏn chŏngch'aek kwa nambuk kaltŭng ŭi kiwŏn" [1945–1948 US-USSR 38th Parallel Policy and the Origins of the North-South Conflict], *Chung-So yŏn'gu* 100 (2003–2004): 184.
21. "38-sŏn kyot'ong t'ongno nŭn (1)" [The Transportation Route Over the 38th Parallel], *Tonga ilbo*, December 16, 1945, 2.
22. Chŏng Pyŏngjun, "1945–1948 Mi-So ŭi 38-sŏn chŏngch'aek kwa nambuk kaltŭng ŭi kiwŏn," 184; Taeyoung Oh, "The Reorganization of Space and Literary Representation of Seoul during the Liberation Period, 1945–1950," *Inter-Asia Cultural Studies* 25, no. 2 (2024): 196 n. 4; "Kukkyŏnghwa hanŭn 38-sŏn: T'onggwa yŏhaeng ŭl purhŏ, kunjŏngch'ŏng oemuch'ŏ palp'yo" [The 38th Parallel that Is Becoming a National Boundary: Journeys across are Forbidden, the Military Government's Bureau of Foreign Affairs Announces], *Tonga ilbo*, May 24, 1946, 2.
23. Kim Insŭng, "Minjok ŭl chom mŏngnŭn 38-sŏn choeaksang" [The 38th Parallel's State of Sin, Which Is Destroying the Nation], *Chosŏn ilbo*, November 19, 1946, 2.
24. Elisabeth Leake, "On Asian Borders: The Value of Comparative Studies," in *Decoding the Sino-North Korean Borderlands*, ed. Adam Cathcart, Christopher Green, and Steven Denney (Amsterdam: Amsterdam University Press, 2021), 51.
25. The role of price differences is mentioned in Yu Kŏnho, "Sŏgŭlp'ŭn 38 wŏlgyŏng" [Sorrowful Crossings of the 38th Parallel], *Chosŏn ilbo*, May 9, 1947, 2.
26. For description of this with participant testimonies, see Cho Kyuha, "Nambuk ŭi taehwa (85)—Chŏngbu surip kwa 6.25 chŏnhu (5)—Nambuk mulcha kyoyŏk (Sang)" [North-South Conversation (85)—Establishment of the Government and the Period Surrounding 6.25 (5)—North-South Goods Trade (1)], *Tonga ilbo*, April 29, 1972, 5.
27. "Nambuk kyoyŏk paeksŏ" [White Paper on North-South Trade], *Maeil kyŏngje*, August 15, 1972, 9.
28. "Nambuk kyoyŏk paeksŏ," 9; Kim Sŏgwŏn, "Nambuk kyoyŏk sakŏn kwa na" [Me and the North-South Trade Event], *Sedae* 87 (October 1970): 189; Cho Kyuha, "Nambuk ŭi taehwa (85)," 5.
29. Kim Sŏgwŏn, "Nambuk kyoyŏk sakŏn kwa na," 189; Cho Kyuha, "Nambuk ŭi taehwa (85)," 5.
30. "Organizations in Kaesŏng, North Korea" (October 23, 1953, CIA-RDP80-00810A002600770010-8), CIA Freedom of Information Act Electronic Reading Room, accessed February 23, 2024, https://www.cia.gov/readingroom/document/cia-rdp80-00810a002600770010-8.

INTRODUCTION 265

31. Kim Hojin, "Ch'ŏl ŭi changmak: 38-sŏn tapsa (7)" [The Iron Curtain: Journey Across the 38th Parallel (7)], *Tonga ilbo*, October 2, 1947, 2.
32. Cho Kyuha, "Nambuk ŭi taehwa (69)—'Mi-So Kongwi' wa 'hapchak undong' (3)—6.25 ro kkŭnnan '38 up'yŏnmul' [North-South Conversation (69)—"The US-USSR Joint Commission" and the "United Front Movement" (3)—The "38 Mail" that Ended with the Korean War], *Tonga ilbo*, March 30, 1972, 5.
33. For all texts published before 1948, when new spelling and pronunciation policies were promulgated in the North, I use "Yi" rather than "Ri." On the language policies implemented in the North in 1948, see An Miae, Hong Miju, and Paek Tuhyŏn, "Pukhan munhwaŏ ŭi ŏdu R, N kyujŏng ŭl t'ong haesŏ pon ŏnŏ chŏngch'esŏng kuch'uk kwa ch'abyŏrhwa pangsik yŏn'gu [The Establishment and Differentiation of Linguistic Identity As Soon Through the Word-Beginning R, N Rule in North Korean Language], *Ŏmun nonch'ong* 76 (June 2018): 85–125.
34. Yi Wŏnjo, "Paengman ch'ŏnman i hyangnak hal munhak ŭl" [Literature that Millions and Tens of Millions Will Enjoy], *Munhak* 3 (April 1947): 96.
35. Yi Wŏnjo, "Paengman ch'ŏnman i hyangnak hal munhak ŭl," 97.
36. Yi Wŏnjo, "Paengman ch'ŏnman i hyangnak hal munhak ŭl," 97.
37. Yi Wŏnjo, "Paengman ch'ŏnman i hyangnak hal munhak ŭl," 96.
38. Cho Yŏnhyŏn, "Han Sŏrya ssi ege ponaenŭn sŏhan: chagi ege tora kara" [A Letter Sent to Han Sŏrya: Return to Your Self], *Taejo* 4, no. 1 (March 1949): 29.
39. For example, see Jerôme de Wit, "Writing under Wartime Conditions: North and South Korean Writers during the Korean War (1950–1953)," PhD diss. (Leiden University, 2015); Joanna Elfving-Hwang, "Cross-Border Representation in South and North Korean Literatures of the Cold War Period," in *Global Cold War Literatures: Western, Eastern and Postcolonial Perspectives,* ed. Andrew Hammond (New York: Routledge, 2012), 43–57; Kim Minsŏn, "1950–1960-nyŏndae Nambukhan SF yŏn'gu" [A Study of 1950s–1960s North and South Korean SF], PhD diss. (Tongguk University, 2020); Dafna Zur, *Figuring Korean Futures: Children's Literature in Modern Korea* (Palo Alto, CA: Stanford University Press, 2017), 191–214; Steven Chung, *Split Screen Korea: Shin Sang-ok and Postwar Cinema* (Minneapolis: University of Minnesota Press, 2014).
40. For example, see Immanuel Kim, "South Korean Activist Readers of North Korean Literature," in *Routledge Handbook of Modern Korean Literature,* ed. Yoon Sun Yang (New York: Routledge, 2020), 156–67; Kang Chuyŏng, "1980-nyŏndae Pukhan ŭi tanp'yŏn sosŏl esŏ ch'aja pon Namhan munhak ŭi hŭnjŏk: Kim Kwanil ŭi 'Ch'ŏngnyŏn kaech'ŏkja ŭi sugi' wa Ro Chŏngbŏp ŭi 'Nae kohyang ŭi chagŭn tari' rŭl chungsim ŭro" [Traces of South Korean Literature Found in 1980s North Korean Short Stories: Focusing on Kim Kwanil's "Record of a Young Pioneer" and Ro Chŏngbŏp's "The Small Bridge in My Hometown"], *Han minjok ŏmunhak* 71 (2015): 621–55; Kim Sŏngsu, "1990-nyŏndae ch'o munyeji ŭi t'ongil tamnon kwa Pukhan munhak chŏnyu pangsik pip'an: Pukhan munyeji *Chosŏn munhak* kwaŭi maech'esajŏk taehwa" [A Critique of the Unification Discourse and Appropriation of North Korean Literature in Literary and Cultural Publications of the Early 1990s: A Media-Historical Conversation with the North Korean Literary and Cultural Journal *Korean Literature*], *Sanghŏ hakpo* 54 (2018): 11–47.

41. Ku Chungsŏ, "Wasŏ chedan pusura" [Come Smash the Altar], *Munhak sinmun*, April 16, 1965, 4.
42. Ku Chungsŏ, "Wasŏ chedan pusura" [Come Smash the Altar], *Choguk t'ongil*, June 12, 1963, 4; Ku Chungsŏ, "Wasŏ chedan pusura" [Come Smash the Altar], *Han'guk ilbo*, April 18, 1963, 5.
43. Ku Chungsŏ, "Wasŏ chedan pusura" [Come Smash the Altar], *Chosŏn sinbo*, April 24, 1963, 3.
44. Lori Watt, *When Empire Comes Home: Repatriation and Reintegration in Postwar Japan* (Cambridge, MA: Harvard University Asia Center, 2009), 25, 39; Sonia Ryang, "Introduction: Resident Koreans in Japan," in *Koreans in Japan: Critical Voices from the Margin* (New York: Routledge, 2000), 3–4.
45. This is evident from foreigner registration records seized in the North by the US military during the Korean War. See the following: "(Tong P'yŏngyang) Ilbonin Kiryubu, Sadong Naemusŏ" [(East Pyongyang) Japanese Temporary Residence Documents, Sadong Internal Affairs Station], Shipping Advice 2005 9/18 part 11, Records of Foreign Documents Seized, RG 242, National Archives, College Park, MD; "Ilbonin Kiryubu, Tong P'yŏngyang sŏ" [Japanese Temporary Residence Documents, East Pyongyang Station], Shipping Advice 2005 9/18 part 13–15, Records of Foreign Documents Seized, RG 242, National Archives, College Park, MD; "Ilbonin Chosap'yo (Tong P'yŏngyang sŏ)" [Investigation Report of Japanese (East Pyongyang Station)], Shipping Advice 2006 Item 75, Records of Foreign Documents Seized, RG 242, National Archives, College Park, MD; "Pukchosŏn chaeryu oegukin 18-se isang chosap'yo (Ilbonin) (Hŭngnam-si Inmin Wiwŏnhoe Naemusŏ, 1949)" [Investigation Report of Foreigners Above 18 Residing in Northern Korea (Japanese) (Bureau of Internal Affairs, Hŭngnam People's Committee, 1949)], Shipping Advice 2005 9/13 part 2, Records of Foreign Documents Seized, RG 242, National Archives, College Park, MD; "Oegukin kiryubu (Ilbonin) (Hŭngnam-si Inmin Wiwŏnhoe Naemusŏ)" [Foreigners' Temporary Residence Documents (Japanese) (Bureau of Internal Affairs, Hŭngnam People's Committee)], Shipping Advice 2006 Item 70, Records of Foreign Documents Seized, RG 242, National Archives, College Park, MD. Above documents digitized by the National Library of Korea. www.nl.go.kr.
46. Matthew Augustine, *From Japanese Empire to American Hegemony: Koreans and Okinawans in the Resettlement of Northeast Asia* (Honolulu: University of Hawaii Press, 2023), 82–83.
47. This is evident from the foreigner registration records seized in the North by the US military during the Korean War. See note 45.
48. "Japanese-North Korean trade and contacts" (April 4, 1950, CIA-RDP82-00457R004 600240002-7), CIA Freedom of Information Act Electronic Reading Room, accessed February 23, 2024, https://www.cia.gov/readingroom/document/cia-rdp82-00457r00 4600240002-7.
49. Matthew Augustine, *From Japanese Empire to American Hegemony*, 130–33.
50. For such work, see Serk-Bae Suh, *Treacherous Translation: Culture, Nationalism, and Colonialism in Korea and Japan from the 1910s to the 1960s* (Berkeley: University of

California Press, 2013), 104–59; Jonathan Glade, "Fracturing Literary Boundaries: Connecting with the Korean Peninsula in Postwar Japan," in *Routledge Handbook of Modern Korean Literature*, ed. Yoon Sun Yang (New York: Routledge, 2020), 116–27; Matthew Augustine, *From Japanese Empire to American Hegemony*.

51. For example, see Song Hyewŏn, *"Chaeil Chosŏnin munhaksa" rŭl wihayŏ: Sori ŏmnŭn moksori ŭi p'ollip'oni* [Toward a "Literary History of Resident Koreans in Japan": The Polyphony of Silent Voices] (Seoul: Somyŏng ch'ulp'an, 2019), which is Song's Korean translation of *"Zainichi Chōsenjin bungakushi" no tame ni: Koe naki koe no porifonī* (Tokyo: Iwanami shoten, 2014); Sonia Ryang and John Lie, eds., *Diaspora Without Homeland: Being Korean in Japan* (Berkeley: University of California Press, 2009); Sonia Ryang, ed., *Koreans in Japan: Critical Voices from the Margin* (New York: Routledge, 2000); Sonia Ryang, *North Koreans in Japan: Language, Ideology, and Identity* (Boulder, CO: Westview Press, 1997); John Lie, *Zainichi (Koreans in Japan): Diasporic Nationalism and Postcolonial Identity* (Berkeley: University of California Press, 2008); Christina Yi, *Colonizing Language*; Cindi Textor, "Representing Radical Difference: Kim Sŏkpŏm's Korea(n) in Japan(ese)," *positions: asia critique* 27, no. 3 (August 2019): 499–529; Cindi Textor, "Zainichi Writers and the Postcoloniality of Modern Korean Literature," in *Routledge Companion to Korean Literature*, ed. Heekyoung Cho (New York: Routledge, 2022). 225–38; Sayaka Chatani, "Revisiting Korean Slums in Postwar Japan: *Tongne* and *Hakkyo* in the Zainichi Memoryscape," *Journal of Asian Studies* 80, no. 3 (August 2021): 587–610; Sayaka Chatani, "Becoming Korean: Japanese Wives in the Boundary Formation of a Leftist Zainichi Community," *Critical Asian Studies* 54, no. 1 (January 2022): 105–27; Deokhyo Choi, "Crucible of the Post-Empire: Decolonization, Race, and Cold War Politics in US-Japan-Korea Relations, 1945–1952," PhD diss. (Cornell University, 2013); Deokhyo Choi, "The Empire Strikes Back from Within: Colonial Liberation and the Korean Minority Question at the Birth of Postwar Japan, 1945–47," *American Historical Review* 126, no. 2 (June 2021): 555–84; Deokhyo Choi, "Fighting the Korean War in Pacifist Japan: Korean and Japanese Leftist Solidarity and American Cold War Containment," *Critical Asian Studies* 49, no. 4 (October 2017): 546–68; Julia Hansell Clark, "Reclaiming Landscape: Place and Personhood in the Literature of Ikaino," PhD diss. (University of California, Los Angeles, 2023).

52. Sunhee Koo, *Sound of the Border: Music and the Identity of Korean Minority in China* (Honolulu: University of Hawaii Press, 2021), 15–16; David S. Roh, *Minor Transpacific: Triangulating American, Japanese, and Korean Fictions* (Palo Alto, CA: Stanford University Press, 2021).

53. Rosie Bsheer and Mohammed Alsudairi, "Introduction: Inter-Asian Cold War Linkages: The Middle East in the World," *Comparative Studies of South Asia, Africa and the Middle East* 43, no. 3 (December 2023): 338.

54. Lorenz Lüthi, *Cold Wars: Asia, the Middle East, Europe* (New York: Cambridge University Press, 2020), 1, 3.

55. Kim T'aegyŏng, "Haesin kwa kugŏ kongbu" [*The Liberation Times* and the Study of the National Language], *Haebang sinmun*, 30 (December 30, 1952), 3.

268   INTRODUCTION

56. Kim T'aegyŏng, "*Haesin* kwa kugŏ kongbu," 3.
57. For example, see the installments for November 5, 1952, September 19, 1953, and September 22, 1953.
58. For a recent discussion of these issues, see Julia Hansell Clark, "Reclaiming Landscape," 177–91.
59. Serk-Bae Suh, *Treacherous Translation*, 135–59.
60. Hino Ashihei, "Kosei no utsukushisa toku: Kitasen no sakka Kan Setsuya [Han Sŏrya] si" [On the Beauty of Individuality: The North Korean Writer Han Sŏrya], *Asahi shimbun*, May 30, 1957, 8.
61. Hŏ's 1955 Japanese-language anthology of Korean literature, *Chōsen shisen*, was imported to South Korea in 1957, where it was confiscated by ROK authorities for its inclusion of North Korean literature. This was reported on widely in the South Korean press at the time. For example, see "Puron sŏjŏk p'anmae ŏpja 5-myŏng chŏngsik kusok" [Five Sellers of Seditious Books Formally Arrested], *Chosŏn ilbo*, July 23, 1957, 2.
62. Ueda Masaaki, "Sŏksang sin'gung kwa Ch'iljido" [The Isonokami Shrine and the Seven-Branched Sword], *Sindonga* 101 (January 1973): 129–37.
63. This characterization of the journal comes from Ri Chinhŭi. For more on this, see chapter 4.
64. Ri Chŏnggu, "Han Namchosŏn ŭi chakka ege" [To A Southern Korean Writer], *Munhak sinmun*, October 6, 1961, 4.
65. Ri Chŏnggu, "Han Namchosŏn ŭi chakka ege," 4.
66. Ri Chŏnggu, "Han Namchosŏn ŭi chakka ege," 4.
67. Im Suil, "Paegŭi ŭi sugi (1–2)" [Record of White Clothes (1–2)], *Munhak sinmun*, 17 August 17–August 24, 1962, 4.
68. For an example of this perspective, see Dennis Cutchins, "Bakhtin, Intertextuality, and Adaptation," in *The Oxford Handbook of Adaptation Studies*, ed. Thomas Leitch (New York: Oxford University Press, 2017), 71–86.

1. REVERBERATIONS

1. Min Sukcha, "Oppa ege" [To My Older Brother], *Sae sedae* 79 (August 1961): 22.
2. Kang Myŏnghŭi, "Oppa wa ŏnni ka wae p'i hŭllyŏnŭnji" [Why My Older Brothers and Sisters Bled], *Chosŏn ilbo*, April 23, 1960, 3.
3. Kang Myŏnghŭi, "Oppa wa ŏnni rŭl ttarŭryŏmnida" [I Will Follow My Older Brothers and Sisters], *Adong munhak* 93 (August 1960): 78–79.
4. Kang Myŏnghŭi, "Uri nŭn oppa wa ŏnni ŭi twi rŭl ttarŭryŏmnida" [We Will Follow Behind Our Older Brothers and Sisters], *Chosŏn minbo*, May 16, 1960, 4.
5. Kang Myŏnghŭi, "Watashi wa shitte imasu" [I know], *Atarashii sedai* 1, no. 6 (July 1960): 13.
6. Kang Myŏnghŭi, "Niisan to neesan wa naze jyū de utareta no desu ka" [Why Were My Older Brothers and Sisters Struck Down with Guns?], in *Chi no shigatsu: Minami*

Chōsen jinmin hōki [An April of Blood: The Southern Korean People's Uprising], (Tokyo: Chōsen bunkasha, 1960), 1–3.

7. Kim Chaeyong, *Pundan kujo wa Pukhan munhak* [The Structure of Division and North Korean Literature] (Seoul: Somyŏng ch'ulp'an, 2012), 34. I use the term "Northern Korea" for discussions of the period prior to 1948.
8. Kee Kwang-seo, "The Historical Origins and Formation of the Monolithic Political System in North Korea," in *Understanding North Korea: Indigenous Perspectives*, ed. Han Jong-woo and Jung Tae-hern (New York: Lexington Books, 2014), 17; Cheehyung Harrison Kim, *Heroes and Toilers: Work as Life in Postwar North Korea, 1953–1961* (New York: Columbia University Press, 2018), 23. According to Kim, land reform redistributed one million *chŏngbo* of land and one *chŏngbo* equals approximately 2.45 acres.
9. Cheehyung Harrison Kim, *Heroes and Toilers*, 23–24.
10. Kee Kwang-seo, "The Historical Origins and Formation of the Monolithic Political System in North Korea," 20.
11. Kee Kwang-seo, "The Historical Origins and Formation of the Monolithic Political System in North Korea," 21.
12. *Nambanbu e kwanhan charyojip* [Collection of Materials about the Southern Half [of our Country]] (Pyongyang: Kungnip inmin ch'ulp'ansa, 1949), n.p. Available as Shipping Advice 2005 Item 2/108, Records of Foreign Documents Seized, RG 242, National Archives, College Park, MD. Digitized by the National Library of Korea. www.nl.go.kr.
13. *Nambanbu e kwanhan charyojip*, 55.
14. *Nambanbu e kwanhan charyojip*, 55–56.
15. *Nambanbu e kwanhan charyojip*, 56–57.
16. "T'oep'ye wa yullak ŭi amdamhan sahoesang" [The Dark Social State of Degeneration and Prostitution], *Rodong sinmun*, January 28, 1949, 3.
17. For other examples from around the same time, see "Konghwaguk nambanbu e taehan Mije ŭi 'kyŏngje wŏnjo' chŏngch'e" [The Identity of the American Imperialists' "Economic Aid" to the Southern Half of Our Republic], *Rodong sinmun*, February 26, 1949, 3; Song Nam, "Nambanbu nongmindŭl ŭl kiman haryŏnŭn 'nongji kaehyŏkpŏp' ch'oan ŭi chŏngch'e" [The Identity of the Draft "Land Reform Law" that Is Attempting to Deceive the Farmers in the Southern Half], *Rodong sinmun*, March 5, 1949, 3; "Migun chudun ha 38-sŏn inam singnyang sat'ae wigi e chŏlbak!" [The US Military-Occupied Region South of the 38th Parallel is Desperate Due to the Crisis of the Food Situation!], *Rodong sinmun*, April 19, 1949, 3.
18. Hong Tuwŏn, "Namchosŏn ŏrinidŭl ŭi pich'amhan ch'ŏji" [The Sorry State of Children in Southern Korea], *Rodong sinmun*, June 1, 1956, 3.
19. Hong Tuwŏn, "Namchosŏn ŏrinidŭl ŭi pich'amhan ch'ŏji," 3.
20. Paek Injun, "Munhak yesul ŭn inmin ege pongmu hayŏya hal kŏt ida: Wŏnsan munhak tongmaeng p'yŏnjip sijip *Ŭnghyang* ŭl p'yŏng ham" [Literary Arts Must Serve the People: Critiquing *Ŭnghyang*, the Poetry Collection Edited by the Wŏnsan Writers' Alliance], *Rodong sinmun*, December 25, 1946, 2. It is unclear what these quotations in the original refer to.

21. "Sijip *Ŭnghyang* e kwanhan Pukchosŏn munhak yesul ch'ongdongmaeng sangim wiwŏnhoe ŭi kyŏlchŏngsŏ" [Decision of the Standing Committee of the Northern Korean Literature and Arts Alliance Regarding the Poetry Collection *Ŭnghyang*], *Rodong sinmun*, December 24, 1946, 3.
22. Kim Sŏngsu, "Pukhan Chosŏn munhak yesul ch'ongdongmaeng ŭi yŏksajŏk pyŏnch'ŏn (1946–1953)" [The Historical Transformation of Northern Korea's Korean Literature and Arts Alliance (1946–53)], *T'ongil chŏngch'aek yŏn'gu* 33, no. 1 (2024): 218–24. As Kim notes, previous scholarship relied upon the decision's February 1947 republication.
23. O T'aeho, "'Ŭnghyang kyŏlchŏngsŏ' rŭl tullŏssan haebanggi mundan ŭi insingnonjŏk ch'ai yŏn'gu" [Research on Epistemological Differences Surrounding the 'Ŭnghyang Decision' in the Liberation-Era Literary Sphere], *Ŏmun nonjip* 48 (November 2011): 37.
24. Tatiana Gabroussenko, *Soldiers on the Cultural Front: Developments in the Early History of North Korean Literature and Literary Policy* (Honolulu: University of Hawaii Press, 2010), 150–60; Brian Myers, *Han Sŏrya and North Korean Literature: The Failure of Socialist Realism in the* DPRK (Ithaca, NY: Cornell East Asia Series, 1994), 81–85.
25. Ŏm Hosŏk, "Uri munhak e issŏsŏ ŭi chayŏnjuŭi wa hyŏngsikchuŭi chanjae waŭi t'ujaeng" [The Struggle Against the Remnants of Naturalism and Formalism in Our Literature], *Rodong sinmun*, January 17, 1952, 2–3.
26. Ŏm Hosŏk, "Uri munhak e issŏsŏ ŭi chayŏnjuŭi wa hyŏngsikchuŭi chanjae waŭi t'ujaeng," 2.
27. Interestingly, Kim himself also took up the renewed critique of *Ŭnghyang* at this time. For example, see Kim Namch'ŏn, "Kim Ilsŏng ryŏngdo ha e changsŏng palchŏn hanŭn Chosŏn minjok munhak yesul" [Korean National Literature and Arts Developing and Maturing under the Leadership of Kim Il Sung], *Munhak yesul* 5, no. 7 (July 1952): 104–21.
28. Han Hyo, "Chayŏnjuŭi rŭl pandae hanŭn t'ujaeng e issŏsŏ ŭi Chosŏn munhak (3)" [Korean Literature in the Struggle Against Naturalism (3)], *Munhak yesul* 6, no. 3 (March 1953): 138.
29. Han Hyo, "Chayŏnjuŭi rŭl pandae hanŭn t'ujaeng e issŏsŏ ŭi Chosŏn munhak (3)," 124–25.
30. Han Hyo, "Chayŏnjuŭi rŭl pandae hanŭn t'ujaeng e issŏsŏ ŭi Chosŏn munhak (3)," 131–35.
31. Kye Puk, "Namchosŏn ŭi pandongjŏk purŭjyoa mihak ŭi chŏngch'e" [The Identity of Southern Korea's Reactionary Bourgeois Aesthetics], *Chosŏn munhak* 106 (June 1956): 182.
32. Kye Puk, "Namchosŏn ŭi pandongjŏk purŭjyoa mihak ŭi chŏngch'e," 182.
33. Wŏn Sŏkp'a, "Ch'oegŭn Namchosŏn pandong si munhak ŭi ponjil" [The Essence of Recent Southern Korean Reactionary Poetry], *Munhak sinmun*, April 12, 1959, 4.
34. Wŏn Sŏkp'a, "Ch'oegŭn Namchosŏn pandong si munhak ŭi ponjil," 4.
35. Ri Hyŏn, "Hŏmu wa p'aedŏk ŭi sŏlgyo: Namchosŏn pandong sosŏl 'Ŏttŏn chijŏm esŏ' e taehayŏ" [A Sermon of Futility and Immorality: On the Southern Korean Reactionary Short Story "At a Certain Point"], *Munhak sinmun*, May 10, 1959, 3.

36. Pak Im, "Namchosŏn pandong munhak pup'aesang ŭi ilmyŏn" [A View of the Decayed State of Southern Korean Reactionary Literature], *Rodong sinmun*, January 13, 1954, 3; Ri Hyo, "Chŏnjaeng ŭl sŏndong hanŭn Namchosŏn pandong munhak" [The War-Provoking Reactionary Literature of Southern Korea], *Rodong sinmun*, October 2, 1954, 3.
37. Ro Kŭmsŏk, "Ch'oegŭn Namchosŏn sosŏl munhak ŭi ponjil [The Essence of Recent Fiction from Southern Korea], *Ch'ŏllima* 38 (November 1961): 70–72.
38. Kim Haegyun, "Namchosŏn pandong munhak esŏŭi p'ŭroidŭjuŭi" [Freudianism in the Reactionary Literature of Southern Korea], *Kŭlloja* 257 (October 1964): 38–44.
39. Ch'ŏng Am, "Noye ŭi munhak kwa panhang ŭi munhak: Purŭjyoajŏk hyumanijŭm ŭi ponjil" [The Literature of the Slave and the Literature of Resistance: The Essence of Bourgeois Humanism], *Chosŏn munhak* 133 (September 1958): 164–71.
40. Ch'ŏng Am, "Noye ŭi munhak kwa panhang ŭi munhak," 164.
41. Ch'ŏng Am, "Noye ŭi munhak kwa panhang ŭi munhak," 170.
42. Balázs Szalontai, *Kim Il Sung in the Khrushchev Era: Soviet-DPRK Relations and the Roots of North Korean Despotism, 1953–1964* (Washington, D.C.: Woodrow Wilson Center Press, 2005), 141.
43. Balázs Szalontai, *Kim Il Sung in the Khrushchev Era*, 140.
44. Cho Pyŏgam, "Choguk t'ongil kwa nambuk Chosŏn munhwa kyoryu rŭl wihayŏ" [For the Unification of the Ancestral Land and Cultural Exchange between Northern and Southern Korea], *Choguk chŏnsŏn*, October 18, 1956, 3.
45. O Chŏngsam, "In'gansŏng ŭi ch'ubang: Ch'oegŭn Namchosŏn munhak ŭi tonghyang" [The Banishment of Humanity: Recent Developments in Southern Korean Literature], *Munhak sinmun*, August 25, 1959, 3.
46. O Chŏngsam, "In'gansŏng ŭi ch'ubang," 3.
47. Ro Kŭmsŏk, "Si munhak esŏ pon Namchosŏn" [Southern Korea as Seen in Poetry], *Ch'ŏllima* 51 (December 1962): 109–11.
48. Kim Kyŏngho, "Saeroun mosaek: Sangbannyŏn ŭi nambanbu mundan kaegwan" [A Survey of the First Half of the Year's Literature in the Southern Half], *Munhak sinmun*, July 5, 1963, 4.
49. Kim Haegyun, "Namchosŏn munhak i kŏrŏ on kil" [The Road that Southern Korean Literature Has Walked], *Chosŏn munhak* 221 (January 1966): 95–100.
50. Kim Song, "Ch'ŏnggaeguri" [Green Frog], *Chosŏn munhak* 118 (June 1957): 50–59. Kim Song is the novelist and translator mentioned in chapter 2. The original text was published in *Munhak yesul* in 1956.
51. Charles R. Kim, *Youth for Nation: Culture and Protest in Cold War South Korea* (Honolulu: University of Hawaii Press, 2017), 176.
52. Balázs Szalontai, *Kim Il Sung in the Krushchev Era*, 155–60.
53. Kim Chonghoe, "Pukhan munhak e nat'anan Masan ŭigŏ wa 4-wŏl hyŏngmyŏng" [The Masan Uprising and April Revolution as Represented in North Korean Literature], *Hyŏndae munhak iron yŏn'gu* 30 (2007): 5–25; Kim Sŏngsu, "Pukhan ŭi Namhan munhwa yesul insik e taehan yŏksajŏk koch'al" [A Historical Exploration of North Korea's

Understanding of South Korean Literary Arts], *T'ongil chŏngch'aek yŏn'gu* 10. vol. 1 (2001): 241–68; Kim Sŏngsu, "4.19 wa 1960-nyŏndae Pukhan munhak—Sŏndong kwa sot'ong sai e: Pukhan chakka ŭi 4.19 tamnon kwa chŏnyu pangsik pip'an" [4.19 and 1960s North Korean Literature—Between Incitement and Communication: A Critique of North Korean Writers' Discourse on 4.19 and their Method of Appropriation], *Han'guk kŭndae munhak yŏn'gu* 30 (2014): 7–40; Yi Sunuk, "Nambuk munhak e nat'anan Masan ŭigŏ ŭi silchŭngjŏk yŏn'gu" [An Empirical Study of the Masan Uprising as Depicted in North and South Korean Literature], *Yŏngju ŏmun* 12 (2006): 267–97; Yi Sunuk, "4-wŏl hyŏngmyŏng kwa Pukhan munhak: Chosŏn Chakka Tongmaeng Chungang Wiwŏnhoe kigwanji *Munhak sinmun* ŭl chungsim ŭro" [The April Revolution and North Korean Literature: Focusing on *Munhak sinmun*, the Official Organ of the Central Committee of the Korean Writers' Association], *Han'guk minjok munhwa* 40 (2011): 133–65.

54. For more on this, see Theodore Q. Hughes, *Literature and Film in Cold War South Korea: Freedom's Frontier* (New York: Columbia University Press, 2012), 129–64.
55. All such texts were marked as South Korean productions, and many were published under labels like "From Southern Korean Publications" (Namchosŏn ch'ulp'anmul esŏ) and "Southern Korea as Seen through Literary Arts" (Munhak yesul ŭl t'ong hae pon Namchosŏn). The names of the original authors were redacted in publications like the *Rodong Sinmun* and *Munhak sinmun* newspapers but not in the *Choguk t'ongil* newspaper. The Kim Song short story published in *Chosŏn munhak* in 1957 also included the original author's name.
56. Kim Sangdon, "Kongp'o wa t'anap kwa pujŏng ŭi togani" [The Crucible Of Fear, Repression, And Injustice], *Rodong sinmun*, March 13, 1958, 3.
57. Kim Sangdon, "Kongp'o wa t'anap kwa pujŏng ŭi togani," 3.
58. Kim Sangdon. "Kongp'o wa t'anap kwa pujŏng ŭi togani," 3.
59. Notably, South Korean current events comics (*sisa manhwa*) had appeared in North Korean publications like the *Rodong sinmun* as early as 1954. Yet textual reproductions did not appear in a sustained fashion until the 1960s.
60. "Chaju chŏngsin, chaju p'andan, kŭrigo chaju ch'ŏriman i chaju minjok kukka rŭl chajujŏk ŭro kkŭlgo kal su innŭn, yangbo hal su ŏmnŭn taewŏnch'ik" [Only an Autonomous Spirit, Autonomous Judgment, And Autonomous Treatment—Principles That Cannot Be Conceded—Are Capable Of Leading An Autonomous Nation-State Autonomously], *Rodong sinmun*, April 2, 1963, 3.
61. "Chaju chŏngsin, chaju p'andan, kŭrigo chaju ch'ŏriman i chaju minjok kukka rŭl chajujŏk ŭro kkŭlgo kal su innŭn, yangbo hal su ŏmnŭn taewŏnch'ik," 3.
62. "Chaju chŏngsin, chaju p'andan, kŭrigo chaju ch'ŏriman i chaju minjok kukka rŭl chajujŏk ŭro kkŭlgo kal su innŭn, yangbo hal su ŏmnŭn taewŏnch'ik," 3.
63. "Yesok ŭro ŭi kil: Woegok toen saengsan kujo, chongsokchŏk kyŏngje ch'eje (I)" [The Road To Dependence: A Distorted Production Structure, A Subservient Economic System (I)], and "Kyŏngje ch'eje ŭi charipchŏk chaep'yŏnsŏng ŭn ch'omi ŭi kŭnmu (II)" [The Self-Sufficient Reorganization Of The Economic System Is The Most Pressing And Urgent Task], *Rodong sinmun*, November 1–4, 1963, 3.

1. REVERBERATIONS   273

64. "Pip'an toeŏya hal Miguk ŭi wŏnjo chŏngch'aek" [US Aid Policies That Must Be Critiqued], *Rodong sinmun*, December 9, 1963, 3.
65. Kim Chongt'ae, "Chaju charip ŭl wi haesŏnŭn oese rŭl paegyŏk haeya handa" [For An Autonomous Self-Sufficiency, We Must Reject Foreign Influence], *Rodong sinmun*, January 30, 1964, 3.
66. Kim Chongt'ae, "Chaju charip ŭl wi haesŏnŭn oese rŭl paegyŏk haeya handa," 3.
67. Chang Habo, "Uri nŭn kkŭnnae chik'irira" [We Will Protect Until The End], *Chosŏn nyŏsŏng* 198 (April 1964): 40. The original poem, published in the *Pusan ilbo* in May 1960, was titled "Yŏgi nŭn amudo oji malla" [No One Come Here] and it was first republished in the North in the *Rodong sinmun* in February 1964; Ko Yangsun, "Au ŭi yŏngjŏn e" [At My Brother's Funerary Altar], *Chosŏn nyŏsŏng* 198 (April 1964): 40
68. "Mot salketta nŭn hasoyŏn ppun" [Nothing But The Grievance That Living Is Impossible], *Chosŏn nyŏsŏng* 203 (September 1964): 36–37; Ham Sŏkhŏn, "Minjung iyŏ no hara!" [People, Feel Rage!], *Chosŏn nyŏsŏng* 206 (December 1964): 67–69.
69. Kim Sangwŏn, "Choguk t'ongil" [National Unification], *Chosŏn nyŏsŏng* 208 (February 1965): 28; "T'ongil ŭl purŭnŭn moksoridŭl" [Voices Calling for Unification], *Chosŏn nyŏsŏng* 208 (February 1965): 29–30.
70. Pak Yŏngil, "Kŭm panji" [Gold Ring], *Chosŏn nyŏsŏng* 210 (April 1965): 104–7.
71. O Yŏngsu, "Anna ŭi yusŏ" [Anna's Will], *Chosŏn nyŏsŏng* 211–213 (May–July 1965): 126–30; 131–34.
72. Yi Insŏk, "Tari" [Bridge], *Sae sedae* 109 (March 1964): 64–65; Kim Kyŏnghŏn, "Kongil nal en chugŏdo chohŭn'ga" [Is It Ok To Die On A Sunday?], *Sae sedae* 109 (March 1964): 65; "I nara animyŏn kugyŏng mothal 'kyoyuk pigŭk'" [An 'Educational Tragedy' That Cannot Be Seen In Any Other Country], *Sae sedae* 109 (March 1964): 64–65.
73. "Ch'aek kap" [Book Prices], *Sae sedae* 110 (April 1964): 72–73; Cho Yŏngho, "Poribap" [Barley Rice], *Sae sedae* 111 (May 1964): 88–89; Ha Chaedŏk, "Nunmul i p'inŭn iyagi" [A Tear-blooming Story], *Sae sedae* 111 (May 1964): 88–89.
74. Sin Hyŏndŭk, "I iyagi rŭl ank'o nŭn kyŏndil su ka ŏpkuna" [Without Telling This Story, I Cannot Survive], *Sae sedae* 112 (June 1964): 139; "Hyosŏng ŭi puksori" [The Drumbeat of Filiality], *Sae sedae* 113 (July 1964): 85–88; Yi Yunhwa, "Parik'et'ŭ" [Barricade], *Sae sedae* 113 (July 1964): 88; "Kongbu hanŭn kŏt poda nŭn pae kop'ŭn kŏt i tŏ kŭphayŏ" [Hunger Is More Urgent Than Studying], *Sae sedae* 116 October 1964, 128; "Salkil ŭn soksumuch'aek" [No Way to Survive], *Sae sedae* 116 (October 1964): 129–30; "Ch'ŏlbuji tongsaeng ŏpko yurang 8-nyŏn kkŭt e Sin sonyŏn ŭn ŏdi ro kanŭnga?" [After Wandering For 8 Years With His Small Sister On His Back, Where Did Young Sin Go?], *Sae sedae* 116 (October 1964): 126–27; Sŏ Sŏkkyu. "Ch'angja rŭl mallinŭn pŏl ŭi choemyŏng ŭn muŏt imnikka?" [For What Crime Is This Vexing Punishment?], *Sae sedae* 116 (October 1964): 127–28; "Na to karyŏnda" [I Will Go Too], *Sae sedae* 116 (October 1964): 130; "Usŭm irhŭn kyosil" [A Classroom that Has Lost its Laughter], *Sae sedae* 117 (November 1964): 133–35; "Manhwa mukkŭm: Namchosŏn p'unggyŏng" [Comic Compilation: The Scene of Southern Korea], *Sae sedae* 117 (November 1964): 138–39; "Tongsim ŭn unda" [The Child's Heart Cries], *Sae sedae* 118 (December 1964):

123–24; "Koyongju e chitpalp'in se sonyŏn" [Three Boys Trampled Upon By Their Employer], *Sae sedae* 118 (December 1964): 124–25.

75. Avram Agov, "North Korea's Alliances and the Unfinished Korean War," *Journal of Korean Studies* 18, no. 2 (2013): 227.
76. On the role of these nations in postwar reconstruction, see Cheehyung Harrison Kim, *Heroes and Toilers*, 82–83.
77. On this, see Benjamin Young, *Guns, Guerillas, and the Great Leader: North Korea and the Third World* (Palo Alto, CA: Stanford University Press, 2021), and Moe Taylor, *North Korea, Tricontinentalism, and the Latin American Revolution, 1959–1970* (New York: Cambridge University Press, 2023).
78. Yi Insŏk, "Tari" [Bridge], *Chayu munhak* 6, no. 9 (September 1961): 171.
79. Yi Insŏk, "Tari" [Bridge], *Munhak sinmun*, July 27, 1962, 4; Yi Insŏk, "Tari" [Bridge], *Choguk t'ongil*, January 22, 1964, 4; Yi Insŏk, "Tari" [Bridge], *Sae sedae* 109 (March 1964): 64–65.
80. Sin Tongmun, "Aa nae choguk" [O My Ancestral Land], *Sasanggye* 120 (April 1963): 397–99.
81. Sin Tongmun, "Aa nae choguk" [O My Ancestral Land]," *Minju ch'ŏngnyŏn*, May 16, 1963, 3; Sin Tongmun, "Aa nae choguk" [O My Ancestral Land], *Choguk t'ongil*, May 18, 1963, 3; Sin Tongmun, "Aa nae choguk" [O My Ancestral Land], *Rodongja sinmun*, May 19, 1963, 3; Sin Tongmun, "Aa nae choguk" [O My Ancestral Land], *Munhak sinmun*, August 3, 1965, 4.
82. Nam Chŏnghyŏn, "Pujujŏn sangsŏ" [Letter to Father], *Sasanggye* 135 (June 1964): 358–75.
83. Nam Chŏnghyŏn, "Pujujŏn sangsŏ" [Letter to Father], *Munhak sinmun*, September 18, 1964, 3; Nam Chŏnghyŏn, "Pujujŏn sangsŏ" [Letter to Father], *Choguk t'ongil* September 16–19, 1964, 4; Nam Chŏnghyŏn, "Pyŏrak ŭn tangsin i mandŭsyŏya hamnida" [You Must Create Your Own Thunderbolt], *Rodong sinmun*, September 21, 1964, 3.
84. Yi Kŭnbae, "4.19 e puch'yŏ" [On 4.19], *Kyŏnghyang sinmun*, April 18, 1964, 5.
85. Yi Kŭnbae, "4.19 e puch'yŏ" [On 4.19], *Choguk t'ongil*, May 23, 1964, 4; Yi Kŭnbae, "4.19 e puch'yŏ" [On 4.19], *Ch'ŏllima* 79 (April 1965): 97.
86. Yi Kŭnbae, "4.19 e puch'yŏ" [On 4.19], *Chosŏn sinbo*, April 19, 1965, 3.
87. Yi Insŏk, "In'gan ŭn sara issŭl kwŏlli ga itta" [A Human Has the Right to Live], *Sasanggye* 118 (March 1963): 370–71.
88. Yi Insŏk, "In'gan ŭn sara issŭl kwŏlli ga itta" [A Human Has the Right to Live], *Choguk t'ongil*, April 27, 1963, 3; Yi Insŏk, "In'gan ŭn sara issŭl kwŏlli ga itta" [A Human Has the Right to Live], *Munhak sinmun*, December 11, 1964, 4; Yi Insŏk, "In'gan ŭn sara issŭl kwŏlli ga itta" [A Human Has the Right to Live], *Chosŏn sinbo*, July 24, 1963, 3.
89. Ku Chungsŏ, "Wasŏ chedan pusura," *Han'guk ilbo*, 5.
90. Ku Chungsŏ, "Wasŏ chedan pusura," *Choguk t'ongil*, 4; Ku Chungsŏ, "Wasŏ chedan pusura," *Munhak sinmun*, 4.
91. Ku Chungsŏ, "Wasŏ chedan pusura," *Chosŏn sinbo*, 3.
92. John Lie, "Korean Diaspora and Diasporic Nationalism," in *The Routledge Handbook of Korean Culture and Society*, ed. Youna Kim (New York: Routledge, 2017), 248.

93. Sayaka Chatani, "Revisiting Korean Slums in Postwar Japan: *Tongne* and *Hakkyo* in the *Zainichi* Memoryscape," *Journal of Asian Studies* 80, no. 3 (August 2021): 593.
94. Deokhyo Choi, "The Empire Strikes Back from Within: Colonial Liberation and the Korean Minority Question at the Birth of Postwar Japan, 1945–47," *American Historical Review* 126, no. 2 (June 2021): 570.
95. Deokhyo Choi, "The Empire Strikes Back from Within," 571.
96. Matthew Augustine, *From Japanese Empire to American Hegemony: Koreans and Okinawans in the Resettlement of Northeast Asia* (Honolulu: University of Hawaii Press, 2023), 70.
97. Matthew Augustine, *From Japanese Empire to American Hegemony*, 48–49, 81.
98. Hiromitsu Inokuchi, "Korean Ethnic Schools in Occupied Japan, 1945–1952," in *Koreans in Japan: Critical Voices from the Margin*, ed. Sonia Ryang (New York: Routledge, 2000), 148–49.
99. Yi Haenghwa and Yi Kyŏnggyu, "Migunjŏnggi ŭi chaeil Chosŏnin kwallyŏn sinmun kisa wa ideollogi" [US Occupation Era Ideology and Newspaper Articles Regarding Koreans in Japan], *Ilbon kŭndaehak yŏn'gu* 64 (May 2019): 200–201.
100. Deokhyo Choi, "Crucible of the Post-Empire: Decolonization, Race, and Cold War Politics in US-Japan-Korea Relations, 1945–1952," PhD diss. (Cornell University, 2013), 206–7.
101. Matthew Augustine, *From Japanese Empire to American Hegemony*, 179.
102. "Nŏlli Ilbon inmin sok ŭro" [Go Broadly within the Japanese People], *Haebang sinmun*, January 1, 1950, 2.
103. Reproduced in Chŏn Chun, *Choch'ongnyŏn yŏn'gu che 2-kwŏn* [Research on Chongryon Vol. 2] (Seoul: Korea University Press, 1972), 29–30. Note: Chŏn's reproduction of these documents includes some inaccurate dates.
104. Chin Hŭigwan, "Chaeil Han'gugin sahoe hyŏngsŏng kwa Choch'ongnyŏn kyŏlsŏng paegyŏng yŏn'gu" [Research on the Formation of Korean Society in Japan and the Background for the Establishment of Chongryon], *T'ongil munje yŏn'gu* 31 (May 1999): 102.
105. Chin Hŭigwan, "Chaeil Han'gugin sahoe hyŏngsŏng kwa Choch'ongnyŏn kyŏlsŏng paegyŏng yŏn'gu," 102; Chŏn Chun, *Choch'ongnyŏn yŏn'gu che 2-kwŏn*, 33.
106. The *Haebang sinmun* was renamed *Chosŏn minbo* in 1957 and *Chosŏn sinbo* in 1961.
107. Kim Hun, "Fukkan no shukusu" [Congratulations on Reissue], *Haebang sinmun*, May 20, 1952, 1.
108. "Fukkan no shi" [Reissue Message], *Haebang sinmun*, May 20, 1952, 1.
109. "Zainichi zendōhō ni uttau: Minsen chūō de apīru" [Call to All Compatriots in Japan: An Appeal at the Minjŏn Central Committee], *Haebang sinmun*, May 20, 1952, 2.
110. Kim Saryang's work oversteps the boundaries between North Korean literature and resident Korean literature. However, these particular works, "From Seoul to Suwŏn" (Sŏul sŏ Suwŏn ŭro, 1950) and "This Is How We Won" (Uri nŭn irŏk'e sawŏtta, 1950) were written and published in the North. Therefore, they fit broadly within the phenomenon under discussion here.
111. Chŏn Chun, *Choch'ongnyŏn yŏn'gu che 2-kwŏn*, 473–74; Chin Hŭigwan, "Choch'ongnyŏn yŏn'gu: Yŏksa wa sŏnggyŏk ŭl chungsim ŭro" [Research on Chongryon: Focused on its History and Character], PhD diss. (Tongguk University, 1998), 86.

112. See advertisements in the November 30, 1952, April 18, 1953, May 16, 1953, September 8, 1953, and December 23, 1954 issues of the *Haebang Sinmun*; see also, "Toksŏ annae" [Reading Guide], *Haebang sinmun*, January 30, 1953, 2.
113. See advertisement in the December 23, 1954 issue of the *Haebang sinmun*.
114. Rim Kwangch'ŏl, "Mujŏkon hago kwŏn hal su innŭn uri 'yŏksa' ch'aek" [A Book on Our 'History' that I Can Absolutely Recommend], *Haebang sinmun*, February 23, 1954, 2.
115. "Toksŏ annae" [Reading Guide], *Haebang sinmun*, January 21, 1954, 2.
116. See advertisement in the August 5, 1954 issue of the *Haebang sinmun*.
117. Chŏn Chun, *Choch'ongnyŏn yŏn'gu che 2-kwŏn*, 474; Chin Hŭigwan, "Choch'ongnyŏn yŏn'gu: Yŏksa wa sŏnggyŏk ŭl chungsim ŭro," 86.
118. See advertisement in the May 16, 1953 issue of the *Haebang sinmun*.
119. Although the Chŏn Chun—and Chin Hŭigwan following him—say that Kuwŏl was established in 1952, this appears incorrect. All documentary sources date its founding to 1954. See, for example, the text by the store's owner: Ro Pyŏngu, "Tosŏsil sŏlch'i cheŭi rŭl chiji handa" [In support of the Proposal to Establish a Reading Room], *Haebang sinmun*, August 11, 1956, 3.
120. See advertisement in the December 23, 1954 issue of the *Haebang sinmun*.
121. Hŏ Namgi, "Nae o ueru hitobito: Kugatsu shobō tanbōki" [The People Who Planted the Seed: A Visit to Kuwŏl Sŏbang], *Chōsen sōren*, May 21, 1958, 2.
122. See advertisements in the July 27, 1954 and August 14, 1954 issues of the *Haebang sinmun*.
123. Sonia Ryang, *North Koreans in Japan: Language, Ideology, and Identity* (Boulder, CO: Westview Press, 1997), 78–91; Sonia Ryang, "Visible and Vulnerable: The Predicament of Koreans in Japan," in *Diaspora without Homeland: Being Korean in Japan*, ed. Sonia Ryang and John Lie (Berkeley: University of California Press, 2009), 65–66.
124. "Sŏnŏn" [Declaration], reproduced in Chŏn Chun, *Choch'ongnyŏn yŏn'gu che 2-kwŏn*, 277.
125. "Kyuyak" [Bylaws], reproduced in Chŏn Chun, *Choch'ongnyŏn yŏn'gu che 2-kwŏn*, 278.
126. "Yŏnggwang e kadŭkch'an choguk ero ŭi kil: Choguk pangmundan kongno ro hyangbal" [The Glorious Road to Our Ancestral Land: The Ancestral Land Delegation Departs by Air], *Haebang sinmun*, September 1, 1955, 2; "Sangho wŏnjo" [Mutual Aid], *Haebang sinmun*, November 26, 1955, 2.
127. "Ŭijang enŭn Kim Ilsŏng wŏnsu oe 6-myŏng: Han Tŏksu ssido ŭijang e, chungang ŭiwŏn 87-myŏng chung en Ri Simch'ŏl, Hwang Ponggu ssido" [Kim Il Sung and Six Others as Chairmen: Han Tŏksu Also a Chairman, Ri Simch'ŏl and Hwang Ponggu Also Appointed to Central Council], *Chosŏn minbo*, December 26, 1957, 2.
128. "Chŏnjin hanŭn munhwa undong: Songnyŏn munhak yesurin chwadamhoe" [The Advancing Cultural Movement: Artists' and Writers' End-of-Year Roundtable], *Chosŏn minbo*, December 28, 1957, 4.
129. "Choguk ŭro put'ŏ kŏaek ŭi kyoyukpi wa changhakkŭm" [A Large Amount of Educational Funds and Scholarships from the Ancestral Land], *Chosŏn minbo*, April 25, 1957, 1.

1. REVERBERATIONS   277

130. "Sŏnjin kwahak t'amgu ŭi chŏndang: Chosŏn Taehak ŭi apkil ŭn yangnyang handa" [Palace of Advanced Scientific Exploration: Korea University's Future Path is Bright], *Chosŏn minbo*, October 19, 1957, 2.
131. Sayaka Chatani, "Revisiting Korean Slums in Postwar Japan," 602, 604.
132. "Choguk munhwa pogŭp ssent'ŏ: Kuwŏl sŏbang saok yaksŏngsik" [Center for Disseminating the Culture of Our Ancestral Land: Completion Ceremony for Kuwŏl Sŏbang's Building], *Chosŏn minbo*, January 28, 1958, 2.
133. Ri Ch'anŭi, "Aegukjuŭi sasang ŭi chego: Chaeil Chosŏnin munhwa undong ŭi hoego wa chŏnmang" [The Improvement of Nationalist Ideology: Retrospection and Outlook on the Cultural Movement of Koreans in Japan], *Haebang sinmun*, January 1, 1956, 5.
134. Ri Ch'anŭi, "Aegukjuŭi sasang ŭi chego," 5.
135. Ri Ch'anŭi, "Aegukjuŭi sasang ŭi chego," 5.
136. Ri Ch'anŭi, "Aegukjuŭi sasang ŭi chego," 5.
137. "Kyuyak" [Bylaws], reproduced in Chŏn Chun, *Choch'ongnyŏn yŏn'gu che 2-kwŏn*, 278.
138. "Chojik sŏnjŏn pangch'im (1952.5.26)" [Plan for Organizational Propaganda (1952.5.26)], reproduced in Chŏn Chun, *Choch'ongnyŏn yŏn'gu che 2-kwŏn*, 36.
139. "Tonggyŏng Hwangch'ŏn [Tōkyō Arakawa], Taep'an [Ōsaka] sŏnŭn Mindan to ch'amka: Kakchi sŏ pŏrŏjinŭn kongdong haengdong" [In Tokyo's Arakawa and in Osaka, Mindan Participates Too: Joint Action Taking Place in Various Places], *Haebang sinmun*, August 16, 1956, 3.
140. For example, see "Kamdong purŭmyŏ ryŏllin misulchŏn chinhaeng: Ch'ongnyŏn-Mindan misurindŭl i son ŭl chapko" [With an Emotional Opening, Art Exhibition Takes Place: Chongryon-Mindan Artists Join Hands], *Chosŏn sinbo*, May 6, 1961, 4.
141. See the November 17, 1955 issue of the *Haebang sinmun*.
142. See, for example, the July 14 and August 2, 1956 issues of the *Haebang sinmun*.
143. "Nambanbu tongp'o waŭi ryŏn'gye haksŭp tŭng" [Liaison with Compatriots from the Southern Half, Study, and More], *Haebang sinmun*, February 23, 1956, 2.
144. The poet Nam Siu recounts listening to a full recording of the congress via the radio in the following roundtable: "Che 2-ch'a Chosŏn chakka taehoe e komu toen chaeil Chosŏn chakkadŭl ŭi saeroun p'obu: chwadamhoe (1)" [The New Aspirations of Korean Writers in Japan Inspired by the Second Congress of Korean Writers: Roundtable (1)], *Haebang sinmun*, October 27, 1956, 4.
145. Hŏ Namgi, ed. and trans., *Chōsen shisen* (Tokyo: Aoki shoten, 1955).
146. For facsimile versions of extant copies, see Unoda Shōya, ed., *Zainichi Chōsen bungakukai kankē shiryō, 1945–1960* (vol 3) [Materials Related to the Korean Literature Association in Japan, 1945–1960 (vol. 3)], commentary by Song Hyewŏn (Tokyo: Ryokuin shobō, 2018), 5–183.
147. Song Hyewŏn, "Kaisetsu" [Commentary], in Unoda Shōya, ed., *Zainichi Chōsen bungakukai kankē shiryō, 1945–1960* (vol 1), xix–xx.
148. Song Hyewŏn, "Kaisetsu," xix.
149. Cho Yŏnhyŏn, "Sŏ" [Preface], in Kim Yun, *Mŏngdŭn kyejŏl: Kim Yun sijip* (Seoul: Hyŏndae munhaksa, 1968), 8–9.
150. Song Hyewŏn, "Kaisetsu", xix.

151. Kang Myŏnghŭi, "Oppa wa ŏnni ka wae p'i hŭllyŏnŭnji," *Chosŏn ilbo*, 3.
152. Lines from the poem appeared in Japanese translation as a caption for a photo of young children in Seoul participating in a demonstration. See page 2 of the May 9, 1960 issue of *Chōsen sōren*.
153. Kang Myŏnghŭi, "Watashi wa shitte imasu," 13; Kang Myŏnghŭi, "Niisan to neesan wa naze jyū de utareta no desu ka," 1–3.
154. Yu Sŏnjun, "Hata" [Flag], *Atarashii sedai* 1, no. 5 (June 1960): 29; Sim Chaesin, "Hajiru" [Embarrassed], *Atarashii sedai* 1, no. 6 (July 1960): 11; Kim Yosŏp, "Gunshū" [Masses], *Atarashii sedai* 1, no. 6 (July 1960): 12. Unlike the other works in this original round of republications, Kim was a professional writer rather than a student amateur.
155. Ko Yangsun, "Otōto no reizen ni" [At My Younger Brother's Funerary Altar], *Atarashii sedai* 2, no. 3 (April 1961): 10–11. Ko's name is mistakenly listed here as Ko Sunhŭi.
156. Yi Wŏnsu, "Ane no reizen ni" [Song of a Younger Sister], *Atarashii sedai* 2, no. 3 (April 1961): 13–14. Ko's name is mistakenly listed here as Ko Sunhŭi.
157. As above, Ko's name is mistakenly listed as Ko Sunhŭi here.
158. For the above texts, see pp. 170–208 of *Chi no shigatsu: Minami Chōsen jinmin hōki*.
159. Kang Myŏnghŭi, "Oppa wa ŏnni nŭn wae ch'ong e majannayo" [Why Were My Older Brothers and Sisters Shot?], *Munhak yesul* 6 (May 1963): 66–67.
160. Kang Myŏnghŭi, "Oppa wa ŏnni nŭn wae ch'ong e majannayo" [Why Were My Older Brothers and Sisters Shot?], *Chosŏn sinbo*, April 19, 1973, 4.
161. Yi Insŏk, "In'gan ŭn sara issŭl kwŏlli ga itta," *Chosŏn sinbo*, 3; Ku Chungsŏ, "Wasŏ chedan pusura," *Chosŏn sinbo*, 3; Cho Pyŏnghwa, "T'ongil iyŏ! Yŏllyŏra" [Open, Unification], *Chosŏn sinbo*, January 22, 1965, 3; Yi Kŭnbae, "4.19 e puch'yŏ" [On 4.19], *Chosŏn sinbo*, 3; Pak Tujin, "A Choguk" [Ah Ancestral Land], *Chosŏn sinbo*, January 27, 1965, 3; Pak Tujin, "A Choguk" [Ah Ancestral Land], *Chosŏn sinbo* April 28, 1973, 4; Pak Tujin, "A Choguk" [Ah Ancestral Land], *Chosŏn sinbo*, April 19, 1975, 2.
162. Kang Sun, "Pulkil" [Blaze], *Munhak sinmun*, April 12, 1960, 1.
163. Kang Sun, "Pulkil," 1.
164. Kang Sun, "Pulkil," 1.
165. "'Hagwŏn e chayu rŭl talla!' Chiptan siwi, kyesok kakchi ro hwaktae" ["Give Schools Freedom!" Mass Demonstrations Continue to Spread to All Locations], *Chosŏn minbo*, March 16, 1960, 2.
166. Kang Sun, "Pulkil" [Blaze], *Chosŏn minbo*, March 28, 1960, 4.
167. See the morning and evening editions of the March 9, 1960 issue of the *Tonga ilbo*.
168. Chŏn Hwagwang, "Han'guk nyusŭ" [South Korean News], *Chosŏn munye* 7 (1957): 18–19. Reproduced in Unoda Shōya, ed., *Zainichi Chōsen bungakukai kankē shiryō, 1945–1960* (vol 2), commentary by Song Hyewŏn (Tokyo: Ryokuin shobō, 2018), 246–47.
169. Chŏn Hwagwang, "Han'guk nyusŭ," 18.
170. Chŏn Hwagwang, "Han'guk nyusŭ," 19.
171. Kim Hongsik, "Tŏ nŭn ch'amŭl su ŏpta" [We Cannot Bear It Anymore], *Chosŏn minbo*, June 8, 1957, 4.
172. Kim Hongsik, "Tŏ nŭn ch'amŭl su ŏpta," 4.

173. "Ŏmma pap chom chuso" [Mom, Please Give Me Some Food], *Chosŏn minbo*, April 13, 1957, 2.
174. Tessa Morris-Suzuki discusses this space and group in detail in *Borderline Japan: Foreigners and Frontier Controls in the Postwar Era* (New York: Cambridge University Press, 2010). See chapter six.
175. Kang Sun, "Yusŏ kat'ŭn mal ŭl namgigo" [Leaving Words Like a Last Testament], *Chosŏn sinbo*, March 4, 1964, 4.
176. Kang Sun, "Yusŏ kat'ŭn mal ŭl namgigo," 4.
177. "Sŏul ŭi pinminch'on Namgajwa-dong sŏ ŭi ch'amgŭk" [The Tragedy in the Seoul Slum of Namgajwa-dong], *Chosŏn ilbo*, January 26, 1964, 7.
178. Kang Sun, "Yusŏ kat'ŭn mal ŭl namgigo," 4.
179. Ch'ae Kyusang, "Hanggŏ hanŭn nyŏsŏngdŭl" [Women Who Resist], *Chosŏn nyŏsŏng* 223 (May 1966): 78–81.
180. "Silchik yŏch'ajang i chasal" [Fired Female Attendant Commits Suicide], *Chosŏn ilbo*, March 17, 1964, 7.
181. Kim Sunhwa, "Sŏul ŭi han yŏch'ajang ŭi unmyŏng" [The Fate of One Female Attendant in Seoul], *Rodong sinmun*, March 8, 1965, 3.
182. Kim Ullyong, "Punno ŭi norae" [Song of Rage], *Munhak sinmun*, April 22, 1960, 4.
183. Pak Seyŏng, "Sech'age t'a pŏnjira hangjaeng ŭi pulkil" [Burn and Spread Powerfully, Flame of Struggle], *Rodong sinmun*, April 21, 1960, 3.
184. "3.15 ŭi punhwagu: Masan sakŏn haebu" [The Volcanic Crater of 3.15: A Dissection of the Masan Incident], *Han'guk ilbo*, March 18, 1960, 2.
185. Yi Hanjik, "Kyŏngnyu e puch'inda (3): Kan pam kkum iyagina han chari" [Dispatch into the Torrent (3): Where We Talked of Things like the Previous Night's Dreams], *Saebyŏk* 7, no. 5 (May 1960): 32.
186. Yi Hanjik, "Kyŏngnyu e puch'inda (3)," 32.
187. Kim Yongho, "Haemada 4-wŏl" [April Every Year], *Chosŏn ilbo*, April 28, 1960, 4.
188. Hwang Kŭmch'an, "Chŏlmŭn sanmaekdŭl" [Young Mountain Ridges], *Chosŏn ilbo*, May 30, 1960, 4.
189. Pak Hwamok, "Sa-wŏl" [April], *Chosŏn ilbo*, May 3, 1960, 4.
190. Yun Ch'angju, "Masan ŭn ponghwa rŭl ch'uk'yŏ tŭrŏtta" [Masan Has Raised the Signal Fire], *Rodong sinmun*, April 14, 1960, 5.
191. "*Punno ŭi hwasan ŭn t'ŏjyŏtta*: Kungnip yŏn'gŭk kŭkchang kongyŏn" [*The Volcano of Rage Has Erupted*: Performance at the National Drama Theater], *Rodong sinmun*, June 5, 1960, 5.
192. Song Yŏng, *Punno ŭi hwasan ŭn t'ŏjyŏtta* [The Volcano of Rage Has Erupted], *Chosŏn munhak* 154 (June 1960): 22.
193. Song Yŏng, *Punno ŭi hwasan ŭn t'ŏjyŏtta*, 49.
194. Song Yŏng, *Punno ŭi hwasan ŭn t'ŏjyŏtta*, 46.
195. Ku Inhwan, "P'anjajip kŭnŭl" [In the Shadow of Shacks], *Hyŏndae munhak* 7, no. 8 (August 1961): 94–113.
196. Ku Inhwan, "P'anjajip kŭnŭl (1–2)" [In the Shadow of Shacks (1–2)], *Munhak sinmun*, December 11–25, 1962, 4.

197. Kim Suyŏng, "Kadao nagadao" [Go, Get Out], *Chosŏn hwabo* 90 (January 1964): n.p.; Kim Suyŏng, "Kadao nagadao" [Go, Get Out], *Rodongja sinmun*, April 19, 1964, 4.
198. Kwŏn Pyŏngsun, "Kudu takki sonyŏ ŭi si" [The Poems of a Shoeshine Girl], *Yŏwŏn* 11, no. 3 (March 1965): n.p.
199. Kwŏn Pyŏngsun, "Kudu takki sonyŏ ŭi si" [The Poems of a Shoeshine Girl], *Chosŏn nyŏsŏng* 213 (July 1965): n.p.
200. "Han kudu takki sonyŏ ka purŭn norae" [The Song Sung by a Shoeshine Girl], *Ch'ŏllima* 81 (June 1965): 112.
201. Pak Myŏngch'ŏl, "Kudu takki sonyŏ" [Shoeshine Girl], *Sonyŏndan* 189 (July 1965): 36.
202. Pak Myŏngch'ŏl, "Kudu takki sonyŏ," 38.
203. Chŏn Ponggu, "Nae insaeng nae chige e chigo (1–3)" [With My Life on My Back (1–3)], *Chosŏn nyŏsŏng* 222–224 (April–June 1966): 70–75, 85–88, 84–88. For the original, see Chŏn Ponggu, *Nae insaeng nae chige e chigo* [With My Life on My Back] (Seoul: Taedong Munhwasa, 1965).
204. Ryu Tohŭi, "Palp'yo toeji mothan kisa" [The Article that Could Not Be Published], *Munhak sinmun*, April 18, 1961: 2, 4.
205. Yi Hoch'ŏl, "P'anmunjŏm," *Sasanggye* 92 (March 1961): 374–95.
206. For more on this, see Theodore Q. Hughes, "Writing the Boundaries of the Divided Nation: The Works of Son Ch'ang-sŏp, Ch'oe In-hun, Nam Chŏng-hyŏn, and Lee Ho-Chul," PhD diss. (University of California-Los Angeles, 2002), 202–6.
207. Ryu Tohŭi, "Palp'yo toeji mothan kisa" [The Article that Could Not Be Published], *Munhak sinmun*, April 18, 1961, 2.
208. Ryu Tohŭi, "Palp'yo toeji mothan kisa," 4.
209. Ryu Tohŭi, "Palp'yo toeji mothan kisa," 4.
210. Ryu Tohŭi, "Palp'yo toeji mothan kisa," 4.
211. Yŏm Muung, "77-nyŏn sosŏl munhak ŭi sanghwang" [The Situation of Fiction of the Year 1977], in *77-nyŏn munje chakp'um 20-sŏnjip*, ed. Yŏm Muung (Seoul: Hanjin ch'ulp'ansa, 1978), 477.
212. "Ilche sigi Okkinawa e kkŭllyŏ on han halmŏni ŭi p'i ŭi kobal" [An Indictment of Blood from a Grandmother Who Was Forcibly Brought to Okinawa during the Japanese Colonial Era], *Chosŏn sinbo*, April 23, 1977, 3; For more on Pae, see C. Sarah Son, *The Comfort Women: Sexual Violence and Postcolonial Memory in Korea and Japan* (Chicago: University of Chicago Press, 2008), 155–57.

2. MOTHER(S) OF THE SOUTH

1. Chŏn Tongu, "Kŭ punno rŭl anko naa kasira! Namchosŏn han ŏmŏni ege" [Go Forward Carrying that Rage! To a Southern Korean Mother], *Munhak sinmun*, April 30, 1963, 4.
2. Chin Yŏngsuk, "Saengmyŏng ŭl pach'yŏ ssauryŏmnida: Ŏmŏni ege namgin yusŏ" [I Will Fight with My Life: A Last Testament Left for My Mother], *Chosŏn ilbo*, May 1,

2. MOTHER(S) OF THE SOUTH   281

    1960, 4; Chin Yŏngsuk, "Na[i] ŏrin sonyŏ Chin Yŏngsuk ŭi yusŏ," [The Last Testament of the Young Woman Chin Yŏngsuk], *Munhak sinmun*, October 4, 1960, 4.
3. Chŏn Tongu, "Kŭ punno rŭl anko naa kasira!" 4.
4. Chŏn Tongu, "Kŭ punno rŭl anko naa kasira!" 4.
5. Ra Sŭngim, "Yŏn'gŭk *Namnyŏk ŭi ŏmŏni* ŭi Sunnyŏ yŏk" [The Role of Sunnyŏ in the Play *Mother of the South*], *Chosŏn yesul* 129 (May–June 1967): 56–59.
6. Ra Sŭngim, "Yŏn'gŭk *Namnyŏk ŭi ŏmŏni* ŭi Sunnyŏ yŏk," 58.
7. Ra Sŭngim, "Yŏn'gŭk *Namnyŏk ŭi ŏmŏni* ŭi Sunnyŏ yŏk," 58.
8. Ra Sŭngim, "Yŏn'gŭk *Namnyŏk ŭi ŏmŏni* ŭi Sunnyŏ yŏk," 59.
9. Suzy Kim, *Everyday Life in the North Korean Revolution, 1945–1950* (Ithaca, NY: Cornell University Press, 2013), 177.
10. Suzy Kim, *Everyday Life in the North Korean Revolution*, 196.
11. Immanuel Kim, *Rewriting Revolution: Women, Sexuality, and Memory in North Korean Fiction* (Honolulu: University of Hawaii Press, 2018), 28.
12. Immanuel Kim, *Rewriting Revolution*, 28.
13. For the original publication of "Hope" in the South, see An Tongnim, "Hŭimang" [Hope], *Hyŏndae munhak* 9, no. 3 (March 1963): 60–71. For the North Korean reprints, see An Tongnim, "Hŭimang" [Hope], *Choguk t'ongil*, February 3–February 6, 1965, 4; An Tongnim, "Hŭimang" [Hope], *Samch'ŏlli* 9 (April 1965): 117–21. For the original South Korean reports on and discussions of Yi Kyedan that were picked up in the North, see, for example, "Nae adŭl changhage chugŏtkuna!" [My Son Died Gloriously!], *Han'guk ilbo*, April 24, 1960, 3; "Naeil ullyŏnda" [I'll Cry Tomorrow], *Han'guk ilbo*, April 25, 1960, 3; Yu Taryŏng, "4.19 wa minjok ŭi changnae" [4.19 and the Future of the Nation], *Sasanggye* 83 (June 1960): 106–10; "Tansik t'ujaeng 3-iltchae: Sŏul mullidae haksaeng 40-yŏ myŏng" [Third Day of Hunger Strikes: Around 40 Students from Seoul National University College of Arts and Sciences], *Kyŏnghyang sinmun*, June 1, 1964, 7. For the North Korean reprints, see: "I ŏmŏni rŭl kuwŏn haja!" [Let's Save this Mother!], *Rodong sinmun*, April 29, 1965, 3; "Nae adŭl changhage chugŏtkuna!" [My Son Died Gloriously!], *Samch'ŏlli* 11 (June 1965): 41; "Nŏ nŭn changhage ssawŏtta" [You Fought Gloriously], *Samch'ŏlli* 11 (June 1965): 40.
14. Han Sunmi, "Han'guk hyŏndae munhak esŏŭi ŏmŏni p'yosang kwa hŭisaeng sŏsa" [The Mother Figure and the Sacrifice Narrative in Modern Korean Literature], *Sŏktang nonch'ong* 50 (2011): 471–74.
15. Yi Pongun, "Ŏmŏni" [Mother], *Tonga ilbo*, April 30, 1960, 4.
16. Yi Pongun, "Ŏmŏni" [Mother], *Munhak sinmun*, October 4, 1960, 4.
17. Kim Myŏngsu, *Namnyŏk ŭi ŏmŏni* (1–2) [Mother of the South (1–2)], *Chosŏn yesul* 114–15 (February–March 1966): 33–48; 33–41.
18. Kim Myŏngsu, *Namnyŏk ŭi ŏmŏni* (1), 40.
19. Kim Myŏngsu, *Namnyŏk ŭi ŏmŏni* (1), 40.
20. An Tongnim, "Hŭimang," *Hyŏndae munhak*, 63.
21. An Tongnim, "Hŭimang," *Hyŏndae munhak*, 63.
22. An Tongnim, "Hŭimang," *Hyŏndae munhak*, 63.

23. "I ŏmŏni rul kuwŏn haja!" [Let's Save this Mother!], *Rodong sinmun*, April 29, 1965, 3.
24. "I ŏmŏni rul kuwŏn haja!" 3.
25. Ri Sŏngbok, "Aegukchŏk ŏmŏni ŭi sŏkpang ŭl wihayŏ ssawŏra" [Fight for the Release of this Patriotic Mother], *Rodong sinmun*, April 27, 1965, 3.
26. Ri Sŏngbok, "Aegukchŏk ŏmŏni ŭi sŏkpang ŭl wihayŏ ssawŏra," 3.
27. Ri Sŏngbok, "Aegukchŏk ŏmŏni ŭi sŏkpang ŭl wihayŏ ssawŏra," 3.
28. Ri Sŏngbok, "Aegukchŏk ŏmŏni ŭi sŏkpang ŭl wihayŏ ssawŏra," 3.
29. Ri Sŏngbok, "Ri Kyedan ŏmŏni nŭn mujokŏn sŏkpang toeyŏya handa" [Mother Yi Kyedan Must Absolutely Must Be Released], *Rodong sinmun*, May 7, 1965, 3.
30. For the original, see: "Nae adŭl changhage chugŏtkuna!" *Han'guk ilbo*, 3. For the North Korean reprint, see: "Nae adŭl changhage chugŏtkuna!" *Rodong sinmun*, 3.
31. Kim Myŏngsu, *Namnyŏk ŭi ŏmŏni* (2), 36–37.
32. Kim Myŏngsu, *Namnyŏk ŭi ŏmŏni* (2), 41.
33. On Gorky, see Suk-Young Kim, *Illusive Utopia: Theater, Film, and Everyday Performance in North Korea* (Ann Arbor: University of Michigan Press, 2010), 223. I am grateful to Robin Visser for the reference to Ding Ling.
34. Jerôme de Wit, "Writing under Wartime Conditions: North and South Korean Writers during the Korean War (1950–1953)," PhD diss. (Leiden University, 2015), 219–22.
35. Pak Hyŏk, *Chosŏn ŭi ŏmŏni* [Mother of Korea], in *Pak Hyŏk hŭigokchip: Chosŏn ŭi ŏmŏni* (Pyongyang: Chosŏn chakka tongmaeng ch'ulp'ansa, 1960), 5–96.
36. Immanuel Kim, *Rewriting Revolution*, 36.
37. Pak Hyŏk, *Chosŏn ŭi ŏmŏni*, 92.
38. Suzy Kim, "Mothers and Maidens: Gendered Formation of Revolutionary Heroes in North Korea," *Journal of Korean Studies* 19, no. 2 (Fall 2014): 262–63.
39. Chŏng Chonghyŏn, "*P'ibada* wa 'chuch'e munhak iron' ŭi kwallyŏn yangsang" [Aspects of Connection between *Sea of Blood* and "Chuch'e Literary Theory"], *Han'guk munhak yŏn'gu* 25 (2002): 343–62.
40. In Song Yŏng's initial account, the mother's youngest son is killed when she refuses to give up the Korean partisan they are hiding. The mother then joins the partisans as a seamstress, accompanying her daughter, who becomes a propaganda operative. See Song Yŏng, *Paekdusan ŭn ŏdisŏna poinda* [Mt. Paekdu Is Visible Everywhere] (Pyongyang: Minju ch'ŏngnyŏnsa, 1956), 139–41. An Hamgwang's initial account presents a similar narrative while suggesting that the mother and daughter ultimately take up arms themselves. It also presents another variant in which the mother is martyred along with her son when she refuses to give up the location of her husband and eldest son. The daughter then takes up arms in response. See An Hamgwang, *Chosŏn munhaksa* [A History of Korean Literature] (Yŏnbyŏn kyoyuk ch'ulp'ansa, 1956; facsimile ed., Han'guk munhwasa, 1956), 199–201. This latter variant is the one that was anthologized in the DPRK Academy of Sciences' *Comprehensive History of Korean Literature* in 1959. See Literary Research Division, Language and Literary Research Institute, DPRK Academy of Sciences, ed., *Chosŏn munhak t'ongsa II* [Comprehensive History of Korean Literature II] (Pyongyang: Kwahagwŏn

ch'ulp'ansa, 1959), 95–96. In another version of this variant introduced in 1961, the mother and son are Chinese, and they are martyred when they refuse to give up the Korean partisan they are hiding. On this last version, see Yun Sep'yŏng, "Hyŏngmyŏng yŏn'gŭk *Hyŏrhae ŭi norae* e taehayŏ" [On the Revolutionary Drama *The Song of Sea of Blood*], *Chosŏn munhak* 164 (April 1961): 94–105; Chŏng Chonghyŏn, "*P'ibada* wa 'chuch'e munhak iron' ŭi kwallyŏn yangsang," 352.

41. Kim Myŏnghwa, *Hyŏngmyŏng ŭi kil esŏ: Hyŏngmyŏng chŏnt'ong yŏn'gu charyo* (Vol. 1) [On the Road of Revolution: Research Materials on the Revolutionary Tradition (Vol. 1)] (Pyongyang: Nodongdang ch'ulp'ansa, 1960), 131; An Hamgwang, "Hyŏngmyŏng munhak yesul e taehan Kim Ilsŏng wŏnsu ŭi chido pangch'im e taehan yakkan ŭi koch'al" [A Consideration of Marshal Kim Il Sung's Guiding Policy toward Revolutionary Literary Arts], *Chosŏn munhak* 165 (May 1961): 104; Chŏng Chonghyŏn, "*P'ibada* wa 'chuch'e munhak iron' ŭi kwallyŏn yangsang," 349.

42. Ri Manyŏng, "Ilp'yŏn tansim ŭl wihayŏ: Hyesan yŏn'gŭktan ŭi yŏn'gŭk *Pukkŭksŏng* ŭl pogo" [Toward Single-Minded Devotion: After Seeing the Hyesan Theater Troupe's Play, *North Star*], *Rodong sinmun*, November 6, 1966, 4.

43. An Chinsŏng, "Ŏmŏni ŭi sunggohan chŏngsin segye: Yŏn'gŭk *Pukkŭksŏng* ŭl pogo" [The Lofty Internal World of a Mother: After Seeing the Play *North Star*], *Chosŏn yesul* 124 (December 1966): 23.

44. Kim Pongyŏp and Ri Kwiyŏng, "Yŏn'gŭk *Pukkŭksŏng*" [The Play *North Star*], *Chosŏn yesul* 130 (July 1967): 41–42.

45. Ryu Ch'ip'yo, "Yŏn'gŭk *Pukkŭksŏng* ŭi Hwang ssi yŏk" [The Part of Hwang in the Play *North Star*], *Chosŏn yesul* 129 (May–June 1967): 55.

46. Kim Subŏm, "P'oong" [Embrace], *Chosŏn munhak* 226 (June 1966): 49–57.

47. Cho Kŭnwŏn, "Chosŏn ŭi ŏmŏni: pulkul ŭi hyŏngmyŏng t'usa Ma Tonghŭi tongji ŭi moch'in Chang Kilbu nyŏsa" [Mother of Korea: Chang Kilbu, the Mother of the Unyielding Revolutionary Fighter, Ma Tonghŭi], *Rodong sinmun*, October 27, 1965, 2.

48. Kim Subŏm, "P'oong," 56.

49. Kim Subŏm, "P'oong," 57.

50. Kim Chaeha, "Hangil mujang t'ujaeng kwajŏng e ch'angjo toen hyŏngmyŏngjŏk yŏn'gŭk (1–4)" [Revolutionary Dramas Created in the Process of the Anti-Japanese Armed Struggle], *Chosŏn yesul* 43–46 (March–June 1960): 9–11; 5–7; 6–8; 7–9, 12; Ri Ryŏng, "Hangil mujang t'ujaeng sigi ŭi hyŏngmyŏng yŏn'gŭk" [Revolutionary Dramas of the Era of Armed Anti-Japanese Struggle], *Rodong sinmun*, June 24, 1962, 4.

51. Yŏn Changnyŏl, "Hyŏngmyŏng yŏn'gŭk *Hyŏrhae* e taehayŏ" [On the Revolutionary Play *Sea of Blood*], *Rodong sinmun*, April 14, 1963, 4; Kim Ojun, "Hangil t'ujaeng sigi e ch'angjo toen hyŏngmyŏngjŏk munhak yesul" [Literary Arts Created During the Era of Anti-Japanese Struggle], *Choguk* 1, no. 6 (June 1964): 88–93.

52. Ri Ryŏng, "Hangil mujang t'ujaeng sigi ŭi hyŏngmyŏngjŏk yŏn'gŭk (3)" [Revolutionary Dramas of the Era of Armed Anti-Japanese Struggle (3)], *Rodong sinmun*, January 13, 1968, 6.

53. "Yŏnggwangsŭrŏun hangil mujang t'ujaeng kwajŏng e ch'angjo toen hyŏngmyŏng yŏn'gŭk (3)" [Revolutionary Dramas Created during the Process of the Glorious Anti-Japanese Armed Struggle (3)], *Chosŏn yesul* 144 (July 1968): 59.
54. Rim Kyŏngsang, "Song sŏbang" [Mr. Song], *Chosŏn munye* 8 (November 1957): 23–32. Facsimile version available in Unoda Shōya, ed., *Zainichi Chōsen bungakukai kankē shiryō, 1945–1960* (vol 2) [Materials Related to the Korean Literature Association in Japan, 1945–1960 (vol. 2)], commentary by Song Hyewŏn (Tokyo: Ryokuin shobō, 2018), 285–94.
55. Rim Kyŏngsang, "Song sŏbang," *Chosŏn munye*, 27.
56. Rim Kyŏngsang, "Song sŏbang," *Chosŏn munye*, 27.
57. Rim Kyŏngsang, "Song sŏbang," *Chosŏn munye*, 27–28.
58. Rim Kyŏngsang, "Song sŏbang (1–5)" [Mr. Song (1–5)], *Chosŏn minbo*, March 1–March 29, 1958, 4.
59. Rim Kyŏngsang, "Song sŏbang (3)," *Chosŏn minbo*, 4.
60. Yun Kwangyŏng, "Tongmu wa ch'in'gu" [Comrade and Friend], *Chosŏn munye* 9 (March 1958): 30–37. Facsimile version available in Unoda Shōya, ed., *Zainichi Chōsen bungakukai kankē shiryō, 1945–1960* (vol 2) [Materials Related to the Korean Literature Association in Japan, 1945–1960 (vol. 2)], commentary by Song Hyewŏn (Tokyo: Ryokuin shobō, 2018), 354–61.
61. Yun Kwangyŏng, "Tongmu wa ch'in'gu," 33.
62. Yun Kwangyŏng, "Tongmu wa ch'in'gu," 37.
63. Tessa Morris-Suzuki, *Exodus to North Korea: Shadows from Japan's Cold War* (New York: Rowman & Littlefield, 2007), 12.
64. Pak Wŏnjun, "Hwansong (1–23)," *Chosŏn sinbo*, March 4–May 20, 1961, 4. Since the title of the story does not include Chinese characters, it can be interpreted as either "send off" (歡送) or "return" (還送).
65. Pak Wŏnjun, "Hwansong (19)," 4.
66. Song Hyewŏn, *"Chaeil Chosŏnin munhaksa" rŭl wihayŏ: Sori ŏmnŭn moksori ŭi p'ollip'oni* [Toward a "Literary History of Resident Koreans in Japan": The Polyphony of Silent Voices] (Seoul: Somyŏng ch'ulp'an, 2019), 367.
67. Kim Min, "Kaeiji annŭn hanŭl" [The Sky that Does Not Clear], *Chosŏn munye* 4 (December 1956): 11–14. Facsimile version available in Unoda Shōya, ed., *Zainichi Chōsen bungakukai kankē shiryō, 1945–1960* (vol 2) [Materials Related to the Korean Literature Association in Japan, 1945–1960 (vol. 2)], commentary by Song Hyewŏn (Tokyo: Ryokuin shobō, 2018), 155–58; Kim Min, "Nun ttŭnŭn inhyŏng (1–5)" [The Eye-Opening Doll], *Chosŏn minbo*, February 1–February 10, 1960, 4.
68. Kim Min, "Kaeiji annŭn hanŭl," 13.
69. Kim Min, "Kaeiji annŭn hanŭl," 13–14.
70. Kim Min, "Kaeiji annŭn hanŭl," 14.
71. Kim Min, "Nun ttŭnŭn inhyŏng (5)," 4.
72. Paek Chuja, "Kippŭm" [Happiness], *Chosŏn minbo*, December 4, 1959, 4.
73. Song Sukhŭi, "Nodokana Pyonyang no machi" [The Comfortable Streets of Pyongyang], *Atarashii sedai* 1, no. 10 (December 1960): 12–14.

2. MOTHER(S) OF THE SOUTH

74. Cindi Textor, "Zainichi Writers and the Postcoloniality of Modern Korean Literature," in *Routledge Companion to Korean Literature*, ed. Heekyoung Cho (New York: Routledge, 2022), 229.
75. Song Hyewŏn, *"Chaeil Chosŏnin munhaksa" rŭl wihayŏ*, 377.
76. Song Hyewŏn, *"Chaeil Chosŏnin munhaksa" rŭl wihayŏ*, 375.
77. Ryu Pyŏk, "Miwansŏng ŭi chahwasang" [Unfinished Self-Portrait], *Chosŏn minbo*, April 5–May 17, 1958, 4.
78. Ryu Pyŏk, "Miwansŏng ŭi chahwasang (1)," 4.
79. Ryu Pyŏk, "Miwansŏng ŭi chahwasang (7)," 4.
80. Ryu Pyŏk, "Charang" [Pride], *Munhak yesul* 2 (March 1960): 79–96.
81. Ryu Pyŏk, "Charang," 91.
82. Chi Myŏngsun, "Kwiguk han kŭriun tongmu ege" [To a Repatriated Friend for Whom I Long], *Chosŏn sinbo*, December 14, 1963, 4.
83. Chi Myŏngsun, "Kwiguk han kŭriun tongmu ege," 4.
84. Pak Kwanbŏm, "Nuna wa hamkke" [With My Elder Sister], in *Kkot p'inŭn kil: Pak Kwanbŏm tanp'yŏnjip* (Pyongyang: Munye ch'ulp'ansa, 1991), 126–48.
85. Pak Kwanbŏm, "Nuna wa hamkke," 140.
86. Pak Kwanbŏm, "Nuna wa hamkke," 148.
87. I have not been able to locate an extant copy of the film. Instead, the analysis in the next section focuses on the script.
88. Kim Chiha, "Ojŏk" [Five Bandits], *Sasanggye* 205 (May 1970): 231–48.
89. According to Chongryon's *Chosŏn sinbo*, the poem appeared in the June 26, 1970, issue. See "Ilbon ŭi chugan chapchi *Chugan choil* [*Shūkan asahi*] (6-wŏl 26-il ho) ka tamsi 'Ojŏk' ŭi chŏnmun ŭl pŏnyŏk hayŏ sirŏtta" [The Japanese Weekly Journal *Shūkan Asahi* (June 26th Issue) Translated and Carried the Entirety of the Narrative Poem "Five Bandits"], *Chosŏn sinbo*, June 18, 1970, 3; Kim Chiha, "Gozoku" [Five Bandits], *Koria hyōron* 113 (August 1970): 50–59; Kim Chiha, "Gozoku" [Five Bandits], *Shin Nihon bungaku* 277 (August 1970): 116–24.
90. Kim Chiha, "Ojŏk" [Five Bandits], *Chosŏn sinbo*, June 4, 1970, 8.
91. For examples of such references, see Kim Yunho, "Hoaebul ŭn t'abŏnjinda" [The Torch Fire Spreads], *Chosŏn sinbo*, July 14, 1970, 4; Ch'ŏng Ak, "Wŏnssudŭl ege pulbyŏrak ŭl" [Fiery Lightning to Our Enemies], *Chosŏn sinbo*, July 23, 1970, 4.
92. Pak Kwangt'aek, "Hyŏndaep'an 'Ojŏk'" [A Modern "Five Bandits"], *Munhak yesul* 33 (August 1970): 53–57.
93. Youngju Ryu, *Writers of the Winter Republic: Literature and Resistance in Park Chung Hee's Korea* (Honolulu: University of Hawaii Press, 2016), 18.
94. Pak Kwangt'aek, "Hyŏndaep'an 'Ojŏk,'" 53.
95. Pak Kwangt'aek, "Hyŏndaep'an 'Ojŏk,'" 57.
96. Chang Chunghyŏn, "Choguk e taehan taham ŏmnŭn ch'an'ga: Yŏn'gŭk *Na ege nŭn choguk i itta* rŭl pogo" [An Endless Paean to the Ancestral Land: After Seeing the Play *I Have an Ancestral Land*], *Rodong sinmun*, January 1, 1965, 6.
97. Chang Chunghyŏn, "Choguk e taehan taham ŏmnŭn ch'an'ga," 6.

98. "Chaeil tongp'odŭl kwa kwiguk tongp'odŭl ŭi saenghwal ŭl panyŏng han yŏn'gŭk: *Na ege nŭn choguk i itta* (P'yŏngyang kŭkchang)" [A Play that Reflects the Lives of Our Compatriots in Japan and our Repatriating Compatriots: *I Have an Ancestral Land* (Pyongyang Theater)], *Chosŏn sinbo*, January 25, 1965, 4.
99. Ham Tŏgil, "Chuin'gong ŭi sŏnggyŏk palchŏn kwa chuje sasang ch'ŏnmyŏng e hullyunghi pongmu han ŭmak: Yesul yŏnghwa *Uri ege nŭn choguk i itta* ŭi ŭmak hyŏngsang ŭl tugo" [Music that Wonderfully Served the Elucidation of the Protagonist's Character Development and the Thematic Ideology: Regarding the Musical Form of the Artistic Film *We Have an Ancestral Land*], *Chosŏn yesul* 146 (September 1968): 83.
100. Hŏ Namgi, *Uri ege nŭn choguk i itta* [We Have an Ancestral Land] (Pyongyang: Munye Ch'ulp'ansa, 1969).
101. Hŏ Namgi, "Uri ege nŭn choguk i itta" [We Have an Ancestral Land] in *Chuch'e ŭi han kil esŏ: Chaeilbon Chosŏnin Ch'ongnyŏnhaphoe yŏltasŏt tol kinyŏm chakp'umjip* (Tokyo: Chaeilbon Chosŏn munhak yesulga tongmaeng, 1970), 65.
102. Hŏ Namgi, "Uri ege nŭn choguk i itta," 66.
103. Hŏ Namgi, "Uri ege nŭn choguk i itta," 66.
104. Kim Myŏngsu, *Namnyŏk ŭi ŏmŏni* (1), 38.
105. Hŏ Namgi, "Uri ege nŭn choguk i itta," 98.
106. Hŏ Namgi, "Uri ege nŭn choguk i itta," 104.
107. Hŏ Ongnyŏ, "Uri ŭi chihyang ŭl magŭl su ŏpta" [They Cannot Block Our Path], *Chosŏn sinbo*, April 23, 1969, 4.
108. Hŏ Ongnyŏ, "Uri ŭi chihyang ŭl magŭl su ŏpta," 4.
109. For more on these phases, see Keun Woo Nam, "Rethinking the North Korean Repatriation Program: The Change from an 'Aid Economy' to a 'Hostage Economy,'" *Korean Social Sciences Review* 2, no. 2 (2012): 219–51.
110. Hŏ Ongnyŏ, "Uri ŭi chihyang ŭl magŭl su ŏpta," 4.
111. Cho Namdu, "Hana ŭi kamhoe" [A Reflection], *Chosŏn sinbo*, March 11, 1961, 4.
112. This story is republished in a recent South Korean anthology of Kim's Korean-language works. See Kim Sŏkpŏm, "Honbaek" [Spirit] in *Honbaek*, ed. Kim Tongyun (Seoul: Pogosa, 2021), 23–34.
113. Kim Sŏkpŏm, "Yoru" [Night], in *Yoru* (Tokyo: Bungei shunshū, 1973), 7–47.
114. Kim Sŏkpŏm, "Yoru" [Night], 46.
115. Kim Sŏkpŏm, "Yoru" [Night], 46.
116. Kim Sŏkpŏm, "Yoru" [Night], 46.
117. Ko Samyŏng, "'Furusato' to no kaikō" [Encounter with My "Hometown"], *Tenbō* 157 (January 1972): 126–35.
118. Ko Samyŏng, "Kaikō" [Encounter], *Kikan sanzenri* 3 (Fall 1975): 198–216. For a Korean translation, see Ko Samyŏng, "Haehu," trans. Sin Sŭngmo, in *Chaeil tiasŭp'ora munhak sŏnjip* vol. 2 (Seoul: Somyŏng, 2018), 147–77.
119. Ko Samyŏng, "Kaikō," 206.
120. For this reason, it is all the more painful for Munsik when his application for naturalization as a Japanese citizen is rejected.
121. Ko Samyŏng, "Kaikō," 210–16.
122. Ko Samyŏng, "Kaikō," 216.

2. MOTHER(S) OF THE SOUTH 287

123. Ko Samyŏng, "Kaikō," 216.
124. Kim Sŏkpŏm, "Shūu" [Cloudburst], *Kikan sanzenri* 2 (Summer 1975): 196–221. For a Korean translation, see Kim Sŏkpŏm, "Ch'wiu" [Cloudburst], trans. Kim Haktong, in *Chaeil tiasŭp'ora munhak sŏnjip* vol. 2 (Seoul: Somyŏng, 2018), 101–45.
125. Kim Sŏkpŏm, "Shūu," 207.
126. Kim Sŏkpŏm, "Shūu," 219.
127. Kim Sŏkpŏm, "Shūu," 219–20.
128. Kim Sŏkpŏm, "Shūu," 220.
129. Kim Sŏkpŏm, "Shūu," 204.
130. Kim Sŏkpŏm, "Shūu," 221.
131. Cindi Textor, "Representing Radical Difference: Kim Sŏkpŏm's Korea(n) in Japan(ese)," *positions: asia critique* 27, no. 3 (August 2019): 524–25.
132. This first appears on pp. 208–9 of "Shūu".
133. Kim Sŏkpŏm, "Shūu," 430.
134. An Chŏnghwa, "Chaeil Hanin chapchi sojae 'Kim Chiha tamnon' ŭi chŏngch'ijŏk ŭimi: *Samch'ŏlli* rŭl chungsim ŭro" [The Political Meaning of "Kim Chiha Discourse" in Journals of Koreans in Japan: Focusing on *Samch'ŏlli*], *Han'guk munhak nonch'ong* 42 (April 2006): 436.
135. On this, see: Youngju Ryu, *Writers of the Winter Republic*, 14; Namhee Lee, *The Making of Minjung: Democracy and the Politics of Representation in South Korea* (Ithaca, NY: Cornell University Press, 2016), 170–71.
136. Wada Haruki, "Kin Shika [Kim Chiha] o tasukerukai no imi" [The Meaning of the Committee to Assist Kim Chiha], *Kikan sanzenri* 1 (Spring 1975): 52–61.
137. On these earlier committees, see Misook Lee, "The Japan-Korea Solidarity Movement in the 1970s and 1980s: From Solidarity to Reflexive Democracy," *Asia-Pacific Journal/Japan Focus* 12, issue 38, no. 1 (September 21, 2014), https://apjjf.org/2014/12/38/Misook-Lee/4187.html.
138. Wada Haruki, "Kin Shika [Kim Chiha] o tasukerukai no imi," 54.
139. "Kan'koku gun'pōkaigi no han'ketsu ni kōgikōdō hirogaru: Kokusaiteki na rentai mo Tōkyō de ha hansuto" [Actions of Resistance to the South Korean Military Tribunal's Decision Spread: The International Solidarity Group Also Has a Hunger Strike in Tokyo], *Asahi shimbun*, July 17, 1974, 19.
140. Wada Haruki, "Kin Shika [Kim Chiha] o tasukerukai no imi," 58.
141. Kim Talsu, "Chōsen bungaku ni okeru yūmoa to fūshi: Kin Ryū [Kim Rip] to Kin Shika [Kim Chiha] no shi o chūshin ni" [Humor and Satire in Korean Literature: Focusing on the Poetry of Kim Rip and Kim Chiha], *Bungaku* 38, no. 11 (November 1970): 54–65. Kim Sŏkpŏm, "Kin Shika [Kim Chiha] to zainichi Chōsenjin bungakusha" [Kim Chiha and Korean Writers in Japan], in *Kotoba no jubaku: Zainichi Chōsenjin bungaku to Nihongo* (Tokyo: Chikuma Shobō, 1972), 267–70; Kim Sŏkpŏm, "Kyōfu de ningen o shihai dekinai" [One Cannot Rule Humans with Fear], "Katare, katare, hikisakareta karada de" [Speak, Speak, With a Torn Body], "Atarashii rentaikan o unda nichi" [The Day that Gave Birth to a New Feeling of Solidarity], and "Yurusenu Pen daihyō no kiben" [The Unforgivable Sophistry of the PEN Representative], in *Guchi aru mono ha katare* (Tokyo: Chikuma Shobō, 1975), 55–97. The four articles in this latter collection were all

originally published in 1974. Ko Samyŏng, "'Gozoku' no shijin" [The Poet of "Five Bandits"], *Waseda bungaku* 6, no. 7 (July 1974): 64–72.

142. For example, see Kim Sŏkpŏm, "'Kon/Han' to *Ryōshin sengen*" ["Han" and the *Declaration of Conscience*] in *Minzoku, kotoba, bungaku* (Tokyo: Sōjusha, 1976), 145–57; Ko Samyŏng, "Kiki no jidae ni oite Kin Shika [Kim Chiha] o omou" [Thinking About Kim Chiha During an Age of Crisis], *Shin Nihon bungaku* 31, no. 12 (December 1976): 40–42.
143. Kim Talsu, "Chōsen bungaku ni okeru yūmoa to fūshi," 61–62.
144. Christina Yi, *Colonizing Language: Cultural Production and Language Politics in Modern Japan and Korea* (New York: Columbia University Press, 2018),73; Cindi Textor, "Zainichi Writers and the Postcoloniality of Modern Korean Literature," 234.
145. "Chakka Yi Hoesŏng [Ri Kaisei], Kim Talsu ssi tŭng 13-myŏng: Choch'ongnyŏn chungangwi sŏ sukch'ŏng" [Thirteen People Including the Writers Ri Kaisei and Kim Talsu: Purged By the Chongryon Central Committee], *Tonga ilbo*, August 1, 1972, 1.

3. CRITICAL CONNECTIONS AND CRITICAL LIMITS IN 1950S SOUTH KOREA

1. "Merry Xmas," *Sint'aeyang* 1, no. 5 (December 1952): n.p.
2. "Kwanggo: 25-si" [Advertisement: *The Twenty-Fifth Hour*], *Sint'aeyang* 1, no. 3 (October 1952): back cover.
3. Kukka poanbŏp (pŏmnyul che 10-ho) [National Security Law, Statute Number 10], Republic of Korea, Enacted December 1, 1948, https://www.law.go.kr/LSW//lsInfoP.do?efYd=19481201&lsiSeq=7221&ancYd=19481201&nwJoYnInfo=N&ancNo=00010&chrClsCd=010202&efGubun=Y#0000.
4. Chŏng Ut'aek, "'Han Haun sijip sakŏn' ŭi ŭimi wa Yi Pyŏngch'ŏl" [The Meaning of the "Han Haun Poetry Anthology Incident" and Yi Pyŏngch'ŏl], *Sanghŏ hakpo* 40 (2014): 163.
5. Kang Sŏnghyŏn, "Han'guk ŭi kukka hyŏngsŏnggi 'yewoe sangt'ae sangnye' ŭi pŏpchŏk kujo: Kukka poanbŏp (1948, 1949, 1950) kwa Kyeŏmbŏp (1949) ŭl chungsim ŭro" [The Legal Structure of the "Usual State of Exception" during the Republic of Korea's Formative Period: Focusing on the National Security Law (1948, 1949, 1950) and Martial Law (1949)], *Sahoe wa yŏksa* 94 (2012): 99.
6. Chŏn Sangsuk, "Sasang t'ongje chŏngch'aek ŭi yŏksasŏng: Pan'gong kwa chŏnhyang" [The Historicity of Policies of Ideological Control: Anticommunism and Conversion], *Han'guk chŏngch'i oegyosa nonch'ong* 27, no. 1 (2005): 91–92.
7. Kukka poanbŏp (pŏmnyul che 85-ho) [National Security Law, Statute Number 85], Republic of Korea, Enacted December 19, 1949, https://www.law.go.kr/LSW//lsInfoP.do?lsiSeq=7222&ancYd=19491219&ancNo=00085&efYd=19500109&nwJoYnInfo=N&efGubun=Y&chrClsCd=010202&ancYnChk=0#0000.
8. Pan'gongbŏp (pŏmnyul che 643-ho) [Anticommunist Law, Statute Number 643], Republic of Korea, Enacted July 3, 1961, https://www.law.go.kr/LSW/lsInfoP.do?lsiSeq=3534&ancYd=19610703&ancNo=00643&efYd=19610703&nwJoYnInfo=N&efGubun=Y&chrClsCd=010202&ancYnChk=0#0000.

9. Kukka poanbŏp (pŏmnyul che 500-ho) [National Security Law, Statute Number 500], Republic of Korea, Enacted December 26, 1958, https://www.law.go.kr/LSW//lsInfoP.do?lsiSeq=7224&ancYd=19581226&ancNo=00500&efYd=19590116&nwJoYnInfo=N&efGubun=Y&chrClsCd=010202&ancYnChk=0#0000.
10. Pan'gongbŏp (pŏmnyul che 643-ho).
11. For more on this, see Theodore Q. Hughes, *Literature and Film in Cold War South Korea: Freedom's Frontier* (New York: Columbia University Press, 2012), 61–89.
12. On these events, see Kim Pyŏngik, *Han'guk mundansa: 1908–1970* [A History of the Korean Literary World: 1908–1970] (Seoul: Munhak kwa chisŏngsa, 2001), 295–99.
13. For a detailed account of these groups, publications, and activities, see Jerôme de Wit, "Writing under Wartime Conditions: North and South Korean Writers during the Korean War (1950–1953)," PhD diss. (Leiden University, 2015), 29–40. See also Sin Yŏngdŏk, *Han'guk chŏnjaeng kwa chonggun chakka* [The Korean War and Embedded Writers] (Seoul: Kukhak charyowŏn, 2002).
14. For more on the culture of wartime mobilization and "war literature," see Yi Yŏngjae, *Cheguk Ilbon ŭi Chosŏn yŏnghwa: Singminji mal ŭi pando, hyŏmnyŏk ŭi simjŏng, chedo, nolli* [The Korean Film of Imperial Japan: The Peninsula in the Late Colonial Period and the Feelings, System, and Logic of Collaboration] (Seoul: Hyŏnsil munhwa, 2008); Kim Yerim, *1930-nyŏndae huban kŭndae insik ŭi t'ŭl kwa miŭisik* [The Frame and Aesthetic Consciousness of the Late 1930s Modern Episteme] (Seoul: Somyŏng ch'ulp'an, 2004); and Yi Hyeryŏng, *Han'guk sosŏl kwa kolsanghakchŏk t'ajadŭl* [Korean Fiction and its Phrenological Others] (Seoul: Somyŏng ch'ulp'an, 2007).
15. This last slogan is mentioned in Ch'oe Inuk, "Chŏnjaeng munhwaron" [Theory of War Culture], *Sinch'ŏnji* 6, no. 1 (January 1951): 77.
16. Kim Kiwan, "Chŏnjaeng kwa munhak" [War and Literature], *Munye* 2, no. 7 (December 1950): 18.
17. Kim Chongmun, "Chŏnjaeng kwa sŏnjŏn" [War and Propaganda], *Chŏnsŏn munhak* 1, no. 1 (October 1950): 22. To avoid confusion, it should be noted that there were two separate journals published under the title *Chŏnsŏn munhak* during the wartime period.
18. Ch'oe Tokkyŏn, "Ch'anggansa" [Inaugural message], *Chŏnsŏn munhak* 1, no. 1 (April 1952): 9.
19. Kim Song, "Minju munhwa ŭi panghyang" [The Direction of Democratic Culture], *Chayu yesul* 1, no. 1 (November 1952): 36.
20. Kim Song, "Minju munhwa ŭi panghyang," 33.
21. Pak Kijun, "Han'guk chakka ŭi pansŏng" [The Introspection of Korean Writers], *Chŏnsŏn munhak* 1, no. 1 (April 1952): 14.
22. Kim Chaejun, "Kŏnsŏljŏk t'ujaeng" [Constructive Struggle], in *Kyesi wa chŭngŏn* (Seoul: Sae saramsa, 1956), 30–31. According to Kim's collected works, this text is from 1953. See *Kim Chaejun chŏnjip (vol. 2): Pogŭm ŭi chayu (1950–1953)* (Osan: Changgong Kim Chaejun moksa kinyŏm saŏphoe, 1992), 265.
23. Pak Hwamok, "Sinbun chŭngmyŏngsŏ" [Identification Card], *Kyŏnghyang sinmun*, June 5, 1952, 2.

24. Yu Chuhyŏn, "Yŏng" [Mountain Pass], *Ch'anggong* 1, no. 1 (March 1952): 26–34. I am grateful to Sonagi Village (the Hwang Sunwŏn Literary Village) for providing me access to their copy of this text. It is the only known copy of the original still extant.
25. Yu Chuhyŏn, "Yŏng," 26.
26. Yu Chuhyŏn, "Yŏng," 30.
27. Yu Chuhyŏn, "Yŏng," 32.
28. Yu Chuhyŏn, "Yŏng," 34.
29. Kwŏn Myŏnga, "Yŏsŏng sunansa iyagi: Minjok kukka mandŭlki wa yŏsŏngsŏng ŭi tongwŏn" [Narratives of Women's Histories of Suffering: Creating the Nation-State and the Mobilization of Femininity], *Yŏsŏng munhak yŏn'gu* 7 (2002): 111–13.
30. Kwŏn Myŏnga, "Yŏsŏng sunansa iyagi," 111–113.
31. Yŏm Sangsŏp, "San tokkaebi" [Mountain Demons], *Sinsajo* 2, no. 1 (September 1951): 95–106.
32. Yŏm Sangsŏp, "San tokkaebi," 103.
33. Yŏm Sangsŏp, "San tokkaebi," 106.
34. Kang Sinjae, "Chŏnt'ugi" [Fighter plane], *K'omet'ŭ* 1, no. 1 (November 1952): 138–41. Digital copy from Air Force of the Republic of Korea, http://afzine.co.kr/home/view.php?host =main&site=20190721_041348_104&listPageNow=0&list2PageNow=0&code=1418 &code2=0&code3=0&optionlisttype=L&listcount=10&searchcode=0&searchcode2 =0 &searchdate=0&searchkey=&searchval=&searchandor=AND&dummy=&&orders=.
35. Kang Sinjae, "San kisŭk" [Foot of the Mountain], *Sinch'ŏnji* 9, no. 3 (March 1954): 266–71.
36. Kang Sinjae, "San kisŭk," 268.
37. Kang Sinjae, "San kisŭk," 271.
38. C. Virgil Gheorghiu, *The Twenty-Fifth Hour*, trans. Rita Eldon (New York: Knopf, 1950), see especially 39–49.
39. "Kwanggo: 25-si," back cover.
40. The Korean version of *Nineteen Eighty-Four* appeared in 1951. See George Orwell, *1984-nyŏn* [Nineteen Eighty-Four], trans. Chi Yŏngmin (Seoul: Munye sŏrim, 1951).
41. Cho Yŏnhyŏn, "Mek'anijŭm eŭi kyŏnggye" [Vigilance toward Mechanism], *Sinsajo* 2, no. 2 (October 1951): 81.
42. Cho Yŏnhyŏn, "Hyŏndae ŭi wigi wa munhak chŏngsin ŭi panghyang" [The Crisis of the Modern and the Direction of the Literary Spirit], *Chayu segye* 1, no. 5 (August–September 1952): 107.
43. Cho Yŏnhyŏn, "Hyŏndae ŭi wigi wa munhak chŏngsin ŭi panghyang," 107.
44. Paek Ch'ŏl, "P'ian" [Going Beyond], *Sinch'ŏnji* 7, no. 3 (May 1952): 49.
45. Paek Ch'ŏl, "Saeroun in'gan kwan'gye ŭi munje: munhwa ongho ŭi 1-p'oint'ŭ" [The Problem of a New Form of Human Relations: One Point Regarding the Defense of Culture], *Chayu segye* 1, no. 3 (April 1952): 177. Facsimile edition in Chŏn Kich'ŏl, ed., *Han'guk pundan munhak pip'yŏng charyojip* (Namhan p'yŏn, vol. 3) [Collection of Materials on the Divided Literary Criticism of Korea (Southern Section, vol. 3)], Seoul: Han'guk yesulsa, 1998), 136.
46. Im Kŭngjae, "Hoeŭi wa mosaek ŭi kyeje" [The Occasion for Skepticism and Searching], *Munhwa segye* 1, no. 1 (July 1953): 35.

3. CRITICAL CONNECTIONS AND CRITICAL LIMITS 291

47. Kwak Chongwŏn, "Sae in'ganhyŏng ŭi hyŏngsŏng e taehan kusang" [Vision of the Formation of a New Human Type], *Sinsajo* 2, no. 1 (September 1951): 16.
48. Kwak Chongwŏn, "Sae in'ganhyŏng ŭi hyŏngsŏng e taehan kusang," 17.
49. Kwak Chongwŏn, "Sae in'ganhyŏng ŭi hyŏngsŏng e taehan kusang," 17.
50. Kwak Chongwŏn, "Sae in'ganhyŏng ŭi hyŏngsŏng e taehan kusang," 18.
51. Kwak Chongwŏn, "Munhak chŏngsin ŭi hwangnip" [The Establishment of the Literary Spirit], *Chayu segye* 1, no. 1 (January 1952): 167.
52. Kwak Chongwŏn, "Munhak undong ŭi puhŭngnon" [On the Renaissance of the Literary Movement], reprinted *Sin in'ganhyŏng ŭi t'amgu* (Seoul: Tongsŏ munhwasa, 1955), 109–10. Originally appeared in the August 1951 issue of *Sinjo*.
53. On the history of this synthesis, see James Chappel, "The Catholic Origins of Totalitarianism Theory in Interwar Europe," *Modern Intellectual History* 8, no. 3 (November 2011): 561–90.
54. Yang Pyŏngsik, "Munhwa wa in'gan: t'ŭkkwŏn ŭisik e panhang hanŭn sin hyumŏnijŭm (1)" [Culture and the Human: A New Humanism in Resistance to the Consciousness of Privilege (1)], *Kyŏnghyang sinmun*, October 23, 1952, 2.
55. Yang Pyŏngsik, "Munhwa wa in'gan (1)," 2.
56. Yang Pyŏngsik, "Munhwa wa in'gan (5)," 2.
57. Yang Pyŏngsik, "Hyŏndae chisŏng ŭi pangyang: Haengdong ŭro iruwŏ chinŭn" [The Direction of Contemporary Intellect: Constituted through Action], *Sudo p'yŏngnon* 1, no. 3 (August 1953): 79.
58. Yang Pyŏngsik, "Chŏnjaeng kwa munhwa ŭi kwaje" [War and the Task of Culture], in *1952-nyŏn* (Seoul: Sudo munhwasa, 1951), 170. Facsimile edition in *Han'guk chŏnjaenggi munhak, sugi, chedo charyojip* (Seoul: K'ep'oibuksŭ, 2013), www.krpia.co.kr/product/main?plctId=PLCT00005230. The Malraux quote inside this quote is reproduced from the English translation by Stuart Gilbert with minor edits. See André Malraux, "Man and Artistic Culture," in *Reflections on Our Age* (New York: Columbia University Press, 1949), 84–99. As noted later in this chapter, Yang's claim that Malraux spoke in opposition to the "two materialisms" of capitalism and communism was an inaccuracy that came from the Japanese critic Komatsu Kiyoshi.
59. Yang Pyŏngsik, "Chŏnjaeng kwa munhwa ŭi kwaje," 196–97.
60. Yang Pyŏngsik, "Chŏnjaeng kwa munhwa ŭi kwaje," 208.
61. Yang Pyŏngsik, "Chŏnjaeng kwa munhwa ŭi kwaje," 198
62. Yang Pyŏngsik, "Chŏnjaeng kwa munhwa ŭi kwaje," 208.
63. Kim Yongsŏng, "Temok'ŭrasi wa che-sam seryŏk" [Democracy and the Third Force], *Sinsajo* 4, no. 2 (May/June 1953): 55.
64. Su Lin Lewis, "Asian Socialism and the Forgotten Architects of Post-Colonial Freedom, 1952–1956," *Journal of World History* 30, no. 1/2 (June 2019): 61.
65. On this, see Herbert R. Lottman, *The Left Bank: Writers, Artists, and Politics from the Popular Front to the Cold War* (Chicago: University of Chicago Press, 1982), 277–79.
66. Su Lin Lewis, "Asian Socialism," 63–66; J. A. A. Stockwin, *The Japanese Socialist Party and Neutralism: A Study of Political Party and Its Foreign Policy* (New York: Cambridge University Press, 1968), 49–50.

67. Jeong Min Kim, "Intimate Exchanges: Korean Women, American GIs and the Making of the Wartime Political Economy of South Korea during the Korean War, 1950–1953," PhD diss. (New York University, 2017), 52. Kim attributes this quotation to the following text: General Headquarters Far East Command (GHQ FEC), Japan, *Rest and Recuperation* (FEC Printing and Publications Center, 1951): 6.
68. On such "R&R" leaves, see Jeong Min Kim, "Intimate Exchanges," 175–224.
69. "Establishment of Prisoner of War Labor Detachment, Tokyo Area (May 17, 1951)," Entry 1182-A-54, 2nd Logistical Command, 1951, Box 28 (3)-2, Records of the US Eighth Army 2nd Logistical Command, 1951, Records of US Army Operational, Tactical, and Support Organizations (World War II and Thereafter), 1917–1993, RG 338, National Archives, College Park, MD. Digitized by the National Institute of Korean History, http://archive.history.go.kr/id/AUS004_28_00C0009_099.
70. This can be gauged via increasingly frequent reports of government confiscations of Japanese texts. For a sample of such reports, see "Ilsŏjŏk pŏnyŏngmul tansok, Yi kongbo ch'ŏjang tam" [Crackdown on Translated Japanese Books, Says Minister of Public Information Yi], *Kyŏnghyang sinmun*, April 7, 1950, 2; "Ilsŏ man'gan," *Kyŏnghyang sinmun*, April 8, 1950, 2; "Ilbon chapchi suip purhŏ" [Japanese Magazines Banned from Importation], *Tonga ilbo*, September 11, 1951, 2; "Ilbon sŏjŏk do, kongbo ch'ŏ hŏga oenŭn ilchŏl ch'wich'e" [Without Permit from Ministry of Public Information, Japanese Books Also Completely Controlled], *Chosŏn ilbo*, October 7, 1951, 2; "Ilbon chapchi sijŏng p'anmae tansok kanghwa" [Strengthening the Crackdown on the Sale of Japanese Magazines in the Market], *Kyŏnghyang sinmun*, November 8, 1952, 2.
71. Komatsu Kiyoshi, "Marurou [Malraux] to Girisia no hakken" [Malraux and the Discovery of Greece], *Risō* 213 (January 1951): 1–16.
72. Komatsu Kiyoshi, "Marurou [Malraux] to Girisia no hakken," 7.
73. Sinh Vinh, "Komatsu Kiyoshi and French Indochina," *Moussons: Recherche en Sciences Humaines sur l'Asie du Sud-Est* 3 (June 2001): 64.
74. Komatsu Kiyoshi, "Futsubungaku no ittenki" [A Turning Point in French Literature], *Kōdō* 2, no. 8 (August 1934): 33.
75. Ramon Fernandez, "Humanisme de l'Action" [Humanism of Action], in *Examen de Conscience* (Cahiers du Mois 21/22), ed. Marcel Arland (Paris: Éditions Émile-Paul Frères, 1926), 93–97.
76. Komatsu Kiyoshi, *Kōdō shugi bungakuron* [Theory of a Literature of Actionism] (Tokyo: Kinokuniya shuppanbu, 1935), 2.
77. For more on this, see I Jonathan Kief, " 'Antagonistic Unity:' Kim Oseong, Dialectical Anthropology, and the Discovery of Literature, 1929–1938," *Review of Korean Studies* 16, no. 2 (December 2013): 81–124.
78. Komatsu Kiyoshi et al., "Zaidankai: Nihon o ika ni shite eiru ka?" [Roundtable: How to Protect Japan?], *Shakai shichō* 33 (March 1951): 25.
79. Komatsu Kiyoshi et al., "Zaidankai," 25–26.
80. Komatsu Kiyoshi, "Hitotsu no kaisō to hitotsu no kibō" [A Recollection and a Hope], *Sekai* 55 (July 1950): 66.
81. Komatsu Kiyoshi, "Chishikijin huronto no dentō: Huransu no bai ni tsuite" [The Tradition of An Intellectuals' Front: On the Case of Japan], *Risō* 208 (August 1950): 65.

3. CRITICAL CONNECTIONS AND CRITICAL LIMITS   293

82. Komatsu Kiyoshi, "Chishikijin huronto no dentō," 68.
83. Komatsu Kiyoshi, "Chishikijin huronto no dentō," 68.
84. Nakahashi Kazuo, "Seiōteki chisei no kyōryoku o" [The Cooperation of Western Intelligence], *Kindai bungaku* 5, no. 5 (May 1950): 25.
85. Nakahashi Kazuo, "Jiyūjin no risōzō: Daisan no tachiba ni tsuite" [The Ideal Image for the Free Person: On the Third Perspective], *Gunzō* 6, no. 3 (March 1951): 87.
86. Nakahashi Kazuo, "Jiyūjin no risōzō," 91.
87. François Mauriac, "La Résistance Spirituelle" [Spiritual Resistance], *Le Figaro*, February 20, 1950, 1. The quote does not actually appear in Nakahashi's article. I reproduce it here in order to illustrate some of his references.
88. Nakahashi Kazuo, "Jiyūjin no risōzō," 88.
89. Yi Haengsŏn, "Keorŭgyu [Gheorghiu] ŭi suyong kwa Han'guk chisŏngsa ŭi 25-si: Chŏnhu munhak, hyumŏnijŭm, silchonjuŭi, munmyŏng pip'an, pan'gongjuŭi, ŏyong chakka" [The Reception of Gheorghiu and Korean Intellectual History's Twenty-Fifth Hour: Postwar Literature, Humanism, Existentialism, Civilizational Critique, Anticommunism, Government-Patronized Writers], *Han'gukhak yŏn'gu* 41 (May 2016): 13.
90. Paek Ch'ŏl, "Oeguk chakp'um kwa kŭ pŏnyŏk: Kŭllae ŭi pŏnyŏk sosŏl ŭl chungsim hayŏ" [Foreign Works and their Translation: On Recent Translated Fiction], *Munye* 4, no. 5 (November 1953): 38.
91. "25-si chakka Georgyu [Gheorghiu] nŭn marhanda" [Gheorghiu, the Author of *The Twenty-Fifth Hour*, Speaks], *Sint'aeyang* 1, no. 5 (December 1952): 75.
92. Hirabayashi Taiko, "25ji no sakusha Giorugyu [Gheorghiu] to monogataru" [Talking with Gheorghiu, the Author of *The Twenty-Fifth Hour*], *Yomiuri shimbun*, June 26, 1952, 5.
93. C. Virgil Gheorghiu, *The Twenty-Fifth Hour*, 49.
94. Nishitani Keiji, "Kyomu kara no dasshutsu: 25ji ni miru Seiyō to Tōyō no mondai" [The Escape from Futility: The Problem of East and West as Seen in *The Twenty-Fifth Hour*], *Kaizō* 31, no. 12 (December 1950): 9.
95. Nishitani Keiji, "Kyomu kara no dasshutsu," 16.
96. Nishitani Keiji, "Kyomu kara no dasshutsu," 14.
97. Nishitani Keiji, "Kyomu kara no dasshutsu," 18.
98. Takeuchi Yoshimi, "Jinruiaku no kokuhatsu: Georgiu [Gheorghiu] 25ji ni tsuite" [The Indictment of Humanity's Evil: On Gheorghiu's *The Twenty-Fifth Hour*], *Nihon hyōron* 25, no. 10 (October 1950): 29.
99. Takeuchi Yoshimi, "Jinruiaku no kokuhatsu," 21.
100. Takeuchi Yoshimi, "Jinruiaku no kokuhatsu," 33.
101. Takeuchi Yoshimi, "Jinruiaku no kokuhatsu," 32.
102. Takeuchi Yoshimi, "Jinruiaku no kokuhatsu," 33.
103. Takeuchi Yoshimi, "Jinruiaku no kokuhatsu," 31.
104. Takeuchi Yoshimi, " 'Tōhō' e no kyōshū" [Nostalgia for "the East"], *Tenbō* 58 (October 1950): 17.
105. Takeda Kiyoko, "Tōyō no jikoku ha?" [What Time Is It in the East?], *Tenbō* 58 (October 1950): 19.
106. Iizuka Kōji, "25ji wa wareware no jikoku" [*The Twenty-Fifth Hour* and Our Time], *Tenbō* 58 (October 1950): 21.

107. Yi Ponggu, "26-si ŭi sŏngji (1)" [Holy Land of the Twenty-Sixth Hour (1)], *Sŏul sinmun*, March 4, 1952, 4.
108. Yi Ponggu, "26-si ŭi sŏngji (1)," 4.
109. Yi Ponggu, "26-si ŭi sŏngji (1)," 4.
110. Yi Ponggu, "26-si ŭi sŏngji (1)," 4.
111. Yi Ponggu, "26-si ŭi sŏngji (1)," 4.
112. Yi Ponggu, "26-si ŭi sŏngji (2)," 4.
113. Yi Ponggu, "Chapch'o" [Weeds], *Hyŏndae munhak* 5, no. 7 (July 1959): 38–53.
114. Kim Chunghŭi, "Ch'adan" [Roadblock], *Sasanggye* 24 (June 1955): 93–103.
115. Kim Chunghŭi, "Ch'adan," 103.
116. Han Yŏnghwan, "Pokkwi" [Return], *Munhak yesul* 2, no. 3 (August 1955): 83–95.
117. Han Yŏnghwan, "Pokkwi," 87.
118. Yang Pyŏngsik, "Hyŏndae chisŏng ŭi panghyang: Haengdong ŭro iruwŏ chinŭn" [The Direction of Contemporary Intellect: Constituted through Action], *Sudo p'yŏngnon* 1, no. 3 (August 1953): 76–77.
119. Marie-Louise Abeille to Kauh Kwang Man (Ko Kwangman), December 3, 1956, UN Korean Reconstruction Agency Foreign Book Retail Store, Vol. III (S-0526-0310-0001), UN Archives, New York, NY.
120. Marie-Louise Abeille to FBRS, November 30, 1956, UNKRA FBRS, Vol. III.
121. Chief of Education Projects Section to Chief of Supply Division, November 24, 1956, UNKRA FBRS, Vol. III.
122. For example, see H. E. Eastwood to Lee Sun Kyun (Yi Sŏn'gŭn), March 29, 1955, UN Korean Reconstruction Agency Foreign Book Retail Store, Vol II (S-0526-0309-0002), UN Archives, New York, NY; Chester W. Wood to Thomas Jamieson, February 4, 1955, UNKRA FBRS, Vol. II; Ewart G. Plank to KD Chin, March 23, 1955, UN Korean Reconstruction Agency Foreign Book Retail Store, Vol II; Marie-Louise Abeille to Oh Jae Kyung (O Chaegyŏng), May 25, 1954, UNKRA FBRS, Vol. II.
123. Chun Suk Auh (O Ch'ŏnsŏk) to Donald K. Faris, September 19, 1952, UNKRA FBRS, Vol. I (S-0526-0309-0002), UN Archives, New York, NY.
124. "Budget: AP's & Allocations etc, 1954/55 (Korea–Administration)," Records of the Asia Foundation, Hoover Archives, Stanford University, Palo Alto, CA.
125. After being approved, it was called UNKRA Project 812D. It was then renamed and divided between UNKRA 9.8-1 (1953 procurement, $50,000) and UNKRA 9.8-2 (1954 procurement, $31,000). The first mention of the program appears in "Daily Journals, Civil Information and Education Section, 1–29 Feb. 1952," Staff Section Report, Public Works, for Month of January 1952 (3 of 3), Entry UNCACK, Box 5753, UN Civil Assistance Command, Korea (UNCACK), 1952, General Correspondence, 1951–1955, Records of U.S. Army Operational, Tactical, and Support Organizations (World War II and Thereafter), 1917–1993, RG 338, National Archives, College Park, MD. Digitized by the National Institute of Korean History. http://archive.history.go.kr/id/AUS004_77_00C0109_009.
126. "812-D Project Agreement, Foreign Book Retail Store," March 4, 1953, UN Korean Reconstruction Agency Foreign Book Retail Store (March 4, 1953–December 30, 1954; S-0526-0091-0007), UN Archives, New York, NY. The agreement appears to have been amended by February 1954, such that the FBRS charged up to 120 percent

3. CRITICAL CONNECTIONS AND CRITICAL LIMITS 295

of the landed costs and then reimbursed UNKRA at 100 percent. See "Agreement: Cost of Books Under UNKRA Tokyo Procurement Order No. 190 for UNKRA Project 9.8-1 [812-D] Foreign Book Retail Store," February 23, 1954, UNKRA FBRS (March 4, 1953–December 30, 1954).

127. There are some inconsistencies in the records regarding the arrival of this first shipment. Official records say June. However, a handwritten note on the book list used for inventorying the shipment says May. See Shipping Advice (June 10, 1953), UNKRA FBRS, Vol. I; "Publications for Project No. 9.8 (ex 812-D) Foreign Book Retail Store," undated, UNKRA FBRS, Vol. I. There was an earlier shipment of books from the US, but it only contained twenty volumes.

128. "Schedule Showing Landed Cost Value of Aid Goods Imported Under Project 9.8-1, Foreign Retail Book Store [sic]," October 14, 1955, UNKRA FBRS, Vol. III.

129. Purchase Requisition, "Foreign Book Retail Store, Supplement No. 4," August 5, 1953, UNKRA FBRS, Vol. I; Project Specification, "Foreign Book Retail Store, Supplement No. 5," September 18, 1953, UNKRA FBRS, Vol. I.

130. Firm Request (Equipment and Supplies: Foreign Book Retail Store), Enclosure #1, September 1954, UNKRA FBRS, Vol. I.

131. "Il puron sŏjŏk ŭl apsu" [Confiscation of Japanese Seditious Texts], *Tonga ilbo*, April 29, 1954, 2; "Chŏsok han Ilbon sŏjŏk, kongbo ch'ŏsŏ ilche apsu" [Debased Japanese Texts, Total Confiscation by Office of Public Information], *Chosŏn ilbo*, April 29, 1954, 2.

132. Volume 5 of *Capital* was listed as out of stock and thus not delivered; see Liaison and Procurement Office (UNKRA Tokyo) to Headquarters Korea (UNKRA), 23 June 1953, UNKRA FBRS, Vol. I. Two volumes of *The Complete Works of Joseph Stalin* and three volumes of the *Selected Works of Marx and Engels* were listed as "missing" upon arrival; see "Publications for Project No. 9.8 (ex 812-D) Foreign Book Retail Store," undated, UNKRA FBRS, Vol. I.

133. Liaison and Procurement Office (UNKRA Tokyo) to Headquarters Korea (UNKRA), June 23, 1953, UNKRA FBRS, Vol. I.

134. "Publications for Project No. 9.8 (ex 812-D) Foreign Book Retail Store," undated, UNKRA FBRS, Vol. I; Issue and Receipt Voucher, July 8, 1953, UNKRA FBRS, Vol. I.

135. Project Specifications: PS 17, April 8, 1954, UNKRA FBRS, Vol. III.

136. J. P. Bradford to William F. Armstrong, May 25, 1954, UNKRA FBRS, Vol. III.

137. Marie-Louise Abeille to E.M. Reed, December 13, 1954, UNKRA FBRS, Vol. III.

138. Yang Homin, *Kongsanjuŭi ŭi iron kwa yŏksa: Marksŭ-Reninjuŭi ŭi pi'pan* [The Theory and History of Communism: A Critique of Marxism-Leninism] (Seoul: Chungang munhwasa, 1956).

139. J. Victor Koshmann, *Revolution and Subjectivity in Postwar Japan* (Chicago: University of Chicago Press, 1996), esp. 136–40.

140. Takakuwa Sumio, "Minshu shugi to hyūmanizumu" [Democracy and Humanism], *Risō* 5, no. 9 (September 1950): 36–39.

141. Takakuwa Sumio, "Shakai shugi no jiyū to dokusai: shizen shugi to rekishi shugi no sōkoku" [The Freedom and Dictatorship of Socialism: The Opposition between Naturalism and Historicism], *Kaizo* 33, no. 7 (May 1952): 31–32.

142. Takakuwa Sumio, *Yuibutsuron to shutaisei* [Materialism and Subjectivity] (Tokyo: Kokudosha, 1948), 2–26, 63–110.

143. J. Victor Koshmann, *Revolution and Subjectivity in Postwar Japan*, 139–40.
144. Paek Ch'ŏl, "Saeroun in'gan kwan'gye ŭi munje: munhwa ongho ŭi 1-p'oint'ŭ," 177.
145. Cho Hyang, "20-segi munye sajo" [Artistic Trends of the Twentieth Century], *Sasang* 1, no. 4 (December 1952): 173.
146. Cho Hyang, "20-segi munye sajo," 175.
147. Yi Haenam, "Han Kangnyŏl kyosu chŏ *In'gan kwa sahoe*" [*The Human and Society* by Professor Han Kangnyŏl], *Kyŏnghyang sinmun*, July 6, 1954, 2.
148. Yi Haenam, "P'asŭk'al [Pascal] ŭi in'ganhak" [Pascal's Anthropology], *Kyŏnghyang sinmun*, May 30, 1954, 4.
149. Yi Hwan, "Ppasŭkkal [Pascal] sŏsŏl" [An Introduction to Pacscal], *Mullidae hakpo* 2, no. 2 (September 1954): 60. Author mistakenly listed as Yi Hang.
150. Yi Hwan, "Ppasŭkkal sŏsŏl," 63.
151. Yi Hwan, "Ppasŭkkal sŏsŏl," 63.
152. Yi Haenam, "P'asŭk'al ŭi in'ganhak," 4.
153. Im Ch'un'gap, "Sasaek ilgi" [Diary of Contemplation], *Hyŏndae kongnon* 1, no. 1 (October 1953): 112.
154. Hong Sajung, "Hyŏndae ŭi chisŏng kwa sin eŭi chŏpkŭn: K'ap'ŭk'a [Kafka] ŭi kyŏng'u (1)" [Contemporary Intelligence and the Encounter with God: The Case of Kafka (1)], *Hyŏndae munhak* 1, no. 11 (November 1955): 161.
155. Kim Hyŏngsŏk, "In'gan ŭi hak kwa hyŏndae ch'ŏrhak: Hyŏndae munje wa in'ganhak ŭl wihan susang" [The Study of the Human and Modern Philosophy: The Problem of the Contemporary and a Contemplation on Anthropology], *Sasanggye* 30 (January 1956): 236.
156. Kim Hyŏngsŏk, "25-si ŭi ing'an ch'ŏrhak: Hyumŏnijŭm ŭi wigi" [Human Philosophy of the Twenty-fifth Hour: The Crisis of Humanism], *Sasanggye* 77 (December 1959): 113.
157. Kim Hat'ae, "Sin chŏngt'ongp'a sinhak e taehan soron" [Short Essay on Neoorthodox Theology], *Sinhak nondan* 3 (March 1957): 15.
158. Chi Tongsik, "Hyŏndaein ŭi wigi wa Yesu K'ŭrisŭt'o [Jesus Christ and the Crisis of the Contemporary Person], *Yŏnhŭi ch'unch'u*, July 3, 1954, 2.
159. Chi Tongsik, "In'gan e taehan sogo: Kidokkyo ŭi ipchang esŏ" [Preliminary Thoughts on the Human: From a Protestant Perspective] *Sasanggye* 1 (April 1953): 54–57.
160. Paul Tillich, "20-segi ŭi in'gansang: Pi in'ganhwa e taehan panhang" [The Human Image of the Twentieth Century: Rebellion Against Dehumanization], *Sasanggye* 32 (March 1956): 22–38, 49.
161. Paul Tillich, "The Person in a Technical Society," in *Christian Faith and Social Action: A Symposium*, ed. John Alexander Hutchinson (New York: Scribner, 1953), 137.
162. Paul Tillich, "The Person in a Technical Society," 139.
163. Paul Tillich, "The Person in a Technical Society," 151.
164. An Pyŏnguk, "Silchonjuŭi ŭi kyebo" [A Genealogy of Existentialism], *Sasanggye* 21 (April 1955): 77–100.
165. An Pyŏnguk, "Hyŏndae sasang kangjwa (7)" [Lectures on Contemporary Thought (7)], *Sasanggye* 33 (April 1956): 313.

166. An Pyŏnguk, "Hyŏndae sasang kangjwa (8)," 78.
167. An Pyŏnguk, "Hyŏndae sasang kangjwa (7)," 310.
168. An Pyŏnguk, "Hyŏndae sasang kangjwa (8)," 78.
169. An Pyŏnguk, "Hyŏndae sasang kangjwa (8)," 84.
170. An Pyŏnguk, "Hyŏndae sasang kangjwa (8)," 79.
171. An Pyŏnguk, "Hyŏndae sasang kangjwa (8)," 80.
172. An Pyŏnguk, "Hyŏndae sasang kangjwa (7)," 314.
173. An Pyŏnguk, "Hyŏndae sasang kangjwa (8)," 82.
174. An Pyŏnguk, "Hyŏndae sasang kangjwa (8)," 81.
175. An Pyŏnguk, "Saeroun segyegwan ŭi mosaek" [The Search for a New Worldview], *Sasanggye* 45 (April 1957): 284.
176. An Pyŏnguk, "Saeroun segyegwan ŭi mosaek," 289.
177. An Pyŏnguk, "Sahoe kigu wa hyumaenijŭm" [Social Organizations and Humanism], *Sasanggye* 51 (October 1957): 34.
178. Ha Kirak, "Hyŏndae ŭi sasangjŏk kwaje" [The Ideological Task of the Contemporary], *Sasanggye* 44 (March 1957): 23–30, 42. Also see Ha Kirak, "In'gan ŭi chokŏn" [The Human Condition], *Sasanggye* 50 (September 1957): 75–82.
179. For more on this, see I Jonathan Kief, "'Antagonistic Unity:' Kim Oseong, Dialectical Anthropology, and the Discovery of Literature, 1929–1938."
180. On this, see "Puron sŏjŏk p'anmae ŏpja 5-myŏng chŏngsik kusok," 2; "Tasŏt p'anmae ŏpcha kusok" [Five Sellers Arrested], *Tonga ilbo*, July 24, 1957, 3.
181. "Puron sŏjŏk p'anmae ŏpja 5-myŏng chŏngsik kusok," *Chosŏn ilbo*, 2.
182. Kim Kwangju, "P'yojŏng: Kangaji ŭi monorogŭ" [Expression: A Puppy's Monologue], *Sinjo* 1, no. 1 (June 1951): 7.
183. Kim Kwangju, "P'yojŏng: Kangaji ŭi monorogŭ," 12.
184. Kim's text is entirely fictional. Hitler's mother was not alive during the Second World War nor was her name Rosa as in Kim's story.
185. Kim Sŏnghan, "Sŏninjang ŭi hangŭi" [Protestation of a Cactus], *Munhwa segye* 2, no. 1 (January 1954): 230.
186. Kim Sŏnghan, "Sŏninjang ŭi hangŭi," 234.
187. Yu Chuhyŏn, "Yujŏn 24-si" [Twenty-four Hours of Flux], *Sasanggye* 22 (May 1955): 159–60.
188. For example, see stories like Yi Kiyŏng's "Tale of Rats" (Chwi iyagi, 1926), Yun Kŭmsuk's "Theft" (Chŏlto, 1953), Kim Song's "Nude Portrait" (Nach'esang, 1953), and Pak Yonggu's "Trash" (Ssŭregi, 1953).
189. Yu Chuhyŏn, "Yujŏn 24-si," 159.
190. Yu Chuhyŏn, "Yujŏn 24-si," 169.
191. Yu Chuhyŏn, "Insaeng ŭl pul sarŭnŭn saramdŭl" [People Who Incinerate Life], *Munhak yesul* 3, no. 8 (August 1956): 59.
192. Yu Chuhyŏn, "Insaeng ŭl pul sarŭnŭn saramdŭl," 60.
193. Yu Chuhyŏn, "Insaeng ŭl pul sarŭnŭn saramdŭl," 60.
194. Yu Chuhyŏn, "Insaeng ŭl pul sarŭnŭn saramdŭl," 59.

195. Kim Sŏngsu, "Chae/wŏlbuk chakka 'haegŭm' choch'i (1988) ŭi yŏn'gusa/munhwasajŏk ŭimi" [The Meaning for Research and Cultural History of the Directive (1988) to "Lift the Ban" on Writers Who Had Gone or Were in the North], *Sanghŏ hakpo* 55 (2019): 13–14.
196. Yi Ponggu, "Sasŭm ch'ŏrŏm" [Like a Deer], *Chayu munhak* 4, no. 12 (December 1959): 14–21.
197. Yi Ponggu, "Saem" [Spring], *Munhwa segye* 1, no. 3 (September 1953): 165–66.
198. Yi Ponggu, "Saem," 166.
199. Paek Sŏk, "Ch'on esŏ on ai" [Child from the Countryside], *Munjang* 3, no. 4 (April 1941): 168–69.
200. Paek Sŏk, "Hŭin parambyŏk i issŏ" [There Is a White Partition Wall], *Munjang* 3, no. 4 (April 1941): 165–67.
201. Yi Ponggu, "Saem," 169.
202. Yi Ponggu, "Yi Sang" *Hyŏndae munhak* 2, no. 3 (March 1956): 18.
203. Yi Ponggu, "Yi Sang," 19.
204. Yi Ponggu, "Yi Sang," 24.
205. Pak T'aewŏn, "Chebi (1)" [Chebi (1)], *Chosŏn ilbo*, February 22, 1939, 5.
206. Yi Ponggu, "Yi Sang," 22.
207. Pak T'aewŏn, "Chebi (2)," 5.
208. Yi Ponggu, "Nosŭt'arŭji" [Nostalgia] *Hyŏndae munhak* 2, no. 7 (July 1956): 63.
209. Yi Ponggu, "Nosŭt'arŭji," 66.
210. Yi Ponggu, "Nosŭt'arŭji," 66.
211. O Changhwan, "The Last Train," in *Hŏnsa* (Seoul: Namman sŏbang, 1939), n.p.
212. Yi Ponggu, "Saja ŭi sŏ" [Book of the Dead], *Hyŏndae munhak* 6, no. 11 (November 1958): 336–46.
213. Yi Ponggu, "Yŏnghoe," *Hyŏndae munhak* 5, no. 9 (September 1956): 234.
214. Yi Ponggu, "Yŏnghoe," 226.
215. In the story, Yi replaces "pride" (*charang*) with "love" (*sarang*).
216. On this poem, see Kevin Shadel, "Ports of Call: A Maritime Study of Korean Modernist Poetry," *Verge: Global Asias* 10, no. 2 (Fall 2024): 191–218.

4. TRAGIC RETURNS

1. Im Chungbin, "Yŏksa munhak pangbŏmnon sŏsŏl" [Introduction to a Methodology of Historical Literature], *Sŏngdae munhak* 13 (1967): 84–93.
2. Im Chungbin, "Yŏksa munhak pangbŏmnon sŏsŏl," 84–85.
3. Im Chungbin, "Yŏksa munhak pangbŏmnon sŏsŏl," 85.
4. Im Chungbin, "Yŏksa munhak pangbŏmnon sŏsŏl," 85.
5. Im Chungbin, "Yŏksa munhak pangbŏmnon sŏsŏl," 87.
6. Im Chungbin, "Yŏksa munhak pangbŏmnon sŏsŏl," 89.
7. Following North Korean convention, Matsumoto calls his protagonist "Rim."
8. Like other texts mentioned below, this list included those who had "gone North" (*wŏlbuk*) and those who were rumored to have been "kidnapped to the North"

(nappuk). At the time, however, such distinctions did not affect whether the writers' works were banned.

9. The question mark appears in the original to suggest irony; Ch'oe T'aeŭng, "Wŏlbuk munhwain ŭi pigŭk (1)" [The Tragedy of Those Who Went North (1)], Sasanggye 115 (December 1962): 270.
10. Ch'oe T'aeŭng, "Wŏlbuk munhwain ŭi pigŭk (1)," 270.
11. Ch'oe T'aeŭng, "Wŏlbuk munhwain ŭi pigŭk (3)," 367.
12. Ch'oe T'aeŭng, "Wŏlbuk munhwain ŭi pigŭk (3)," 367.
13. Ch'oe T'aeŭng, "Wŏlbuk munhwain ŭi pigŭk (4)," 389.
14. Ch'oe T'aeŭng, "Wŏlbuk munhwain ŭi pigŭk (5)," 350.
15. Ch'oe Chinsŏk, "Naengjŏn'gi Han'guk chisigin ŭi pŏnyŏk silch'ŏn: 1960-nyŏndae Sasanggye ŭi pŏnyŏk charyo sŏnbyŏl ŭl chungsim ŭro" [Cold War–Era Korean Intellectuals' Translation Practice: Focusing on the Selection of Translated Materials in Sasanggye of the 1960s], Inmun kwahak 85 (May 2022): 176.
16. Tibor Méray, "Han siin ŭi ch'uŏk: Sŏl Chŏngsik ŭi pigŭk" [Memories of a Poet: The Tragedy of Sŏl Chŏngsik], trans. Han Ch'ŏlmo, Sasanggye 111 (September 1962): 222–27.
17. Ch'oe T'aeŭng, "Wŏlbuk munhwain ŭi pigŭk (1)," 264.
18. Ch'oe T'aeŭng, "Wŏlbuk munhwain ŭi pigŭk (3)," 359–65.
19. A useful synopsis of the novel is provided in John Whittier Treat, "Im Hwa Before and After Japan," Trans-Humanities 8, no. 1 (2015): 5–26.
20. For translations by Kim, see, for example, the second installment of the novel. For the trial record translations, see: Abakareta inbō: Amerika no supai Boku Ken'ei [Pak Hŏnyŏng], Ri Shōka [Ri Sŭngyŏp] ichimi no kōhan kiroku [An Exposed Conspiracy: Record of the Trials of the Clique of the American Spies Pak Hŏnyŏng and Ri Sŭngyŏp], trans. Gendai Chōsen Kenkyūkai (Tokyo: Sundaisha, 1954), 91–97.
21. For example, see Matsumoto Seichō, "Minami Chōsen no gunji seiken ni omou" [Thoughts on the Southern Korean Military Regime], Atarashii sedai 2, no. 8 (October 1961): 34–35; Matsumoto Seichō, "Seiji mondai to ha betsu ni kangaeyo," Chōsen jihō, October 12, 1963, 3.
22. For a recent account, see Yi Pongbŏm, "Puk ŭi siin [Kita no shijin] kwa naengjŏn chŏngch'isŏng: 1960-nyŏndae ch'o Han'guk suyong kwa hyŏnhaet'an nonjŏn ŭl chungsim ŭro" [Poet of the North and Cold War Politicality: Focusing on Its Early-1960s Reception in Korea and the Cross-Strait Debate], Han'guk yŏn'gu 6 (December 2020): 203–52.
23. "K'ŭn p'adong irŭk'in changp'yŏn Puk ŭi siin [Kita no shijin]" [Poet of the North, the Novel that Has Caused a Large Stir], Kyonghyang sinmun, December 29, 1962, 5.
24. Cho Chaech'ŏn, "Songbon Ch'ŏngjang [Matsumoto Seichō] ege munnŭnda" [Questions for Matsumoto Seichō], Tonga ch'unch'u 1, no. 1 (December 1962): 82–94.
25. Cho Chaech'ŏn, "Sasil ŭl waegok haji malla: Ilbon wŏl chapchi Chungang kongnon [Chūō kōron] e ponaenŭn konggae sŏhan" [Do Not Distort Facts: An Open Letter Sent to the Japanese Monthly Journal Chūō kōron], Han'guk ilbo, January 8, 1963, 7.
26. "Kankoku moto hosho ni kamitsukareta Matsumoto Seichō shi" [Mr. Matsumoto Seichō Excoriated by First South Korean Minister of Justice], Shūkan yomiuri 21, no. 52 (December 1962): 20–24.

27. "Han'guk wŏn pŏpsang ege murŏ ttŭtkin Songbon Ch'ŏngjang [Matsumoto Seichō] ssi" [Mr. Matsumoto Seichō Excoriated by First South Korean Minister of Justice], *Tonga ch'uch'u* 2, no. 2 (February 1963): 134–39.
28. Chang T'aeksang, "Sok—Songbon Ch'ŏngjang [Matsumoto Seichō] ege munnŭnda" [Questions for Matsumoto Seichō, Continued], *Tonga ch'uch'u* 2, no. 1 (January 1963): 214–20; Cho P'ungyŏn, "Songbon Ch'ŏngjang [Matsumoto Seichō]-ron" [On Matsumoto Seichō], *Tonga ch'uch'u* 2, no. 1 (January 1963): 222–27; Cho P'ungyŏn, "Chinsil ŭi tam'gu rŭl wihayŏ" [For the Pursuit of Truth], *Tonga ch'uch'u* 2, no. 2 (February 1963): 140–46.
29. Yi Ch'ŏlju, "Pukhan ŭi chakka, yesulga (1): Kŭnŭl ŭl kasŭm e anko" [North Korea's Writers and Artists (1): With a Shade in My Heart], *Sasanggye* 123 (July 1963): 249. Yi Pongbŏm also mentions this in "*Puk ŭi siin* kwa naengjŏn chŏngch'isŏng," see 211.
30. Yi Ch'ŏlju, "Pukhan ŭi chakka, yesulga (13): Sŭlp'ŭn unmyŏng ŭi kunsangdŭl" [North Korea's Writers and Artists (13): Crowds of a Sad Fate], *Sasanggye* 137 (August 1964): 252.
31. Yi Ch'ŏlju, "Pukhan ŭi chakka, yesulga (1)," 249.
32. For more on the journal, including a discussion of its discontinuation, see Yi Pongbŏm, "*Puk ŭi siin* kwa naengjŏn chŏngch'isŏng," 223–25.
33. The exact circumstances under which the latter two writers went North remains unclear. Nevertheless, they were considered *wŏlbuk chakka* (writers who went North) at the time.
34. "Wŏlbuk chakka ŭi munhakchŏk chaep'an" [The Literary Judgment of the Writers Who Went North], *Tonga ch'unch'u* 2, no. 4 (April 1963): 305.
35. "Wŏlbuk chakka ŭi munhakchŏk chaep'an," 305.
36. Although these works were from the pre-1945 era, I refer to the authors as Rim Hwa and Ri T'aejun because the feature was published in the 1960s.
37. Cho Yŏnhyŏn, "Sinhwa wa pigŭk ŭl samk'in Im Hwa [Rim Hwa]" [Rim Hwa, Who Swallowed Myth and Tragedy], *Tonga ch'unch'u* 2, no. 4 (April 1963): 347.
38. Cho Yŏnhyŏn, "Sinhwa wa pigŭk ŭl samk'in Im Hwa [Rim Hwa]," 348.
39. Cho Yŏnhyŏn, "Sinhwa wa pigŭk ŭl samk'in Im Hwa [Rim Hwa]," 349.
40. "Ibuk innŭn kajok ege p'yŏnji pangsong kaesi" [Commencement of Broadcasting of Letters to Family Members in the North], *Tonga ilbo*, May 22, 1960, 3.
41. "P'anmunjŏmhaeng yŏbi mogŭm undong chŏn'gae k'iro" [Development of a Movement to Collect Money to Travel to P'anmunjŏm], *Kyŏnghyang sinmun*, May 13, 1961, 3.
42. Yi Ponggu, "Munhakchŏk sanbo (2)" [A Literary Stroll (2)], *Hyŏndae munhak* 6, no. 11 (November 1960): 210.
43. Yi Ponggu, "Munhakchŏk sanbo (5)" [A Literary Stroll (5)], *Hyŏndae munhak* 7, no. 3 (March 1961): 159.
44. Yi Ponggu, "Munhakchŏk sanbo (4)" [A Literary Stroll (4)], *Hyŏndae munhak* 7, no. 2 (February 1961): 296–306.
45. Yi Ponggu, "Munhakchŏk sanbo (7)" [A Literary Stroll (7)], *Hyŏndae munhak* 7, no. 6 (June 1961): 90.
46. Yi Ponggu, "Munhakchŏk sanbo (7)," 90–91.
47. Yi Ponggu, "Munhakchŏk sanbo (7)," 91–93.

48. Yi Ponggu, "Munhakchŏk sanbo (7)," 93–96.
49. Yi Ponggu, "Ssŭlssŭrhan nŏ ŭi kohyang e" [In Your Desolate Hometown], *Chayu munhak* 4, no. 4 (April 1962): 26–38.
50. Yi Ponggu, "Hwaryŏhan kodok" [Splendid Solitude], *Munhak ch'unch'u* 9 (December 1964): 29.
51. Yi Ponggu, *Kŭriun irŭm ttara: Myŏngdong 20-nyŏn* [In Pursuit of Names I Long For: 20 Years in Myŏngdong] (Seoul: Yushin munhwasa, 1966), 60–61; Yi Ponggu, "Myŏngdong 20-nyŏn (6)" [20 Years in Myŏngdong (6)], *Chosŏn ilbo*, August 12, 1965, 4.
52. Yi Ponggu, *Kŭriun irŭm ttara*, 60–61; Yi Ponggu, "Myŏngdong 20-nyŏn (6)," 4.
53. Yi Ponggu, "Hŏmanghan paehoe" [Futile Wandering], *Hyŏndae munhak* 14, no. 6 (June 1968): 49–83.
54. Yi Ponggu, "Hŏmanghan paehoe," 50.
55. Yi Ponggu, "Hŏmanghan paehoe," 49–50.
56. Yi Ponggu, "Hŏmanghan paehoe," 73.
57. Yi Ponggu, "Hŏmanghan paehoe," 75.
58. Yi Ponggu, "Ch'ilmyŏnjo" [Turkey], *Wŏlgan munhak* 5, no. 2 (February 1972): 12–30.
59. Yi Ponggu, "Ch'ilmyŏnjo," 25.
60. In Korean, the word for turkey literally means "seven-sided bird." It has thus been linked to changeability and apostasy.
61. On the real individual, whose path closely mirrors the one in the story, see, for example, Yi Chongsik, "Ton ilk'o ch'ŏja ilk'o" [Lost His Money, Lost His Family], *Chosŏn ilbo*, June 14, 1970, 7.
62. Yi Ponggu, "Ch'ilmyŏnjo," 23.
63. Yi Ponggu, "Ch'ilmyŏnjo," 22.
64. Yi Ponggu, "Ch'ilmyŏnjo," 26–27.
65. Yi Ponggu, "Ch'ilmyŏnjo," 28–29.
66. Hirabayashi Taiko, Kim Tongni, and Yŏ Sŏkki, "Han-Il munhak ŭl marhanda: Ilbon yŏryu chakka P'yŏngnim Taija [Hirabayashi Taiko] wa hamkkye" [Discussing Korean and Japanese Literature: With the Female Writer Hirabayashi Taiko], *Sasanggye* 110 (August 1962): 245.
67. "Kankoku moto hosho ni kamitsukareta Matsumoto Seichō shi," 20.
68. Ōmura Masuo, "Kaihōgo no Rin Wa [Im Hwa]" [Rim Hwa After Liberation], *Shakai kagaku tōkyū* 13, no. 1 (1967): 99–125; Chang Munsŏk, "Yŏndae ŭi inyŏm esŏ chuch'esŏng ŭi segye ro: Naengjŏn'gi Ilbon ŭi Chosŏn munhak yŏn'gu wa Chosŏnŏ" [From the Idea of Solidarity to the World of Subjectivity: Cold War–Era Japan's Research on Korean Literature and Korean Language], *Ilbon pip'yŏng* 27 (August 2022): 93–94.
69. Kim Pyŏngik, "Memarŭn Ilbon e ssakt'ŭnŭn Han'guk munhak" [Korean Literature Sprouting in Parched Japan], *Tonga ilbo*, July 5, 1971, 5.
70. Kim Pyŏngik, "Sansil (2): Munhak p'yŏngnon'ga Kim Yunsik" [Delivery Room (2): Literary Critic Kim Yunsik], *Tonga ilbo*, October 23, 1972, 5.
71. Chang Munsŏk, "1960-1970-nyŏndae Ilbon ŭi Han'guk munhak yŏn'gu wa 'Chosŏn munhak ŭi hoe:' Taech'on Ikpu [Ōmura Masuo] kyosu ege chilmun handa" [Research on Korean Literature in 1960s–1970s Japan and the "Korean Literature Association:"

Questions for Professor Ōmura Masuo], *Han'gukhak yŏn'gu* 40 (February 2016): 181, 198–99.
72. Chang Munsŏk, "1960-1970-nyŏndae Ilbon ŭi Han'guk munhak yŏn'gu wa 'Chosŏn munhak ŭi hoe,'" 202.
73. Kim Yunsik, "Im Hwa [Rim Hwa] yŏn'gu: Pip'yŏngkaron ki-7" [Research on Rim Hwa: On Critics, Installment 7], *Nonmunjip: Inmun sahoe kwahak p'yŏn* 4 (April 1972): 35–64. I am grateful to Hyonhui Choe for pointing me in the direction of this article.
74. Kim Yunsik, "Im Hwa yŏn'gu," 38.
75. Kim Yunsik, "Im Hwa yŏn'gu," 64.
76. Kim Yunsik, "Im Hwa yŏn'gu," 48–50.
77. Kim Yunsik, "Im Hwa yŏn'gu," 45–47.
78. Kim Yunsik, "Im Hwa yŏn'gu," 52.
79. Kim Yunsik, "Im Hwa yŏn'gu," 59–60.
80. Kim Yunsik, "Im Hwa yŏn'gu," 59–60.
81. Kim Yunsik, "Im Hwa yŏn'gu," 64.
82. Kim Yunsik, "Im Hwa yŏn'gu," 60.
83. Kim Yunsik and Kim Hyŏn, "Yŏng-Chŏngjo esŏ 4.19 e irŭnŭn Han'guk munhaksa (1)" [A History of Korean Literature from the Reigns of Yŏngjo and Chŏngjo to 4.19 (1)], *Munhak kwa chisŏng* 3, no. 1 (March 1972): 202–10.
84. Kim Yunsik and Kim Hyŏn, "Yŏng-Chŏngjo esŏ 4.19 e irŭnŭn Han'guk munhaksa (1)," 202–3.
85. Kim Yunsik and Kim Hyŏn, "Yŏng-Chŏngjo esŏ 4.19 e irŭnŭn Han'guk munhaksa (1)," 203.
86. Kim Yunsik and Kim Hyŏn, "Yŏng-Chŏngjo esŏ 4.19 e irŭnŭn Han'guk munhaksa (1)," 203.
87. Kim Yunsik and Kim Hyŏn, "Yŏng-Chŏngjo esŏ 4.19 e irŭnŭn Han'guk munhaksa (1)," 209.
88. Im Hŏnyŏng, "Kŭndae sosŏl sahoesa sigo" [An Exploration in the Social History of Modern Fiction], *Kiwŏn* 1, no. 3 (December 1973): 123–24.
89. Yŏm Muung, "Singminji sidae munhak ŭi insik" [The Perception of Colonial-Era Literature], *Sindonga* 121 (September 1974): 346–57.
90. For example, see So Chaeyŏng, "Kodae sosŏlsa 40-nyŏn ŭi haengjŏk: T'onggyesang ŭro pon pansŏngjŏm kwa munje ŭi chegi" [The Record of 40 Years of the Literary History of Ancient Fiction: Points for Reflection and Problems to Be Raised As Seen Through Data], *Sae kugŏ kyoyuk* 13 (December 1969): 46–54; Chŏng Kyubok, "'Namjŏnggi' ŭi chŏjak tonggi e taehayŏ: Kim Hyŏnyong ssi ŭi 'Sassi namjŏnggi yŏn'gu' rŭl ilkko" [On the Motivation for the Composition of "Lady Sa's Journey to the South:" After Reading Mr. Kim Hyŏnyong's "Research on Lady Sa's Journey to the South"], *Sŏngdae munhak* 15/16 (February 1970): 35–39.
91. A copy of this 1972 facsimile is held in the National Assembly Library in Seoul.
92. Kim Yunsik and Kim Hyŏn, "Yŏng-Chŏngjo esŏ 4.19 e irŭnŭn Han'guk munhaksa (1)," 221.

93. Im Hŏnyŏng, "Kŭndae munhaksa non'go" [A Study on Modern Literary History], *Ch'angjak kwa pip'yŏng* 10, no. 1 (March 1975): 69–88.
94. Cho Haeil, "Im Kkŏkchŏng," *Hyŏndae munhak* 19, no. 3 (March 1973): 218–25.
95. Kang Yŏngju, "*Im Kkŏkchŏng* ŭi ch'angjak kwajŏng kwa *Chosŏn wangjo sillok*" [The Process of Composition of *Im Kkŏkchŏng* and the Veritable Records of the Chosŏn Dynasty], *Han'guk hyŏndae munhak yŏn'gu* 20, no. 20 (December 2006): 13–47; Yun Sunyong, "Pyŏkch'o *Im Kkŏkchŏng* e nat'anan paekjŏng ŭi silch'e wa munhakchŏk hyŏngsanghwa" [The Reality and Literary Representation of the Butcher as Seen in Pyŏkch'o's *Im Kkŏkchŏng*], MA thesis (Kongju University, 2011), 44.
96. Cho Haeil, "Im Kkŏkchŏng 2," in *Wangsimni* (Seoul: Samjungdang, 1975), 29.
97. Cho Haeil, "Im Kkŏkchŏng 2," 28.
98. Cho Haeil, "Chakka ŭi mal" [Writer's Note], in *Im Kkŏkchŏng e kwanhan ilgop kae ŭi iyagi* (Seoul: Ch'aek sesang, 1986; repr., 2000), 153.
99. Cho Haeil, *Im Kkŏkchŏng e kwanhan ilgop kae ŭi iyagi* [Seven Stories about Im Kkŏkchŏng] (Seoul: Ch'aek sesang, 1986; repr., 2000), 137–38. The only installment that does not make this sourcing claim is the first one, in which Hŏ Sun is introduced as a character in the text.
100. Cho Haeil, *Im Kkŏkchŏng e kwanhan ilgop kae ŭi iyagi*, 125.
101. "Hong Myŏnghŭi chak *Im Kŏjŏng* p'an'gŭm" [Sale of *Im Kŏjŏng* by Hong Myŏnghŭi Prohibited], *Tonga ilbo*, October 7, 1985, 6.
102. "Hong Myŏnghŭi chak *Im Kŏjŏng* p'an'gŭm," 6.
103. Chang Munsŏk, "Wŏlbuk chakka ŭi haegŭm kwa chakp'umjip ch'ulp'an (1): 1985-1989-nyŏn sigi rŭl chungsim ŭro" [The Lifting of the Ban on Writers Who Went North and the Publication of Literary Collections (1): Focusing on the 1985–1989 Period], *Kubo hakpo* 19 (2018): 56.
104. "Hong Myŏnghŭi chak *Im Kŏjŏng* p'an'gŭm," 6.
105. Chang Munsŏk, "Wŏlbuk chakka ŭi haegŭm kwa chakp'umjip ch'ulp'an (1)," 56.
106. Chang Munsŏk, "Wŏlbuk chakka ŭi haegŭm kwa chakp'umjip ch'ulp'an (1)," 56.
107. Chang Munsŏk, "Wŏlbuk chakka ŭi haegŭm kwa chakp'umjip ch'ulp'an (1)," 59.
108. "'Asŭk'a'-ch'on ŭi Nambuk taehwa—Nam: 'tangsin ch'aek ilgŏtta,' Puk: Yu Hongnyŏl kyosu wa tongch'ang" [South-North Dialogue in "Asuka" Village—South: "I Read Your Book," North: I Was a Classmate of Professor Yu Hongnyŏl], *Tonga ilbo*, October 5, 1972, 3.
109. "'Asŭk'a'-ch'on ŭi Nambuk taehwa," 3.
110. "'Asŭk'a'-ch'on ŭi Nambuk taehwa," 3.
111. E. Taylor Atkins, *Primitive Selves: Koreana in the Japanese Colonial Gaze, 1910–1945* (Berkeley: University of California Press, 2010), 102.
112. Kim Sŏkhyŏng, "Samhan Samguk ŭi Ilbon ryŏlto nae pun'guktŭl e taehayŏ" [On the Subordinate States of the Three Han and Three Kingdoms in the Japanese Archipelago], *Ryŏksa kwahak* 9, no. 1 (January 1963): 1–32.
113. Kim Sŏkhyŏng, "Samhan Samguk ŭi Ilbon ryŏlto nae pun'guktŭl e taehayŏ," 9–23.
114. Kim Sŏkhyŏng, "Samhan Samguk ŭi Ilbon ryŏlto nae pun'guktŭl e taehayŏ," 32.

115. Kim Sŏkhyŏng, "Samhan Samguk ŭi Ilbon ryŏlto nae pun'guktŭl e taehayŏ," 21.
116. Kim Sŏkhyŏng, *Ch'ogi Cho-Il kwan'gye yŏn'gu* [Research on Early Korean-Japanese Relations] (Pyongyang: Sahoe kwahagwon ch'ulp'ansa, 1966).
117. Kim Ch'aesu, "Kangsang P'abu [Egami Namio] ŭi kima minjok chŏngboksŏl ŭi ch'urhyŏn paegyŏng e kwanhan koch'al" [An Examination of the Background of the Appearance of Egami Namio's Horse-Rider Theory], *Tongbuga munhwa yŏn'gu* 21 (2009): 565–87.
118. Kim Sanggi, "Irin i waegok han Han'guksa (5): Kodae ŭi Han-Il sagwan" [The History of Korea Distorted by the Japanese (5): Perspective on the History of Ancient Korea-Japan Relations], *Kyŏnghyang sinmun*, February 2, 1966, 5.
119. Wi Kaya, "Samhan Samguk pun'guksŏl ŭi kusang kwa p'agŭp" [The Formation and Dissemination of the Three Han and Three Kingdoms Subordinate States Theory], *Sahak yŏn'gu* 137 (March 2020): 113–14.
120. Kim Sŏkhyŏng, "Sankan Sangoku no Nihon rettō nai no bunkuni ni tsuite (1–3)" [On the Subordinate States of the Three Han and Three Kingdoms in the Japanese Archipelago (1–3)], trans. Chŏng Chinhwa, *Rekishi hyōron* 165, 168, 169 (May, August, September 1964): 19–28; 34–47; 45–54.
121. Ri Chinhŭi, *Haehyŏp: Han chaeil sahakcha ŭi pan p'yŏngsaeng* [Straits: Half the Life of a Resident Korean Historian in Japan], trans. Yi Kyusu (Seoul: Samin, 2003), 120. Even after leaving Chongryon, Ri appears to have continued to use "Ri." I follow that convention here even for citations of his work published in South Korea.
122. Ri Chinhŭi, *Haehyŏp*, 120.
123. Ri Chinhŭi, *Haehyŏp*, 112.
124. Ri Chinhŭi, *Haehyŏp*, 106–9.
125. For a brief discussion of this exposé, see I Jonathan Kief, "Closed Borders and Open Letters in the Postcolonial Koreas," in *Routledge Companion to Korean Literature*, ed. Heekyoung Cho (New York: Routledge, 2022), 436.
126. Ri Chinhŭi, *Haehyŏp*, 106–9.
127. Ri Chinhŭi, *Haehyŏp*, 163–69, 334.
128. Ri Chinhŭi, *Kōkaido-ō ryōhi no kenkyū* [Research on the King Kwanggaet'o Burial Mound Stele] (Tokyo: Yoshikawa kōbunkan, 1972), 59; Kim Sŏkhyŏng, "Samhan Samguk ŭi Ilbon ryŏlto nae pun'guktŭl e taehayŏ," 7–8.
129. Pak Sihyŏng, *Kwanggaet'owang Rŭngbi* [The King Kwanggaet'o Burial Mound Stele] (Pyongyang: Sahoe kwahakwŏn ch'ulp'ansa, 1966).
130. Hong Chonguk, "Yŏksa hakcha Pak Sihyŏng ŭi minjok kwa kwahak" [The Nation and Science of the Historian Pak Sihyŏng], *Yŏksa kyoyuk* 165 (March 2023): 27–28.
131. Ri Chinhŭi, *Kōtaiōhi no nazo: Nihon kodaishi o kaki kaeru* [Investigating the King Hot'ae Stele: Rewriting Ancient Japanese History] (Tokyo: Kodansha, 1973), 117–25; Ri Chinhŭi, *Kwanggaet'o wangbi ŭi t'amgu* [Investigating the King Kwanggaet'o Stele], trans. Yi Kidong (Seoul: Iljogak, 1982), 85–91.
132. In fact, as Ri noted, it was not an ordinary rubbing (Kr. *t'akpon*, Jp. *takuhon*) at all, but rather a kind of calligraphic stencil (Kr. *sanggu kamukpon*, Jp. *sōkakagika sumimoto*); Ri Chinhŭi, *Kōtaiōhi no nazo*, 169–81; Ri Chinhŭi, *Kwanggaet'o wangbi ŭi t'amgu*, 121–33.

133. Ri Chinhŭi, *Kōtaiōhi no nazo*, 125–36; Ri Chinhŭi, *Kwanggaet'o wangbi ŭi t'amgu*, 91–99.
134. Ri Chinhŭi, *Kōtaiōhi no nazo*, 41–55; Ri Chinhŭi, *Kwanggaet'o wangbi ŭi t'amgu*, 32–41.
135. Ri Chinhŭi, *Haehyŏp*, 13.
136. Ri Chinhŭi, *Haehyŏp*, 13.
137. Ri Chinhŭi, *Kōkaido-ō ryōhi no kenkyū*, 57.
138. Kim Chŏngbae, "Kodae Han-Il kwan'gyesa ŭi il-tanmyŏn: Kwanggaet'o taewangnŭng pimun ŭi munjejŏm" [One Aspect of the History of Ancient Korean-Japanese Relations: The Problem of the King Kwanggaet'o Burial Mound Stele Inscription], *Sindonga* 96 (August 1972): 132–38.
139. Kim Chŏngbae, "Kodae Han-Il kwan'gyesa ŭi il-tanmyŏn," 133–34.
140. Kim Ch'ŏljun, "Paekche sahoe wa kŭ munhwa (3)" [Paekche Society and Its Culture], *Kyŏnghyang sinmun*, December 17, 1973, 5.
141. Ri Chinhŭi, *Haehyŏp*, 334.
142. Ri Chinhŭi, *Haehyŏp*, 152.
143. Ri Chinhŭi, *Haehyŏp*, 152–53.
144. Ueda Masaaki, "Sŏksang sin'gung kwa Ch'iljido," *Sindonga* 101 (January 1973): 129–36; Ueda Masaaki, "Isonokami jingu to Shichishitō" [The Isonokami Shrine and the Seven-Branched Sword], *Nihon no naka no Chōsen bunka* 9 (March 1971): 4–14.
145. Kim Sŏkhyŏng, "Samhan Samguk ŭi Ilbon ryŏlto nae pun'guktŭl e taehayŏ," 19.
146. Ueda Masaaki, "Sŏksang sin'gung kwa Ch'iljido," 135–36.
147. Ueda Masaaki et al., "Nihon no naka no Chōsen" [Korea Within Japan], *Nihon no naka no Chōsen bunka* 1 (March 1969): 29–30.
148. Ueda Masaaki, "Sŏksang sin'gung kwa Ch'iljido," 129.
149. Ueda Masaaki, "Sŏksang sin'gung kwa Ch'iljido," 129.
150. "Chakka Yi Hoesŏng [Ri Kaisei], Kim Talsu ssi tŭng 13-myŏng: Choch'ongnyŏn chungangwi sŏ sukch'ŏng," *Tonga ilbo*, August 1, 1972, 1.
151. "Kwŏn Il," *Encyclopedia of Overseas Korean Culture*, accessed September 4, 2023, http://www.okpedia.kr/Contents/ContentsView?localCode=jpn&contentsId=GC95200330. Unfortunately, this encyclopedia, hosted by the Academy of Korean Studies, has been deactivated.
152. For the first, see Hagiwara Toshihiko, "Wangin kwa Paekche wangssi" [Wangin and the Paekche Wangs], *Ilbon munje* 3 (Summer 1973): 160–65; Hagiwara Toshihiko, "Wani to Kudara ōshi" [Wangin and the Paekche Wangs], *Nihon no naka no Chōsen bunka* 10 (June 1971): 4–9. For the second, see Okada Seishi, "Edo makbu sidae ŭi 'Chosŏnin kado'" [The Korean Street of the Edo Bakufu Era], *Ilbon munje* 3 (Summer 1973): 144–51; Okada Seishi, "'Chōsenjin kaidō' no koto" [On the Korean Street], *Nihon no naka no Chōsen bunka* 6 (June 1970): 38–44.
153. Kim Talsu, Tanigawa Ken'ichi, and Okazaki Takashi, "Nihon bunka to Chōsen bunka: Genkainada no rekishiteki imi" [Japanese Culture and Korean Culture: The Historical Meaning of the Genkai Strait], *Bessatsu keizai hyōron* 10 (September 1972): 16–30; Kim Talsu, Tanigawa Ken'ichi, and Okazaki Takashi, "Han'guk munhwa wa Ilbon munhwa" [Korean Culture and Japanese Culture], *Ilbon munje* 2 (Spring 1973): 134–55.

154. Kim Talsu et al., "Han'guk munhwa wa Ilbon munhwa," 145, 153, 155.
155. Kim Talsu, "Chōsen to Man'yōshū" [Korea and the Man'yōshū], *Kokubungaku* 17, no. 6 (May 1972): 157–62.
156. "Kodae Irŏ e tturyŏthan uri mal yŏnghyang" [The Clear Influence of Our Language on Ancient Japanese], *Tonga ilbo*, February 13, 1973, 5.
157. "Tonggyŏng esŏ yŏllin ŏnŏ simp'ojium: Koguryŏ ŏnŏ, Kodae Ilbonŏ e k'ŭn yŏnghyang" [Language Symposium Held in Tokyo: Koguryŏ Language, Large Influence on Ancient Japanese], *Kyŏnghyang sinmun*, February 13, 1973, 5.
158. Ri Chinhŭi, "Kodaishi o kakikaete 34-nen" [34 Years of Rewriting Ancient History], *Higashi Aji no kodai bunka* 137 (January 2009): 189.
159. See the fourth and fifth issues of the journal, published in January and June 1975.
160. "Int'ŏbyu: Ilbon sŏ munbak hagwi padŭn Kim Unhak sŭnim" [Interview: The Monk Kim Unhak, Who Received a Doctorate in Literature in Japan], *Tonga ilbo*, April 28, 1973, 5.
161. Kim Unhak, "Hyangga wa Manyŏpchip" [Hyangga and the Man'yōshū], *Hyŏndae munhak* 21, no. 12 (October 1975): 38–53. The *Nihon no naka no Chōsen bunka* citation does not appear in this version.
162. Kim Unhak, "Hyangga wa Ilbon kayo waŭi kwan'gye" [Hyangga and Its Relationship with Japanese Songs], *Tongguk taehakkyo nonmunjip* 13 (December 1974): 114.
163. Kim Talsu et al., "Ilbon sok ŭi Han'guk/Han'guk munhwa" [Korea/Korean Culture within Japan], *Sindonga* 201 (May 1981): 108–19.
164. "'Chosŏn sidae t'ongsinsa:' Chaeil kogohakcha Yi Chinhŭi [Ri Chinhŭi] ssi kangyŏn" ["The Chosŏn-Era T'ongsinsa": Lecture by the Resident Korean Archeologist Ri Chinhŭi], *Maeil kyŏngje*, January 25, 1982, 9.
165. "Chaeil sahakcha Yi Chinhŭi [Ri Chinhŭi] ssi, Han-Il kwan'gyesa t'amgu wihae naehan" [Resident Korean Historian Ri Chinhŭi, Visiting Korea to Investigate the History of Korean-Japanese Relations] *Kyŏnghyang sinmun*, May 3, 1982, 2.
166. "Chaeil sahakcha Yi Chinhŭi [Ri Chinhŭi] ssi, Han-Il kwan'gyesa t'amgu wihae naehan," 2.
167. "Chaeil sahakcha Yi Chinhŭi [Ri Chinhŭi] kyosu, Chŏng Kuho ponsa sajang yebang" [Professor Ri Chinhŭi, Resident Korean Historian, Visits Company President Chŏng Kuho], *Kyŏnghyang sinmun*, January 22, 1982, 10.
168. Ri Chinhŭi, *Kwanggaet'o wangbi ŭi t'amgu*. As noted in Yi Kidong's translator's note, these selections were selected by the author and drawn from Yi's 1973 work on the Kwanggaet'o Stele (*Kōtaiōhi no nazo*) and his 1980 work on the Seven-Branched Sword and other issues (*Kōkaido-ō ryōhi to Shichishitō*).
169. "Ilbon kodaesa nŭn uri sŏnjodŭl ŭi iminsa" [The Ancient History of Japanese is the History of Our Ancestors' Migration], *Chosŏn ilbo*, October 22, 1986, 7.
170. Ch'oe Inho, "I ch'aek ŭl ilki chŏn e: Chakka ŭi mal" [Before Reading this Book: Writer's Message], in *Irhŏbŏrin wangguk* (Seoul: Usŏk, 1986), 13–16.
171. Mun Chŏngch'ang, *Ilbon sanggosa* [Ancient History of Japan] (Seoul: Paengmundang, 1970), 115; Mun Chŏngch'ang, "Kodae Ilbon ŭi chibaech'ŭng kwa Samhan Samguk: Kodae Han-Il kwan'gye ŭi silsang" [The Ruling Class of Ancient Japan and the Three

Han and Three Kingdoms: The Reality of Ancient Korean-Japanese Relations], *Sindonga* 101 (January 1973): 94.

172. Mun Chŏngch'ang, *Ilbon sanggosa*, 171–73.
173. Sheila Miyoshi Jager, *Narratives of Nation-Building in Korea: A Genealogy of Patriotism* (New York: Routledge, 2003), 80–86; Robert Oppenheim, *Kyŏngju Things: Assembling Place* (Ann Arbor: University of Michigan Press, 2008), 28–29.
174. Robert Oppenheim, *Kyŏngju Things*, 34–39.
175. Yun Sangdŏk, "Pukhan ŭi Silla kokogak yŏn'gu hyŏnhwang kwa t'ŭkching" [The Current State and Characteristics of North Korea's Archeological Research on Silla], *Munhwajae* 53, no. 2 (June 2020): 270–85.
176. "'Ilbon munhwa ŭi wŏllyu'" ["The Roots of Japanese Culture"], *Rodong sinmun*, March 16, 1986, 4.
177. Ch'oe Inho, "Irhŏbŏrin wangguk (669)" [The Lost Kingdom (669)], *Chosŏn ilbo*, May 8, 1987, 7.
178. Ch'oe Inho, ""Irhŏbŏrin wangguk (944)" [The Lost Kingdom (944)], *Chosŏn ilbo*, March 30, 1988, 9.
179. "Ilbon sok e Hanminjoksa t'ambang: sago" [Field Trip on the History of the Korean Nation in Japan: Company Notice], *Chosŏn ilbo*, November 6, 1987, 1.
180. "Che-2-hoe Ilbon sok e Hanminjoksa t'ambang: sago" [The Second Field Trip on the History of the Korean Nation in Japan: Company Notice], *Chosŏn ilbo*, October 22, 1988, 1.
181. Kim Yunsik, "Wŏlbuk chakka haegŭm ŭn munhaksa sae chŏn'gi" [The Lifting of the Ban on Writers Who Went North Is a New Turning Point], *Tonga ilbo*, July 20, 1988, 8. According to Kim Sŏngsu and Chang Munsŏk, the 1978 loosening of restrictions on research applied to the nonideological, colonial-era works of writers who were no longer alive, and this was expanded in 1987. See Kim Sŏngsu. "Chae/wŏlbuk chakka 'haegŭm' choch'i (1988) ŭi yŏn'gusa/munhwasajŏk ŭimi," *Sanghŏ hakpo* 55 (2019): 13, n. 4. Chang Munsŏk, "Wŏlbuk chakka ŭi haegŭm kwa chakp'umjip ch'ulp'an (1)," 44.
182. "Wŏlbuk chakka 5-myŏng ch'ulp'an ch'uga haegŭm" [Additional Lifting of the Ban on Publication of Five Writers Who Went North], *Kyŏnghyang sinmun*, February 20, 1989, 1.
183. In 1988, South Korean publishing companies began republishing North Korean works and selling them in the ordinary marketplace. In late 1988 and early 1989, the South Korean state cracked down on this. See, for example, Song Yŏngŏn, "Pukhan wŏnjŏn tansok e nollan i k'ŭda" [Largescale Controversy Regarding the Crackdown on Texts Reprinted from North Korea], *Tonga ilbo*, April 11, 1989, 5.

EPILOGUE. THE COLD WAR IN KOREA

1. Chang Sejin, "Wŏnhan, nosŭt'aeljia, kwahak: Wŏllam chisigindŭl kwa 1960-nyŏndae Pukhan hakji ŭi sŏngnip sajŏng [Ressentiment, Nostalgia, Science: Defector Intellectuals from North Korea and the Conditions Surrounding the Establishment of North Korean Studies in the 1960s], *Sai* 17 (November 2014): 141–80.

2. Youna Kim, "Illicit Media, Reflexivity and Sociocultural Change in North Korea," *International Journal of Cultural Studies* 27, no. 2 (March 2024): 166.
3. Sonny Yoon, "South Korean Media Reception and Youth Culture in North Korea," in *South Korean Popular Culture and North Korea*, ed. Youna Kim (New York: Routledge, 2019), 124.
4. Youna Kim, "Illicit Media, Reflexivity and Sociocultural Change in North Korea," 166.

BIBLIOGRAPHY

Abakareta inbō: Amerika no supai Boku Ken'ei [Pak Hŏnyŏng], *Ri Shōka* [Ri Sŭngyŏp] *ichimi no kōhan kiroku.* Translated by Gendai Chōsen Kenkyūkai. Tokyo: Sundaisha, 1954.

Agov, Avram. "North Korea's Alliances and the Unfinished Korean War." *Journal of Korean Studies* 18, no. 2 (2013): 225–62.

An, Chinsŏng. "Ŏmŏni ŭi sunggohan chŏngsin segye: Yŏn'gŭk *Pukkŭksŏng* ŭl pogo." *Chosŏn yesul* 124 (December 1966): 23–25.

An, Chŏnghwa. "Chaeil Hanin chapchi sojae 'Kim Chiha tamnon' ŭi chŏngch'ijŏk ŭimi: *Samch'ŏlli* rŭl chungsim ŭro." *Han'guk munhak nonch'ong* 42 (April 2006): 419–39.

An, Hamgwang. *Chosŏn munhaksa.* Yŏnbyŏn: Yŏnbyŏn kyoyuk ch'ulp'ansa, 1956. Facsimile edition. Seoul: Han'guk munhwasa, 1999.

An, Hamgwang. "Hyŏngmyŏng munhak yesul e taehan Kim Ilsŏng wŏnsu ŭi chido pangch'im e taehan yakkan ŭi koch'al." *Chosŏn munhak* 165 (May 1961): 99–104.

An, Mak. "Minjok yesul kwa minjok munhak kŏnsŏl ŭi kosanghan sujun ŭl wihayŏ." *Munhwa chŏnsŏn* 5 (1947): 2–16.

An, Miae, Hong Miju, and Paek Tuhyŏn. "Pukhan munhwaŏ ŭi ŏdu R, N kyujŏng ŭl t'ong haesŏ pon ŏnŏ chŏngch'esŏng kuch'uk kwa ch'abyŏrhwa pangsik yŏn'gu." *Ŏmun nonch'ong* 76 (June 2018): 85–125.

An, Pyŏnguk. "Hyŏndae sasang kangjwa (1–8)." *Sasanggye* 27–34 (October 1955–May 1956): 215–22; 174–99; 136–64; 238–62; 146–60; 153–86, 152; 309–19; 72–86.

An, Pyŏnguk. "Saeroun segyegwan ŭi mosaek." *Sasanggye* 45 (April 1957): 283–90.

An, Pyŏnguk. "Sahoe kigu wa hyumaenijŭm." *Sasanggye* 51 (October 1957): 26–34.

An, Pyŏnguk. "Silchonjuŭi ŭi kyebo." *Sasanggye* 21 (April 1955): 77–100.

An, Tongnim. "Hŭimang." *Hyŏndae munhak* 9, no. 3 (March 1963): 60–71.

An, Tongnim. "Hŭimang." *Choguk t'ongil*, February 3–February 6, 1965, 4.

An, Tongnim. "Hŭimang." *Samch'ŏlli* 9 (April 1965): 117–21.
"'Asŭk'a'-ch'on ŭi Nambuk taehwa—Nam: 'tangsin ch'aek ilgŏtta,' Puk: Yu Hongnyŏl kyosu wa tongch'ang." *Tonga ilbo*, October 5, 1972, 3.
Atkins, E. Taylor. *Primitive Selves: Koreana in the Japanese Colonial Gaze, 1910–1945*. Berkeley: University of California Press, 2010.
Augustine, Matthew. *From Japanese Empire to American Hegemony: Koreans and Okinawans in the Resettlement of Northeast Asia*. Honolulu: University of Hawaii Press, 2023.
Bsheer, Rosie, and Mohammed Alsudairi. "Inter-Asian Cold War Linkages: The Middle East in the World." *Comparative Studies of South Asia, Africa and the Middle East* 43, no. 3 (December 2023): 337–42.
"Budget: AP's & Allocations etc., 1954/55 (Korea–Administration)." Records of the Asia Foundation. Hoover Archives, Stanford University. Palo Alto, CA.
"Chaeil sahakcha Yi Chinhŭi [Ri Chinhŭi] kyosu, Chŏng Kuho ponsa sajang yebang." *Kyŏnghyang sinmun*, January 22, 1982, 10.
"Chaeil sahakcha Yi Chinhŭi [Ri Chinhŭi] ssi, Han-Il kwan'gyesa t'amgu wihae naehan." *Kyŏnghyang sinmun*, May 3, 1982, 2.
"Chaeil tongp'odŭl kwa kwiguk tongp'odŭl ŭi saenghwal ŭl panyŏng han yŏn'gŭk: *Na ege nŭn choguk i itta* (P'yŏngyang kŭkchang)." *Chosŏn sinbo*, January 25, 1965, 4.
"Ch'aek kap." *Sae sedae* 110 (April 1964): 72–73.
"Chaju chŏngsin, chaju p'andan, kŭrigo chaju ch'ŏriman i chaju minjok kukka rŭl chajujŏk ŭro kkŭlgo kal su innŭn, yangbo hal su ŏmnŭn taewŏnch'ik." *Rodong sinmun*, April 2, 1963, 3.
"Chakka Yi Hoesŏng [Ri Kaisei], Kim Talsu ssi tŭng 13-myŏng: Choch'ongnyŏn chungangwi sŏ sukch'ŏng." *Tonga ilbo*, August 1, 1972, 1.
Chang, Chunghyŏn. "Choguk e taehan taham ŏmnŭn ch'an'ga: Yŏn'gŭk *Na ege nŭn choguk i itta* rŭl pogo." *Rodong sinmun*, January 1, 1965, 6.
Chang, Habo. "Uri nŭn kkŭnnae chik'irira." *Chosŏn nyŏsŏng* 198 (April 1964): 40.
Chang, Munsŏk. "1960–1970-nyŏndae Ilbon ŭi Han'guk munhak yŏn'gu wa 'Chosŏn munhak ŭi hoe': Taech'on Ikpu [Ōmura Masuo] kyosu ege chilmun handa." *Han'gukhak yŏn'gu* 40 (February 2016): 171–218.
Chang, Munsŏk. "Wŏlbuk chakka ŭi haegŭm kwa chakp'umjip ch'ulp'an (1): 1985–1989-nyŏn sigi rŭl chungsim ŭro." *Kubo hakpo* 19 (2018): 39–110.
Chang, Munsŏk. "Yŏndae ŭi inyŏm esŏ chuch'esŏng ŭi segye ro: Naengjŏn'gi Ilbon ŭi Chosŏn munhak yŏn'gu wa Chosŏnŏ." *Ilbon pip'yŏng* 27 (August 2022): 76–119.
Chang, Sejin. "Wŏnhan, nosŭt'aeljia, kwahak: Wŏllam chisigindŭl kwa 1960-nyŏndae Pukhan hakji ŭi sŏngnip sajŏng." *Sai* 17 (November 2014): 141–80.
Chang, T'aeksang. "Sok-Songbon Ch'ŏngjang [Matsumoto Seichō] ege munnŭnda." *Tonga ch'uch'u* 2, no. 1 (January 1963): 214–20.
Chappel, James. "The Catholic Origins of Totalitarianism Theory in Interwar Europe." *Modern Intellectual History* 8, no. 3 (November 2011): 561–90.
Chatani, Sayaka. "Becoming Korean: Japanese Wives in the Boundary Formation of a Leftist Zainichi Community." *Critical Asian Studies* 54, no. 1 (January 2022): 105–27.
Chatani, Sayaka. "Revisiting Korean Slums in Postwar Japan: *Tongne* and *Hakkyo* in the Zainichi Memoryscape." *Journal of Asian Studies* 80, no. 3 (August 2021): 587–610.

"Che 2-ch'a Chosŏn chakka taehoe e komu toen chaeil Chosŏn chakkadŭl ŭi saeroun p'obu: chwadamhoe (1)." *Haebang sinmun*, October 27, 1956, 4.

"Che 2-hoe Ilbon sok e Hanminjoksa t'ambang: sago." *Chosŏn ilbo*, October 22, 1988, 1.

Chi, Myŏngsun. "Kwiguk han kŭriun tongmu ege." *Chosŏn sinbo*, December 14, 1963, 4.

Chi, Tongsik. "Hyŏndaein ŭi wigi wa Yesu K'ŭrisŭt'o." *Yŏnhŭi ch'unch'u*, July 3, 1954, 2.

Chi, Tongsik. "In'gan e taehan sogo: Kidokkyo ŭi ipchang esŏ." *Sasanggye* 1 (April 1953): 53–60.

Chin, Hŭigwan. "Chaeil Han'gugin sahoe hyŏngsŏng kwa Choch'ongnyŏn kyŏlsŏng paegyŏng yŏn'gu." *T'ongil munje yŏn'gu* 31 (May 1999): 80–106.

Chin, Hŭigwan. "Choch'ongnyŏn yŏn'gu: Yŏksa wa sŏnggyŏk ŭl chungsim ŭro." PhD dissertation. Tongguk University, 1998.

Chin, Yŏngsuk. "Na[i] ŏrin sonyŏ Chin Yŏngsuk ŭi yusŏ." *Munhak sinmun*, October 4, 1960, 4.

Chin, Yŏngsuk. "Saengmyŏng ŭl pach'yŏ ssauryŏmnida: Ŏmŏni ege namgin yusŏ." *Chosŏn ilbo*, May 1, 1960, 4.

Cho, Chaech'ŏn. "Songbon Ch'ŏngjang [Matsumoto Seichō] ege munnŭnda." *Tonga ch'unch'u* 1, no. 1 (December 1962): 82–94.

Cho, Chaech'ŏn. "Sasil ŭl waegok haji malla: Ilbon wŏl chapchi *Chungang kongnon* [Chūō kōron] e ponaenŭn konggae sŏhan." *Han'guk ilbo*, January 8, 1963, 7.

Cho, Haeil. *Im Kkŏkchŏng e kwanhan ilgop kae ŭi iyagi*. Seoul: Ch'aek sesang, 1986. Reprint, 2000.

Cho, Haeil. "Im Kkŏkchŏng 2." In *Wangsimni*, 28–34. Seoul: Samjungdang, 1975.

Cho, Haeil. "Im Kkŏkchŏng." *Hyŏndae munhak* 19, no. 3 (March 1973): 218–25.

Cho, Hyang. "20-segi munye sajo." *Sasang* 1, no. 4 (December 1952): 159–77.

Cho, Kyuha. "Nambuk ŭi taehwa (69)–'Mi-So Kongwi' wa 'hapchak undong' (3)—6.25 ro kkŭnnan '38 up'yŏnmul.'" *Tonga ilbo*, March 30, 1972, 5.

Cho, Kyuha. "Nambuk ŭi taehwa (85)–Chŏngbu surip kwa 6.25 chŏnhu (5)–Nambuk mulcha kyoyŏk (Sang)." *Tonga ilbo*, April 29, 1972, 5.

Cho, Kŭnwŏn. "Chosŏn ŭi ŏmŏni: pulkul ŭi hyŏngmyŏng t'usa Ma Tonghŭi tongji ŭi moch'in Chang Kilbu nyŏsa." *Rodong sinmun*, October 27, 1965, 2.

Cho, Namdu. "Hana ŭi kamhoe." *Chosŏn sinbo*, March 11, 1961, 4.

Cho, Pyŏgam. "Choguk t'ongil kwa nambuk Chosŏn munhwa kyoryu rŭl wihayŏ." *Choguk chŏnsŏn*, October 18, 1956, 3.

Cho, Pyŏnghwa. "T'ongil iyŏ! Yŏllyŏra." *Chosŏn sinbo*, January 22, 1965, 3.

Cho, P'ungyŏn. "Chinsil ŭi tam'gu rŭl wihayŏ." *Tonga ch'uch'u* 2, no. 2 (February 1963): 140–46.

Cho, P'ungyŏn. "Songbon Ch'ŏngjang [Matsumoto Seichō]-ron." *Tonga ch'uch'u* 2, no. 1 (January 1963): 222–27.

Cho, Yŏngho. "Poribap." *Sae sedae* 111 (May 1964): 88–89.

Cho, Yŏnhyŏn. "Han Sŏrya ssi ege ponaenŭn sŏhan: chagi ege tora kara." *Taejo* 4, no. 1 (March 1949): 28–32.

Cho, Yŏnhyŏn. "Hyŏndae ŭi wigi wa munhak chŏngsin ŭi panghyang." *Chayu segye* 1, no. 5 (August–September 1952): 101–9.

Cho, Yŏnhyŏn. "Mek'anijŭm eŭi kyŏnggye." *Sinsajo* 2, no. 2 (October 1951): 79–81.

Cho, Yŏnhyŏn. "Sinhwa wa pigŭk ŭl samk'in Im Hwa [Rim Hwa]." *Tonga ch'unch'u* 2, no. 4 (April 1963): 347–51.

Cho, Yŏnhyŏn. "Sŏ." In Kim Yun, *Mŏngdŭn kyejŏl: Kim Yun sijip*, 8–9. Seoul: Hyŏndae munhaksa, 1968.

"Choguk munhwa pogŭp ssent'ŏ: Kuwŏl sŏbang saok yaksŏngsik." *Chosŏn minbo*, January 28, 1958, 2.

"Choguk ŭro put'ŏ kŏaek ŭi kyoyukpi wa changhakkŭm." *Chosŏn minbo*, April 25, 1957, 1.

Choi, Deokhyo. "Crucible of the Post-Empire: Decolonization, Race, and Cold War Politics in US-Japan-Korea Relations, 1945–1952." PhD dissertation. Cornell University, 2013.

Choi, Deokhyo. "Fighting the Korean War in Pacifist Japan: Korean and Japanese Leftist Solidarity and American Cold War Containment." *Critical Asian Studies* 49, no. 4 (October 2017): 546–68.

Choi, Deokhyo. "The Empire Strikes Back from Within: Colonial Liberation and the Korean Minority Question at the Birth of Postwar Japan, 1945–47." *American Historical Review* 126, no. 2 (June 2021): 555–84.

"Ch'ŏlbuji tongsaeng ŏpko yurang 8-nyŏn kkŭt e Sin sonyŏn ŭn ŏdi ro kanŭnga?" *Sae sedae* 116 (October 1964): 126–27.

"Chŏnjin hanŭn munhwa undong: Songnyŏn munhak yesurin chwadamhoe." *Chosŏn minbo*, December 28, 1957, 4.

"Chŏsok han Ilbon sŏjŏk, kongbo ch'ŏsŏ ilche apsu." *Chosŏn ilbo*, April 29, 1954, 2.

"'Chosŏn sidae t'ongsinsa:' Chaeil kogohakcha Yi Chinhŭi [Ri Chinhŭi] ssi kangyŏn." *Maeil kyŏngje*, January 25, 1982, 9.

Chung, Steven. *Split Screen Korea: Shin Sang-ok and Postwar Cinema*. Minneapolis: University of Minnesota Press, 2014.

Chŏn, Chun. *Choch'ongnyŏn yŏn'gu che 2-kwŏn*. Seoul: Korea University Press, 1972.

Chŏn, Hwagwang. "Han'guk nyusŭ." *Chosŏn munye* 7 (1957): 18–19. Facsimile edition in Unoda Shōya, ed., *Zainichi Chōsen bungakukai kankē shiryō, 1945–1960* (vol. 2). Commentary by Song Hyewŏn. Tokyo: Ryokuin shobō, 2018, 246–47.

Chŏn, Ponggu. *Nae insaeng nae chige e chigo*. Seoul: Taedong Munhwasa, 1965.

Chŏn, Ponggu. "Nae insaeng nae chige e chigo (1–3)." *Chosŏn nyŏsŏng* 222–224 (April–June 1966): 70–75, 85–88, 84–88.

Chŏn, Sangsuk. "Sasang t'ongje chŏngch'aek ŭi yŏksasŏng: Pan'gong kwa chŏnhyang." *Han'guk chŏngch'i oegyosa nonch'ong* 27, no. 1 (2005): 75–110.

Chŏn, Tongu. "Kŭ punno rŭl anko naa kasira! Namchosŏn han ŏmŏni ege." *Munhak sinmun*, April 30, 1963, 4.

Chŏng, Chonghyŏn. "*P'ibada* wa 'chuch'e munhak iron' ŭi kwallyŏn yangsang." *Han'guk munhak yŏn'gu* 25 (2002): 343–62.

Chŏng, Kyubok. "'Namjŏnggi' ŭi chŏjak tonggi e taehayŏ: Kim Hyŏnyong ssi ŭi 'Sassi namjŏnggi yŏn'gu' rŭl ilkko." *Sŏngdae munhak* 15/16 (February 1970): 35–39.

Chŏng, Pyŏngjun. "1945–1948 Mi-So ŭi 38-sŏn chŏngch'aek kwa nambuk kaltŭng ŭi kiwŏn." *Chung-So yŏn'gu* 100 (2003–2004): 179–204.

Chŏng, Ut'aek. "'Han Haun sijip sakŏn' ŭi ŭimi wa Yi Pyŏngch'ŏl." *Sanghŏ hakpo* 40 (2014): 147–84.

Ch'ae, Kyusang. "Hanggŏ hanŭn nyŏsŏngdŭl." *Chosŏn nyŏsŏng* 223 (May 1966): 78–81.

Ch'oe, Chinsŏk. "Naengjŏn'gi Han'guk chisigin ŭi pŏnyŏk silch'ŏn: 1960-nyŏndae *Sasanggye* ŭi pŏnyŏk charyo sŏnbyŏl ŭl chungsim ŭro." *Inmun kwahak* 85 (May 2022): 157–92.
Ch'oe, Inho. "I ch'aek ŭl ilki chŏn e: Chakka ŭi mal." In *Irhŏbŏrin wangguk* 1, 13–16. Seoul: Usŏk, 1986.
Ch'oe, Inho. "Irhŏbŏrin wangguk (669)." *Chosŏn ilbo*, May 8, 1987, 7.
Ch'oe, Inho. "Irhŏbŏrin wangguk (944)." *Chosŏn ilbo*, March 30, 1988, 9.
Ch'oe, Inuk. "Chŏnjaeng munhwaron." *Sinch'ŏnji* 6, no. 1 (January 1951): 77–81.
Ch'oe, Tokkyŏn. "Ch'anggansa." *Chŏnsŏn munhak* 1, no. 1 (April 1952): 9.
Ch'oe, T'aeŭng. "Wŏlbuk munhwain ŭi pigŭk (1, 2a, 2b, 3, 4, 5, 6)." *Sasanggye* 115–120 (December 1962–June 1963): 264–70; 288–94; 315–21; 359–67; 388–94; 344–51; 295–301.
Ch'ŏng, Ak. "Wŏnssudŭl ege pulbyŏrak ŭl." *Chosŏn sinbo*, July 23, 1970, 4.
Ch'ŏng, Am "Noye ŭi munhak kwa panhang ŭi munhak: Purŭjyoajŏk hyumanijŭm ŭi ponjil." *Chosŏn munhak* 133 (September 1958): 164–71.
Ch'ŏng, Am. "Namchosŏn esŏ Mije ka ryup'o hanŭn purŭjyoa pandong mihak ŭi ponjil." *Chosŏn munhak* 122 (October 1957): 120–32.
Clark, Julia Hansell. "Reclaiming Landscape: Place and Personhood in the Literature of Ikaino." PhD dissertation. University of California, Los Angeles, 2023.
Cutchins, Dennis. "Bakhtin, Intertextuality, and Adaptation." In *The Oxford Handbook of Adaptation Studies*, edited by Thomas Leitch, 71–86. New York: Oxford University Press, 2017.
"Daily Journals, Civil Information and Education Section, 1–29 Feb. 1952." Staff Section Report, Public Works, for Month of January 1952 (3 of 3), Entry UNCACK, Box 5753, UN Civil Assistance Command, Korea (UNCACK), 1952. General Correspondence, 1951–1955. Records of US Army Operational, Tactical, and Support Organizations (World War II and Thereafter), 1917–1993, RG 338. National Archives. College Park, MD. Digitized by the National Institute of Korean History. http://archive.history.go.kr/id/AUS004_77_00C0109_009.
Elfving-Hwang, Joanna. "Cross-Border Representation in South and North Korean Literatures of the Cold War Period." In *Global Cold War Literatures: Western, Eastern and Postcolonial Perspectives*, edited by Andrew Hammond, 43–57. New York: Routledge, 2012.
"Establishment of Prisoner of War Labor Detachment, Tokyo Area (May 17, 1951)." Entry 1182-A-54, 2nd Logistical Command, 1951, Box 28 (3)-2. Records of the US Eighth Army 2nd Logistical Command, 1951. Records of US Army Operational, Tactical, and Support Organizations (World War II and Thereafter), 1917–1993, RG 338. National Archives, College Park, MD. Digitized by the National Institute of Korean History. http://archive.history.go.kr/id/AUS004_28_00C0009_099.
Fernandez, Ramon. "Humanisme de l'Action." In *Examen de Conscience* (Cahiers du Mois 21/22), edited by Marcel Arland, 93–97. Paris: Éditions Émile-Paul Frères, 1926.
"Fukkan no shi." *Haebang sinmun*, May 20, 1952, 1.
Gabroussenko, Tatiana. *Soldiers on the Cultural Front: Developments in the Early History of North Korean Literature and Literary Policy*. Honolulu: University of Hawaii Press, 2010.
Gheorghiu, C. Virgil. *The Twenty-Fifth Hour*. Translated by Rita Eldon. New York: Knopf, 1950.

Glade, Jonathan. "Fracturing Literary Boundaries: Connecting with the Korean Peninsula in Postwar Japan." In *Routledge Handbook of Modern Korean Literature*, edited by Yoon Sun Yang, 116–27. New York: Routledge, 2020.
Ha, Chaedŏk. "Nunmul i p'inŭn iyagi." *Sae sedae* 111 (May 1964): 88–89.
Ha, Kirak. "Hyŏndae ŭi sasangjŏk kwaje." *Sasanggye* 44 (March 1957): 23–30, 42.
Ha, Kirak. "In'gan ŭi chokŏn." *Sasanggye* 50 (September 1957): 75–82.
Hagiwara, Toshihiko. "Wangin kwa Paekche wangssi." *Ilbon munje* 3 (Summer 1973): 160–65.
Hagiwara, Toshihiko. "Wani to Kudara ōshi." *Nihon no naka no Chōsen bunka* 10 (June 1971): 4–9.
"'Hagwŏn e chayu rŭl talla!' Chiptan siwi, kyesok kakchi ro hwaktae." *Chosŏn minbo*, March 16, 1960, 2.
Ham, Sŏkhŏn. "Minjung iyŏ no hara!" *Chosŏn nyŏsŏng* 206 (December 1964): 67–69.
Ham, Tŏgil. "Chuin'gong ŭi sŏnggyŏk palchŏn kwa chuje sasang ch'ŏnmyŏng e hullyunghi pongmu han ŭmak: Yesul yŏnghwa *Uri ege nŭn choguk i itta* ŭi ŭmak hyŏngsang ŭl tugo." *Chosŏn yesul* 146 (September 1968): 83–90.
"Han'guk wŏn pŏpsang ege murŏ ttŭtkin Songbon Ch'ŏngjang [Matsumoto Seichō] ssi." *Tonga ch'uch'u* 2, no. 2 (February 1963): 134–39.
Han, Hyo. "Chayŏnjuŭi rŭl pandae hanŭn t'ujaeng e issŏsŏ ŭi Chosŏn munhak (3)." *Munhak yesul* 6, no. 3 (March 1953): 110–54.
"Han kudu takki sonyŏ ka purŭn norae." *Ch'ŏllima* 81 (June 1965): 112.
Han, Sunmi. "Han'guk hyŏndae munhak esŏŭi ŏmŏni p'yosang kwa hŭisaeng sŏsa." *Sŏktang nonch'ong* 50 (2011): 465–96.
Han, Yŏnghwan. "Pokkwi." *Munhak yesul* 2, no. 3 (August 1955): 83–95.
Hino, Ashihei. "Kosei no utsukushisa toku: Kitasen no sakka Kan Setsuya [Han Sŏrya] si." *Asahi shimbun*, May 30, 1957, 8.
Hirabayashi, Taiko, Kim Tongni, and Yŏ Sŏkki. "Han-Il munhak ŭl marhanda: Ilbon yŏryu chakka P'yŏngnim Taija [Hirabayashi Taiko] wa hamkkye." *Sasanggye* 110 (August 1962): 238–47.
Hirabayashi, Taiko. "25ji no sakusha Giorugyu [Gheorghiu] to monogataru." *Yomiuri shimbun*, June 26, 1952, 5.
Hiromitsu, Inokuchi. "Korean Ethnic Schools in Occupied Japan, 1945–1952." In *Koreans in Japan: Critical Voices from the Margin*, edited by Sonia Ryang, 140–56. New York: Routledge, 2000.
Hong, Chonguk. "Yŏksa hakcha Pak Sihyŏng ŭi minjok kwa kwahak." *Yŏksa kyoyuk* 165 (March 2023): 1–46.
Hong, Sajung. "Hyŏndae ŭi chisŏng kwa sin eŭi chŏpkŭn: K'ap'ŭk'a [Kafka] ŭi kyŏng'u (1–2)." *Hyŏndae munhak* 1, nos. 11–12 (November–December 1955): 158–64; 142–48.
Hong, Tuwŏn. "Namchosŏn ŏrinidŭl ŭi pich'amhan ch'ŏji." *Rodong sinmun*, June 1, 1956, 3.
Hughes, Theodore Q. *Literature and Film in Cold War South Korea: Freedom's Frontier*. New York: Columbia University Press, 2012.
Hughes, Theodore Q. "Writing the Boundaries of the Divided Nation: The Works of Son Ch'ang-sŏp, Ch'oe In-hun, Nam Chŏng-hyŏn, and Lee Ho-Chul." PhD dissertation. University of California, Los Angeles, 2002.
Hwang, Kŭmch'an. "Chŏlmŭn sanmaektŭl." *Chosŏn ilbo*, May 30, 1960, 4.

Hŏ, Namgi, ed. and trans. *Chōsen shisen*. Tokyo: Aoki shoten, 1955.
Hŏ, Namgi. *Uri ege nŭn choguk i itta*. Pyongyang: Munye ch'ulp'ansa, 1969.
Hŏ, Namgi. "Nae o ueru hitobito: Kugatsu shobō tanbōki." *Chōsen sōren*, May 21, 1958, 2.
Hŏ, Namgi. "Uri ege nŭn choguk i itta." In *Chuch'e ŭi han kil esŏ: Chaeilbon Chosŏnin Ch'ongnyŏnhaphoe yŏltasŏt tol kinyŏm chakp'umjip*, 7–104. Tokyo: Chaeilbon Chosŏn munhak yesulga tongmaeng, 1970.
Hŏ, Ongnyŏ. "Uri ŭi chihyang ŭl magŭl su ŏpta." *Chosŏn sinbo*, April 23, 1969, 4.
"Hong Myŏnghŭi chak *Im Kŏjŏng* p'an'gŭm." *Tonga ilbo*, October 7, 1985, 6.
"Hyosŏng ŭi puksori." *Sae sedae* 113 (July 1964): 85–88.
"I nara animyŏn kugyŏng mothal 'kyoyuk pigŭk.'" *Sae sedae* 109 (March 1964): 64–65.
"I ŏmŏni rŭl kuwŏn haja!" *Rodong sinmun*, April 29, 1965, 3.
"Ibuk innŭn kajok ege p'yŏnji pangsong kaesi." *Tonga ilbo*, May 22, 1960, 3.
Iizuka, Kōji. "25ji wa wareware no jikoku." *Tenbō* 58 (October 1950): 19–21.
"Il puron sŏjŏk ŭl apsu." *Tonga ilbo*, April 29, 1954, 2.
"Ilbon chapchi sijŏng p'anmae tansok kanghwa." *Kyŏnghyang sinmun*, November 8, 1952, 2.
"Ilbon chapchi suip purhŏ." *Tonga ilbo*, September 11, 1951, 2.
"Ilbon kodaesa nŭn uri sŏnjodŭl ŭi iminsa." *Chosŏn ilbo*, October 22, 1986, 7.
"Ilbon munhwa ŭi wŏllyu." *Rodong sinmun*, March 16, 1986, 4.
"Ilbon sok e Hanminjoksa t'ambang: sago." *Chosŏn ilbo*, November 6, 1987, 1.
"Ilbon sŏjŏk do, kongbo ch'ŏ hŏga oenŭn ilchŏl ch'wich'e." *Chosŏn ilbo*, October 7, 1951, 2.
"Ilbon ŭi chugan chapchi *Chugan choil* [*Shūkan asahi*] (6-wŏl 26-il ho) ka tamsi 'Ojŏk' ŭi chŏnmun ŭl pŏnyŏk hayŏ sirŏtta." *Chosŏn sinbo*, June 18, 1970, 3.
"Ilbonin Chosap'yo (Tong P'yŏngyang sŏ)." Shipping Advice 2006 Item 75. Records of Foreign Documents Seized, RG 242. National Archives, College Park, MD. Digitized by the National Library of Korea. www.nl.go.kr.
"Ilbonin Kiryubu, Tong P'yŏngyang sŏ." Shipping Advice 2005 9/18 part 13–15. Records of Foreign Documents Seized, RG 242. National Archives, College Park, MD. Digitized by the National Library of Korea. www.nl.go.kr.
"Ilche sigi Okkinawa e kkŭllyŏ on han halmŏni ŭi p'i ŭi kobal." *Chosŏn sinbo*, April 23, 1977, 3.
"Ilsŏ man'gan." *Kyŏnghyang sinmun*, April 8, 1950, 2.
"Ilsŏjŏk pŏnyŏngmul tansok, Yi kongbo ch'ŏjang tam." *Kyŏnghyang sinmun*, April 7, 1950, 2.
Im, Chungbin. "Yŏksa munhak pangbŏmnon sŏsŏl." *Sŏngdae munhak* 13 (1967): 84–93.
Im, Ch'un'gap. "Sasaek ilgi." *Hyŏndae kongnon* 1, no. 1 (October 1953): 110–12.
Im, Hŏnyŏng. "Kŭndae munhaksa non'go." *Ch'angjak kwa pip'yŏng* 10, no. 1 (March 1975): 69–88.
Im, Hŏnyŏng. "Kŭndae sosŏl sahoesa sigo." *Kiwŏn* 1, no. 3 (December 1973): 123–36.
Im, Kŭngjae. "Hoeŭi wa mosaek ŭi kyeje." *Munhwa segye* 1, no. 1 (July 1953): 30–35.
Im, Suil. "Paegŭi ŭi sugi (1–2)." *Munhak sinmun*, August 17–August 24, 1962, 4.
"Int'ŏbyu: Ilbon sŏ munbak hagwi padŭn Kim Unhak sŭnim." *Tonga ilbo*, April 28, 1973, 5.
Jager, Sheila Miyoshi. *Narratives of Nation-Building in Korea: A Genealogy of Patriotism*. New York: Routledge, 2003.
"Japanese-North Korean trade and contacts" (April 4, 1950, CIA-RDP82-00457 R004600240002-7). CIA Freedom of Information Act Electronic Reading Room.

Accessed February 23, 2024. https://www.cia.gov/readingroom/document/cia-rdp82-00457r004600240002-7.
"Kamdong purŭmyŏ ryŏllin misulchŏn chinhaeng: Ch'ongnyŏn-Mindan misurindŭl i son ŭl chapko." *Chosŏn sinbo*, May 6, 1961, 4.
Kang, Chuyŏng. "1980-nyŏndae Pukhan ŭi tanp'yŏn sosŏl esŏ ch'aja pon Namhan munhak ŭi hŭnjŏk: Kim Kwanil ŭi 'Ch'ŏngnyŏn kaech'ŏkja ŭi sugi' wa Ro Chŏngbŏp ŭi 'Nae kohyang ŭi chagŭn tari' rŭl chungsim ŭro." *Han minjok ŏmunhak* 71 (2015): 621–55.
Kang, Myŏnghŭi. "Niisan to neesan wa naze jyū de utareta no desu ka." In *Chi no shigatsu: Minami Chōsen jinmin hōki*. Tokyo: Chōsen bunkasha, 1960.
Kang, Myŏnghŭi. "Oppa wa ŏnni ka wae p'i hŭllyŏnŭnji." *Chosŏn ilbo*, April 23, 1960, 3.
Kang, Myŏnghŭi. "Oppa wa ŏnni nŭn wae ch'ong e majannayo." *Chosŏn sinbo*, April 19, 1973, 4.
Kang, Myŏnghŭi. "Oppa wa ŏnni nŭn wae ch'ong e majannayo." *Munhak yesul* 6 (May 1963): 66–67.
Kang, Myŏnghŭi. "Oppa wa ŏnni rŭl ttarŭryŏmnida." *Adong munhak* 93 (August 1960): 78–79.
Kang, Myŏnghŭi. "Uri nŭn oppa wa ŏnni ŭi twi rŭl ttarŭryŏmnida." *Chosŏn minbo*, May 16, 1960, 4.
Kang, Myŏnghŭi. "Watashi wa shitte imasu." *Atarashii sedai* 1, no. 6 (July 1960): 13.
Kang, Sinjae. "Chŏnt'ugi." *K'omet'ŭ* 1, no. 1 (November 1952): 138–41. Digital copy from Air Force of the Republic of Korea, http://afzine.co.kr/home/view.php?host=main&site=20190721_041348_104&listPageNow=0&list2PageNow=0&code=1418&code2=0&code3=0&optionlisttype=L&listcount=10&searchcode=0&searchcode2=0&searchdate=0&searchkey=&searchval=&searchandor=AND&dummy=&&orders=.
Kang, Sinjae. "San kisŭk." *Sinch'ŏnji* 9, no. 3 (March 1954): 266–71.
Kang, Sun. "Pulkil." *Chosŏn minbo*, March 28, 1960, 4.
Kang, Sun. "Pulkil." *Munhak sinmun*, April 12, 1960, 1.
Kang, Sun. "Yusŏ kat'ŭn mal ŭl namgigo." *Chosŏn sinbo*, March 4, 1964, 4.
Kang, Sŏnghyŏn. "Han'guk ŭi kukka hyŏngsŏnggi 'yewoe sangt'ae sangnye' ŭi pŏpchŏk kujo: Kukka poanbŏp (1948, 1949, 1950) kwa Kyeŏmbŏp (1949) ŭl chungsim ŭro." *Sahoe wa yŏksa* 94 (2012): 87–128.
Kang, Yŏngju. "*Im Kkŏkchŏng* ŭi ch'angjak kwajŏng kwa *Chosŏn wangjo sillok*." *Han'guk hyŏndae munhak yŏn'gu* 20, no. 20 (December 2006): 13–47.
"Kankoku moto hosho ni kamitsukareta Matsumoto Seichō shi." *Shūkan yomiuri* 21, no. 52 (December 1962): 20–24.
"Kankoku gun'pōkaigi no han'ketsu ni kōgikōdō hirogaru: Kokusaiteki na rentai mo Tōkyō de ha hansuto." *Asahi shimbun*, July 17, 1974, 19.
Kee, Kwang-seo. "The Historical Origins and Formation of the Monolithic Political System in North Korea." In *Understanding North Korea: Indigenous Perspectives*, edited by Han Jong-woo and Jung Tae-hern, 13–35. New York: Lexington Books, 2014.
Kief, I Jonathan. "Closed Borders and Open Letters in the Postcolonial Koreas." In *Routledge Companion to Korean Literature*, edited by Heekyoung Cho, 427–40. New York: Routledge, 2022.
Kief, I Jonathan. "'Antagonistic Unity:' Kim Oseong, Dialectical Anthropology, and the Discovery of Literature, 1929–1938." *Review of Korean Studies* 16, no. 2 (December 2013): 81–124.

Kief, I Jonathan. "In the Southern Half of Our Republic: Cross-Border Writing and Performance in 1960s North Korea." *Journal of Asian Studies* 81, no. 1 (February 2022): 81–100.

Kief, I Jonathan. "Reading Seoul in Pyongyang: Cross-Border Mediascapes in Early Cold War North Korea." *Journal of Korean Studies* 26, no. 2 (October 2021): 325–48.

Kim, Chaeha. "Hangil mujang t'ujaeng kwajŏng e ch'angjo toen hyŏngmyŏngjŏk yŏn'gŭk (1–4)." *Chosŏn yesul* 43–46 (March–June 1960): 9–11; 5–7; 6–8; 7–9, 12.

Kim, Chaejun. *Kim Chaejun chŏnjip (vol. 2): Pogŭm ŭi chayu (1950–1953)*. Osan: Changgong Kim Chaejun moksa kinyŏm saŏphoe, 1992.

Kim, Chaejun. "Kŏnsŏljŏk t'ujaeng." In *Kyesi wa chŭngŏn*, 21–31. Seoul: Sae saramsa, 1956.

Kim, Chaeyong. *Pundan kujo wa Pukhan munhak*. Somyŏng ch'ulp'an, 2012.

Kim, Charles R. *Youth for Nation: Culture and Protest in Cold War South Korea*. Honolulu: University of Hawaii Press, 2017.

Kim, Cheehyung Harrison. *Heroes and Toilers: Work as Life in Postwar North Korea, 1953–1961*. New York: Columbia University Press, 2018.

Kim, Chiha. "Gozoku." *Koria hyōron* 113 (August 1970): 50–59.

Kim, Chiha. "Gozoku." *Shin Nihon bungaku* 277 (August 1970): 116–24.

Kim, Chiha. "Ojŏk." *Chosŏn sinbo*, June 4, 1970, 8.

Kim, Chiha. "Ojŏk." *Sasanggye* 205 (May 1970): 231–48.

Kim, Chonghoe. "Pukhan munhak e nat'anan Masan ŭigŏ wa 4-wŏl hyŏngmyŏng." *Hyŏndae munhak iron yŏn'gu* 30 (2007): 5–25.

Kim, Chongmun. "Chŏnjaeng kwa sŏnjŏn." *Chŏnsŏn munhak* 1, no. 1 (October 1950): 10–22.

Kim, Chongt'ae. "Chaju charip ŭl wi haesŏnŭn oese rŭl paegyŏk haeya handa." *Rodong sinmun*, January 30, 1964, 3.

Kim, Chunghŭi. "Ch'adan." *Sasanggye* 24 (June 1955): 93–103.

Kim, Chŏngbae. "Kodae Han-Il kwan'gyesa ŭi il-tanmyŏn: Kwanggaet'o taewangnŭng pimun ŭi munjejŏm." *Sindonga* 96 (August 1972): 132–38.

Kim, Ch'aesu. "Kangsang P'abu [Egami Namio] ŭi kima minjok chŏngboksŏl ŭi ch'urhyŏn paegyŏng e kwanhan koch'al." *Tongbuga munhwa yŏn'gu* 21 (2009): 565–87.

Kim, Ch'ŏljun. "Paekche sahoe wa kŭ munhwa (3)." *Kyŏnghyang sinmun*, December 17, 1973, 5.

Kim, Haegyun. "Namchosŏn munhak i kŏrŏ on kil." *Chosŏn munhak* 221 (January 1966): 95–100.

Kim, Haegyun. "Namchosŏn pandong munhak esŏŭi p'ŭroidŭjuŭi." *Kŭlloja* 257 (October 1964): 38–44.

Kim, Hat'ae. "Sin chŏngt'ongp'a sinhak e taehan soron." *Sinhak nondan* 3 (March 1957): 7–15.

Kim, Hojin. "Ch'ŏl ŭi changmak: 38-sŏn tapsa (7)." *Tonga ilbo*, October 2, 1947, 2.

Kim, Hongsik. "Tŏ nŭn ch'amŭl su ŏpta." *Chosŏn minbo*, June 8, 1957, 4.

Kim, Hun. "Fukkan o shukusu." *Haebang sinmun*, May 20, 1952, 1.

Kim, Hyŏngsŏk. "25-si ŭi in'gan ch'ŏrhak: Hyumŏnijŭm ŭi wigi." *Sasanggye* 77 (December 1959): 106–13.

Kim, Hyŏngsŏk. "In'gan ŭi hak kwa hyŏndae ch'ŏrhak: Hyŏndae munje wa in'ganhak ŭl wihan susang." *Sasanggye* 30 (January 1956): 227–37.

Kim, Immanuel. *Rewriting Revolution: Women, Sexuality, and Memory in North Korean Fiction*. Honolulu: University of Hawaii Press, 2018.

Kim, Immanuel. "South Korean Activist Readers of North Korean Literature." In *Routledge Handbook of Modern Korean Literature*, edited by Yoon Sun Yang, 156–67. New York: Routledge, 2020.

Kim, Insŭng. "Minjok ŭl chom mŏngnŭn 38-sŏn choeaksang." *Chosŏn ilbo*, November 19, 1946, 2.

Kim, Jeong Min. "Intimate Exchanges: Korean Women, American GIs and the Making of the Wartime Political Economy of South Korea during the Korean War, 1950–1953." PhD dissertation. New York University, 2017.

Kim, Kiwan. "Chŏnjaeng kwa munhak." *Munye* 2, no. 7 (December 1950): 18–19.

Kim, Kwangju. "P'yojŏng: Kangaji ŭi monorogŭ." *Sinjo* 1, no. 1 (June 1951): 7–12.

Kim, Kyŏngho. "Saeroun mosaek: Sangbannyŏn ŭi nambanbu mundan kaegwan." *Munhak sinmun*, July 5, 1963, 4.

Kim, Kyŏnghŏn. "Kongil nal en chugŏdo chohŭn'ga." *Sae sedae* 109 (March 1964): 65.

Kim, Min. "Kaeiji annŭn hanŭl." *Chosŏn munye* 4 (December 1956): 11–14. Facsimile edition in Unoda Shōya, ed., *Zainichi Chōsen bungakukai kankē shiryō, 1945–1960* (vol. 2). Commentary by Song Hyewŏn. Tokyo: Ryokuin shobō, 2018, 155–58.

Kim, Min. "Nun ttŭnŭn inhyŏng (1–5)." *Chosŏn minbo*, February 1–February 10, 1960, 4.

Kim, Minsŏn. "1950–1960-nyŏndae Nambukhan SF yŏn'gu." PhD dissertation. Tongguk University, 2020.

Kim, Monica. *Interrogation Rooms of the Korean War*. Princeton, NJ: Princeton University Press, 2019.

Kim, Myŏnghwa. *Hyŏngmyŏng ŭi kil esŏ: Hyŏngmyŏng chŏnt'ong yŏn'gu charyo* (Vol. 1). Pyongyang: Nodongdang ch'ulp'ansa, 1960.

Kim, Myŏngsu, *Namnyŏk ŭi ŏmŏni* (1–2). *Chosŏn yesul* 114–115 (February–March 1966): 33–48; 33–41.

Kim, Namch'ŏn. "Kim Ilsŏng ryŏngdo ha e changsŏng palchŏn hanŭn Chosŏn minjok munhak yesul." *Munhak yesul* 5, no. 7 (July 1952): 104–21.

Kim, Ojun. "Hangil t'ujaeng sigi e ch'angjo toen hyŏngmyŏngjŏk munhak yesul." *Choguk* 1, no. 6 (June 1964): 88–93.

Kim, Pongyŏp, and Ri Kwiyŏng. "Yŏn'gŭk *Pukkŭksŏng*." *Chosŏn yesul* 130 (July 1967): 41–42.

Kim, Pyŏngik. "Memarŭn Ilbon e ssakt'ŭnŭn Han'guk munhak." *Tonga ilbo*, July 5, 1971, 5.

Kim, Pyŏngik. "Sansil (2): Munhak p'yŏngnon'ga Kim Yunsik." *Tonga ilbo*, October 23, 1972, 5.

Kim, Pyŏngik. *Han'guk mundansa: 1908–1970*. Seoul: Munhak kwa chisŏngsa, 2001.

Kim, P'albong [Kim Kijin]. "Pungnyŏk edo pom i onŭnde: Yi Kiyŏng [Ri Kiyŏng] ege." *Pukhan* 1, no. 2 (February 1972): 103–4.

Kim, Sangdon. "Kongp'o wa t'anap kwa pujŏng ŭi togani." *Rodong sinmun*, March 13, 1958, 3.

Kim, Sanggi. "Irin i waegok han Han'guksa (5): Kodae ŭi Han-Il sagwan." *Kyŏnghyang sinmun*, February 2, 1966, 5.

Kim, Sangwŏn. "Choguk t'ongil." *Chosŏn nyŏsŏng* 208 (February 1965): 28.

Kim, Song. "Ch'ŏnggaeguri." *Chosŏn munhak* 118 (June 1957): 50–59.

Kim, Song. "Minju munhwa ŭi panghyang." *Chayu yesul* 1, no. 1 (November 1952): 32–36.

Kim, Subŏm. "P'oong." *Chosŏn munhak* 226 (June 1966): 49–57.

Kim, Suk-Young. *Illusive Utopia: Theater, Film, and Everyday Performance in North Korea*. Ann Arbor: University of Michigan Press, 2010.

Kim, Sunhwa. "Sŏul ŭi han yŏch'ajang ŭi unmyŏng." *Rodong sinmun*, March 8, 1965, 3.
Kim, Suyŏng. "Kadao nagadao." *Chosŏn hwabo* 90 (January 1964): n.p.
Kim, Suyŏng. "Kadao nagadao." *Rodongja sinmun*, April 19, 1964, 4.
Kim, Suzy. *Everyday Life in the North Korean Revolution, 1945–1950*. Ithaca, NY: Cornell University Press, 2013.
Kim, Suzy. "Mothers and Maidens: Gendered Formation of Revolutionary Heroes in North Korea." *Journal of Korean Studies* 19, no. 2 (Fall 2014): 257–89.
Kim, Sŏgwŏn. "Nambuk kyoyŏk sakŏn kwa na." *Sedae* 87 (October 1970): 188–92.
Kim, Sŏkhyŏng. *Ch'ogi Cho-Il kwan'gye yŏn'gu*. Pyongyang: Sahoe kwahagwon ch'ulp'ansa, 1966.
Kim, Sŏkhyŏng. "Samhan Samguk ŭi Ilbon ryŏlto nae pun'guktŭl e taehayŏ." *Ryŏksa kwahak* 9, no. 1 (January 1963): 1–32.
Kim, Sŏkhyŏng. "Sankan Sangoku no Nihon rettō nai no bunkuni ni tsuite (1–3)." Translated by Chŏng Chinhwa. *Rekishi hyōron* 165, 168, 169 (May, August, September 1964): 19–28; 34–47; 45–54.
Kim, Sŏkpŏm. *Guchi aru mono ha katare*. Tokyo: Chikuma Shobō, 1975.
Kim, Sŏkpŏm. "Ch'wiu." In *Chaeil tiasŭp'ora munhak sŏnjip* vol. 2, 101–45. Translated by Kim Haktong. Seoul: Somyŏng, 2018.
Kim, Sŏkpŏm. "Honbaek." In *Honbaek*, edited by Kim Tongyun, 23–34. Seoul: Pogosa, 2021.
Kim, Sŏkpŏm. "Kin Shika [Kim Chiha] to zainichi Chōsenjin bungakusha." In *Kotoba no jubaku: Zainichi Chōsenjin bungaku to Nihongo*, 267–70. Tokyo: Chikuma Shobō, 1972.
Kim, Sŏkpŏm. "Shūu." *Kikan sanzenri* 2 (Summer 1975): 196–221.
Kim, Sŏkpŏm. "Yoru." In *Yoru*, 7–47. Tokyo: Bungei shunshū, 1973.
Kim, Sŏkpŏm. "'Kon/Han' to *Ryōshin sengen*." In *Minzoku, kotoba, bungaku*, 145–57. Tokyo: Sōjusha, 1976.
Kim, Sŏnghan. "Sŏninjang ŭi hangŭi." *Munhwa segye* 2, no. 1 (January 1954): 226–37.
Kim, Sŏngsu. "1990-nyŏndae ch'o munyeji ŭi t'ongil tamnon kwa Pukhan munhak chŏnyu pangsik pip'an: Pukhan munyeji *Chosŏn munhak* kwaŭi maech'esajŏk taehwa." *Sanghŏ hakpo* 54 (2018): 11–47.
Kim, Sŏngsu. "4.19 wa 1960-nyŏndae Pukhan munhak–Sŏndong kwa sot'ong sai e: Pukhan chakka ŭi 4.19 tamnon kwa chŏnyu pangsik pip'an." *Han'guk kŭndae munhak yŏn'gu* 30 (2014): 7–40.
Kim, Sŏngsu. "Chae/wŏlbuk chakka 'haegŭm' choch'i (1988) ŭi yŏn'gusa/munhwasajŏk ŭimi." *Sanghŏ hakpo* 55 (2019): 11–49.
Kim, Sŏngsu. "Pukhan Chosŏn munhak yesul ch'ongdongmaeng ŭi yŏksajŏk pyŏnch'ŏn (1946–1953)." *T'ongil chŏngch'aek yŏn'gu* 33, no. 1 (2024): 209–36.
Kim, Sŏngsu. "Pukhan ŭi Namhan munhwa yesul insik e taehan yŏksajŏk koch'al." *T'ongil chŏngch'aek yŏn'gu* 10, no. 1 (2001): 241–68.
Kim, Talsu. "Chōsen bungaku ni okeru yūmoa to fūshi: Kin Ryū [Kim Rip] to Kin Shika [Kim Chiha] no shi o chūshin ni." *Bungaku* 38, no. 11 (November 1970): 54–65.
Kim, Talsu. "Chōsen to Man'yōshū." *Kokubungaku* 17, no. 6 (May 1972): 157–62.
Kim, Talsu, ed., Kim Pyŏngwŏn, trans., "Ri Kiei [Ri Kiyŏng] no shōgai to chosaku." *Shin Nihon bungaku* 10, no. 8 (August 1955): 131–39.

Kim, Talsu, Ri Chinhŭi, Kang Chaeŏn, and Ch'oe Yŏnghŭi. *Sindonga* 201 (May 1981): 108–19.

Kim, Talsu, Tanigawa Ken'ichi, and Okazaki Takashi. "Han'guk munhwa wa Ilbon munhwa." *Ilbon munje* 2 (Spring 1973): 134–55.

Kim, Talsu, Tanigawa Ken'ichi, and Okazaki Takashi. "Nihon bunka to Chōsen bunka: Genkainada no rekishiteki imi." *Bessatsu keizai hyōron* 10 (September 1972): 16–30.

Kim, T'aegyŏng. "*Haesin* kwa kugŏ kongbu." *Haebang sinmun*, December 30, 1952, 3.

Kim, Ullyong. "Punno ŭi norae." *Munhak sinmun*, April 22, 1960, 4.

Kim, Unhak. "Hyangga wa Ilbon kayo waŭi kwan'gye." *Tongguk taehakkyo nonmunjip* 13 (December 1974): 97–117.

Kim, Unhak. "Hyangga wa Manyŏpchip." *Hyŏndae munhak* 21, no. 12 (October 1975): 38–53.

Kim, Yerim. *1930-nyŏndae huban kŭndae insik ŭi t'ŭl kwa miŭisik*. Seoul: Somyŏng ch'ulp'an, 2004.

Kim, Yongho. "Haemada 4-wŏl." *Chosŏn ilbo*, April 28, 1960, 4.

Kim, Yongsŏng. "Temok'ŭrasi wa che-sam seryŏk." *Sinsajo* 4, no. 2 (May/June 1953): 54–60.

Kim, Yosŏp. "Gunshū." *Atarashii sedai* 1, no. 6 (July 1960): 12.

Kim, Youna. "Illicit Media, Reflexivity and Sociocultural Change in North Korea." *International Journal of Cultural Studies* 27, no. 2 (March 2024): 165–80.

Kim, Yun. *Möngdŭn kyejŏl: Kim Yun sijip*. Seoul: Hyŏndae munhaksa, 1968.

Kim, Yunho. "Hoaebul ŭn t'abŏnjinda." *Chosŏn sinbo*, July 14, 1970, 4

Kim, Yunsik, and Kim Hyŏn. "Yŏng-Chŏngjo esŏ 4.19 e irŭnŭn Han'guk munhaksa (1)." *Munhak kwa chisŏng* 3, no. 1 (March 1972): 202–10.

Kim, Yunsik. "Im Hwa [Rim Hwa] yŏn'gu: Pip'yŏngkaron ki-7." *Nonmunjip: Inmun sahoe kwahak p'yŏn* 4 (April 1972): 35–64.

Kim, Yunsik. "Wŏlbuk chakka haegŭm ŭn munhaksa sae chŏn'gi." *Tonga ilbo*, July 20, 1988, 8.

Ko, Samyŏng. "'Furusato' to no kaikō." *Tenbō* 157 (January 1972): 126–35.

Ko, Samyŏng. "Haehu." In *Chaeil tiasŭp'ora munhak sŏnjip* vol. 2, 147–77. Translated by Sin Sŭngmo. Seoul: Somyŏng, 2018.

Ko, Samyŏng. "Kiki no jidae ni oite Kin Shika [Kim Chiha] o omou." *Shin Nihon bungaku* 31, no. 12 (December 1976): 40–42.

Ko, Samyŏng. "'Gozoku' no Shijin." *Waseda bungaku* 6, no. 7 (July 1974): 64–72.

Ko, Samyŏng. "'Kaikō." *Kikan sanzenri* 3 (Fall 1975): 198–216.

Ko, Yangsun. "Au ŭi yŏngjŏn e." *Chosŏn nyŏsŏng* 198 (April 1964): 40.

Ko, Yangsun. "Otōto no reizen ni." *Atarashii sedai* 2, no. 3 (April 1961): 10–11.

"Kodae Irŏ e tturyŏthan uri mal yŏnghyang." *Tonga ilbo*, February 13, 1973, 5.

Komatsu, Kiyoshi. "Chishikijin huronto no dentō: Huransu no bai ni tsuite." *Risō* 208 (August 1950): 63–68.

Komatsu, Kiyoshi. "Futsubungaku no ittenki." *Kōdō* 2, no. 8 (August 1934): 22–33.

Komatsu, Kiyoshi. "Hitotsu no kaisō to hitotsu no kibō." *Sekai* 55 (July 1950): 65–69.

Komatsu, Kiyoshi. *Kōdō shugi bungakuron*. Tokyo: Kinokuniya shuppanbu, 1935.

Komatsu, Kiyoshi. "Marurou [Malraux] to Girisia no hakken." *Risō* 213 (January 1951): 1–16.

Komatsu, Kiyoshi et al. "Zaidankai: Nihon o ika ni shite eiru ka?" *Shakai shichō* 33 (March 1951): 24–33.

"Kongbu hanŭn kŏt poda nŭn pae kop'ŭn kŏt i tŏ kŭphayŏ." *Sae sedae* (October 1964): 128.
"Konghwaguk nambanbu e taehan Mije ŭi 'kyŏngje wŏnjo' chŏngch'e." *Rodong sinmun*, February 26, 1949, 3.
Koo, Sunhee. *Sound of the Border: Music and the Identity of Korean Minority in China*. Honolulu: University of Hawaii Press, 2021.
Koshmann, J. Victor. *Revolution and Subjectivity in Postwar Japan*. Chicago: University of Chicago Press, 1996.
"Koyongju e chitpalp'in se sonyŏn." *Sae sedae* 118 (December 1964): 124–25.
Ku, Chungsŏ. "Han'guk munhaksa pangbŏmnon yŏn'gu." MA thesis. Myŏngji University, 1977.
Ku, Chungsŏ. "Wasŏ chedan pusura." *Choguk t'ongil*, June 12, 1963, 4.
Ku, Chungsŏ. "Wasŏ chedan pusura." *Chosŏn sinbo*, April 24, 1963, 3.
Ku, Chungsŏ. "Wasŏ chedan pusura." *Han'guk ilbo*, April 18, 1963, 5.
Ku, Chungsŏ. "Wasŏ chedan pusura." *Munhak sinmun*, April 16, 1965, 4.
Ku, Inhwan. "P'anjajip kŭnŭl (1–2)." *Munhak sinmun*, December 11–25, 1962, 4.
Ku, Inhwan. "P'anjajip kŭnŭl." *Hyŏndae munhak* 7, no. 8 (August 1961): 94–113.
Kukka poanbŏp (pŏmnyul che 10-ho). Republic of Korea. Enacted December 1, 1948. https://www.law.go.kr/LSW//lsInfoP.do?efYd=19481201&lsiSeq=7221&ancYd=19481201&nwJoYnInfo=N&ancNo=00010&chrClsCd=010202&efGubun=Y#0000.
Kukka poanbŏp (pŏmnyul che 85-ho). Republic of Korea. Enacted December 19, 1949. https://www.law.go.kr/LSW//lsInfoP.do?lsiSeq=7222&ancYd=19491219&ancNo=00085&efYd=19500109&nwJoYnInfo=N&efGubun=Y&chrClsCd=010202&ancYnChk=0#0000.
Kukka poanbŏp (pŏmnyul che 500-ho). Republic of Korea. Enacted December 26, 1958. https://www.law.go.kr/LSW//lsInfoP.do?lsiSeq=7224&ancYd=19581226&ancNo=00500&efYd=19590116&nwJoYnInfo=N&efGubun=Y&chrClsCd=010202&ancYnChk=0#0000.
"Kukkyŏnghwa hanŭn 38-sŏn: T'onggwa yŏhaeng ŭl purhŏ, kunjŏngch'ŏng oemuch'ŏ palp'yo." *Tonga ilbo*, May 24, 1946, 2.
"K'ŭn p'adong irŭk'in changp'yŏn *Puk ŭi siin* [Kita no shijin]." *Kyŏnghyang sinmun*, December 29, 1962, 5.
Kwak, Chongwŏn. "Munhak chŏngsin ŭi hwangnip." *Chayu segye* 1, no. 1 (January 1952): 161–67.
Kwak, Chongwŏn. "Munhak undong ŭi puhŭngnon." Reprinted in *Sin in'ganhyŏng ŭi t'amgu*, 103–13. Seoul: Tongsŏ munhwasa, 1955.
Kwak, Chongwŏn. "Sae in'ganhyŏng ŭi hyŏngsŏng e taehan kusang." *Sinsajo* 2, no. 1 (September 1951): 16–21.
"Kwanggo: 25-si." *Sint'aeyang* 1, no. 3 (October 1952): back cover.
Kwŏn, Myŏnga. "Yŏsŏng sunansa iyagi: Minjok kukka mandŭlki wa yŏsŏngsŏng ŭi tongwŏn." *Yŏsŏng munhak yŏn'gu* 7 (2002): 105–34.
Kwŏn, Pyŏngsun. "Kudu takki sonyŏ ŭi si." *Chosŏn nyŏsŏng* 213 (July 1965): n.p.
Kwŏn, Pyŏngsun. "Kudu takki sonyŏ ŭi si." *Yŏwŏn* 11, no. 3 (March 1965): n.p.
Kye, Puk. "Namchosŏn ŭi pandongjŏk purŭjyoa mihak ŭi chŏngch'e." *Chosŏn munhak* 106 (June 1956): 166–82.
Leake, Elisabeth. "On Asian Borders: The Value of Comparative Studies." In *Decoding the Sino-North Korean Borderlands*, edited by Adam Cathcart, Christopher Green, and Steven Denney, 45–58. Amsterdam: Amsterdam University Press, 2021.

Lee, Misook. "The Japan-Korea Solidarity Movement in the 1970s and 1980s: From Solidarity to Reflexive Democracy." *Asia-Pacific Journal/Japan Focus* 12, iss. 38, no. 1 (September 21, 2014). https://apjjf.org/2014/12/38/Misook-Lee/4187.html.

Lee, Namhee. *The Making of Minjung: Democracy and the Politics of Representation in South Korea*. Ithaca. NY: Cornell University Press, 2016.

Lewis, Su Lin. "Asian Socialism and the Forgotten Architects of Post-Colonial Freedom, 1952–1956." *Journal of World History* 30, no. 1/2 (June 2019): 55–88.

Lie, John. *Zainichi (Koreans in Japan): Diasporic Nationalism and Postcolonial Identity*. Berkeley: University of California Press, 2008.

Lie, John. "Korean Diaspora and Diasporic Nationalism." In *The Routledge Handbook of Korean Culture and Society*, edited by Youna Kim, 245–54. New York: Routledge, 2017.

Literary Research Division, Language and Literary Research Institute, DPRK Academy of Sciences, ed. *Chosŏn munhak t'ongsa II*. Pyongyang: Kwahagwŏn ch'ulp'ansa, 1959.

Lottman, Herbert R. *The Left Bank: Writers, Artists, and Politics from the Popular Front to the Cold War*. Chicago: University of Chicago Press, 1982.

Lüthi, Lorenz. *Cold Wars: Asia, the Middle East, Europe*. New York: Cambridge University Press, 2020.

Malraux, André. "Man and Artistic Culture." In *Reflections on Our Age*, 84–99. New York: Columbia University Press, 1949.

"Manhwa mukkŭm: Namchosŏn p'unggyŏng." *Sae sedae* 117 (November 1964): 138–39.

Matsumoto, Seichō. "Minami Chōsen no gunji seiken ni omou." *Atarashii sedai* 2, no. 8 (October 1961): 34–35.

Matsumoto, Seichō. "Seiji mondai to ha betsu ni kangaeyo." *Chōsen jihō*, October 12, 1963, 3.

Mauriac, François. "La Résistance Spirituelle." *Le Figaro*, February 20, 1950, 1.

"Merry Xmas." *Sint'aeyang* 1, no. 5 (December 1952): n.p.

"Migun chudun ha 38-sŏn inam singnyang sat'ae wigi e chŏlbak!" *Rodong sinmun*, April 19, 1949, 3.

Min, Sukcha. "Oppa ege." *Sae sedae* 79 (August 1961): 22–23.

Morris-Suzuki, Tessa. *Borderline Japan: Foreigners and Frontier Controls in the Postwar Era*. New York: Cambridge University Press, 2010.

Morris-Suzuki, Tessa. *Exodus to North Korea: Shadows from Japan's Cold War*. New York: Rowman & Littlefield, 2007.

"Mot salketta nŭn hasoyŏn ppun." *Chosŏn nyŏsŏng* 203 (September 1964): 36–37.

Mun, Chŏngch'ang. *Ilbon sanggosa*. Seoul: Paengmundang, 1970.

Mun, Chŏngch'ang. "Kodae Ilbon ŭi chibaech'ŭng kwa Samhan Samguk: Kodae Han-Il kwan'gye ŭi silsang." *Sindonga* 101 (January 1973): 84–95.

Myers, Brian. *Han Sŏrya and North Korean Literature: The Failure of Socialist Realism in the DPRK*. Ithaca, NY: Cornell East Asia Series, 1994.

Méray, Tibor. "Han siin ŭi ch'uŏk: Sŏl Chŏngsik ŭi pigŭk." Translated by Han Ch'ŏlmo. *Sasanggye* 111 (September 1962): 222–27.

"Na to karyŏnda." *Sae sedae* 116 (October 1964): 130.

"Nae adŭl changhage chugŏtkuna!" *Han'guk ilbo*, April 24, 1960, 3.

"Nae adŭl changhage chugŏtkuna!" *Samch'ŏlli* 11 (June 1965): 41.

"Naeil ullyŏnda." *Han'guk ilbo*, April 25, 1960, 3.
Nail, Thomas. *Theory of the Border*. New York: Cambridge University Press, 2012.
Nakahashi, Kazuo. "Jiyūjin no risōzō: Daisan no tachiba ni tsuite." *Gunzō* 6, no. 3 (March 1951): 87–91.
Nakahashi, Kazuo. "Seiōteki chisei no kyōryoku o." *Kindai bungaku* 5, no. 5 (May 1950): 24–27.
Nam, Chŏnghyŏn. "Pujujŏn sangsŏ." *Choguk t'ongil*, September 16–19, 1964, 4.
Nam, Chŏnghyŏn. "Pujujŏn sangsŏ." *Munhak sinmun*, September 18, 1964, 3
Nam, Chŏnghyŏn. "Pujujŏn sangsŏ." *Sasanggye* 135 (June 1964): 358–75.
Nam, Chŏnghyŏn. "Pyŏrak ŭn tangsin i mandŭsyŏya hamnida." *Rodong sinmun*, September 21, 1964, 3.
Nam, Keun Woo. "Rethinking the North Korean Repatriation Program: The Change from an 'Aid Economy' to a 'Hostage Economy.'" *Korean Social Sciences Review* 2, no. 2 (2012): 219–51.
Nambanbu e kwanhan charyojip. Pyongyang: Kungnip inmin ch'ulp'ansa, 1949. Shipping Advice 2005 Item 2/108. Records of Foreign Documents Seized, RG 242. National Archives, College Park, MD. Digitized by the National Library of Korea. www.nl.go.kr.
"Nambanbu tongp'o waŭi ryŏn'gye haksŭp tŭng." *Haebang sinmun*, February 23, 1956, 2.
"Nambuk kyoyŏk paeksŏ." *Maeil kyŏngje*, August 15, 1972, 9.
"Namchosŏn kyoyuk ŭi pup'aesang." *Rodong sinmun*, March 19, 1955, 3.
"National Accounts Estimates of Main Aggregates: Per capita GDP at current prices–US dollars." United Nations Statistics Division. Accessed November 30, 2024. https://data.un.org/Data.aspx?d=SNAAMA&f=grID%3A101%3BcurrID%3AUSD%3BpcFlag%3A1.
Nishitani, Keiji. "Kyomu kara no dasshutsu: 25ji ni miru Seiyō to Tōyō no mondai." *Kaizō* 31, no. 12 (December 1950): 9–18.
"Nŏ nŭn changhage ssawŏtta." *Samch'ŏlli* 11 (June 1965): 40.
"Nŏlli Ilbon inmin sok ŭro." *Haebang sinmun*, January 1, 1950, 2.
O, Changhwan. "The Last Train." In *Hŏnsa*, n.p. Seoul: Namman sŏbang, 1939.
O, Chŏngsam. "In'gansŏng ŭi ch'ubang: Ch'oegŭn Namchosŏn munhak ŭi tonghyang." *Munhak sinmun*, August 25, 1959, 3.
O, T'aeho. "'Ŭnghyang kyŏlchŏngsŏ' rŭl tullŏssan haebanggi mundan ŭi insingnonjŏk ch'ai yŏn'gu." *Ŏmun nonjip* 48 (November 2011): 37–46.
O, Yŏngsu. "Anna ŭi yusŏ." *Chosŏn nyŏsŏng* 211–213 (1965): 126–30; 131–34.
"Oegukin kiryubu (Ilbonin) (Hŭngnam-si Inmin Wiwŏnhoe Naemusŏ)." Shipping Advice 2006 Item 70. Records of Foreign Documents Seized, RG 242. National Archives, College Park, MD. Digitized by the National Library of Korea. www.nl.go.kr.
Oh, Taeyoung. "The Reorganization of Space and Literary Representation of Seoul during the Liberation Period, 1945–1950." *Inter-Asia Cultural Studies* 25, no. 2 (2024): 185–98.
Okada, Seishi. "Edo makbu sidae ŭi 'Chosŏnin kado.'" *Ilbon munje* 3 (Summer 1973): 144–51.
Okada, Seishi. "'Chōsenjin kaidō' no koto." *Nihon no naka no Chōsen bunka* 6 (June 1970): 38–44.
Ŏm, Hosŏk, "Uri munhak e issŏsŏ ŭi chayŏnjuŭi wa hyŏngsikchuŭi chanjae waŭi t'ujaeng." *Rodong sinmun*, January 17, 1952, 2–3.

"Ŏmma pap chom chuso." *Chosŏn minbo*, April 13, 1957, 2.

Ōmura, Masuo. "Kaihōgo no Rin Wa [Rim Hwa]." *Shakai kagaku tōkyū* 13, no. 1 (1967): 99–125.

Oppenheim, Robert. *Kyŏngju Things: Assembling Place*. Ann Arbor: University of Michigan Press, 2008.

"Organizations in Kaesŏng, North Korea" (October 23, 1953, CIA-RDP80–00810A0026-00770010–8). CIA Freedom of Information Act Electronic Reading Room. Accessed February 23, 2024. https://www.cia.gov/readingroom/document/cia-rdp80-00810a002600 770010-8.

"Ŏrinidŭl ŭi haengbok ŭl wihaesŏ." *Rodong sinmun*, June 1, 1956, 2.

Orwell, George. *1984-nyŏn*. Translated by Chi Yŏngmin. Seoul: Munye sŏrim, 1951.

Paek, Chuja. "Kippŭm." *Chosŏn minbo*, December 4, 1959, 4.

Paek, Ch'ŏl. "Oeguk chakp'um kwa kŭ pŏnyŏk: Kŭllae ŭi pŏnyŏk sosŏl ŭl chungsim hayŏ." *Munye* 4, no. 5 (November 1953): 36–43.

Paek, Ch'ŏl. "P'ian." *Sinch'ŏnji* 7, no. 3 (May 1952): 47–49.

Paek, Ch'ŏl. "Saeroun in'gan kwan'gye ŭi munje: munhwa ongho ŭi 1-p'oint'ŭ." *Chayu segye* 1, no. 3 (April 1952): 176–82. Facsimile edition in *Han'guk pundan munhak pip'yŏng charyojip* Namhan p'yŏn, vol. 3, edited by Chŏn Kich'ŏl, 135–41. Seoul: Han'guk yesulsa, 1998.

Paek, Injun. "Munhak yesul ŭn inmin ege pongmu hayŏya hal kŏt ida: Wŏnsan munhak tongmaeng p'yŏnjip sijip *Ŭnghyang* ŭl p'yŏng ham." *Rodong sinmun*, December 25, 1946, 2–3.

Paek, Sŏk. "Ch'on esŏ on ai." *Munjang* 3, no. 4 (April 1941): 168–69.

Paek, Sŏk. "Hŭin parambyŏk i issŏ." *Munjang* 3, no. 4 (April 1941): 165–67.

Pak, Ch'unhŭi. "Kigŭn chiok ŭro hwa han Namchosŏn." *Ch'ŏllima* 29 (February 1961): 77–79.

Pak, Hwamok. "Sa-wŏl." *Chosŏn ilbo*, May 3, 1960, 4.

Pak, Hwamok. "Sinbun chŭngmyŏngsŏ." *Kyŏnghyang sinmun*, June 5, 1952, 2.

Pak, Hyŏk. *Chosŏn ŭi ŏmŏni*. In *Pak Hyŏk hŭigokchip: Chosŏn ŭi ŏmŏni*, 5–96. Pyongyang: Chosŏn chakka tongmaeng ch'ulp'ansa, 1960.

Pak, Im. "Namchosŏn pandong munhak pup'aesang ŭi ilmyŏn." *Rodong sinmun*, January 13, 1954, 3.

Pak, Kijun. "Han'guk chakka ŭi pansŏng." *Chŏnsŏn munhak* 1, no. 1 (April 1952): 13–15.

Pak, Kwanbŏm, "Nuna wa hamkke." In *Kkot p'inŭn kil: Pak Kwanbŏm tanp'yŏnjip*, 126–48. Pyongyang: Munye ch'ulp'ansa, 1991.

Pak, Kwangt'aek. "Hyŏndaep'an 'Ojŏk.'" *Munhak yesul* 33 (August 1970): 53–57.

Pak, Min'gyu. "*Ŭnghyang* sakŏn ŭi paegyŏng kwa yŏp'a." *Hanminjok munhwa yŏn'gu* 44 (2013): 285–318.

Pak, Myŏngch'ŏl. "Kudu takki sonyŏ." *Sonyŏndan* 189 (July 1965): 36–39.

Pak, Seyŏng. "Sech'age t'a pŏnjira hangjaeng ŭi pulkil." *Rodong sinmun*, April 21, 1960, 3.

Pak, Sihyŏng. *Kwanggaet'owang Rŭngbi*. Pyongyang: Sahoe kwahagwŏn ch'ulp'ansa, 1966.

Pak, Tujin. "A Choguk." *Chosŏn sinbo* April 28, 1973, 4.

Pak, Tujin. "A Choguk." *Chosŏn sinbo*, April 19, 1975, 2.

Pak, Tujin. "A Choguk." *Chosŏn sinbo*, January 27, 1965, 3.

Pak, T'aewŏn. "Chebi (1–2)." *Chosŏn ilbo*, February 22–February 23, 1939, 5.

Pak, Wŏnjun. "Hwansong (1–23)." *Chosŏn sinbo*, March 4–May 20, 1961, 4.

Pak, Yŏngil. "Kŭm panji." *Chosŏn nyŏsŏng* 210 (April 1965): 104–7.

Pan'gongbŏp (pŏmnyul che 643-ho). Republic of Korea. Enacted July 3, 1961. https://www.law .go.kr/LSW/lsInfoP.do?lsiSeq=3534&ancYd=19610703&ancNo=00643&efYd=19610703 &nwJoYnInfo=N&efGubun=Y&chrClsCd=010202&ancYnChk=0#0000.

"P'anmunjŏmhaeng yŏbi mogŭm undong chŏn'gae k'iro." *Kyŏnghyang sinmun*, May 13, 1961, 3.

"Pip'an toeŏya hal Miguk ŭi wŏnjo chŏngch'aek." *Rodong sinmun*, December 9, 1963, 3.

"Pukchosŏn chaeryu oegukin 18-se isang chosap'yo (Ilbonin) (Hŭngnam-si Inmin Wiwŏnhoe Naemusŏ, 1949)." Shipping Advice 2005 9/13 part 2. Records of Foreign Documents Seized, RG 242. National Archives, College Park, MD. Digitized by the National Library of Korea. www.nl.go.kr.

"Punno ŭi hwasan ŭn t'ŏjyŏtta: Kungnip yŏn'gŭk kŭkchang kongyŏn." *Rodong sinmun*, June 5, 1960, 5.

"Puron sŏjŏk p'anmae ŏpja 5-myŏng chŏngsik kusok." *Chosŏn ilbo*, July 23, 1957, 2.

Ra, Sŭngim. "Yŏn'gŭk *Namnyŏk ŭi ŏmŏni* ŭi Sunnyŏ yŏk." *Chosŏn yesul* 129 (May–June 1967): 56–59.

Ri, Chinhŭi. *Haehyŏp: Han chaeil sahakcha ŭi pan p'yŏngsaeng*. Translated by Yi Kyusu. Seoul: Samin, 2003.

Ri, Chinhŭi. *Kwanggaet'o wangbi ŭi t'amgu*. Translated by Yi Kidong. Seoul: Iljogak, 1982.

Ri, Chinhŭi. *Kōkaido-ō ryōhi no kenkyū*. Tokyo: Yoshikawa kōbunkan, 1972.

Ri, Chinhŭi. *Kōtaiōhi no nazo: Nihon kodaishi o kaki kaeru*. Tokyo: Kodansha, 1973.

Ri, Chinhŭi. "Kodaishi o kakikaete 34-nen." *Higashi Aji no kodai bunka* 137 (January 2009): 189.

Ri, Chŏnggu. "Han Namchosŏn ŭi chakka ege." *Munhak sinmun*, October 6, 1961, 4.

Ri, Ch'anŭi. "Aegukjuŭi sasang ŭi chego: Chaeil Chosŏnin munhwa undong ŭi hoego wa chŏnmang." *Haebang sinmun*, January 1, 1956, 5.

Ri, Hyo. "Chŏnjaeng ŭl sŏndong hanŭn Namchosŏn pandong munhak." *Rodong sinmun*, October 2, 1954, 3.

Ri, Hyŏn. "Hŏmu wa p'aedŏk ŭi sŏlgyo: Namchosŏn pandong sosŏl 'Ŏttŏn chijŏm esŏ' e taehayŏ." *Munhak sinmun*, May 10, 1959, 3.

Ri, Manyŏng. "Ilp'yŏn tansim ŭl wihayŏ: Hyesan yŏn'gŭktan ŭi yŏn'gŭk *Pukkŭksŏng* ŭl pogo." *Rodong sinmun*, November 6, 1966, 4.

Ri, Ryŏng, "Hangil mujang t'ujaeng sigi ŭi hyŏngmyŏng yŏn'gŭk." *Rodong sinmun*, June 24, 1962, 4.

Ri, Ryŏng. "Hangil mujang t'ujaeng sigi ŭi hyŏngmyŏngjŏk yŏn'gŭk (3)." *Rodong sinmun*, January 13, 1968, 6.

Ri, Sŏngbok. "Aegukchŏk ŏmŏni ŭi sŏkpang ŭl wihayŏ ssawŏra." *Rodong sinmun*, April 27, 1965, 3.

Ri, Sŏngbok. "Ri Kyedan ŏmŏni nŭn mujokŏn sŏkpang toeyŏya handa." *Rodong sinmun*, May 7, 1965, 3.

Rim, Kwangch'ŏl. "Mujŏkon hago kwŏn hal su innŭn uri 'yŏksa' ch'aek." *Haebang sinmun*, February 23, 1954, 2.

Rim, Kyŏngsang. "Song sŏbang (1–5)." *Chosŏn minbo*, March 1–March 29, 1958, 4.

Rim, Kyŏngsang. "Song sŏbang." *Chosŏn munye* 8 (November 1957): 23–32. Facsimile edition in Unoda Shōya, ed., *Zainichi Chōsen bungakukai kankē shiryō, 1945–1960* (vol. 2). Commentary by Song Hyewŏn. Tokyo: Ryokuin shobō, 2018, 285–94.

Ro, Kŭmsŏk. "Ch'oegŭn Namchosŏn sosŏl munhak ŭi ponjil." *Ch'ŏllima* 38 (November 1961): 70–72.

Ro, Kŭmsŏk. "Si munhak esŏ pon Namchosŏn." *Ch'ŏllima* 51 (December 1962): 109–11.

Ro, Pyŏngu. "Tosŏsil sŏlch'i cheŭi rŭl chiji handa." *Haebang sinmun*, August 11, 1956, 3.

Robinson, Michael. *Cultural Nationalism in Korea, 1920–1925*. Seattle: University of Washington Press, 1988.

Roh, David S. *Minor Transpacific: Triangulating American, Japanese, and Korean Fictions*. Palo Alto: Stanford University Press, 2021.

Ryang, Sonia. *North Koreans in Japan: Language, Ideology, and Identity*. Boulder, CO: Westview Press, 1997.

Ryang, Sonia. "Introduction: Resident Koreans in Japan." In *Koreans in Japan: Critical Voices from the Margin*, 1–12. New York: Routledge, 2000.

Ryang, Sonia. "Visible and Vulnerable: The Predicament of Koreans in Japan." In *Diaspora without Homeland: Being Korean in Japan*, edited by Sonia Ryang and John Lie, 62–80. Berkeley: University of California Press, 2009.

Ryang, Sonia, ed. *Koreans in Japan: Critical Voices from the Margin*. New York: Routledge, 2000.

Ryang, Sonia, and John Lie, eds. *Diaspora Without Homeland: Being Korean in Japan*. Berkeley: University of California Press, 2009.

Ryu, Ch'ip'yo. "Yŏn'gŭk *Pukkŭksŏng* ŭi Hwang ssi yŏk." *Chosŏn yesul* 129 (May–June 1967): 49–55.

Ryu, Pyŏk. "Charang." *Munhak yesul* 2 (March 1960): 79–96.

Ryu, Pyŏk. "Miwansŏng ŭi chahwasang." *Chosŏn minbo*, April 5–May 17, 1958, 4.

Ryu, Tohŭi. "Palp'yo toeji mothan kisa." *Munhak sinmun*, April 18, 1961, 2, 4.

Ryu, Youngju. *Writers of the Winter Republic: Literature and Resistance in Park Chung Hee's Korea*. Honolulu: University of Hawaii Press, 2016.

"Salkil ŭn soksumuch'aek." *Sae sedae* 116 (October 1964): 129–30.

Salter, Mark. "Theory of the /: The Suture and Critical Border Studies." *Geopolitics* 17, no. 4 (November 2012): 734–55.

"Sangho wŏnjo." *Haebang sinmun*, November 26, 1955, 2.

Shadel, Kevin. "Ports of Call: A Maritime Study of Korean Modernist Poetry." *Verge: Global Asias* 10, no. 2 (Fall 2024): 191–218.

"Sijip *Ŭnghyang* e kwanhan Pukchosŏn munhak yesul ch'ongdongmaeng sangim wiwŏnhoe ŭi kyŏlchŏngsŏ." *Rodong sinmun*, December 24, 1946, 3.

"Silchik yŏch'ajang i chasal." *Chosŏn ilbo*, March 17, 1964, 7.

Sim, Chaesin. "Hajiru." *Atarashii sedai* 1, no. 6 (July 1960): 11.

Sin, Hyŏndŭk. "I iyagi rŭl ank'o nŭn kyŏndil su ka ŏpkuna." *Sae sedae* 112 (June 1964): 139.

Sin, Tongmun. "Aa nae choguk." *Choguk t'ongil*, May 18, 1963, 3.

Sin, Tongmun. "Aa nae choguk." *Minju ch'ŏngnyŏn*, May 16, 1963, 3.

Sin, Tongmun. "Aa nae choguk." *Munhak sinmun*, August 3, 1965, 4.

Sin, Tongmun. "Aa nae choguk." *Rodongja sinmun*, May 19, 1963, 3.

Sin, Tongmun. "Aa nae choguk." *Sasanggye* 120 (April 1963): 397–99.
Sin, Yŏngdŏk. *Han'guk chŏnjaeng kwa chonggun chakka*. Seoul: Kukhak charyowŏn, 2002.
So, Chaeyŏng. "Kodae sosŏlsa 40-nyŏn ŭi haengjŏk: T'onggyesang ŭro pon pansŏngjŏm kwa munje ŭi chegi." *Sae kugŏ kyoyuk* 13 (December 1969): 46–54.
Son, C. Sarah. *The Comfort Women: Sexual Violence and Postcolonial Memory in Korea and Japan*. Chicago: University of Chicago Press, 2008.
Song, Sukhŭi. "Nodokana Pyonyan no machi." *Atarashii sedai* 1, no. 10 (December 1960): 12–14.
Song, Hyewŏn. "Chaeil Chosŏnin munhaksa" rŭl wihayŏ: Sori ŏmnŭn moksori ŭi p'ollip'oni. Seoul: Somyŏng ch'ulp'an, 2019.
Song, Hyewŏn. "Zainichi Chōsenjin bungakushi" no tame ni: Koe naki koe no porifonī. Tokyo: Iwanami shoten, 2014.
Song, Nam. "Nambanbu nongmindŭl ŭl kiman haryŏnŭn 'nongji kaehyŏkpŏp' ch'oan ŭi chŏngch'e." *Rodong sinmun*, March 5, 1949, 3.
Song, Yŏng. *Paekdusan ŭn ŏdisŏna poinda*. Pyongyang: Minju ch'ŏngnyŏnsa, 1956.
Song, Yŏng. *Punno ŭi hwasan ŭn t'ŏjyŏtta*. *Chosŏn munhak* 154 (June 1960): 22–51.
Song, Yŏngŏn. "Pukhan wŏnjŏn tansok e nollan i k'ŭda." *Tonga ilbo*, April 11, 1989, 5.
"Sŏnjin kwahak t'amgu ŭi chŏndang: Chosŏn Taehak ŭi apkil ŭn yangnyang handa." *Chosŏn minbo*, October 19, 1957, 2.
"Sŏul ŭi pinminch'on Namgajwa-dong sŏŭi ch'amgŭk." *Chosŏn ilbo*, January 26, 1964, 7.
Stockwin, J.A.A. *The Japanese Socialist Party and Neutralism: A Study of Political Party and its Foreign Policy*. New York: Cambridge University Press, 1968.
Suh, Serk-Bae. *Treacherous Translation: Culture, Nationalism, and Colonialism in Korea and Japan from the 1910s to the 1960s*. Berkeley: University of California Press, 2013.
Szalontai, Balázs. *Kim Il Sung in the Khrushchev Era: Soviet-DPRK Relations and the Roots of North Korean Despotism, 1953–1964*. Washington, D.C.: Woodrow Wilson Center Press, 2005.
Sŏ, Sŏkkyu. "Ch'angja rŭl mallinŭn pŏl ŭi choemyŏng ŭn muŏt imnikka?" *Sae sedae* 116 (October 1964): 127–28.
Takakuwa, Sumio. *Yuibutsuron to shutaisei*. Tokyo: Kokudosha, 1948.
Takakuwa, Sumio. "Minshu shugi to hyūmanizumu." *Risō* 5, no. 9 (September 1950): 35–46.
Takakuwa, Sumio. "Shakai shugi no jiyū to dokusai: shizen shugi to rekishi shugi no sōkoku." *Kaizo* 33, no. 7 (May 1952): 25–32.
Takeda, Kiyoko. "Tōyō no jikoku ha?" *Tenbō* 58 (October 1950): 17–19.
Takeuchi, Yoshimi. "Jinruiaku no kokuhatsu: Georgiu [Gheorghiu] 25ji ni tsuite." *Nihon hyōron* 25, no. 10 (October 1950): 28–33.
Takeuchi, Yoshimi. "'Tōhō' e no kyōshū." *Tenbō* 58 (October 1950): 16–17.
"Tansik t'ujaeng 3-iltchae: Sŏul mullidae haksaeng 40-yŏ myŏng." *Kyŏnghyang sinmun*, June 1, 1964, 7.
"Tasŏt p'anmae ŏpcha kusok." *Tonga ilbo*, July 24, 1957, 3.
Taylor, Moe. *North Korea, Tricontinentalism, and the Latin American Revolution, 1959–1970*. New York: Cambridge University Press, 2023.
Textor, Cindi. "Representing Radical Difference: Kim Sŏkpŏm's Korea(n) in Japan(ese)." *Positions: asia critique* 27, no. 3 (August 2019): 499–529.

Textor, Cindi. "Zainichi Writers and the Postcoloniality of Modern Korean Literature." In *Routledge Companion to Korean Literature*, edited by Heekyoung Cho, 225–38. New York: Routledge, 2022.
"38-sŏn kyot'ong t'ongno nŭn (1)." *Tonga ilbo*, December 16, 1945: 2.
"3.15 ŭi punhwagu: Masan sakŏn haebu." *Han'guk ilbo*, March 18, 1960, 2.
Tillich, Paul. "20-segi ŭi in'gansang: Pi in'ganhwa e taehan panhang." *Sasanggye* 32 (March 1956): 22–38, 49.
Tillich, Paul. "The Person in a Technical Society." In *Christian Faith and Social Action: A Symposium*, edited by John Alexander Hutchinson, 137–53. New York: Scribner, 1953.
"Toksŏ annae." *Haebang sinmun*, January 21, 1954, 2.
"Toksŏ annae." *Haebang sinmun*, January 30, 1953, 2.
"Tonggyŏng Hwangch'ŏn [Tōkyō Arakawa], Taep'an [Ōsaka] sŏnŭn Mindan to ch'amka: Kakchi sŏ pŏrŏjinŭn kongdong haengdong." *Haebang sinmun*, August 16, 1956, 3.
"(Tong P'yŏngyang) Ilbonin Kiryubu, Sadong Naemusŏ." Shipping Advice 2005 9/18 part 11. Records of Foreign Documents Seized, RG 242. National Archives, College Park, MD. Digitized by the National Library of Korea. www.nl.go.kr.
"Tonggyŏng esŏ yŏllin ŏnŏ simp'ojium: Koguryŏ ŏnŏ, Kodae Ilbonŏ e k'ŭn yŏnghyang." *Kyŏnghyang sinmun*, February 13, 1973, 5.
"Tongsim ŭn unda." *Sae sedae* 118 (December 1964): 123–24.
"T'oep'ye wa yullak ŭi amdamhan sahoesang." *Rodong sinmun*, January 28, 1949, 3.
"T'ongil ŭl purŭnŭn moksoridŭl." *Chosŏn nyŏsŏng* 208 (February 1965): 29–30.
Treat, John Whittier. "Im Hwa Before and After Japan." *Trans-Humanities* 8, no. 1 (2015): 5–26.
"25-si chakka Keolgyu [Gheorghiu] nŭn marhanda." *Sint'aeyang* 1, no. 5 (December 1952): 75.
Ueda, Masaaki, Kim Talsu, Shiba Ryōtarō, and Murai Yasuhiko. "Nihon no naka no Chōsen." *Nihon no naka no Chōsen bunka* 1 (March 1969): 17–34.
Ueda, Masaaki. "Isonokami jingu to Shichishitō." *Nihon no naka no Chōsen bunka* 9 (March 1971): 4–14.
Ueda, Masaaki. "Sŏksang sin'gung kwa Ch'iljido." *Sindonga* 101 (January 1973): 129–37.
"Ŭijang enŭn Kim Ilsŏng wŏnsu oe 6-myŏng: Han Tŏksu ssido ŭijang e, chungang ŭiwŏn 87-myŏng chung en Ri Simch'ŏl, Hwang Ponggu ssido." *Chosŏn minbo*, December 26, 1957, 2.
"UN Korean Reconstruction Agency Foreign Book Retail Store, Vol. III" (S-0526-0310-0001). UN Archives. New York, NY.
"UN Korean Reconstruction Agency Foreign Book Retail Store, Vols. I–II" (S-0526-0309-0002). UN Archives. New York, NY.
"UN Korean Reconstruction Agency Foreign Book Retail Store (March 4, 1953–December 30, 1954)" (S-0526-0091-0007). UN Archives. New York, NY.
Unoda Shōya, ed. *Zainichi Chōsen bungakukai kankē shiryō, 1945–1960* (vol 1–3). Commentary by Song Hyewŏn. Tokyo: Ryokuin shobō, 2018.
"Usŭm irhŭn kyosil." *Sae sedae* 117 (November 1964): 133–35.
Vinh, Sinh. "Komatsu Kiyoshi and French Indochina." *Moussons: Recherche en Sciences Humaines sur l'Asie du Sud-Est* 3 (June 2001): 57–86.

Wada, Haruki. "Kin Shika [Kim Chiha] o tasukerukai no imi." *Kikan sanzenri* 1 (Spring 1975): 52–61.
Watt, Lori. *When Empire Comes Home: Repatriation and Reintegration in Postwar Japan*. Cambridge, MA: Harvard University Asia Center, 2009.
Wi, Kaya. "Samhan Samguk pun'guksŏl ŭi kusang kwa p'agŭp." *Sahak yŏn'gu* 137 (March 2020): 89–124.
de Wit, Jerôme. "Writing under Wartime Conditions: North and South Korean Writers during the Korean War (1950–1953)." PhD dissertation. Leiden University, 2015.
"Wŏlbuk chakka 5-myŏng ch'ulp'an ch'uga haegŭm." *Kyŏnghyang sinmun*, February 20, 1989, 1.
"Wŏlbuk chakka ŭi munhakchŏk chaep'an." *Tonga ch'unch'u* 2, no. 4 (April 1963): 304–5.
Wŏn, Sŏkp'a. "Ch'oegŭn Namchosŏn pandong si munhak ŭi ponjil." *Munhak sinmun*, April 12, 1959, 4.
Yang, Homin. *Kongsanjuŭi ŭi iron kwa yŏksa: Marksŭ-Reninjuŭi ŭi pi'pan*. Seoul: Chungang munhwasa, 1956.
Yang, Pyŏngsik. "Chŏnjaeng kwa munhwa ŭi kwaje." In *1952-nyŏn*, 137–207. Seoul: Sudo munhwasa, 1951. Facsimile edition in *Han'guk chŏnjaenggi munhak, sugi, chedo charyojip*. Seoul: K'ep'oibuksŭ, 2013. www.krpia.co.kr/product/main?plctId=PLCT00005230.
Yang, Pyŏngsik. "Hyŏndae chisŏng ŭi panghyang: Haengdong ŭro iruwŏ chinŭn." *Sudo p'yŏngnon* 1, no. 3 (August 1953): 75–80.
Yang, Pyŏngsik. "Munhwa wa in'gan: t'ŭkkwŏn ŭisik e panhang hanŭn sin hyumŏnijŭm (1–5)." *Kyŏnghyang sinmun*, October 23–October 31, 1952, 2.
"Yesok ŭro ŭi kil: Woegok toen saengsan kujo, chongsokchŏk kyŏngje ch'eje (I–II)." *Rodong sinmun*, November 1–4, 1963, 3.
Yi, Chongsik. "Ton ilk'o ch'ŏja ilk'o." *Chosŏn ilbo*, June 14, 1970, 7.
Yi, Christina. *Colonizing Language: Cultural Production and Language Politics in Modern Japan and Korea*. New York: Columbia University Press, 2018.
Yi, Ch'ŏlju. "Pukhan ŭi chakka, yesulga (1): Kŭnŭl ŭl kasŭm e anko." *Sasanggye* 123 (July 1963): 248–59.
Yi, Ch'ŏlju. "Pukhan ŭi chakka, yesulga (13): Sŭlp'ŭn unmyŏng ŭi kunsangdŭl." *Sasanggye* 137 (August 1964): 244–52.
Yi, Haenam. "Han Kangnyŏl kyosu chŏ *In'gan kwa sahoe*." *Kyŏnghyang sinmun*, July 6, 1954, 2.
Yi, Haenam. "P'asŭk'al [Pascal] ŭi in'ganhak." *Kyŏnghyang sinmun*, May 30, 1954, 4.
Yi, Haenghwa, and Yi Kyŏnggyu. "Migunjŏnggi ŭi chaeil Chosŏnin kwallyŏn sinmun kisa wa ideollogi." *Ilbon kŭndaehak yŏn'gu* 64 (May 2019): 200–201.
Yi, Haengsŏn. "Keorŭgyu [Gheorghiu] ŭi suyong kwa Han'guk chisŏngsa ŭi *25-si*: Chŏnhu munhak, hyumŏnijŭm, silchonjuŭi, munmyŏng pip'an, pan'gongjuŭi, ŏyong chakka." *Han'gukhak yŏn'gu* 41 (May 2016): 9–41.
Yi, Hanjik. "Kyŏngnyu e puch'inda (3): Kan pam kkum iyagina han chari." *Saebyŏk* 7, no. 5 (May 1960): 32–33.
Yi, Hoch'ŏl. "P'anmunjŏm." *Sasanggye* 92 (March 1961): 374–95.
Yi, Hwan. "Ppasŭkkal [Pascal] sosŏl." *Mullidae hakpo* 2, no. 2 (September 1954): 60–71.
Yi, Hyeryŏng. *Han'guk sosŏl kwa kolsanghakchŏk t'ajadŭl*. Seoul: Somyŏng ch'ulp'an, 2007.

Yi, Insŏk. "In'gan ŭn sara issŭl kwŏlli ga itta." *Choguk t'ongil*, April 27, 1963, 3.
Yi, Insŏk. "In'gan ŭn sara issŭl kwŏlli ga itta." *Chosŏn sinbo*, July 24, 1963, 3.
Yi, Insŏk. "In'gan ŭn sara issŭl kwŏlli ga itta." *Munhak sinmun*, December 11, 1964, 4.
Yi, Insŏk. "In'gan ŭn sara issŭl kwŏlli ga itta." *Sasanggye* 118 (March 1963): 370–71.
Yi, Insŏk. "Tari." *Chayu munhak* 6, no. 9 (September 1961): 171.
Yi, Insŏk. "Tari." *Choguk t'ongil*, January 22, 1964, 4.
Yi, Insŏk. "Tari." *Munhak sinmun*, July 27, 1962, 4.
Yi, Insŏk. "Tari." *Sae sedae* 109 (March 1964): 64–65.
Yi, Kŭnbae. "4.19 e puch'yŏ." *Choguk t'ongil*, May 23, 1964, 4.
Yi, Kŭnbae. "4.19 e puch'yŏ." *Chosŏn sinbo*, April 19, 1965, 3.
Yi, Kŭnbae. "4.19 e puch'yŏ." *Ch'ŏllima* 79 (April 1965): 97.
Yi, Kŭnbae. "4.19 e puch'yŏ." *Kyŏnghyang sinmun*, April 18, 1964, 5.
Yi, Pongbŏm. "*Puk ŭi siin* [Kita no shijin] kwa naengjŏn chŏngch'isŏng: 1960-nyŏndae ch'o Han'guk suyong kwa hyŏnhaet'an nonjŏn ŭl chungsim ŭro." *Han'guk yŏn'gu* 6 (December 2020): 203–52.
Yi, Ponggu. *Kŭriun irŭm ttara: Myŏngdong 20-nyŏn*. Seoul: Yushin munhwasa, 1966.
Yi, Ponggu. "26-si ŭi sŏngji (1–3)." *Sŏul sinmun*, March 4–March 6, 1952, 4.
Yi, Ponggu. "Chapch'o." *Hyŏndae munhak* 5, no. 7 (July 1959): 38–53.
Yi, Ponggu. "Ch'ilmyŏnjo." *Wŏlgan munhak* 5, no. 2 (February 1972): 12–30.
Yi, Ponggu. "Hwaryŏhan kodok." *Munhak ch'unch'u* 9 (December 1964): 16–29.
Yi, Ponggu. "Hŏmanghan paehoe." *Hyŏndae munhak* 14, no. 6 (June 1968): 49–83.
Yi, Ponggu. "Munhakchŏk sanbo (2)." *Hyŏndae munhak* 6, no. 11 (November 1960): 208–18.
Yi, Ponggu. "Munhakchŏk sanbo (4)." *Hyŏndae munhak* 7, no. 2 (February 1961): 296–306.
Yi, Ponggu. "Munhakchŏk sanbo (5)." *Hyŏndae munhak* 7, no. 3 (March 1961): 159–65.
Yi, Ponggu. "Munhakchŏk sanbo (7)." *Hyŏndae munhak* 7, no. 6 (June 1961): 90–97.
Yi, Ponggu. "Myŏngdong 20-nyŏn (6)." *Chosŏn ilbo*, August 12, 1965, 4.
Yi, Ponggu. "Nosŭt'arŭji." *Hyŏndae munhak* 2, no. 7 (July 1956): 62–76.
Yi, Ponggu. "Saem." *Munhwa segye* 1, no. 3 (September 1953): 160–69.
Yi, Ponggu. "Saja ui sŏ." *Hyŏndae munhak* 6, no. 11 (November 1958): 336–46.
Yi, Ponggu. "Sasŭm ch'ŏrŏm." *Chayu munhak* 4, no. 12 (December 1959): 14–21.
Yi, Ponggu. "Ssŭlssŭrhan nŏ ŭi kohyang e." *Chayu munhak* 4, no. 4 (April 1962): 26–38.
Yi, Ponggu. "Yi Sang." *Hyŏndae munhak* 2, no. 3 (March 1956): 18–28.
Yi, Ponggu. "Yŏnghoe." *Hyŏndae munhak* 5, no. 9 (September 1956): 226–36.
Yi, Pongun. "Ŏmŏni." *Munhak sinmun*, October 4, 1960, 4.
Yi, Pongun. "Ŏmŏni." *Tonga ilbo*, April 30, 1960, 4.
Yi, Sunuk. "4-wŏl hyŏngmyŏng kwa Pukhan munhak: Chosŏn Chakka Tongmaeng Chunggang Wiwŏnhoe kigwanji *Munhak sinmun* ŭl chungsim ŭro." *Han'guk minjok munhwa* 40 (2011): 133–65.
Yi, Sunuk. "Nambuk munhak e nat'anan Masan ŭigŏ ŭi silchŭngjŏk yŏn'gu." *Yŏngju ŏmun* 12 (2006): 267–97.
Yi, Wŏnjo. "Paengman ch'ŏnman i hyangnak hal munhak ŭl." *Munhak* 3 (April 1947): 96–97.
Yi, Yunhwa. "Parik'et'ŭ." *Sae sedae* 113 (July 1964): 88.

Yi, Yŏngjae. *Cheguk Ilbon ŭi Chosŏn yŏnghwa: Singminji mal ŭi pando, hyŏmnyŏk ŭi simjŏng, chedo, nolli*. Seoul: Hyŏnsil munhwa, 2008.
Yŏm, Muung. "77-nyŏn sosŏl munhak ŭi sanghwang." In *77-nyŏn munje chakp'um 20-sŏnjip*, edited by Yŏm Muung, 461–80. Seoul: Hanjin ch'ulp'ansa, 1978.
Yŏm, Muung. "Singminji sidae munhak ŭi insik." *Sindonga* 121 (September 1974): 346–57.
Yŏm, Sangsŏp. "San tokkaebi." *Sinsajo* 2, no. 1 (September 1951): 95–106.
Yŏn, Changnyŏl. "Hyŏngmyŏng yŏn'gŭk *Hyŏrhae* e taehayŏ." *Rodong sinmun*, April 14, 1963, 4.
"Yŏnggwang e kadŭkch'an choguk ero ŭi kil: Choguk pangmundan kongno ro hyangbal." *Haebang sinmun*, September 1, 1955, 2.
"Yŏnggwangsŭrŏun hangil mujang t'ujaeng kwajŏng e ch'angjo toen hyŏngmyŏng yŏn'gŭk (3)." *Chosŏn yesul* 144 (July 1968): 58–63.
Yoon, Sonny. "South Korean Media Reception and Youth Culture in North Korea." In *South Korean Popular Culture and North Korea*, edited by Youna Kim, 120–32. New York: Routledge, 2019.
Young, Benjamin. *Guns, Guerillas, and the Great Leader: North Korea and the Third World*. Palo Alto, CA: Stanford University Press, 2021.
Yu, Chuhyŏn. "Insaeng ŭl pul sarŭnŭn saramdŭl." *Munhak yesul* 3, no. 8 (August 1956): 51–60.
Yu, Chuhyŏn. "Yujŏn 24-si." *Sasanggye* 22 (May 1955): 159–81.
Yu, Chuhyŏn. "Yŏng." *Ch'anggong* 1, no. 1 (March 1952): 26–34.
Yu, Kŏnho. "Sŏgŭlp'ŭn 38 wŏlgyŏng." *Chosŏn ilbo* May 9, 1947, 2.
Yu, Sŏngho. "Haebang chikhu Pukhan mundan hyŏngsŏnggi ŭi sijŏk hyŏngsang: *Kwansŏ siinjip* ŭl chungsim ŭro." *Inmunhak yŏn'gu* 46 (August 2013): 325–49.
Yu, Sŏnjun. "Hata." *Atarashii sedai* 1, no. 5 (June 1960): 29.
Yu, Taryŏng. "4.19 wa minjok ŭi changnae." *Sasanggye* 83 (June 1960): 106–10.
Yun, Ch'angju. "Masan ŭn ponghwa rŭl ch'uk'yŏ tŭrŏtta." *Rodong sinmun*, April 14, 1960, 5.
Yun, Kwangyŏng. "Tongmu wa ch'in'gu." *Chosŏn munye* 9 (March 1958): 30–37. Facsimile edition in Unoda Shōya, ed., *Zainichi Chōsen bungakukai kankē shiryō, 1945–1960* (vol. 2). Commentary by Song Hyewŏn. Tokyo: Ryokuin shobō, 2018, 354–61.
Yun, Namhŭi. "Pukhaenggi." *T'aep'ung* 18 (February 1949): 66–71.
Yun, Sangdŏk. "Pukhan ŭi Silla kokogak yŏn'gu hyŏnhwang kwa t'ŭkching." *Munhwajae* 53, no. 2 (June 2020): 270–85.
Yun, Sep'yŏng. "Hyŏngmyŏng yŏn'gŭk *Hyŏrhae ŭi norae* e taehayŏ." *Chosŏn munhak* 164 (April 1961): 94–105.
Yun, Sunyong. "Pyŏkch'o *Im Kkŏkchŏng* e nat'anan paekjŏng ŭi silch'e wa munhakchŏk hyŏngsanghwa." MA thesis. Kongju University, 2011.
"Zainichi zendōhō ni uttau: Minsen chūō de apīru." *Haebang sinmun*, May 20, 1952, 2.
Zur, Dafna. *Figuring Korean Futures: Children's Literature in Modern Korea*. Palo Alto, CA: Stanford University Press, 2017.

INDEX

Page numbers in **bold** indicate tables. Page numbers followed by n indicate notes.

Abeille, Marie-Louise, 175, 179
active humanism, 159–61, 163, 174, 190
A Day in the Life of Kubo the Novelist (Pak T'aewŏn), 219
Adong munhak (journal), 25, 49, 57
Agov, Avram, 43
Aihara Shigeru, 178
"Ailing Seoul" (O Changhwan), 220–21
Akizawa Shūji, 188
"A Literary Stroll" (Yi Ponggu), 218
Alsudairi, Mohammed, 14
ambiguity and liminality, 194–96
An Chaehong, 53
ancient Korean-Japanese relations, 247, 248–54
An Hamgwang, 103, 282–83n40
An Hoenam, 218
An Pyŏnguk, 188–90, 192
Anticommunist Law of 1961, 146
An Tongnim, 38, 98, 99
Aoki Shoten, 55, 191
April Revolution of 1960, 25, 39–40; and cross-border literary reception, 24–25, 55–58; and cross-border writing, 58–60, 64–68; and reclamation of banned texts, 217–19; and South Korean literature, 55–56, 64–74
Aragon, Louis, 160
archeology: and ancient history as sites of popular interest, 242–47; discoveries connecting Korea and Japan, 235–42
artifacts and colonial historiography, 243
Atarashii sedai (journal), 25, 56–57
Atkins, E. Taylor, 236

banned texts/literature, 208; reclamation of, 196–205, 213–25, 225–31, 231–35. *See also* censorship
ban on Japanese-language imports, 180–81
Barth, Karl, 186
Bergson, Henri, 167
binary structures of war: blurring of, 148–55; critique of, 156–61
"Blaze" (Kang Sun), 58–60

bodily autonomy as political expression, 203–5
"Book of the Dead" (Yi Ponggu), 203
border, complex dynamics of: economic and material exchange, 8–9; literary and textual exchange, 9–10; persistent connections despite division, 10–11; as space of exchange, 4–5
border-crossing anthology of modern Korean poetry, 190–91
"Bridge" (Yi Insŏk), 42, 44
Brunner, Emil, 186
Bsheer, Rosie, 14

canonical figures of revolutionary motherhood, 105–6
Capital (Marx), 178
Cartesian rationalism, 184
censorship: colonial and postcolonial, 31–33, 145–46, 197, 254–55. *See also* banned texts/literature
Central Committee of the Korean Writers' Alliance, 11
Ch'ae Kyusang, 63
Ch'anggong (journal), 149
Chang Habo, 41
Chang Munsŏk, 226, 234, 307n181
Chatani, Sayaka, 45, 51
Chatterjee, Partha, 97
Chayu munhak (journal), 42, 220
Cheju dialect, 134–37
Chi Myŏnggwan, 246
Chi Myŏngsun, 115–17
Chin Hŭigwan, 47
Chin Yŏngsuk, 57, 98
Chi Tongsik, 186
Cho Chaech'ŏn, 212
Ch'oe Inho, 140, 235, 247, 248–54
Ch'oe Inuk, 37
Ch'oe Kyunam, 176
Ch'oe Myŏngik, 48
Ch'oe Okcha, 57
Ch'oe T'aeŭng, 209–11

Ch'oe Tokkyŏn, 147
Cho, Eunsung, 97
Ch'oe Yŏnghŭi, 247
Choguk chŏnsŏn (newspaper), 49
Choguk t'ongil (newspaper), 11, 44
Chogwang (journal), 231
Cho Haeil, 231, 232–34
Cho Hyang, 182
Cho Kich'ŏn, 48
Cho Kyudong, 33
Ch'ŏllima (journal), 35–36, 38, 44, 69
Chomsky, Noam, 138
Cho Myŏnghŭi, 54
Cho Namdu, 127–28
Chŏn Chun, 47
Ch'ŏndogyo (Religion of the Heavenly Way), 190
Ch'ŏng Am, 36–37, 38
Chŏng Chinhwa, 238
Chŏng Chiyong, 54, 210, 213, 214, 218, 221, 222–23, 254
Chŏng Chomun, 242
Chŏng Chonghyŏn, 103
Chŏng Hansuk, 38
Chŏng Inbo, 239–40
Chŏng Kongch'ae, 38
Chŏng Kuch'ang, 38
Ch'ŏngnyŏn saenghwal (journal), 49
Chongryon organization, 3, 25, 43, 44, 49, 50, 242; co-optive engagement with the South, 53–54; founding of, 13, 50–51; ideological shift, 52–53; involvement with South Korean literature, 54–58; realignment with DPRK, 51–52; and repatriation of Koreans in Japan to North Korea 108–12, 112–19, 120–33; upheavals and splits, 128, 131, 133–34
Chŏn Hwagwang, 60–61
Chŏn Kwangyong, 38
Ch'ŏn Kwanu, 246
Chŏn Ponggu, 70
Chŏn Sangsuk, 145
Chŏn Tongu, 94–95

INDEX 335

Cho Pyŏgam, 37, 54
Cho Pyŏnghwa, 57
Chōsen Bunkasha, 26
Chōsen shisen (Hŏ Namgi), 54–55, 268n61
Chōsen sōren (newspaper), 56
Chosŏn dynasty (1392–1910), 67
Chosŏn hanmunhaksa, 230
Chosŏn hwabo (journal), 69
Chosŏn ilbo (newspaper), 34, 42, 56, 62, 63, 95, 231, 248, 253, 254
Chosŏn minbo (newspaper), 25, 56, 59, 61, 111, 113.
Chosŏn munhak (journal), 34, 37, 38, 39, 49, 67, 208
Chosŏn munje yŏn'gu (journal), 49
Chosŏn munye (journal), 60, 109
Chosŏn nyŏsŏng (journal), 41, 42, 49, 63, 69, 70
Chosŏn sinbo (newspaper), 12, 44, 57, 62, 109, 115–16, 120, 122, 126
Chosŏn yesul (journal), 96
Cho-Sso ch'insŏn (journal), 49
Cho Yŏnghch'ul, 255
Cho Yŏnhyŏn, 34, 156–57, 216–17, 221, 229
Cho Yunje, 34
Choi, Deokhyo, 45
Christian existentialism, 144–45, 180, 181.
Christian socialism, 189
Chūō kōron (journal), 212
Chu Yŏnghŏn, 236
Citizens Have a Right to Know (Hani Gorō), 178
"Cloudburst" (Kim Sŏkpŏm), 134–37
Collection of Materials about the Southern Half (of our Country), 28
collective engagement, 107–108
colonial consciousness, 228
colonial domination, 98, 216, 237
colonial-era historiography: and ancient relations, 242–47; challenging, 237–40
"Come Smash the Altar" (Ku Chungsŏ), 11–12, 44, 58
"Comfort women." *See* wartime sexual slavery

commercialization and simplification of nuanced history, 253–54
Complete Works of Joseph Stalin, 178
co-option, 3, 11; engagement with the South, 20–21, 37, 53–58; and ideological adaptation, 119–28; of Korean residents in Japan, 53; literature and repatriation, 109–10; of South Korean critique, 121; of those affiliated with Chongryon, 108–9, 135
creative rewriting: as political act, 71–74; of South Korean literature, 58–64
A Critique of Contemporary Philosophy (Amakasu Sekisuke), 178
A Critique of German Idealism (Komatsu Setsurō), 178
cross-border communication, reimagining, 217–20
cross-border literary and textual engagement: in adaptation of South Korean texts in Japan, 58–60, 61–63; in adaptation of South Korean texts in North Korea, 66–68, 69–74, 98–102; in reclaiming of in South Korea, 196–205, 213–25, 225–31, 231–35; in references to South Korean texts in North Korea, 25–26, 27–30, 33–36, 36–39, 40–43; in republication of South Korean texts in Japan, 54–58, 59–60, 119–20, 138–40; in republication of South Korean texts in North Korea, 25, 40–42, 44, 57–58, 68–71, **78–93**, 96–102; in South Korean interactions with former Chongryon members, 245–46, 247–54; in South Korean reception of European literature and philosophy, 142, 143–44, 156–61, 169–71, 181–90; in South Korean reception of influences from Japan, 162–66, 166–71, 179–81, 188, 190, 211–13, 246; in South Korean republication of texts from Japan, 242–45, 248; in triangular circulation of texts, 2–3, 11–12, 14–15, 44–45, 54–58, 95–96, 102–3, 122–26, 207–8, 209–14, 225–31, 236, 241–42, 247–54

cross-border travels: immediate post-Liberation transits, 4–8; North-South meeting at Takamatsuzuka Tumulus, 235–36; Ri Chinhŭi, Kim Talsu, and Kang Chaeŏn's trip to South Korea, 247–48; South Korean writers' and scholars' visits to Japan, 226, 245, 248–49. *See also* repatriation
"Customs of the Sun" (Kim Kirim), 214

de Beauvoir, Simone, 138
Dedication (O Changhwan), 202
Deer (Paek Sŏk), 198
deferred repatriation: as revolutionary commitment, 112–19, 125–28; in post-Chongryon narratives, 128–34
dehumanization, dual critique of technocratic "mechanism," 156–61, 165
Democratic People's Republic of Korea (DPRK). *See* North Korea
"diasporic agency," 14
diasporic identity as alternative political space, 132, 133–34
disidentification, 133–34
A Doll's House (Ibsen), 214
dual forces of "mechanism" vs. "humanism," 156–61, 165

East-West dichotomy in intellectual discourse, 166–69
editorial manipulation, 165–66
Egami Namio, 235, 237
"embedded writers," 147
"Embrace" (Kim Subŏm), 104, 122
Emergency Citizens' Propaganda Brigade, 147
"Encounter" (Ko Samyŏng), 131–33
Examen de Conscience, 163
existentialism: 181–90; historical context and evolution, 181–82; integration of religious and atheistic existentialism, 185–86; religious existentialism, 182–88; syncretic connections between Marx and existentialism, 186–90; theme of "mechanism" as modern crisis, 182
"Expression: A Puppy's Monologue" (Kim Kwangju), 191–92

Faris, Donald K., 175–76
Fernandez, Ramon, 163
"Fighter Plane" (Kang Sinjae), 153
"Five Bandits" (Kim Chiha): and its reappropriation, 119–22
The Flower that Bloomed on the Roadside (Kim Chinsu), 34
"Foot of the Mountain" (Kang Sinjae), 153–55
Foreign Book Retail Store (FBRS), 175–79
"For Whom to Write?" (Ri T'aejun), 214
Fujikawa Satoru, 178
"Futile Wandering" (Yi Ponggu), 221

Gabroussenko, Tatiana, 32
gendered representations in narratives of war, 149–52
generational perspectives in poetry, 65
Gheorghiu, C. Virgil, 141, 143, 156, 165–66, 226
"The Girl Next Door" (Pak T'aewŏn), 214
"Glass Window" (Kim Kirim), 220
"Gold Ring" (Pak Yŏngil), 42
"Green Frog" (Kim Song), 39

Haebang sinmun (newspaper), 15–16, 46, 47–49
haegŭm proclamation, 254
Hagu Sŏbang, 49
Hagwŏn (journal), 42
Ha Kirak, 190
Ham Sŏkhŏn, 42
Han'guk hwabo, 30
Han'guk ilbo (newspaper), 12, 40, 42, 44, 65, 101, 212
Han'guk kyŏngje (journal), 41
Han'guk yŏn'gam (journal), 30
Han Haun, 55
Han Hyo, 33

Hani Gorō, 178
Han Kyŏngja, 57
Han Sangun, 122
Han Sŏrya, 37, 48, 255
Han Sunmi, 98
Han Tŏksu, 49, 51
Han Yŏnghwan, 173–74
Han Yongun, 54
Hariu Ichirō, 139
hidden Japanese sources, 165–66
Higashi Ajia no kodai bunka (journal), 245
Hino Ashihei, 17
Hirabayashi Taiko, 166, 225–26
Hiromitsu Inokuchi, 46
historical ambiguity and shame, dealing with, 252–53
historical travelogue as a cultural form, 247–54
History of the Russian Revolution (Trotsky), 178
Hometown (Ri Kiyŏng), 4
Hŏ Namgi, 17, 51, 54–55, 96, 119, 122, 125, 190–91
Hong Hyomin, 34
Hong Kihwang, 51
Hong Kimun, 221
Hong Myŏnghŭi, 51, 231, 255
Hong Sajung, 185–86
Hong Sŏkchung, 234
Hong Tuwŏn, 30
Hŏ Ongnyŏ, 126
"Hope" (An Tongnim), 98, 99, 102
"Horse 1" (Chŏng Chiyong), 223
"Horse-Rider Theory," 237
Hŏ Yunsŏk, 33
Hughes, Theodore, 39, 272n54, 280n206, 289n11
Hŭimangsa, 214
The Human Condition (Malraux), 159
humanism, 144, 156–64, 166–67, 174, 190; "bourgeois humanism," 36–37; religious critique of, 183–86; socialist humanism, 179. *See also* active humanism

human limitations and critical potential, 184–85
human self-alienation, 189
Hwang Kŏn, 48
Hwang Kŭmch'an, 38, 66
Hwang Ponggu, 51
Hwang Sunwŏn, 33, 151
"Hwansong" (Pak Wŏnjun), 109
Hyesan Theater Troupe, 104
Hyŏn Chaehun, 36
Hyŏndae kongnon (journal), 30, 185
Hyŏndae munhak (journal), 19, 34, 35, 42, 198–99, 202, 203, 231, 246

Ibsen, Henrik, 214
identification: cards, 149; misrecognition and blurred, 148–55
ideological confrontation, 27–30; and literary criticism, 31–36
ideological shift for Koreans in Japan, 52–53
Ideology and Practice (Yamada Sakaji), 178
Ide Takashi, 178
I Have An Ancestral Land (play), 122–25
Iizuka Kōji, 169
Ilbon munje (journal), 244, 245
Im Ch'un'gap, 185
Im Chungbin, 207–8, 211, 230
Im Hŏnyŏng, 231
Im Hwa. *See* Rim Hwa
"Im Kkŏkchŏng" (Cho Haeil), 231, 232–34
Im Kkŏkchŏng (Hong Myŏnghŭi), 231–232, 234
Im Kŭngjae, 158
Im Okin, 37
importation of Japanese texts, 175–79; ban on, 180–81
Im Suil, 38
Information Center on North Korea, 258
Inmin (journal), 49
institutional purges, 32
interpretations of ancient East Asian history, changing, 236–42
Isonokami Shrine, 243

Jager, Sheila Miyoshi, 251
Japan: access to North Korean texts in, 48–50; ethnic Korean population in, 45–48; as mediating space for Korean academic exchange, 238–39; republication of South Korean texts in, 44, 55–58, 59–60, 62–63
Japanese colonial historiography, 239
Japanese Communist Party, 46, 47, 131
Japanese culture formation, migration from Korea and, 247, 248–54
Japanese influences: on South Korean intellectual trends, 162–66, 166–71, 179–181, 188, 190, 211–13
Japanese presence in Korea, postcolonial era, 12–13
Japanese texts: hidden sources, 165–66; importation of, 175–79; importation of, ban on, 180–81
Japanese translations: of European texts, 166, 207–8, of Korean historiography, 236; of Korean poetry, 48, 54, 56, 119, 227; of Rim Hwa's writings, 212, 227
Jaspers, Karl, 190
Jingū, Empress, 236
Jiyū to hitsuzen (Yamada Sakaji), 178
Joyce, James, 219

Kafka, Franz, 185
Kaishin Maru (Japanese merchant ship), 177, 178
Kang Chaeŏn, 131, 247
Kang Myŏnghŭi, 25, 56–57
Kang Pansŏk, 97, 103, 106
Kang Pongwŏn, 122
Kang Sinjae, 153–55
Kang Sun, 55, 58–60, 62–63
KAPF (Korea Artista Proletaria Federatio), 217, 226
katakana, 132, 137
Kawakami Hajime, 178
Kawamori Yoshizō, 165–66
Kaya, kingdom of, 236

Kazuo Nakahashi, 165–66
Kierkegaard, 185, 187
Kikan sanzenri (journal), 131, 133–34, 138–39, 247
Kim Chaejun, 148
Kim Ch'aesu, 237
Kim Chaewŏn, 38
Kim Chaeyong, 26
Kim, Charles R., 39
Kim, Cheehyung Harrison, 27
Kim Chiha, 119, 121, 138–39
Kim Chinsu, 33, 34
Kim Ch'ŏljun, 238, 241–42
Kim Chŏngbae, 241
Kim Chŏnghan, 74–75
Kim Chongmun, 147
Kim Chŏngsuk, 97
Kim Chongt'ae, 41
Kim Ch'ŏnhae, 51
Kim Chunghŭi, 171–72
Kim Ch'unsu, 55
Kim Chuyŏl, 67
Kim Haegyun, 36, 38
Kim Hat'ae, 185–86, 187
Kim Hongsik, 61–62
Kim Hun, 47
Kim Hyŏn, 229, 230
Kim Hyŏngsŏk, 185–86
Kim Il Sung (Kim Ilsŏng), 25, 27, 51, 103, 121; biography of, 49
Kim, Immanuel, 97, 103
Kiminsa, 234
Kim, Jeong Min 162
Kim Kijin, 1–4, 34
Kim Kirim, 54, 213, 214, 219, 220, 221, 254
Kim Kwangju, 36, 191
Kim Kwangsŏp, 33
Kim Kyŏngho, 38
Kim Kyŏngsu, 35
Kim Kyudong, 55
Kim Min, 51, 109–11
Kim Myŏnghwa, 103
Kim Myŏngsu, 96, 97, 99, 103–4

Kim Namch'ŏn, 32–33
Kim P'albong. *See* Kim Kijin
Kim Rip, 140
Kim Osŏng, 163, 190
Kim Sangdon, 40
Kim Sanggi, 238
Kim Sangok, 55
Kim Sangwŏn, 42, 55
Kim Sangyong, 54
Kim Saryang, 48, 275n110
Kim Sayŏp, 245–46
Kim Sijong, 138
Kim Sŏkhyŏng, 48, 236, 239, 240, 241–42, 243, 246, 250
Kim Sŏkpŏm, 128, 131, 134, 138, 139
Kim Song, 39, 55, 143
Kim Sŏnghan, 37, 192
Kim Sŏngsu, 31, 197, 307n181
Kim Sŏnhyŏn, 57
Kim Sowŏl, 54
Kim Subŏm, 104
Kim Suyŏng, 68–69
Kim, Suzy, 97, 103
Kim T'aegyŏng, 15
Kim T'aejun, 208, 230
Kim Talsu, 3, 131, 138–39, 140, 212, 242, 244–45, 246, 247–48
Kim Tarhyŏn, 51
Kim Tongil, 55
Kim Tongni, 146–47
Kim Tongsŏk, 221
Kim Unhak, 246
Kim Wŏllyong, 235, 236–38
Kim Yangsu, 34
Kim Yongho, 65–66
Kim Yongjun, 222
Kim Yŏngnang, 33
Kim Yongsŏng, 161
Kim Yosŏp, 57
Kim, Youna, 259
Kim Yujŏng, 218
Kim Yun, 55
Kim Yunsik, 226–31, 254
Kim Yunsŏng, 34, 55
Kobayashi Ryōsei, 178
Kōdō (journal), 162–63
Koguryŏ culture, 251
Koguryŏ murals, 235, 236
Kojiki, 236
Kōkogaku kenkyū (journal), 238
Kōkogaku zasshi (journal), 238, 239
Ko Kwangman, 175
Komatsu Kiyoshi, 162–64, 190
Komatsu Setsurō, 178
Koo, Sunhee, 14
Korean ancient cultural influence on Japanese language and writing, 245–47
Korean Commercial Company, 13
Korean resident population in Japan: DPRK link with, 46–52; and US occupation authorities, 45–46. *See also* Chongryon organization
Korean Wave or Hallyu, 259
Koria hyōron (journal), 119
Kōsaka Masaaki, 188
Ko Samyŏng, 130–31, 139
Koschmann, J. Victor, 180
Ko Wan'gi, 41
Ko Yangsun, 41, 57–58
Ku Chungsŏ, 11–12, 44, 57, 58
Ku Inhwan, 68
Kukche sinbo (newspaper), 42
Kukche sinmun (newspaper), 29
Kŭlloja (journal), 36, 49
Kuwŏl Sŏbang (bookstore), 49–50
Kwahagwŏn hakpo (journal), 50
Kwak Chongwŏn, 158–59, 163
Kwak Hasin, 33
Kwanggaet'o Stele, King, 239, 241, 243, 246, 248
Kwŏn Il, 244
Kwŏn Myŏnga, 151
Kye Puk, 34
Kyŏnghyang sinmun (newspaper), 42, 44, 182, 183, 213, 241, 248
Kyŏngje kŏnsŏl (journal), 50

Kyŏngje saenghwal (journal), 49–50
Kyŏngju (Silla capital), 251
Kyowŏn sinmun (newspaper), 49

labels on reproduced texts, 272n55
"Land of Excrement" (Nam Chŏnghyŏn), 39
Land Reform Act, 27
La Psychologie de l'Art (Malraux), 162
"The Last Train" (O Changhwan), 202, 203
League of Koreans and US occupation authorities, 45–46
Le Figaro, 165
"Letters from Okinawa" (Kim Chŏnghan), 74–75.
Lewis, Su Lin, 161
liminality, 194–96; and ambiguity, 194–96; liminal spaces as sites of resistance, 202–3
linguistic influence of ancient Korean on ancient Japanese texts, 245–47
linguistic play between Japanese and Korean, 134–37
literary figures: as symbols of national division, 209–214, 216–17, 223
literary history: and colonialism, 228–30; as political act, 231–35
literary migration, 32, 54–55
literary reclamation of banned texts and authors, 196–205, 213–25, 225–31, 231–35
literary resistance: evolution of, 223–25; memory as, 219–20; third space of, 138–39
local identity vs. national identity, 134–38
Lohia, Ram Manohar, 161
The Lost Kingdom (Ch'oe Inho), 140, 247, 248–54
Ludwig Feuerbach and the End of Classical German Philosophy (Engels), 178
Lukacs, Gyorgy, 207–8
Luther, Martin, 179
Luthi, Lorenz, 14–15

Malraux, Andre, 159–60, 162, 163
Mammonism, 189

Man'yōshū, the eighth-century anthology, 245, 246
Marcel, Gabriel, 165, 168, 182
Marxism, 189; and existentialism, 186–90; Japanese translations of, 178–79
Matsugi Nobuhiko, 138–39
Matsumoto Seichō, 209, 211–13, 223
Mauriac, François, 165
mechanism: and alienation, 188–89; critique of dual forces of, 156–61; and dehumanization, 194–96
Memorabilia of the Three Kingdoms, 245–46
Méray, Tibor, 211
migration from Korea and Japanese culture formation, 247, 248–54
Miki Kiyoshi, 178
Mindan (Korean Residents Union in Japan), 53, 108, 135
Minju ch'ŏngnyŏn (newspaper), 44, 49
Minju Chosŏn (newspaper), 49
Minju ilbo (newspaper), 29
Min Pyŏnggyun, 48
Min Sukcha, 24–26
misrecognition and blurred identification, 148–55
moral critique of the human, 193–96
More, Thomas, 179
Mother of Korea (Pak Hyŏk), 103–4
Mother of the South (Kim Myŏngsu), 96–100, 101–2, 125
"Mother" (Yi Pongun), 98
Mounier, Emmanuel, 165, 185
"Mountain Demons" (Yŏm Sangsŏp), 152–53
"Mountain Pass" (Yu Chuhyŏn), 149–51
Mo Yunsuk, 33
"Mr. Song" (Rim Kyŏngsang), 106
Mun Chŏngch'ang, 250
Munhak kwa chisŏng (journal), 229
Munhak sinmun (newspaper), 11–12, 19, 35, 38, 44, 58, 70, 94
Munhak yesul (Chongryon journal), 57, 120, 128
Munhak yesul (North Korean journal), 33

Munhak yesul (South Korean journal), 34, 194
Munhwa segye (journal), 34, 192, 197
Munye (journal), 34, 147, 166
Muryŏng, King, 235
mutual aid, 189
Myers, Brian, 32

Nakahashi Kazuo, 165, 166
Nam Chŏnghyŏn, 38, 39, 44
Nam Siu, 51, 277–78n144
Nanbō Yoshimichi, 138
National Federation of Democratic Youth and Students case, 138
National Institute of Korean History, 247, 256–58
National Salvation Brigade, 147
National Security Law, 145, 146, 191
neoorthodox Protestantism, 186–87
"neutralism," 224, 225
"neutralists," 53
"neutrality" and navigating political risk, 161, 164
newsreel, 60–61
Niebuhr, Reinhold, 186
Nihon no naka no Chōsen bunka (journal), 17, 242, 244, 246, 248
Nihon shoki, 236, 252
Nineteen Eighty-Four (Orwell), 156–57, 165
Nishitani Keiji, 167–68
Northern Council for the Promotion of Peaceful Unification, 37, 53
North Korea: alliances, 43; link with Korean resident population in Japan, 46–50; literature importation to Japan, 48–50; media in, 50, 60, 106; publications in Japan, 51; state formation, 26–27; support to Chongryon, 51–52
North Korean literary criticism: evolution of, 36–43; as political control, 31–36
North Korean writers: adaptation and rewriting of South Korean texts, 66–68, 69–74, 98–102; references to South Korean texts, 25–26, 27–30, 33–36, 36–39, 40–43; representation of April Revolution, 24–25, 64–68; vision of revolutionary motherhood, 96–106
North Star (Pak Hyŏk), 104, 122
"Nostalgia" (Yi Ponggu), 202
Notels (the combined "notebook" and "television" multimedia players), 259–60
Nouvelle Revue Française, 162

O Changhwan, 202, 203, 220–21
O Chŏngsam, 38
O Chongsik, 34
O Ch'ŏnsŏk, 175–76
O Ildo, 54
Oka Masao, 237
Okazaki Takashi, 244
O Kwisŏng, 238–39
Ŏm Hosŏk, 32–33
Ŏm Hŭngsŏp, 48
Ōmura Korean Literature Association, 62
Ōmura Masuo, 226
On Individuality (Takakuwa Sumio), 178, 179, 180
Ō no Yasumaro, 252, 253
Oppenheim, Robert, 251
"Orchid" (Chŏng Chiyong), 214
Orwell, George, 156–57, 165
O Sangsun, 54
O Sangwŏn, 38
O T'aeho, 32
Ōtsuka Hisao, 178
O Yŏngsu, 38, 42
O Yugwŏn, 36

Pacific War, 147
Paekche as a political alternative to state-sanctioned histories, 245, 249–53
Paek Ch'ŏl, 34, 157, 166, 181, 216, 229, 230
Paekdusan (Cho Kich'ŏn), 48
Paek Inbin, 38
Paek Injun, 31, 255
Paek Nakchun, 176

Paek Sŏk, 198
Paengmin (journal), 149
"Paengnoktam" (Chŏng Chiyong), 214
Pae Ponggi, 75
Pak Chaeok, 122
Pak Ch'anmo, 48
Pak Chiwŏn, 140
Pak Chŏnghŭi. See Park Chung Hee
Pak Chonghwa, 34
Pak Chongt'ae, 191
Pak Hwamok, 66, 149
Pak Hyŏk, 103, 104
Pak Kiwŏn, 55
Pak Kwanbŏm, 117
Pak Kwangt'aek, 120–21
Pak Kyŏngsik, 238
Pak Myŏngch'ŏl, 69
Pak P'aryang, 54
Pak Seyŏng, 54, 64–66
Pak Sihyŏng, 48, 240, 241
Pak T'aewŏn, 200, 213, 214, 219
Pak Tujin, 55, 57
Pak Wŏnjun, 109
Pak Yanggyun, 55
Pak Yongch'ŏl, 54
Pak Yonggu, 37, 216
Pak Yŏngil, 42
Pak Yŏngjun, 37
p'ansori oral genre, 120
Parhae, 251
Park Chung Hee (Pak Chŏnghŭi), 70, 97, 220, 251, 258–59
Pascal, Blaise, 179–80, 182–83
Peace Preservation Laws, 145–46
People's Assembly of Northern Korea, 27
"People Who Incinerate Life" (Yu Chuhyŏn), 194–96
perceptions of writers who went North: changes in South Korea, 209–17
Personalist movement, 165
"The Pier of Yokohama Under the Umbrella" (Rim Hwa) 227
Podo (journal), 29

Poet of the North (Matsumoto Seichō), 212–13, 223, 225
political canonization process, 105–6
political marginalization of "moderates," 222–23
political persecution and literary victimhood, 211.
political rehabilitation: of previously taboo scholars, 242–47; of previously taboo writers, 209–17
postcolonial era: criticism, 226–27; literary politics, 221–22; migration of Japanese to Korea, 12–13; reassessment of ancient Korean-Japanese relations, 242–47; reassessment of colonial-era historiography, 236–43; reassessment of colonial-era literary history, 228–31; repatriation of Japanese from Korea, 12; repatriation of Koreans from Japan, 12, 45–46
"Pride" (Ryu Pyŏk), 114
"The Protestation of a Cactus" (Kim Sŏnghan), 192
Provisional People's Committee of Northern Korea, 26–27
publication crossovers, 248–49
Pukhan (journal), 1, 3
Pulssi (journal), 55, 58
Pusan ilbo (newspaper), 30, 42
P'yŏnghwa sinmun (newspaper), 29

radio broadcasts, 67–68; and writing, 59
Rassemblement Democratique Revolutionnaire (Revolutionary Democratic Assembly), 164–65
Ra Sŭngim, 96–97
"The Real Estate Office" (Ri T'aejun), 214
"Record of White Clothes" (Im Suil), 19
reimagining cross-border communication, 217–20
religious existentialism, 180–81
repatriation: of Japanese from Korea, 12; of Koreans from Japan, 12, 45–46; of

Koreans in Japan to North Korea 108–12, 112–19, 120–33
Reporting League, 222
reproduction/republication: of Chongryon writers' work in North Korea, 58; of colonial-era banned texts in South Korea, 197–205, 213–25; of North Korean literary texts in South Korea, 227; of South Korean literary and journalistic texts in Japan, 55–58, 59–60, 119–20; of South Korean literary texts in North Korea, 25, 40–42, 44, 57–58, 68–71, **78–93**, 96–102; of North Korean scholarship in Japan, 236, 238. *See also* rewriting
Republic of Korea (ROK). *See* South Korea
Research Institute on the Korean Problem, 49, 51
Research on the Stele Inscription of King Kwanggaet'o, 239
Résistance, 159, 164–5
"Return" (Han Yŏnghwan), 173–74
reunification politics, literature portraying, 42, 119–28, 133
revolutionary coproduction of South Korean texts, 96–102
revolutionary mother figure: in Japan, 119–28; in North Korea, 96–106
rewriting: as political strategy, 119–22; of repatriation-era texts, 111–12; South Korean literary texts, 68–71. *See also* reproduction/republication
Rhee, Syngman (Yi Sŭngman), 11, 25, 39, 68, 110
Ri Ch'anŭi, 52–53
Ri Chin'gyu, 48
Ri Chinhŭi, 131, 138, 139, 238–41, 242, 245, 246, 247–48, 249
Ri Chŏnggu, 19–20
The Riddle of the King Kwanggaet'o Stele, 239
Ri Hyŏn, 35
Ri Kaisei, 138, 244
Ri Kiyŏng, 1–2, 4

Ri Sŏngha, 55
Rim Haksu, 54
Rim Hwa, 32, 209, 210–11, 212, 213; reengagement with literary historical work of, 226–31
Rim Kyŏngsang, 106
Rim Sundŭk, 48
Ri Pungmyŏng, 48
Ri Simch'ŏl, 51
Risō (journal), 164
Ri Sŏngbok, 100–101
Ri T'aejun, 32, 48, 213–214, 221
Ri Kiyŏng, 255
Ri Yongak, 221
Ri Yŏng, 51
"Roadblock" (Kim Chunghŭi), 171–72
Rodongja sinmun (newspaper), 44, 69
Rodong sinmun (newspaper), 29–30, 40–41, 44, 49, 63, 64, 66–67; and cross border reading, 31–33, 35; South Korean publications referenced in, **76–77**
Roh, David S., 14
Ro Kŭmsŏk, 35–36, 38
The Rose of Sharon Handkerchief (drama, film), 105
Rousset, David, 164–65
"R&R" leaves, 162
Ryŏksa kwahak (journal), 237, 238
Ryŏ Sanghyŏn, 223–25
Ryu Pyŏk, 113–14
Ryu Tohŭi, 70–74
Ryu, Youngju, 120

Saebyŏk (journal), 65
Sae sedae (journal), 24, 42, 44
Sagyejŏl, 234
Saint-Simon, Henri de, 189
Sakizaka Itsurō, 178
Sako Kagenobu, 240, 249
saogi, 137
Sartre, Jean-Paul, 138, 164–65, 181
Sasanggye (journal), 34, 40, 42, 44, 71, 119, 180–81, 182, 186, 188, 189, 211

Scenes from Ch'ŏnggye Stream (Pak T'aewŏn), 219
scholarly networks, transnational, 236–42
scholars: exchange between North and South Korean, 235–42; political rehabilitation of previously taboo, 242–47
The Sea and the Butterfly (Kim Kirim), 220
Sea of Blood (drama, film, opera), 103, 105
Second Congress of Korean Writers, 37, 54
Sedae (journal), 41
Segye ilbo (newspaper), 29
Sekai (journal), 164
Selected Works of Mao Zedong, 178
Selected Works of Marx and Engels, 178
self-critique and introspection in Korean literature, 170–74
"self-liberation," 109
self-portraits, 114
self-transformation through revolutionary work, 113–15
Seven-Branched Sword, 243, 248
Shakai shichō (journal), 163
shifting boundaries of acceptable discourse, 234–35
Shin Nihon bungaku (journal), 3, 119
Shin Nihon Bungaku Kai, 3
Shisō (journal), 239, 241
Shisō to jissen (Yamada Sakaji), 178
Shūkan asahi, 119
shutaisei, 180
Sinch'ŏnji (journal), 33
Sindonga (journal), 17, 241, 242–43, 247, 250
Sinjo (journal), 191
sinmyo year of 391, 239
Sin Pulch'ul, 48
Sin Sangok, 11
Sinsegye (journal), 41
Sin Sŏkchŏng, 54
Sint'aeyang (journal), 34, 141, 143, 149, 166
Sin Tongmun, 44
Skirts Ahoy! (film), 141
Socialist Party of Japan, 161
Sŏ Kŭnbae, 36

Sŏl Chŏngsik, 211, 221, 222
Son Usŏng, 34
Sŏngdae munhak (journal), 207
Song Hyewŏn, 55, 109, 113
Song Sangok, 38
Song Sugyŏng, 36
Song Yŏng, 67, 103, 282–83n40
Sonia Ryang, 50
Sonyŏndan (journal), 49, 69
Sonyŏn sinmun (newspaper), 49
Sŏul sinmun (newspaper), 169
South Korean high school textbooks, 238
South Korea: legal statutes related to North Korea, North Korean texts, and those who had gone North, 145–46, 197, 254–55; importation of Japanese texts, 175–80; importation of Japanese texts, ban on, 180–81
South Korean literature: Chongryon and post-Chongryon involvement with, 54–58, 138–140; reprinted in Japan, 55–58, 119–20; reprinted in North Korea, 25, 40–42, 44, 57–58, 68–71, **78–93**, 96–102. See also reproduction/republication
South Korean writers: calls for new "humanism" and critiques of Cold War "mechanism," 156–61; engagement with former Chongryon members, 245–46, 247–54; internal critique, of writerly self, 166–74; internal critique, of human, 191–96; reception of European literature and philosophy, 142, 143–44, 156–61, 169–71, 181–90; reception of influences from Japan, 162–66, 166–71, 179–81, 188, 190, 211–13, 246; reclamation of banned writers from the colonial era, 196–205, 213–25, 225–31, 231–35; representations of misrecognition and "friendly fire," 149–155, 171–174; turn toward precolonial past, 231–35, 245–47, 248–54; wartime mobilization, 147–48
"Spirit" (Kim Sŏkpŏm), 128–29

"Splendid Solitude" (Yi Ponggu), 220
"Spring" (Yi Ponggu), 197–98
Standing Committee of the Northern Korean Literature and Arts Alliance, 31
stele inscription, 239–40, 241
"The Strait of Korea" (Rim Hwa), 214
The Stranger (Camus), 182
"subordinate state theory," 236–38, 241–42, 246, 249–50
subterranean democracy, 65–66
Sudo p'yŏngnon (journal), 174
Sŭlgi, 234
"Suni at the Crossroads" (Rim Hwa), 217
"supervising translator," 166
Susumu Nakanishi, 245
symbolic maternal transformation, 96–102
Szabad Nép, 211
Szalontai, Balázs, 37

Taegu maeil sinmun, 41
T'aep'ung (journal), 29
Takahashi Shinkichi, 204
Takakuwa Sumio, 178, 179–80, 189
Takamatsuzuka Tumulus, 235
Takeda Kiyoko, 169
Takeuchi Yoshimi, 168–69
Tanigawa Ken'ichi, 244
Taylor, Moe, 43
temporal metaphors and "hours" of civilization, 169–70
Tenbō (journal), 130, 169
Textor, Cindi 137
theistic existentialism, 186
The Theory and History of Communism: A Critique of Marxism-Leninism (Yang Homin), 179
Theory of Crisis (Uno Kōzō), 178
"theory of cultural transplantation," 230
"There Is A White Partition Wall" (Paek Sŏk), 198
"They Cannot Block Our Advance" (Hŏ Ongnyŏ), 126–27

third way/third force position, 161–165, 174
Tillich, Paul, 180, 186–88, 189
"Together with My Elder Sister" (Pak Kwanbŏm), 117–18
Tonga ch'unch'u (journal), 212, 213, 214
Tonga ilbo (newspaper), 30, 42, 59, 62, 235, 245, 246
Tonga munhwasa, 143
tragic narratives of division, displacement, and migration, 128, 209–17, 221–25, 226–28
transnational literary circulation. *See* cross-border literary and textual engagement
Trotsky, Leon, 178
Tsurumi Shunsuke, 138, 139
Tsushima Tadayuki, 178
Ttolttoli (comic), 16
"Turkey" (Yi Ponggu), 223–24
The Twenty-fifth Hour (Gheorghiu), 141, 143, 156, 157–58, 165–66
"Twenty-Four Hours of Flux" (Yu Chuhyŏn), 192–95
Twenty Years in Myŏngdong (Yi Ponggu), 220

Ueda Masaaki, 243
Uehara Senroku, 178
Ŭija, King, 252
U Kyaw Nyein, 161
Ulysses (Joyce), 219
Umemoto Katsumi, 178
Ŭnghyang (poetry collection), 31–32
United Democratic Front of Koreans in Japan, 46–47
United Nations Korean Reconstruction Agency (UNKRA). *See* Foreign Book Retail Store (FBRS)
Uno Kōzō, 178
Uri choguk (journal), 49
US occupation authorities and League of Koreans, 45–46

The Volcano of Rage Has Erupted (Song Yŏng), 67–68

Wada Haruki, 138
wartime sexual slavery, 74–75
war trauma and national identity, 170
"Weeds" (Yi Ponggu), 171
We Have An Ancestral Land (Hŏ Namgi), 96, 119, 122
Wi Kaya, 238
Williams, Esther, 141
With My Life on My Back (Chŏn Ponggu), 70
wŏlbuk chakka, 214, 298–99n8, 300n33
Wŏlgan munhak (journal), 223
Wŏn Sŏkp'a, 35
Workers' Party of Korea, 27

Yamada Sakaji, 178
Yamanoue no Okura, 245, 252
Yang Chudong, 54
Yang Homin, 179
Yang Pyŏngsik, 160–61, 163, 174, 182
Yi Changhŭi, 54
Yi Ch'obu, 182
Yi Ch'ŏlju, 213
Yi Chonghak, 35
Yi, Christina, 3
Yi Haenam, 182–84
Yi Haengsŏn, 166
Yi Hanjik, 55, 65–66
Yi Hoch'ŏl, 70–71
Yi Hwan, 183–84
Yi Hyŏnggi, 55
Yi Insŏk, 38, 42, 44, 57
Yi Kibaek, 236
Yi Kiyŏng. *See* Ri Kiyŏng

Yi Kŭnbae, 44, 57
Yi Kyedan, 98, 100–101, 102
Yi Muyŏng, 34
Yi Pŏmsŏn, 36
Yi Pongbŏm, 212
Yi Ponggu, 33, 169–71, 182, 197–99, 200–203, 217–25
Yi Pongun, 98
Yi Sang, 54, 198–201
Yi Sanghwa, 54
Yi Sangno, 216
Yi Sŭngman. *See* Rhee, Syngman
Yi T'aejun. *See* Ri T'aejun
Yi Tongju, 55
Yi Ukchong, 35
Yi Wŏnsu, 57, 58
Yi Yuksa, 54
Yomiuri shimbun (newspaper), 166
Yŏm Muung, 74, 230
Yŏm Sangsŏp, 33–34, 36, 37, 152
"Yŏnghoe" (Yi Ponggu), 203–4
Young, Benjamin, 43
Yŏwŏn (journal), 69
Yu Ch'ihwan, 34, 54
Yu Ch'ijin, 33
Yu Chuhyŏn, 33, 149–51, 192–95
Yu Hangnim, 48
Yun Ch'angju, 66–67
Yung, Prince, 252–53
Yun Kwangyŏng, 108
Yun Kwŏnt'ae, 57
Yun Sangdŏk, 251
Yun Tongju, 54
Yurishima Maru (Japanese merchant ship), 177, 178

Zinn, Howard, 138

GPSR Authorized Representative: Easy Access System Europe, Mustamäe tee
50, 10621 Tallinn, Estonia, gpsr.requests@easproject.com

www.ingramcontent.com/pod-product-compliance
Lightning Source LLC
Chambersburg PA
CBHW022028290426
44109CB00014B/789